THE ECSTASY
BEYOND KNOWING

THE ECSTASY BEYOND KNOWING

A MANUAL OF MEDITATION

by

PIR VILAYAT INAYAT KHAN

Sulūk Press
Omega Publications
New Lebanon New York

Published by Sulūk Press
an imprint of Omega Publications Inc.
New Lebanon, New York
www.omegapub.com

Cover photo of Chamonix mountains by Ahab Cobb
Cover photo of eagle from Shutterstock.com
Cover design by Yasodhara Sandra Lillydahl
Photographs of Pir Vilayat Inayat Khan courtesy of the Sufi Order International

Quotations reprinted by permission from *The Sufi Path of Knowledge: Ibn al-Arabi's Metaphysics of Imagination* by William C. Chittick, the State University of New York Press @1989, State University of New York. All rights reserved.

Quotations from CORBIN, Henry: CREATIVE IMAGINATION IN THE SUFISM OF IBN ʿARABI ©1969 Princeton University Press, 1997 renewed PUP Reprinted by Permission of Princeton University Press

Quotations from ELIADE, MIRCEA: YOGA. © 1958 Princeton University Press, 1969 paperback edition, 2009 paperback with new introduction. Reprinted by permission of Princeton University Press.

Quotations from MASSIGNON, LOUIS: THE PASSION OF AL-HALLAJ. ©1982 Princeton University Press. Reprinted by permission of Princeton University Press.

Quotations from PEARSON, NANCY: SPIRITUAL BODY AND CELESTIAL EARTH; FROM MAZDEAN IRAN TO SHI'ITE IRAN. ©1977 by Princeton University Press. Reprinted by permission of Princeton University Press.

This edition is printed on acid-free paper that meets ANSI standard X39-48.
Printed and bound in the United States of America

Inayat Khan, Pir Vilayat (1916–2004)
Ecstasy Beyond Knowing
A Manual of Meditation
Includes foreword, glossary, index, biographical note
ISBN 978–1–941810019
1.Sufism I. Title

Library of Congress Control Number: 2014936675

Table of Contents

Table of Contents

Table of Contents

Foreword

Bonelli! Bonelli![1] is the call that I heard in the midi Pyrenees when visiting my friend and mentor Pir Vilayat Inayat Khan. Pir Vilayat's call of the eagle sighting and his unexpressed longing to fly with the eagles was a constant theme near the medieval city of Carcassone. The beautiful and natural setting in these beautiful lands in the south of France, and the special home with its own water system and solar panels proved the possibility of being self-sufficient and individually responsible in a trailblazing way. There was a separate, octagonal pod structure, overlooking the hills and valleys to inspire us with the vastness that surrounds us.

My regular visits to visit Pir Vilayat were in sync with the work of writing and editing his superb books that tried to capture the experience of deep meditations and the insights of in-depth retreats. My physics jobs at that time included developing new experimental payloads for scientific and military experiments, various conceptual star wars missions and other classified missions. Working with Pir Vilayat, was a continuation of my day work, with incredible realizations, the experience of portals into new unknown regions, and the discovery of the secrets of the inner spiritual worlds that we open and explore. It was my task with Pir Vilayat to provide continuity with the realms of new and recent physics insights, and occasionally, teachings of the Kabbalah, as part of the integrated whole. We continued to push our meditative realizations into new and uncharted meditative possibilities with the incorporation of Gauss' right hand rule of electromagnetism in describing the energy up and down the spinal column; the alternative particle and wave interplay; the opening of light fields; the Heisenberg uncertainty principle and its impact on the limits of sensory perception; the principles

---

1 The Bonelli's Eagle (Aquila fasciata) is a large bird of prey. Like all eagles, it belongs to the family Accipitridae. It breeds in southern Europe, Africa both north and south of the Sahara Desert and across the Indian subcontinent to Indonesia.

of quantum mechanics; implicate and explicit worlds of hidden variables; the realm of probabilities replacing the deterministic world; and the understandings of the nature of the multiverse and the evolving shape of the universe.

In 1995, Pir Vilayat was undertaking the task of writing his masterpiece on the integration of the practices and understandings of meditations in a complete and whole book that spanned different traditions. He collected insights and meditations from the Hindu tradition, the Buddhist traditions, the Jewish tradition, the Christian tradition, the Sufi traditions, and others less known. He included his own realizations, many of which were not shared before. A few of us fortunate souls were given the opportunity to read a first draft and provide our feedback. The material was awesome, but we felt the audience was not yet prepared to take on this challenging text. Now, a decade after his passing, we are happy to be able to offer this text to a more developed spiritual community that can appreciate and understand such work.

One of Pir Vilayat's challenges was to always try to speak that which was not speakable and not to settle for less. This book, the culminating integration and synthesis of Pir Vilayat's lifelong efforts to learn and teach the hidden realms of our world, seen and unseen, is that realization—the articulation of that which cannot be spoken. May his blessing continue to guide our transformation.

Raqib Ickovits
January 2014

INVOCATION

We invoke the One
Whose Body is the cosmos of the galaxies and our own bodies,
Whose Mind courses through our thinking,
And Whose Ecstasy arouses our acts of glorification;
Whose Personality is customized as our personalities,
Whose Presence is always there,
Whose Consciousness is focalized as our consciousness,
And Whose Reality is beyond our reach.

PREAMBLE

Chapter One
Preparing for the Journey

As a preliminary to starting any meditation there are some basic realizations that are of the utmost importance to spark your motivation and your orientation.

In the words of Hazrat Inayat Khan:

ﻪ

True exaltation of the spirit resides in the fact that it has come to earth and has realized there its spiritual existence.[1]

ﻪ

The soul manifests in the world in order that it may experience the different phases of manifestation, and yet not lose its way, but regain its original freedom in addition to the experience and knowledge it has gained in the world.[2]

ﻪ

Perfect realization can only be gained by passing through all the stages between man, the manifestation, and God, the only Being: knowing and realizing ourselves from the lowest to the highest point of existence, and so accomplishing the heavenly journey.[3]

ﻪ

There is a time in life when a passion is awakened in the soul, which gives the soul a longing for the unattainable; and if the soul does not take that direction, then it certainly misses something in life for which it has an innate longing, and in which lies its ultimate satisfaction.[4]

ﻪ

---

1 Inayat Khan, *The Sufi Message* series, *The Alchemy of Happiness*, 242.
2 Inayat Khan, *The Complete Sayings of Hazrat Inayat Khan*, 208.
3 Inayat Khan, *The Sufi Message* series, *The Sufi Message of Spiritual Liberty*, 17.
4 Inayat Khan, *The Sufi Message* series, *The Unity of Religious Ideals*, 85.

5

This craving for the attainment of what is unattainable, gives the soul a longing to reach life's utmost heights. It is the nature of the soul to try to discover what is behind the veil; it is the soul's constant longing to climb heights which are beyond its power; it is the desire of the soul to see something that it has never seen; it is the constant longing of the soul to know something it has never known. But the most wonderful thing about it is that the soul already knows there is something behind this veil of perplexity; that there is something to be sought for in the highest spheres of life; that there is some beauty to be seen; that there is Someone to be known who is knowable. This desire, this longing, is not acquired; this desire is a dim knowledge which the soul has within itself.[5]

The love for the unattainable object has every possibility of developing, whereas when the object of love is within reach, this is often a check upon love.[6]

There is a stage at which, by touching a particular phase of existence, one feels raised above the limitations of life, and is given that power and peace and freedom, that light and life which belong to the source of all beings...but also dissolved in it, for the source is one's self.[7]

One can lift oneself beyond worldly conditions at the command of one's will.[8]

So our first lesson is our preparation for the journey.

We are all on the journey; life itself is a journey. No one is settled here; we are all passing onward, and therefore, it is not true to say that if we are taking a spiritual journey we have to break our settled life; there is no one living a settled life here; all are unsettled, all are on their way. Only, by taking the spiritual journey you are taking another way, one which is easier, better and more pleasant. Those who do not take this way, they also will come in the end: the difference is in the way. One way is easier, smoother, better; the other way is full of difficulties; and as life has no end of difficulties from the time one has opened one's eyes on this earth, so one may just as well choose the smoother way to arrive at the destination at which all souls will sometime arrive.
By inner life is meant a life directed towards perfection....The inner life is not necessarily in an opposite direction to the worldly life, but the inner life is a fuller life. The worldly life means the limitation of life; the inner life means

5 Ibid., 83.
6 Inayat Khan, *The Sufi Message* series, *The Sufi Message of Spiritual Liberty*, 153.
7 Inayat Khan, *The Sufi Message* series, *Healing, Mental Purification, The Mind World*, 115.
8 Inayat Khan, *Esoteric Papers*.

a complete life. The ascetics who have taken a direction quite opposite to the worldly life, have done so in order to have the facility to search into the depth of life; but going in one direction alone does not make a complete life. Therefore, the inner life means the fullness of life.[9]

The inner life is a journey, and before starting to take it there is a certain preparation necessary. If one is not prepared, there is always the risk of having to return before one has arrived at one's destination. When a person goes on a journey, and when he has to accomplish something, he must know what is necessary on the path and what he must take with him, in order that the journey may become easy and that he may accomplish what he has started to accomplish....One must have everything prepared, so that after reaching a certain distance one may not have to turn back.

The first thing that is necessary is to see that there is no debt to be paid. Every soul has a certain debt to pay in life; it may to be to his mother or father, his brother or sister, to his husband or wife or friend, or to his children, his race, or to humanity; and if he has not paid what is due, then there are cords with which he is inwardly tied, and they pull him back. Life in the world is fair trade, if one could only understand it, if one knew how many souls there are in this world with whom one is connected or related in some way, or whom we meet freshly every day. To everyone there is something due; and if one has not paid one's obligations, the result is that afterwards, one has to pay with interest.

There is the inner justice which is working beyond the worldly justice; and when man does not observe that inner law of justice, it is because at that time he is intoxicated, his eyes are closed, and he does not really know the law of life. But that intoxication will not last; there will come a day when the eyes of every soul will be opened; and it is a pity if the eyes open when it is too late.... To some, consideration is due; to some, respect; to some, service; to some, tolerance; to some, forgiveness; to some, help. In some way or other, in every relationship, in every connection there is something to pay; and one must know before starting the journey that one has paid it, and be sure that one has paid it in full, so there is nothing more to be paid. Besides this, it is necessary that man, before starting his journey, realizes that he has fulfilled his duties, his duty to those around him and his duty to God. But the one who considers his duty to those around him sacredly, does his duty to God.

Man must also consider, before starting on his journey, whether he has learned all he desired to learn from this world. If there is anything he has not learned, he must finish it before starting the journey. For if he thinks, "I will start the journey, although I had the desire to learn something before starting," in that case he will not be able to reach his goal; that desire to learn something will draw him back. Every desire, every ambition, every aspiration that he has

9 Inayat Khan, *The Sufi Message* series, *The Way of Illumination*, 67–68.

7

in life must be gratified. Not only this, man must have no remorse of any kind when starting on his journey, and no repentance afterwards. If there is any repentance or remorse, it must be finished before starting.

There must be no grudge against anybody, and no complaining of anyone having done him harm, for all these things which belong to this world, if man took them along, would become a burden on the spiritual path. The journey is difficult enough, and it becomes more difficult if there is a burden to be carried. If a person is lifting a burden of displeasure, dissatisfaction, discomfort, it is difficult to bear it on that path. It is a path to freedom, and to start on this path to freedom, man must free himself; no attachment should pull him back, no pleasure should lure him back.

Besides this preparation, one needs a vehicle, a vehicle in which one journeys. That vehicle has two wheels, and they are balance in all things. A man who is onesided, however great his power of clairvoyance or clairaudience, whatever be his knowledge, yet is limited; he cannot go very far, for it requires two wheels for the vehicle to run. There must be a balance, the balance of the head and the heart, the balance of power and wisdom, the balance of activity and repose. It is the balance which enables man to stand the strain of this journey and permits him to go forward, making his path easy. Never imagine for one moment that those who show lack of balance can ever proceed further on the spiritual journey, however greatly in appearance they may seem to be spiritually inclined. It is only the balanced ones who are capable of experiencing the external life as fully as the inner life; to enjoy thought as much as feeling; to rest as well as to act. The center of life is rhythm, and rhythm creates balance.

On this journey certain coins are necessary also, to spend on the way. And what are these coins? They are thoughtful expressions in word and in action. On this journey man must take provision to eat and drink, and that provision is life and light. And on this journey man has to take something in which to clothe himself against wind, and storm, and heat, and cold; and that garment is the vow of secrecy, the tendency to silence. On this journey man has to bid farewell to others when starting, and that farewell is loving detachment; before starting on this journey he has to leave something behind with his friends, and that is happy memories of the past.[10]

---

10 Ibid., 65–67.

Chapter Two
On God and Faith

On the Use of the Word God

In the light of present-day thinking, I need to caution readers regarding the use of the word *God* in the present work. We tend easily to forget that when we use the word *God*, we are referring to our concept of God, and whatever this concept is, it cannot fail to be either anthropomorphic or so remote as to prove elusive. On the other hand, if we deny our mind any means of referring to its infinite outreach, or the ability to think holistically, we limit ourselves to our commonplace middle-range thinking. From the moment that we realize to what extent our assessment of reality is distorted by referring everything to our notion of ourselves, we appreciate our ability to look at things in the reverse; for example: *I am seen* rather than *I see*, or *I am thought of* instead of *I think*, or *I am the convergence (or the unfurling) of an infinite and eternal reality* instead of *I experience reality*. Martin Luther called this the *significatio passiva*.[1]

We need a term. We could use the word *reality*, but that sounds rather amorphous and metaphysical. If we adopt the word *universe*, we are confining that reality to its physical expression. Since the word *God* is in common usage, why not opt for that?

However, since we cannot possibly define what we mean by that word, we can at least define what we do not mean. Our very concept of God embodies our desperate quest for meaningfulness at the edge of our understanding. One might illustrate this by a body cell; for example, a blood cell in its odyssey through the complex avenues of the capillaries, intrigued by the incredibly complex circuitry of the brain, trying to make sense of it, trying to grasp the software of the body. Hypothetically, by dint of its commendable efforts, the

1 Pondering upon the verse *In Justicia tua libera me*, Luther, at a young age, saw the relationship between an attribute imputed to God and ourselves. Hence *Thy justice* led to *Thy justice whereby we are led into just men.*

cell's understanding would grow far beyond what it would have been if it had remained jammed between the more stationary cells of the bone or hair tissue. Consequently, it is trying to grasp the thinking of the brain, rather than just sort out its circuitry. This would rather aptly illustrate our utopian efforts to represent what we mean by the word *God*.

Moreover, the illustration above would need to be complemented by the holistic perspective. Rather than being like a cell of the body, we could see ourselves as exemplars carrying, potentially, the bounty present in the template or archetype which we exemplify. This elicits a completely different relationship with the totality we project as God.

Those to whom Unity is revealed see the Absolute whole in the parts; yet each is in despair at its particularization from the whole....Behold the world entirely contained in yourself....The heart of a barley seed conceals a hundred harvests.[2]
Mahmud Shabistari

Therefore one thinks that one is made in the likeness of God, instead of realizing that one is representing God in one's own likeness. Curiously, in the light of the holistic paradigm, we can now see that everything carries, potentially, the code of the totality.

However, there is a more profound way of looking at this; it would not make sense to deny this reality manifesting as a personality in our personality.

It would be a great mistake to say that God is only a personality, but it is a still greater mistake when man denies the personality of God....Man, in the flowering of his personality, expresses the personality of God.[3]
Hazrat Inayat Khan

All this conceptualization only serves to clarify our thoughts in our grappling with reality—so meaningful to us, but only the stepping stone. Belief serves as a stepping stone, but the breakthrough is experience. Our objective in this book is to provide skills that may support experience rather than belief.

The hitch is that our experience is masked and distorted by our interpretations of what is experienced. This is why the Sufis hold that God can never be the object of experience. However, one may keep discovering that which transpires behind what appears, in infinite regress. Conversely, our notion of being the observer can be moved backwards in infinite regress, as one identifies more and more with the universe, or that reality, or God as the Spectator.

---

2 Shabistari, *Gulshan-i Raz.*
3 Inayat Khan, *The Unity of Religious Ideals,* 70.

Knowing and grasping is just a very early first step; believing what one has grasped intuitively is certainly a surer foundation than faith in authority. The breakthrough is in awakening the God within.

The time comes when the belief in God is replaced by the experience of God.[4]

Hazrat Inayat Khan

Distinguishing Between Faith and Belief

As seen from the serenity of a spiritual retreat, the disastrous effect of an ideology upon the destinies of masses of people stands out clearly. The excesses of cruelty that people will wreak upon others in the name of sheer opinion, not based upon real life experience, is appalling!

One needs to make a clear distinction between belief and faith. Belief is opinion based upon authority or custom, routine conditioning. Faith is reinforced by opinion, but is based upon experience.

The mind gets easily caught in a bind. A bind is a situation in which thoughts follow one another in a circular fashion—popularly called a *vicious circle*. The pending catastrophe is rooted in the storms in human thinking. Thoughts thus caught, just as in a whirlwind, become compulsory and gain great emotional support by their very addictive nature until they explode in violence. Imagine: it is this very flaw in the functioning of the mind that begets conflicts, disasters, ordeals of terrible human suffering and terror.

The mystics of the various religious denominations seek after real experience, whereas the thinking of the followers is governed by belief. The originating revelation is gradually distorted by what Hazrat Inayat Khan calls the *followers of the followers*. Therefore the Sufis hold that one needs to base one's concept of God upon one's discovery of the traces (*ayat*) of God in real life. There is a reference in Islam to *the God created in the faiths, al-Haqq-al-makhluq fi'l -i'tiqadat.*

The God who is in a faith...is the God whose form the heart contains, who discloses Himself to the heart in such a way that the heart recognizes Him. Thus the eye sees only the God of the faith....The faith reveals the measure of the heart's capacity. That is why there are many different faiths. To each believer, the Divine Being is He who is disclosed to him in the form of his faith. If God manifests Himself in a different form, the believer rejects Him and that is why the dogmatic faiths combat one another.[5]

Muhyi ad-Din Ibn 'Arabi

---

4 Inayat Khan, *Esoteric Papers.*
5 Corbin, *Creative Imagination in the Sufism of Ibn 'Arabi*, 197.

Thus the Qur'an says, *For each of you we have established a law and a way.*[6]

If at some point doubts should arise as to why the mind finds difficulty in relating the belief to actual real life experience, then the mind can be plunged into the dark night of understanding.

He who is in darkness, blind as to his own proper and natural light, shall see supernaturally. And he who shall rely on any light of his own, the greater will be his blindness.[7]

St. John of the Cross

The same theme is found amongst the Sufis: that very light that the contemplative ascribes to God as other is present in oneself:

Before that brilliant presence, wisdom's light
Must hide its head, diminished as mankind before the sun.
When to the eye of man the source of light approacheth
In the attempt to fathom it, that eye grows weak and dim.
Think that the light of God's existence lies within thy eyeballs![8]

Mahmud Shabistari

Paradoxically, that very light blinds the monk and appears as darkness, yet it is in this darkness of the deepest part of the night of the soul that the monk is liberated from the illusory light cast by his own understanding.

The mind baulks at its inadequacy while blinded by a higher wisdom that, by dint of its very brightness, appears as darkness. However, St. John cleaves to an tenuous spark of light in his understanding: the dawning of meaningfulness.

Trust yourself to this fragile light as you advance towards it. It will grow as the effulgence of dawn. It represents a level of thinking beyond the kind of thinking that spins inexorably in a vicious circle. It dawns upon one's understanding as the horizon of understanding expands. Therefore the Sufis consider that it is revealed when one has found freedom from opinion.

What is the criterion for distinguishing between this intuitive mode of cognizance and opinion based upon belief? One would need to investigate the levels of thinking of the human mind.

At the bottom line, experiences of the physical environment, imputed through the senses and hearsay, opinion, and psychological data, are interpreted from the limited vantage point of our commonplace consciousness. At a higher level, our minds project their grasp of reality, which our consciousness cannot

---

6 Qur'an V:48.
7 St. John of the Cross, *Ascent of Mount Carmel*, Book the Second, IV:7.
8 Shabistari, *Gulshan-i Raz*.

encompass, into metaphors. This is why mystics express their conviction in the splendor behind real life in terms of poetry. To value what comes through in the experience of the world, one needs to tap one's inborn sense of beauty and meaningfulness.

This virtual sense is revealed if one does not limit one's opinion to the way things look from the vantage point of consciousness, focalized by our commonplace notion of *I-ness*, nor to opinions borrowed from others.

The 'Iraqi dervish, 'Abd al-Jabbar an-Niffari, bears testimony to these mystic revelations in which the human point of view is suspended and bypassed by a divine dimension of thinking:

Do not cease from this staying until I make myself known unto thee, and address thee, and command thee.[9]

It is the way the meaningfulness of the universe as a total being erupts in each fraction of that being, when that fraction reaches out beyond its horizon and plugs into the thinking of the universe. Here lies the next phase in human evolution.

Evolution advances by dismissing the conditioning to which it has been subjected. Evolution is sparked by revolution.

---

9 An-Niffari, *The Mawakif and Mukhatabat*, 109. Arberry translates the word *mawkif* (which is etymologically related to *wakf*, which means endowment) by the words *spiritual stayings*.

Chapter Three
Introduction to Meditation

General Introduction

Meditation has now become a household word. Naturally, it is cultivated by those who pursue high ideals and who have a strong need to honor the sacred aspects of their being and to capture some sense of the totality of which they are a part. Meditation is also for those who experience the need to find peace in the midst of the stress of modern life, of recharging themselves with renewed energy, of unfurling the potentialities latent in their personalities, and of gaining deeper insight into their problems with a view to achieving their purpose in life.

Unfortunately, the methods of meditation—mainly imported from the East—were devised for contemplatives. However, the know-how culled by monks and ascetics over the ages constitutes an inestimably rich inheritance for exploring the uncharted reaches of the psyche. Can this rich pool of resourcefulness be tapped to help us in our day and age, involved as we are with the challenges of our modern civilization?

What are the basic needs that people are feeling more intensely than ever? Coping with suffering, resentment, guilt, self-denigration, protection against vulnerability, the need to learn to relax, unwind, to have insight into problems, to be creative. What are the solutions that meditation has to offer? At first they would seem incalculable. But could we venture a partial list as a sampling?

Let us start by advancing an overall view. As a norm, we are programmed in our societies to function within a relatively small range of the potentialities of our psyche. Just as physics discovers properties of matter previously unknown when it adopts a wider space-time and more sophisticated logical framework, even so, meditators can gain access to vaster potentialities of the psyche. The perspective thus gained can make all the difference in one's self-image, assessment of circumstances, and creativity. This is precisely the field being explored in this book. A need is felt to apply the know-how garnered through the traditional methods of meditation to help us deal with our pain, unfurl our potentialities, and enhance our effectiveness in our quest for genuine achievement.

While the present trend is toward dealing with real life situations and confronting personal problems, at some point it becomes clear that one cannot assess situations reliably while one is too engrossed in them: you cannot see the woods for the trees. Moreover, one's personal vantage point in a situation cannot be more than relatively accurate, just as a landscape is distorted when seen through a lens: *the map is not the territory.*[1]

A more holistic view of our problems could be achieved by learning to alternately shift the focus of our consciousness, so as to view both ourselves and our life situations in a wider context. From this perspective, most of the time we are grappling with our concepts of our problems instead of grasping where the real issues lie.

This is where meditation proves to be invaluable—not just as a stress-alleviating technique, but as a training in a more apt use of consciousness. Furthermore, meditation could be applied to fostering the creativity of our personality, an objective which we will keep in mind continually throughout this guide.

It might prove enriching to extrapolate between the psychotherapist's approach to human problems and those gained by meditation. A psychological approach might seem more appropriate for some of the problems we shall consider; for example, grief for the loss of a loved one, remorse, a sense of failure or inadequacy, resentment at being abused, humiliation, and addiction. Psychological therapy and meditation actually offer complementary approaches. Therapists teach clients to articulate their pent up emotions and to own them. However, owning even the entire range of personal emotions would still not take into account the transpersonal range, which needs to be highlighted in order to understand our whole being. For the Sufis, the crux of these issues is the adequacy of our self-image. What we think of as being ourselves is only the tip of the iceberg. Meditation teaches us to discover and identify with the whole person. We easily get bogged down in our personal perspective. Sufism points to a way of reaching beyond that personal bind, by giving vent to our need for the sacred: the divine dimension of our being. This is important because, in the deeper sense, it is our self-esteem which is crucial; and that is precisely what is devastated by despair. It is our discovery

1 Kozybski, *Science and Sanity*, 58.

15

of the wider dimensions of our being that confers upon us a sense of self-validation.

Gaining access to this wider range of our identity requires training, following systematic guidelines. Moreover, a more inclusive sense of identity will trigger off a more comprehensive realization of meaningfulness, which will, in fact, open new circuits in the nervous and endocrine networks of our physical bodies. How does suffering fit into this larger sense of meaningfulness? Suffering is one of the factors in a growth process. Understanding the overall process helps us to monitor it consciously and voluntarily, rather than to feel victimized and helpless.

Considerable light is thrown upon this growth process by the *ars regia*, the royal art of the alchemists, who attempted to cull information from the process of the incubation of metals in the womb of the earth over eons of time, in order to better understand the stages in the transformation of the human psyche. Just as the progress in the transmutation of metals may be accelerated by judicious manipulation, so can the process of human transformation be enhanced by a knowledge of the developmental stages, supplemented by masterly monitoring.

We tend to react to circumstances rather than acting on our own initiative. In so doing, we fail to avail ourselves of the enormous pool of resourcefulness lying in wait in our psyche. Meditation provides us with a buffer between the challenges from external circumstances and our ability to gain access to the potentialities latent in our personality.

Preliminaries

There are certain preliminaries that must be taken into consideration before we start our course.

First of all, let us bear in mind that as soon as we reach beyond the middle range of our thinking (just as in non-Euclidean geometry or relativity), the commonplace logic breaks down and proves inadequate; for example, we sometimes need to deal with complementarity instead of thinking in terms of categories. Furthermore, rather than being like a section of an orange, we are like a whirlpool, inextricably enmeshed in a wave interference pattern. Such a realization shakes our self-image drastically. Or again, we are a continuity in change. This contradicts the usual view according to which a part of us, the spirit, is eternal, while another part, the body, is transient. What this means is that our being, considered as a whole (that is, holistically), is without boundary and is a continuity in change, in a state of ongoing transition. And furthermore, while one pole of our being is transient, the other remains unchanged.

Another important point to consider when meditating is that we cannot induce transformation, nor even concentration, by our will, since our individual will is as limited as consciousness is when focused at the individual setting. The approach to the problem is subtle: one may train the unconscious by dint of one's will, or one may learn how to enlist an impersonal will in action.

It might be helpful to borrow the metaphor of a cone. In our commonplace thinking, we may imagine that we are the apex, and the universe is the base; we converge the fabric and thinking, even the consciousness, of the universe. But there is a more advanced model: we are the whole cone, not just the apex. We can shift our identity to include the whole cone. This is the ultimate in meditation. When we achieve this, our will becomes overwhelmingly powerful, because it customizes the will of the universe. Perhaps we sometimes feel the immensity and bounty behind the limited way we deal with ourselves. It is this hunch that will spur us to strive to discover and marshal the wider dimensions of our being. The art of training oneself to do this is meditation.

There is yet one further noteworthy consideration before we embark on our work: let us bear in mind that it is emotion—not the will—that triggers off a shift in the focus of consciousness. Ecstasy could be defined as an emotion that involves our whole being. Our whole being is coextensive with the whole seedbed (that is, the cosmos) in which it extends, rather than a sub-whole encapsulated in its notion of itself and thus alienated from its source. Ecstasy breaks through every time we are suddenly freed from a constraint, whether it be our biased assessment of a situation, our emotional dependence upon a person or circumstances, or our limited self-image.

A Note of Warning

The art of meditation has been devised and elaborated, in the course of history, as the findings of men and women who have explored the inner and transcendental spaces of the psyche. This required solitude and austerity, the way of the recluse, which may seem incompatible with the way of the householder. Many sects and charismatic groups have been accused of encouraging otherworldliness in their disciples. A term has been coined for it: *spiritual bypass*. In contrast to this, we are here endeavoring to grasp the techniques and know-how that the contemplatives have culled, and apply them to dealing with our problems in action, in worldly life. It is worth the challenge. Just imagine how it would be if we could maintain a stalwart peace and serenity in the midst of a stressful situation, grasp the hidden springs behind the programming of our lives, and develop intuition, mastery, and radiance.

At a certain point in our search for meaningfulness, it may suddenly dawn upon us that the attraction of trance-like meditations or retreats may arise from a perhaps unconscious wish to escape from a life situation; for example, parental authority, or the ruthless, merciless civilization we are living in with its violence, greed, and manipulation.

Some people enter into a retreat (khalwa) because they are wary of society and oppressed by the experience of the world, or even of their families, seeking solace in the tranquility of a retreat. Others look for a retreat to be in a euphoric state. These motivations are counterproductive.

Muhyi ad-Din Ibn 'Arabi[2]

Moreover, it has become evident in recent years that meditation practices can, and sometimes do, lead people to drop out of life in general and eschew taking responsibility in their lives for loved ones or fellow beings. Furthermore, we just may be trying to validate our own personality in our own view, or that of others, by being special or different. Actually, we may be missing out on the inestimable value of that which has been acquired by humans throughout the ages in terms of beauty, material convenience, and orderliness: the marvel, the excitement, the courage, the vulnerability and the enriching effect of sharing joy and pain; relationship, friendship, loyalty, and service, in which God is to be found as a living reality. It is tragic to cloister oneself in an anesthetized psyche that shields one from confronting the challenges of the drama of life, which both actuates the celebration in the heavens in a concrete way, and tests our mettle. There is a way of being high without being spaced out.

When meditating (or prescribing meditation), it is important to be clear about the aftereffect that the shift of focus of consciousness may be expected to have upon our personality, attunement, and worldview, and to know which practices trigger off which effect.

1) When extending consciousness, since our notion of ourselves needs to be expanded as we contemplate vaster and vaster reaches of space, we identify with zones of our being beyond our notion of a skin-bound material body. We may become aware of and identify with our magnetic field or aura. As these do not have a boundary, we then envision ourselves as being like a vortex (boundless). What is more, we tend to assume that we lose ourselves by merging with the totality of the universe.

It is important here to keep in mind that one is both a vortex, and at the same time, something like a cell, bounded by a membrane, albeit porous. We need to work with both in combination, not just one or the other. Our

---

2 Ibn 'Arabi, *Études Traditionelles*, trans. Valsan, March 1969, Nr. 412; Fut., Chap. 78.

minds, in their commonplace thinking mode, find it difficult to reconcile these two paradigms.[3] Our bodies (including the subtle bodies, the psyche, personality, and consciousness, etc.) are holistically related to the totality of the fabric of the universe. This means that they potentially carry the bounty of the totality of the fabric of the universe, just as every drop of water has the same properties as the water of the ocean. In fact, every cell of the body has the same genes as every other cell, but some genes will be activated in one cell and different ones in others, so that, by diversifying, they create the chance to cooperate. Thus they differ while being potentially identical, and in that sense, may be considered as discrete entities. It is in this diversity that our freedom is rooted. A vortex is open to its environment, and in fact, incorporates its environment indiscriminately; whereas a cell, thanks to its membrane, may select the elements it takes in from the environment or secretes to the environment, while still being open to some measure of osmosis.

If we identify just with the vortex model, we are overlooking the containment that ensures our protection against undesirable impressions, honors our idiosyncrasies, and confers upon us our incentive. If we neglect our boundaries, we run the psychological risk of finding ourselves disoriented, spaced out, and unable to confront circumstances as real; sometimes the concept of *maya* is invoked to justify this disability. What is more, just as we generally fail to realize that an eddy does not lose its identity by joining with other eddies in a wave interference pattern (whirlpool), and can even be retrieved, we tend to believe that we lose ourselves as we merge blissfully with the totality of the universe or the Being of God; however, the purpose of the whole universe is that the bounty of the totality should be customized in each of its sub-wholes in a unique way. *Fana* (annihilation) does not mean that one loses oneself, but only one's commonplace notion of oneself.

2) In meditating, we learn to turn within, which can easily be misconstrued as encapsulating ourselves in our psyche while blocking any impressions, physical or psychological, from the environment. Here it is the opposite: by setting up a boundary segregating ourselves from the environment, we tend to merge with the totality in an inverted space. A person unfamiliar with physics would find it difficult to have any clue as to what one might mean by *inverted space.* It may, therefore, be preferable to envision that our magnetic field or aura intersperses with other such fields, like the eddies on the surface

---

3 This problem is similar to the one that physicists encountered in accepting the fact that since photons of light behave either as waves or as particles according to the way the experiment is conducted, they may be considered as displaying both of these two properties. So it is with our notion of ourselves.

of a lake as they combine to form a wave interference pattern. It is difficult for us to realize that this does not imply that they spread out or diffract in space. A good analogy would be to imagine a short musical theme, each note following the other. Now can you imagine the notes forming a chord without being stretched out as a melody? This happens in our dreams, where impressions are jumbled; in order to retrieve them in our memory, we sort them out in a space-time framework.

If, however, as we turn within in meditation, instead of setting up a boundary encapsulating ourselves in our thoughts, we envision that we are protected by a porous membrane that filters impressions from the environment at all levels of reality, and that we are consequently able to radiate into the environment, then we will enjoy an incomparably richer experience. Now envision that you are not just filtering these impressions but transmuting them, just as we digest our food in order to use it, since we can only deal with amino acid chains that match our own. Just as in digestion, we need to break down the ingested elements, rebuild them on the model of our own idiosyncrasies, and reject those elements which, being too alien to our own beings, would prove too difficult to incorporate, or even harmful. Here our sense of having boundaries will help us, on the one hand, reject unwanted impressions or, on the other hand, filter and transmute those impressions that can be put to good use if adjusted to our particular attunement.

3) Transcendence. There can be no doubt that while our involvement with life at its lowest common denominator fosters greed, limitations in the field of consciousness, and conflict, our quest for freedom from conditioning opens the doors to the wonder and meaningfulness behind what seems to be happening at the existential level.

Another final way of putting this, is to say that we must instill something of the way of the hermit into the way of the knight. Our need for freedom is as compelling as our need for involvement. Are they necessarily mutually exclusive? There is a way of reconciling the irreconcilables. One example is to love without being dependent upon being loved. In meditation, detachment frees one from the conditioning of one's thinking and the constraint of one's self-image. Freedom from the usual setting of consciousness will enable us to shift consciousness into an inner space or, alternatively, into a mode of self-transcendence.

General Instructions

The practices in this manual are intended for all meditators, including beginners, those with some experience in meditation, and also advanced meditators who wish to explore further dimensions or different approaches.

Meditations inspired by the Sufi tradition are emphasized. However, in the interest of further clarity, parallels are sometimes made with other traditions. This is quite appropriate, since Sufis have often interfaced with the contemplatives of neighboring spiritual communities. In fact, it may sometimes prove helpful to start with the practices as taught in Yoga or Buddhism, and then add the Sufi way.[4]

In addition, in order to give this manual the scope that could be expected by those aware of the broad, eclectic thinking of our day, a brief summary of practices of some of the major schools are included. To do justice to the methods of meditation of these traditions, you are advised to refer directly to their authenticated representatives.

Most initiatic schools, including the Sufi orders, insist that those who practice meditation receive their instructions directly from the authorized teachers in their tradition. The reason for departing from this custom here is that it is not always feasible to find such a teacher, at least not within reach. Consequently, quite a few people are meditating on the basis of perfunctory instructions, often simply playing it by ear, letting their thoughts idle randomly, or simply spacing out. By so doing, one incurs the risk of becoming other-worldly, and perhaps even dropping out of society, whereas meditation should ideally help one to fulfill one's real purpose in life. Meditation, like any craft or skill or art, requires competence and expertise.

Since meditation is the art of modulating consciousness beyond the middle range in which most people are entrapped for most of the time, it marks a step forward in the evolution of the human species. It is as skillful and elaborate an art as learning to play a musical instrument, compose music, paint or sculpt, act, dance, or acquire the skill of the artisan, or scientist, or technologist—perhaps even more.

It is my hope that this manual may help to throw new light on the practices of those working on their own, and moreover, add some new ideas to their repertoire. The objective of this manual is to help you understand how each practice works, rather than just listing instructions. In my experience, in some cases it is preferable to just start doing the practice, and then figure out later how and why it works. In other cases, it is better to become acquainted with the principles first. Therefore, the principles upon which the practices are based sometimes precede and sometimes follow the instructions, although it might seem more consistently logical to start with the principles. I feel it is best left to you to decide whether you prefer to read the principles first or start with the practices.

---

4 Many Indian Sufi practices (except the *dhikr*) are adaptations of Yogic practices: See Mir Valiuddin, *Contemplative Disciplines in Sufism*.

21

Since these practices involve body and mind, they clearly have implications in physics and psychology. Therefore, to my mind, it is worthwhile for the modern meditator to have a working knowledge of those sciences. It may prove desirable to update that knowledge, at least insofar as it applies to the way the practices affect us. However, some meditators are not interested in science, and may even be put off by any references to science. To make this information available to those for whom it may be of interest, information on scientific views is included, mainly in the footnotes.

You are advised to keep a logbook, including a schedule (revising the schedule after trying out the practices), and a diary articulating what was experienced or how it reflected upon your life. A simplified outline of a proposed systematic schedule is offered here; the practices are listed under different headings such as breathing, light, etc. that are categorized in stages. They proceed from the initial stages to the more elaborate ones. Each practice is graded so that the practitioner will be aware of the level of skill required before undertaking the practice.

The practices are graded as general practices or advanced. If you are just starting out, do not attempt the advanced practices until the general practices have been mastered. Be careful of over-stressing yourself by exploring practices which are beyond your scope; it may simply discourage and disappoint you. If you move through the practices at a pace suited to your temperament and capacity, you stand a far better chance of eventually succeeding in the more difficult ones. Even if there are some you can never manage, you will certainly have derived the benefit that was right for you. Successfully doing all the practices in this manual might require more than a lifetime's practice. For those already familiar with meditation, this might be considered a refresher course. In many cases, you will find that the Sufi versions of the practices are quite different from the similar practices taught in many of the major schools.

Design your curriculum according to the time which you assign to your daily practices. Some possibilities are: (1) a half hour in the morning, a half hour in the evening; (2) an hour in the morning, a half hour in the evening; (3) an hour in the morning, an hour in the evening; (4) a half hour in the morning, a half hour at midday, and a half hour in the evening; (5) an additional half hour or hour at three o'clock in the morning.

Draw up a curriculum for one year. You can always modify it as you go along. Traditionally, it is advised to start each new phase with the new moon, increasing the practices until the full moon, then letting off gradually as the moon wanes, and perhaps playing it by ear during the last quarter. At the beginning of each new lunar month, revise your practices, including one or more new ones, or replacing one or more practices with new ones. You could follow the sequence of practices given in the manual, starting with the easier ones and systematically upgrading.

It is always helpful to start each meditation session with a breathing practice. Follow with a practice using visualizations, then sound (*mantram* or *wazifa*). Then move to the more elaborate practices: cosmic, introspective, transcendent, self-transcendent. Finally, do the more comprehensive ones, for example, the *dhikr*.

By persevering, doing these practices regularly and assiduously, you will feel much more personal energy, more zest for life, more serenity, more joy, and a greater sense of meaningfulness and fulfillment in your life.

PART ONE

WORKING WITH THE BREATH

Introduction

It is best to begin all meditation sessions with a breathing practice. The control of breath has a decisive effect on meditation. There are several reasons for this.

1) Well-Being

Perhaps one of the most elementary objectives of meditation is to foster overall well-being at all levels: physical, mental, emotional, and beyond. The components of our being at these different levels interact meaningfully, which promotes healing, growth, and evolution in general.

To start with, since in average circumstances our lungs only utilize one fifth of their capacity, it is imperative to clear the accumulated polluted gases, radically and systematically. However, we need to be careful not to strain the breath too much (with the exception of advanced Yoga students, or in the case of brisk walking or jogging, where breath can be stressed to the point of panting within reasonable measure). It is wholesome to become aware of the natural ebb and flow of energy in one's being and synchronize one's breath with that rhythm. Furthermore, breath can be modulated in a variety of ways, matched with mental patterns or emotional attunements.

2) *Working with Energy*

From the holistic viewpoint, the action of absorbing oxygen from the environment and expelling polluted gases from the lungs is only one factor in an ongoing exchange of energy between the organism and the universe.

At this point, simply consider the energy exchange with the physical environment. Just by directing our attention towards the ebb of energy as we exhale, then the flow as we inhale, we enhance energy culled from the environment. Since our life field does not have a boundary, this exchange is something like the way the water in a lake is drawn towards the center of the whirlpool; the whirlpool is coextensive with the lake.

As we inhale, energy from the environment and outer space converges, building up our life field; as we exhale, it diffuses or diffracts into the atmosphere. Just as the center of a cyclone, for example, is a vacuum, so one senses a kind of void in one's solar plexus, which is the center of one's life field. As one becomes highly sensitized, one realizes that one's spinal cord seems to suck the ambient energy into a void.

3) Breath as a Link Between Mind and Energy

Another skill developed from breathing techniques is learning to alternate between two complementary psychological archetypes, and to reconcile them. For example, as we absorb energy from the environment while turning within, we attune to the thought of detachment and freedom; whereas when we radiate energy as we exhale, we attune to the thought of generosity.

Moreover, you may notice that if you identify with your subtle body or aura, or think of yourself as being like gossamer or an energy field, your level of thinking will be very different from what it is when you identify with your physical body. There are, in fact, different levels of thinking which correspond to grades of energy.

4) Breathing to Promote Regeneration

Breathing practices may, of course, be applied to alternate methods of healing, or to enhancing energy in specific sites in the body, i.e. the *chakras*.[1] The method consists in concentrating upon the site in the body—for example, the chakra that one wishes to dynamize—while exhaling or inhaling or holding the breath, as the case may be. Concentrate the flow of energy into a stream directed towards the organ or site selected. For advanced meditators, a similar method could be applied to working with the subtle bodies. To affect these subtle bodies, the meditator will need to galvanize the more subtle grades of energy. Indeed, the magnetism emanating from the hands of a healer can range from rather gross energy to very fine. When healers speak about healing with the Holy Spirit, they are referring to this fine energy. Experience confirms that in order to radiate this finer energy, the practitioner needs to sense the subtle bodies and identify with one or the other; the higher the subtle body, the more subtle the energy radiated. In the course of inhaling, one learns to shift one's sense of identity into higher levels of being.

5) Psychological Adjustment

The control of breath offers us a way to modulate our emotional involvement with the ambient circumstances. Consequently, we learn to organize our

---

1 The Sanskrit word *chakra* denotes junctions in the interconnecting network of the subtle energy body or etheric body, rather like the *chi* points in acupuncture. Actually, they correspond to the plexuses of the autonomic nervous system.

mental processes, and eventually learn to regulate our thinking at various levels at will. This is due to the fact that there is clearly a relationship between the metabolic rate at the physical level and the setting of our psychic energy that shifts between two poles: the catabolic state, illustrated by an animal in a state of alertness, ready to spring into action to catch its prey or defend itself against predators; and the anabolic state, in which the animal is at rest and protected in its cave or lair. In the case of the human being, this would be when one is geared to the ambient circumstances, physical or psychic, illustrated by the athlete or the telephone operator, as opposed to a situation where one is able to reflect upon the implications of a problem. In the first case, one reacts; one adapts oneself to prevailing circumstances, in which case one short circuits and does not avail oneself of all one's resources. In the second case, one is in a state that favors enjoying an overview, taking stock of a situation, and getting in touch with the way one feels, not only with regard to the outside, but as generated from within; and one is aware of one's identity and potentials.

In our civilizations, we are normally conditioned excessively into the catabolic mode. Slowing down breath shifts the metabolic rate into the anabolic setting; accelerating breathing shifts into the catabolic. Just by becoming aware of your breathing, you slow it down automatically. We must also bear in mind that the more relaxed we are, the slower we breathe and the less oxygen we need, and therefore, the longer we are able to retain our breath. Yogis and Tibetans carry this to a spectacular limit, holding their breath for hours. The secret of this is probably that the hibernation instinct is still latent (recessive) in human beings, and may be retrieved by the appropriate techniques. This slowing down of the bodily functions creates a stilling effect upon the mind.

There is a monolithic correspondence, albeit extremely intricate, between the plexuses of the autonomic nervous system and our endocrine glands. We may observe the impact of mind over body by observing the effect upon our endocrine glands of concentrating on the corresponding plexuses, which correspond to the chakras on the energetic level. For example, if you concentrate on the throat chakra, you enhance the function of the thyroid; concentrate on the solar plexus and you affect not just the breakdown of proteins by the pancreas, but your ability to process pain or stressful emotion as it is ingested in the psyche; concentrate on the *hara* center of Zen, you will affect the balance between the medullar and cortical adrenal glands, and by the same token, your ego (and aggressiveness).[2]

---

2 In a series of electroencephalograph experiments, Dr. Motayama demonstrated that "the electro potential and frequency recorded in the case of electrodes placed in proximity of a chakra easily emitting energy through the subject's will were remarkably different from those data obtained when the electrodes were placed near a chakra not readily emitting

6) *The Sense of Location in Space*

Our sense of location is indeed relevant to our sense of identity, since we limit our ability to avail ourselves of our latent potentialities by our skin-packaged sense of identity, which is founded upon our commonplace sense of space. Actually, space is the framework—evidencing the limitation in our ability to extrapolate between sensorial impressions—that our psyche imposes upon reality.

For example, if we limit our representation of a tree to solid matter, one tree will occupy one place in space and another tree will occupy a different place. If, however, we think of radio waves, they are interspersed, and consequently, everything is everywhere. Our mind in its commonplace thinking has difficulty conceiving that things can be everywhere rather than located at a particular place in space.

Furthermore, we are getting used to accepting that space can be inverted, and to trying to force our imaginative faculty to represent it. This confirms an experience encountered in meditation. In the twelfth century, the Persian Sufi Shihab ad-Din Suhrawardi referred to a condition out of space he called *na koja abad*,[3] the space out of space.

7) *Our Sense of Time*

Our sense of the passage of time is, no doubt, based upon a large number of physical, physiological, and psychological factors, most of which escape our ordinary awareness. One could venture a partial catalogue: sidereal time, based upon the rotation of the fixed stars and the precession of the equinoxes; the seasons on the planet; the circadian rhythms of daylight and darkness, as evidenced by cellular time; the rate of recovery of wounds; and psychological time, which moves very slowly, for example, if one is waiting, and very fast, if events crowd in densely upon one.

The difficulty in unscrambling this paradox comes from our commonplace assumption that time is one-dimensional. If we are able to envision at least two dimensions of time—the process of becoming, the arrow of time (let us call it the horizontal vector), and the transcendent dimension (let us call it

energy through the will of the subject." See *Future Science*, Hiroshi Motayama, "Measuring Psychic Energy," ed. John White and Stanley Krippner, 1977; 445ff.

3 According to Suhrawardi, Abu Talib al-Makki said of the Prophet that *space had enfolded upon him*. Incidently, the new paradigms of physics, Dr. David Bohm's implicate order, are now positing that which the Sufi contemplatives had grasped in the medieval ages in Iran. Speaking the language of metaphor, Suhrawardi refers to the allegorical figures: nostalgia, desire, and beauty: Nostalgia visits Joseph in Canaan, and when he asks her from where she came, she said; "*Na koja abad*," (the land of nowhere). The same theme appears again in Suhrawardi's epistle translated by Professor Corbin under "Le bruisement de l'Aile de Gabriel," in which the sage declares that he and his brethren have come from the "land of nowhere." Corbin, *Suhrawardi d'Alep: fondateur de la doctrine illuminative (ishraqi)*, 34.

the vertical dimension of time, moving from transiency to eternity)—then we encounter the challenge of extrapolating between these two dimensions. Eventually, we learn to reconcile our eternal being with our transiency. The mind, bypassing its middle range, dismisses the conditioning it has been subjected to.

My Lord invested His perennity upon my transiency to the point of annihilating my transiency in His perennity. Consequently no other quality subsists in me but that of His perennity and the faculty of expressing myself by dint of this quality.[4]

Mansur al-Hallaj

The relationship between these is somewhat similar to that of a seed, whose DNA remains fairly constant, mutating very slowly if at all, and a plant, which unfolds the seed in an incomparably faster time sequence.

8) Directions of Breath

By concentrating, we can direct our breath right, left, up, down, centrifugally, centripetally, in spirals, etc.

The Cosmic Dimension

In the course of our practice, we shall be learning how to direct the energy of the life field outward upon exhaling, by visualizing the vastness of space; and conversely, to absorb cosmic energy upon inhaling, as converging inward, by representing space inverted in a vacuum inside.

Turning Within

To avoid encapsulating ourselves when turned within, as we exhale we learn to extend from within, which gives us a feeling that our being now unfolds after enfolding; whereas when inhaling, as we direct our consciousness into inverted space, we come to realize that we are really unfolding after having been enfolded in what we usually understand by space.[5]

The Transcendent Dimension

Understanding what this means requires us to discover the way that our notion of space is linked with our identification with the physical nature of our body. Space only has meaning for matter. At the more transcendent levels of our thinking, space is irrelevant; it is only meaningful in the imaginary

---

4 Massignon and Kraus. *Akhbār al-Hallāj, texte ancien relatif à la prédiction et au supplice du mystique musulman al-Hosayn b. Mansour al-Hallāj*, 55.
5 We are getting used to accepting that space can be inverted, and to trying to force our imaginative faculty to represent it. This confirms an experience encountered in meditation. This admittedly sounds paradoxical until one becomes versed in David Bohm's *Wholeness and the Implicate Order*.

representations of our minds. There is a gradual transition between these two extremes.

You will notice that, if when inhaling, we remember always having existed, we will, by the same token, lose our sense of space; whereas if upon exhaling, we think of ourselves as having descended through the spheres down to the existential level, we find ourselves once more located in space.

Self-Transcendence

While representing ourselves as timeless and spaceless, we can envision our psyche and body as being equally ourselves, but transient—a continuity in change. Here, in a real tour de force defying our mind's conditioning, we are extrapolating between spacelessness and space. This is the perspective of self-transcendence. The suspension of the breath establishes this condition.

9) The Notion of Time

Our commonplace notion of time is equally written into our programming. Little do we realize the extent to which our sense of the passage of time is based upon that biological metronome, the rhythm of our breath. If we slow down our breath, we will find that we are less involved in, and therefore, less dependent upon, existential circumstances—hence, the wonderful sense of freedom of the contemplative. Now if we arrest our breath altogether, we find that we have lost the notion of the process of becoming, which is associated with the existential state; and we discover a timeless, transpersonal state.

In this state, we have the feeling of remembering having existed prior to our birth, or rather, conception, on Planet Earth—a wonderfully euphoric feeling. Paradoxically, we realize that at this level of our being we are still that which we always were and ever will be, even though our personality seems to have changed, and similarly, our circumstances.

You will remember that it is the practice of suspending breath between inhaling and exhaling that triggers off this sudden shift in the sense of time.

10) The Sufi Vantage Point

According to the Sufis, our breath simply reflects the ebb and flow of the divine breath. Seen from the divine vantage point, the divine exhaling is an expression of the divine nostalgia to manifest and to actuate the potentialities latent within the Divine Being. Conversely, in the divine inhaling, which liberates from conditioning, the quintessence of what is gained by the existential condition is recycled in the divine programming; for example, celestial splendor is materialized as beauty, or the divine harmony as orderliness, which begets power and majesty. The divine magnanimity manifests in some people as generosity; or the quite understandable human sense of fulfillment in building a beautiful house; or joy at listening to beautiful music or enjoying splendid works of art; or projecting our thoughts and aspirations in a creative way so that they are materialized.

Something is gained by a thought materializing as an act or object or being. Besides, an immeasurable yield is gained by the interactions between these beings, because it is thanks to this that the divine software reprograms itself with our input and participation. This is exactly why Ibn 'Arabi warns about the seclusion practiced by monks and hermits because, he says, we might miss out on the divine revelation vouchsafed in the existential state.

On the other hand, we humans also harbor a need for freedom. Unless we balance our involvement with life with our freedom from dependence upon the gratification it may offer us, and unless we open the doors to the wonder and meaningfulness behind what we witness in the world, we may find that our field of consciousness narrows down to our personal interest. Then we may open ourselves to an escalation of our tendency for greed.

Chapter One
Purification Practices with the Elements

Perhaps the most basic and essential breathing practice prescribed in the Sufi Order International is what has come to be known as the four purification breaths, or element breaths. These are based upon four fundamental alchemical processes: (i) filtering, (ii) liquifying, (iii) burnishing, and (iv) distilling.[1]

The corresponding modes of breath are: (i) inhale through the nose, exhale through the nose; (ii) inhale through the nose, exhale through the mouth; (iii) inhale through the mouth, exhale the through nose; (iv) inhale through the mouth, exhale through the mouth.

Each mode of breathing is performed three or five times. The rhythm of the breath must be natural, not forced. There is no retention of breath in these practices. It is best to perform them in nature, in communion with the elements. These practices may be considered as baptisms with the four elements: (i) earth, (ii) water, (iii) fire, (iv) air.

As we exhale, we will be consciously purifying our life field from its many different kinds of pollution; and as we inhale, we will consciously draw fresh energy from the elements, recharging our magnetic field and thus ensuring the regeneration of our tissues.

At a first stage, we identify with our magnetic field, then with our life field more generally, and then, ultimately, with our subtle bodies.[2] At a further

---

1 Incidentally, the Mazdean tradition, known to us through the Magi and continued in Zoroastrianism, was based upon the rituals of knighthood, and has been perpetuated in the Sufi orders. The Mazdean experience of the elements was invariably linked with a contemplation of the archangels of whom these elements are considered to be the bodies. This is now done in the Ziraat ceremony of the Sufi Order, founded in 1910 by Hazrat Inayat Khan, which aims at re-establishing our connection with the universe as composed of living beings, rather than as matter that we can manipulate.

2 See description in Part Five, Chapter Two, "Embodying the States of Awakening."

stage, we will consciously purify our emotions and thoughts from anything that we do not feel comfortable with.[3]

Baptism With Earth *Filtering*

As you exhale, imagine that you drain any polluted energy from your magnetic field into the earth. For healing purposes, envision the lymphatic system serviced by the lymph glands, which acts as a plumbing system in the body and has its counterpart in the subtle bodies. Seize this opportunity to rid yourself of any idiosyncrasies of your being that you dislike.

As you inhale through the nostrils, concentrate upon drawing tellurian (earth) magnetism from the soles of your feet upward along the spine, reaching the crown chakra. Think of your body as a plant that is drawing energy from the earth. However, take heed of the fact that in the human being, earth energy (contrasting with what is traditionally called *spirit*) needs to be transmuted as it rises. Enter into the consciousness of the cells of your body, which thrive as they are regenerated by availing themselves of new bouts of energy.

Baptism With Water *Liquifying*

As you inhale through the nostrils, shifting your attention from your lowest chakra upwards, you will notice that the energy of the higher chakras is more subtle than the lower ones.[4] Towards the end of the upward thrust of your inhalation, you will develop a sense of what is meant by this subtle form of energy, of spirit. This sense of a subtle form of energy will give you a clue to what is meant by your etheric body or subtle bodies.

Fine-tune your sensitivity to the variety of frequencies of wavelengths of the energy composing your field; earmark this particularly fine form of energy: spirit. You will discover, at the core of your being, something of the nature of gossamer—quintessential. Try to identify with it. It strikes one as being immaculate; Pir-o-Murshid Inayat Khan describes it as a mirror that can never become tarnished by whatever impressions it reflects. In a high state of consciousness, you identify with pure spirit. It might prove helpful to represent pure spirit as the finest possible form of energy, corresponding to the immaculate origin of one's being in its pristine state. Imagine that this immaculate core of your being is still present within the distortions or defilements coming from the very fact of existence.

---

3 See description in Part Three, Chapter Two, "The Sufi Dhikr."

4 It may prove helpful to parallel the contrast between pure spirit and tellurian energy with the difference between a high voltage, but comparatively low amperage, current with a low voltage, high amperage one.

As you exhale through the lips, imagine that the energy of the essence of your being, the spirit, is acting as a catalyst to unleash the latent energy at the biological level, descending like a cascade symbolizing the waters of life—the quickening by the Holy Spirit.

Advanced practice: At a further stage, you may discover that you exist at several levels. Your identity is many-tiered. You may reach a point at which you come to terms with the fact that this quintessential energy, which we call spirit, is actually a component of your own life field.

Sometimes this high-powered energy seems to break through as an outburst, rather like a waterfall. Consequently, you may have the impression that it descends upon you, shattering and regenerating you. This is due to the release of tension between the two poles of your own being.

Now envision this energy field as permeating your magnetic field, just like an eddy in a wave interference pattern. You may have the impression that this fine energy filters through your magnetic field while being interspersed with it, rather as the river Rhone diffuses through Lake Geneva.

Baptism with Fire *Burnishing*

As you inhale through the lips, imagine what it would be like to be an incandescent coal sucking air from the environment.[5] You may identify with this igneous body, which flashes as you inhale and exhale. You may have the impression of undergoing a more drastic kind of purification than with the preceding elemental breaths. The baptism of fire is a wonderful opportunity to work with your psyche, to help rid yourself of those idiosyncrasies you dislike most in yourself: hatred, cruelty, guile, deviousness, anything that humiliates one's spirit because it falls below one's loftiest ideal. You have the impression of incinerating them in the flame of truthfulness.

As you exhale through the nose, imagine the center of your spine to be incandescent, like a flame; and represent to yourself the different colors in a flame, starting with a scarlet red at the bottom, then passing through the colors of the spectrum from orange, to yellow, green, and blue, until you reach the top of your head, where the blue hues merge into violet, and of course, even though we do not see it, ultraviolet.

Imagine the center of your aura in the area of your spine to be like that flame. The clue to doing this is to watch the way the particular type of energy you feel in one chakra tends to shift its frequency as it flows into the next one. You will find that when you concentrate on the lower chakras, the radiance of your aura is in the infrared or red frequency range; in the solar plexus, it

5 In fact, the body is in a process of combustion, a process called phosphorescence. The resulting radiation emanating from the body is a bioplasmic effusion. This is particularly enhanced in the firefly or deep sea fish, or in some bats living in underground caves.

is orange; and in the higher chakras it is shifting from green through blue to violet. The effect of this visualization is that the infrared radiance of your aura will automatically be transmuted into light in the visible spectrum, and eventually into ultraviolet. In the traditional schools this is referred to as transmuting fire into light. Your aura now appears as a spectrum of diaphanous hues, glistening like a rainbow.

Baptism With Air *Distilling*

As you inhale through the lips, while your consciousness extends into outer space, envision yourself as a vulnerable formation—actually, an eva-nescent vortex in the universe. It is helpful at this stage to realize that it is not really true that a wave emerges from the ocean, but rather each wave is the apex of the upward thrust of the whole ocean; the whole ocean is involved in the motion of each of its parts. On the one hand, it is a gratifying feeling to think of oneself as an expression of the whole universe. On the other hand, we have pointed out that we are both a vortex and a relatively permanent sub-whole of the universe, each endowed with our personal idiosyncrasies. Consequently, while the whole universe is somehow involved in the very nature of our being, we still have a choice of which of the elements that we borrow from the universe we wish to highlight.

Advanced practice: As you exhale through the lips, experience the joy of being dispersed into outer space, and eventually, in the subtler space. While diffusing, one is also radiating at infinite distances. However, we can never lose ourselves or merge in the universe, as some meditators have the impression of, or seek for when meditating; instead, our life field gets intermeshed, or interspersed, with the environment. Like an eddy in a lake, we may lose sight of it as it combines with other eddies to form a wave interference pattern,[6] but it can be retrieved, and therefore, still maintains its integrity within its very dispersal.

It may be the other way round: you are afraid of losing yourself. Your understandable fear of losing yourself is due to the very compulsiveness of the most basic of all instincts: self-preservation. However, realizing that we could not lose ourselves even if we tried, should give you some reassurance. One of the aims of the ascetics is overcoming fear. When the fear of the

---

6 An illustration of a wave interference pattern would be as follows: if you should drop gravel into a lake, each particle will form eddies that will extend further and further. These eddies will combine to form what, in physics, is called a wave interference pattern. Looking at this wave interference pattern, one cannot detect the individual eddies; if two wave fronts cross one another, they will be able to extricate themselves from their composition unscathed. In the same way, these eddies that elude detection can be extricated, using techniques in physics such as Fourier analysis.

unknown is overcome, you become an adept on the spiritual path. However, as stated in the preface, do not overstress yourself. Just stay at the edge of your capacity.

Advanced practice

Furthermore, as you exhale, expand your consciousness so that it becomes all-encompassing. As you disperse the frontiers of your being, you may have the impression that your consciousness is all-encompassing. Your consciousness seems now to be the consciousness of the universe, the cosmic observer watching what you thought was yourself. The Buddha described his experience thus: the personal notion of consciousness is carried over into cosmic consciousness without any break in continuity, and consequently, no break in memory.

You may, therefore, enjoy letting go of yourself, knowing that by so doing you will not lose yourself irretrievably. The condition for change, and therefore, improvement is to flow with that law of the universe outlined by alchemists: everything needs to break down, fall apart, and dissolve before it can be reformed in a new configuration. This will give you a sense of freedom from your self-image; from your opinions; from being bogged down in your personal emotions, or emotional dependence, or addictions, or the success or failure of your undertakings, or adulation, or rejection, or, ultimately, from your personal will (or personal cussedness).

Now as you inhale, as the bits and pieces of your being are once more pieced together, having removed these erstwhile limits of your personal purview, you will discover the way the whole universe restructures you, just as the whole sea can be seen as emerging in each wave. Yet paradoxically, you will discover your inherent freedom in customizing this creative faculty of the self-organizing universe, in accordance with the way you wish to be, emancipated from the past that had become sclerosed in you.

In addition, you will find that your personal vantage point and personal self-image will adumbrate the immensity of divine consciousness, the splendor of the divine majesty.

Now shift your sense of identity to your etheric or subtle body, and envision yourself as volatile, somewhat like gossamer, interfused with a kind of celestial matter that lies hidden behind gross matter.

As you exhale, free yourself from your commonplace notion of substance and experience yourself as dematerializing, and then rematerializing as you inhale, to the point where the vortex of your being seems to merge with the totality; and then reemerge.

The beauty of this mode of purification is that those aspects of oneself that one does not relish dissolve in the process. Then one has found freedom from bodiness, from one's mental constructs, from personal emotions, from one's personality, and ultimately, from one's individuality.

Advanced practice

At a more advanced stage, rather than envisioning yourself as a formation in which the bounty of the universe is converged, identify yourself with pure intelligence. All the other aspects of your being may now be considered as a support system. Think of yourself as meaningfulness, rather than trying to grasp meaningfulness. You are not only a participant in the very thinking and programming of the universe, you are the congruence of the meaningfulness of the universe. In fact, rather than imagining the universe as its hardware, one imagines it as its software, as fundamentally a program—pure meaningfulness.[7]

Advanced practice

Toward the end of the outward breath, extend your consciousness into the vastness of outer space, and think of the whole universe as an enormous force field that is partly crystallized in the fabric of the galaxies. Now, if you emphasize that feature of your life field that seems like a vortex, that is without boundary, you will see yourself inextricably intermeshed with the stars in the cosmic immensity. When consciousness becomes thus all-encompassing, the amount of energy converged into the vortex of the magnetic field becomes incomparably greater; energy builds up. The clue is freeing oneself from one's limited self-image. Here the relationship between consciousness and energy becomes particularly evident.

---

7 Can you grasp the difference between vibration and sound? The patterns of frequencies of energy manifest to our senses as, for example, the pulsing of air affecting our eardrums. The meaningfulness behind the universe could be translated in terms of a blueprint of sheer vibration; this is precisely what Pythagoras meant by the symphony of the spheres: energy imprinted with meaning, carrying meaning like radio signals. Thus, the mind rides the wind.

Chapter Two
Influence of the Elements Upon Our Psyche

To apply the breathing practices with the elements in order to unfurl poten-
tialities in our personality, we need to gauge the kind of qualities in our soul
that correspond with earth, water, fire, and air. These will remain concepts
unless we experience them.

Let us try to feel, to sense the difference between how you experience the
elements when you find them in yourself if you are turning within, or if you
are reaching upwards in the transcendental dimension.

As you breathe in, you are not just withdrawing from the environment,
but you are also drawing the environment into yourself, while converting or
transmuting it. As you hold your breath after inhaling, suspend any thoughts.
Now, as you exhale, you may sense the emergence in yourself of something
new, which is not the way you ingest the environment, but something that
lay in wait within you and that emerges when catalysed by its counterpart in
the environment. We are recurrently reborn.

Earth

Let us start by concentrating on the earth. As you exhale, you may notice
that something of the nature of the reliability, the resilience, the strength
of the earth latent in you surfaces. Now, on inhaling, concentrate on those
features of the earth in yourself. This is an effective method of concretizing
these qualities. Instead of just thinking of the element as something outside
of yourself, you will arouse representations and emotion in your self that
match the emotion that you feel in the earth. The emotion is more powerful
than the thought; you discover in yourself the very same power that moves
the universe, the stars, the sap in the trees, the very molecules of the earth. In
the weight of your body, you may feel the gravity pull of the earth—gravity is
more intensified where matter is closely knit, and is rarified in outer space:
space is landscaped. Gravity is a kind of power; it may be the most basic of

all powers. It may be looked upon as an expression of the power latent in space.

Therefore, I suggest that as we walk, we concentrate on two things at the same time. One is the power that holds the molecules or atoms of the earth together; they would fly off in all directions if it weren't for that cohesive power that is holding them together. We find that same power in our body and also in our psyche.

Consider the difference between the kind of self-organizing faculty of the universe that we've discovered in matter, organizing itself out of chaos, and on the other hand, at a certain stage in the evolution, our human will that comes in and intervenes in that self-organizing faculty. This constitutes a further development of the self-organizing faculty that passes through our individuality, and is customized by our personal will—two factors.

Stand up now, and see if you can feel the contact between the soles of your feet and the floor or ground. Now try to get into the consciousness of all those molecules of the earth that have this faculty of holding its components together. It will give you the sense of the cohesion of your own being too. This faculty confers upon you some kind of resilience against any impact which might tend to shoot you off balance. It will keep you centered, and also help you to stand your ground, whatever happens

Think of it as the divine will, customized as your will. Feel the power in your being. Move slowly, consciously, willfully, absolutely under control. To match the work we are doing with the *waza'if*, think of the wazifa *ya wali*, which means mastery.

The same power that moves the universe is to be found in you, and when you are aware of it, it gives you mastery.

Hazrat Inayat Khan

I see some of the rishis and sannyasins and dervishes walking with the power of God. It's not the ego power, it's the power of God, spiritual power. You can feel that power in your feet, in the contact of your feet with the earth.

Water

Try to feel your contact with water in the environment: the rain, the river or stream, the ocean. We want to explore those faculties in our psyche that can be matched with water. It's a totally different feeling than the earth: it's flowing. Now turn within and see if you can feel a kind of flowing, the emergence of life. This is the rebirthing that is taking place in you, which moves forward inexorably, recurrently. The whole evolutionary march is not only written into your body but also into your psyche. We block it sometimes, when we become cantankerous and self-destructive. To move forward like this, you always have to look forward, as if you are riding a horse; you always have to look forward so that the pull of the future is stronger than the push of the past. You leave the past behind: you are advancing. And you've got to laugh. You must not take yourself too seriously. Power is rather serious, but water gives you this wonderful sense of *Yes, OK, it's wonderful, of course*, and so on. Just be ready for whatever happens, whatever comes on your path. Even with your projections for the future, you must be prepared for them all to break down. But they might turn out to be better than you thought, different; and maybe if you think that it's a catastrophe, you might find that what seems to be a catastrophe may aver itself, ultimately, to be a victory. The water faculty in our psyche enjoins upon us not to be pigheaded or stubborn, or just blocked by one's will.

Fire

Fire is uncompromising in its cathartic action. It will set up a sudden change, perhaps unexpectedly—in the instant of time, as we learn in Sufism. The instant of time is different from the moment in time. In the moment in time, the past overlaps the future; if you are listening to music, you can hear the notes that you've just heard, and when you hear the next notes, you still hear the notes that you just heard—there's an overlap. Whereas, in music there is such a thing as an apostrophe, a dead beat, and that marks the instant of time: a sudden change from one situation to the other. We think that everything is the consequence of the past, but there are new dispensations that take place, which emerge from a kind of subliminal universe, *ex nihilo*, impromptu. Consequently, we need to be prepared for the unexpected, the non-determined. In fact, here lies the foundation of your freedom: freedom from conditioning, freedom from causality, even from retrocausality. And that which triggers off your freedom is your decision, your option. Think to yourself: *Well, what if? What if I did it differently?* Be prepared for taking the risk, whatever it is, but think differently. Avail yourself of all kinds of possibilities. For the Sufis, God is all possibility.

Paradoxically, in addition to investing you with the courage of letting go of an addiction, or just a blocked situation, and making a fresh start, this frees you from having to make a decision; it frees you from any prefiguration of the future that you have. Freedom from the past, freedom from the future: that's fire.

One of the aspects of fire, which is to be found in our character, is anger. I would rather say outrage rather than rage. When one's sense of propriety has been shocked, a kind of force emerges in one's being to right the wrong.

You become a knight by following your outrage. That's why my sister Noor did what she did: she was outraged by what the Nazis were doing.[1] And if you don't have that outrage, then you are spineless. We have to be careful about escapism from life, because then one doesn't know how to experience outrage. Outrage is not the same as rage; rage is personal, one has been hurt and one is angry—but outrage is cosmic. Of course, nature teaches us that in thunder. It awakens something in us. Some people are afraid of it, but I like to walk right out in the open when there is thunder, and when there is a risk. One of the classical descriptions of thunder is to be found in the Sixth Symphony of Beethoven.

Air

Air differs from earth, in that the molecules of air are not as susceptible to the gravity pull of the planet as the molecules of earth. However, the tendency of the molecules of air to disperse is balanced by the gravity pull. Likewise, we have a need for freedom, yet the combination in us of earth and air gives us some balance. Those whose quota of air in their psyche overbalances their quota of earth have a tendency to escape life and in certain circumstances, become a hermit or sannyasin. Our sense of responsibility, enhanced by the challenge offered by stress, counters our escapism. But there are several dimensions of freedom. You have to find freedom in yourself: freedom from one's opinion, as in the words of Buddha. This will lead you through the dark night of the mind, where you question all that you ever thought—all your assumptions; for example, when you use the word *God*, you think that you are talking about God, and you are assuming tacitly that you understand what you mean. But you are not talking about God. You are talking about what you think is God. More generally, we use all kinds of words like *spirituality*, but what does spirituality mean? And *meditation*, but what does meditation mean? All of these words are just clichés. There comes a time when you think that it is not real. I'm living in a world of mental constructs; I want real experience. And that's what we're trying to do: to have real experience; but then, the trouble is that we interpret our experience in terms of our mental constructs. Surreptitiously, the mental projections of our psyche come through the back door. So as we awaken to a more advanced sense of meaningfulness, we learn to free ourselves from those mental constructs by replacing them with others. Eventually, you reach further ones and so on; because if the air faculty in you leads you to destroy your mental constructs, and you have nothing at <u>all, then you are</u> lost. And that's the reason why it's wiser to keep on shifting to

1 Noor Inayat Khan (1914-1944) sacrificed her life in the cause of freedom through her role as an underground wireless radio operator in Paris in World War II. See Basu, *Spy Princess: the Life of Noor Inayat Khan.*

more intelligent mental constructs, and finally, to let the divine intelligence take over, emancipated from its distortions due to our faulty notion of ourselves.

Moreover, we need to consider freedom from the way the divine emotion in us may be distorted by our personal bias, which is often one's personal emotions. Personal emotion, divine emotion—what does it mean? Are they different categories? How do they relate? In theory, they are the two poles of the same thing, so don't think of them as two different things. But it is interesting is to see how divine emotion can manifest right into human emotion, and how human emotion can be transfigured into what one might call divine emotion. Somehow, by freeing oneself from emotional addiction, the emotions become sublimated and very beautiful. Actually, what one means by addiction is dependence, isn't it? If you are seeking freedom, you want to be free from dependence, to do without any crutches at all. We are dependent upon people, but there is such a thing as codependency. Be careful with the concept of codependency, as it means seeing things unilaterally, from the personal bias, and disregarding our interdependence, which, admittedly, needs to be balanced. There is a danger of being purely selfish.

Therefore, the great art is to know how to find freedom inside, while incurring some modicum of dependence outside. How you do that is very subtle. That's where the teaching of the East has a very special message; because one is adding a further dimension to our lives, it has a kind of cosmic value.

This time, in our breathing practices, instead of turning within or reaching outwards, we will apply the ascending-descending mode of breathing. As you inhale, transfer your attention from one chakra to the next.[2] Concentrate on each chakra, in turn, on one inbreath. Hold your breath, turn your eyeballs upwards, and as you exhale, transfer your attention down the spinal cord, concentrating on each chakra in turn. Notice the difference between the energy of the bottom chakra and the energy of the crown chakra. I like to illustrate the bottom chakra as a current that has a lot of wattage but not much voltage, and the top chakra as an electric potential that has a lot of voltage but not much wattage or amperage. You could illustrate it as a heavy river running down a very gentle slope, or as a mountain stream gushing down, like a waterfall. It is a different type of energy.

---

2 See list of chakras on p. 81.

Chapter Three
Sensing the Life Field

Perhaps when studying elementary physics at school, you tried your hand at pouring metal filings around a magnet and were able to witness the typical pattern thus generated. Think of yourself both as a magnet, and also as the magnetic field surrounding it, and as a matter of fact, permeating it. The body as a whole exhibits the properties of a magnet. In fact, the electromagnetic field emitted by the body can be measured under laboratory conditions. Moreover, differences may be observed in the intensity of the electromagnetic potential in the proximity of the different chakras (the plexus of the autonomous nervous system). Most significant for meditators is the evidence of the impact of the meditator's concentration on the different chakras upon the potential emitted.[1]

Principles

It is helpful to start meditating by sensing the zones of energy around the body, particularly around the shoulders and in front of the heart plexus, and also surrounding the head. Eventually you can feel them permeating the cells, but this takes great sensitivity.

These energy fields are referred to in the more progressive scientific circles as the *life field*. Having ascertained their reality yourself, you will be able to identify with them, step by step.

If you are very sensitive, you will note the difference between (*i*) a static magnetic field; for example, when combing your hair, you may sense sparks; (*ii*) an electromagnetic field coming from the dynamic nature of body functions; for example, the jiggling of the cells, particularly as they divide in the process of mitosis; (*iii*) a gravitational field that becomes mainly noticeable when the g-force increases or diminishes; for example in an elevator;

1 See White, John, and Stanley Krippner, eds. *Future Science: Life Energies and the Physics of Paranormal Phenomena.* Hiroshi Motoyama, 445.

(*iv*) the *chi* force, experienced when shifting one's concentration from one chakra to the next, and which is also ascertained when an acupuncturist pulls the needle out; (*v*) the etheric body, which pulses with your breath; (vi) the aura, called *bioluminescence*; and (*vii*) your celestial body, which is experienced in advanced meditation and referred to by different esoteric traditions, particularly the Sufis.

By identifying with these energy fields, you will enhance their energy level. And by the sheer fact of becoming aware of these various forms of energy and working with them, you will feel yourself emitting more personal magnetism, or radiance.

You will find that these fields seem to have jagged ends, and keep replenishing themselves from the environment, just like a vortex; for example, a whirl-pool. Furthermore, they seem to intersperse or dovetail with one another like Chinese boxes or a many-tiered complex. Although they do not have a boundary, one may notice that they seem to extend themselves in a kind of zone. Consequently, one can only infer that they are a cross between a vortex and a discrete entity, like a cell bounded by a permeable membrane.

The energy in the human electromagnetic field flows in manifold ways. You may distinguish: *i*) a centripetal-centrifugal pulsing, synchronized with your breath; *ii*) an ascending-descending current, alternating, and possibly crisscrossing; *iii*) left-right polarization; *iv*) rotational motion; *v*) spiraling, ascending and descending; *vi*) streamers (plumes of energy); and *vii*) fluctuations in dimensions other than the three dimensions of our commonplace reductionist view of space; for example, in the nature of gravitational expansion and compression, or fluctuations in voltage and amperage. The life field includes the electrostatic and electromagnetic fields, the aura, the sonic field, and perhaps fields of other alternate forces such as the chi force, and is a complex phenomenon. It embodies a large range of forms of manifestation of pure energy. The difference in the grades of energy that you will earmark in your life field could be illustrated by the vast range of energy between a current having high voltage and low amperage, and a current having low voltage and high amperage. Or by the difference between a jet of water projected at high speed and a heavy stream meandering down a gentle slope.

The ancients envisioned the streamers that a highly sensitive person may sense, for example, above the head, as the Pentecostal tongues of flame; or the flashing from the temples as the winged thoughts of Greek mythology; or as appearing behind the shoulder blades. Whereas the wings of the Sera-phim include the plumes around the temples, those around the shoulder blades and those around the ankles can also be found in images of Hermes or Mercury.

46

The radiance of the streamers emanating from the shoulder blades has, when unfolded, often been compared by Sufis with a mantle of light. In the Parsifal legends, it was because there were holes in the mantle of Anfortas that the evil forces of the night were able to attack him.

If we attribute validity to the existence of higher bodies or, let us say, fields that have so far not yielded to the measurement of our scientific instruments, then we could account for some of the uncanny bouts of energy referred to by contemplatives. There is, for example, the quickening of the Holy Spirit reported by Christian mystics, with its equivalent in Sufism, *Ruh al-quddus,* or among Jewish mystics, the *Shekina.* Actually, we have been going along with the assumption that the body emits these fields, but what if the electromagnetic field, in fact, all the components of the life field, were the templates, the mold, in which the body is being formed? There is some solid argument in favor of this view. This might help one to understand what is meant by the *quickening of the Holy Spirit,* as opposed to the telluric energy that one hauls from the earth in kundalini practice.

Esoteric schools do not simply work with the electromagnetic field, or even the aura. The Sufis fashion the *celestial bodies* (a Mazdean tradition),[2] and the Tibetans work with the *illusory body,* the *emanation body,* the *body of splendor,* the *truth body,* and so forth.

Practices

1) You may check your body magnetism if you wave your hand in front of the heart chakra in a rotational manner, counterclockwise. By so doing, you will be churning your magnetic field. The area in front of your solar plexus may prove to be even more sensitive. Likewise, you may feel the energy around your temples, and at the top of your head.

2) Recall the law of Gauss: by swirling the area of your field counterclockwise, you induce a centrifugal current, which releases pent up energy into the environment.[3] By so doing, you draw in magnetism, which has a therapeutic effect. The Native Americans do this by waving eagle or hawk feathers. When they cleanse their auras with eagle feathers, holding out their arms like antennae, drawing energy from the four corners of the Earth, they have,

---

2 Corbin, *Spiritual Body and Celestial Earth,* 180.

3 You will, no doubt, remember from your school days the law of Gauss: supposing your right hand were a dynamo, should you rotate it in the direction of your curled fingers, you would be inducing an electric current in the direction of your extended thumb. The converse is also true: an electric current flowing in the opposite direction will set the dynamo turning in the opposite direction. This is important because, by virtue of the impact of mind over body, we can learn to enhance the flow of ions moving up the spine or down the spine, and consequently, fluctuate our electromagnetic field.

indeed, found an effective way of connecting with the electromagnetic field of the Earth and drawing it into their own electromagnetic field, to promote healing and gain healing power. They declare that they are not just working with telluric power, but with spirit. However, their secret most likely lies in triggering off the more subtle power by dint of the physical forces.

3) Place your hands next to your temples, holding them as if you were going to unscrew a jar. Turn each hand in a counterclockwise position (which means they will be going in opposite directions, with the right hand turning backwards and the left hand turning forwards). Then gradually move the hands outward, away from the temples, while continuing the turning movement. You will find a point, at some distance from the temples and different for each person, where there is a threshold between one level of energy and another. At this critical point, any fluctuating motion of your fingers is felt immediately in your temples.

4) Imagine your heart chakra to be like a miniature sun, dispensing a lot of energy forward, enhanced by your empathy.

5) A practice that could be applied to healing would consist in placing your hand (or hands) in the vicinity of your solar plexus, and then, while rotating your right hand counterclockwise, move it a few inches away, flushing polluted energy that has become stagnant. Then proceed in the same manner with your lymph glands.

6) Try to feel the streamers emanating from your shoulder blades. Envision them as unfolded and draped around your back, affording a kind of protection, or even as the robe investing the initiate into the Hermetic tradition. All the above practices will need to be extended to the aura of light.

7) The ankles and the soles of your feet complement each other, as do the heart chakra and the solar plexus. The soles of the feet are an inlet that can be blocked; therefore, consciously draining polluted energy into the earth through the soles of the feet as you exhale, will prove salutary. Alternate this with consciously drawing telluric energy from the Earth as you inhale. The enhancement of the plumes in the ankles is a feature of movement: jogging, and particularly, dancing. Picking up the right foot, as the whirling dervishes do, induces a current in the gap between the right foot and the left foot.

8) Lastly, there is a rather beautiful movement performed at the end of the Muslim prayer: the hands, which are cupped before the face, are raised over the head, and then parted and slowly lowered to either side, rather like pouring water on oneself. It is actually blessing oneself by directing the high-powered energy aroused in the prayer or meditation above the head, and spreading it over the whole body.

Chapter Four
Breath Directed
Centrifugally Versus Centripetally

If you expand your picture of your life field as you exhale, you will find that you will enhance the converging of the energy from the environment (or outer space) as you inhale. Furthermore, you will want to sublimate it as it closes in. Contrasting with this, we can glean fresh energy emerging from the unsounded depths of our being by turning within. Consequently, when we exhale, we do not just boomerang back the energy drawn in from outer space, but, in addition, we radiate fresh energy into the environment.

Practices

Before meditating, always be sure that you are sitting with your spine straight. Always begin a breathing practice by exhaling, prolonging the exhalation further at each breath.

As you exhale, always contract the abdomen first before the chest. And as you inhale, first dilate the abdomen, then the chest.

1) As you exhale, identify with your magnetic field and expand it. You will notice that although it does not have a boundary, it seems to extend in definite zones, as in the spectrum of light, in which there seems to be a quantum leap from one zone to another and not a gradual transition. This is where we can reconcile the model of the vortex with the model of a discrete entity, illustrated by a cell with a permeable membrane. In fact, it is a vortex which is multi-tiered into definite zones. Like our psyche, our life field is zoned by a number of defense barriers. This being accepted, you will notice that your life field does extend and expand in leaps and bounds.

2) When you inhale, imagine the magnetic field of the universe converging in such a manner that, as it gets closer, it intersperses with your magnetic field while galvanizing it. However, there is no way of locating where the

threshold lies. Once more you will notice the zones.[1] Although we do ingest the universe at all levels, physical, subtle, psychic, etc, thanks to the protective thresholds, the defense barriers that zone our life field, we are able to select those elements of impressions that we wish for or feel comfortable with, and reject those which we dislike or cannot cope with.

3) As you exhale, reject those elements in your life field from which you wish to free yourself. As you inhale, be attentive to those elements you wish to incorporate, by filtering out those you wish to eschew.

4) You may wish to hold your breath between inhaling and exhaling. As the energy thus sublimated proceeds further within, it will seem that space is inverted at the core of your being. This is difficult to imagine because it defies our commonplace norms. You encounter, at the inner core of your field, what seems at first to be a vacuum. As you cease inhaling and are about to hold your breath, concentrating on the solar plexus, it seems as though all the converged energy is sucked into a black hole; however, as you are about to start exhaling, it appears that, from your heart chakra, you are radiating the fresh energy emerging from the solar plexus. As a matter of fact, the heart chakra and the solar plexus are two poles of the same reality, one being an inlet, the other an outlet.

In the cosmic dimension, as you exhale, identify with your magnetic field, which does not have a boundary. Imagine that it is like a centrifugal spiral, expanding infinitely.

When you inhale, imagine the magnetic field of the universe converging like a centripetal spiral, so that as it gets closer it overlaps (or better, is interspersed with) your magnetic field, which does not have a boundary. There is no way of defining a threshold in the transition, because it is like the wave and the ocean.

5) Now, as you inhale, consciously transmute or sublimate the magnetism ingested from the environment (from the geomagnetic field, or from outer space). It will appear to be of an increasingly subtler nature as you proceed inward. As already mentioned, an example that might prove helpful could be found in the difference between a high voltage electric current having not very much amperage (pure spirit), and a lesser voltage current having more amperage (grosser energy).

---

1 If an eddy intersperses with another eddy, no spatial threshold can be defined separating them. Another example: In the case of the whole ocean emerging as a wave, one could assign a threshold at the average mean height of the water of the ocean. A rather similar situation presents itself with the branch of a tree. The whole tree comes through each branch; although, at least in this case, one could make a demarcation to establish where the branch starts and the tree ends (but it could not fail to be arbitrary).

Chapter Five
Directions of Breath
Ascending and Descending

One of the skills you will develop in the breathing techniques of meditation is that of stepping up energy, directed in such a manner as to hoist consciousness into higher levels of awareness. What this means exactly calls for further clarification.

In the preceding chapter, we learned, as we exhale, to become aware of the outreach of our life field in its cosmic dimension, and as we inhale, of the implicate order of our life field. In the present chapter we are going to explore the transcendent dimension of our life field as we inhale, shifting from identifying with our physical body to ever subtler levels of our life field; and then, as we exhale, we will experience the manner in which the subtler counterparts of our body crystallize into the configuration of our body's architectonics, right into our very body cells.

Practices

1) As you inhale, feel the telluric energy of the magnetism of the planet (the geomagnetic field). Feel it threading upwards in your spine, after entering through the soles of your feet, or the bottom of your spine if you are sitting cross-legged. Distinguish between this kind of energy and the energy you feel descending along your spine from the fontanelle (the top of your head), which is the energy which we like to consider as pure spirit.

2) Try to transmute the telluric energy as it leaps from one chakra to the next. It will appear to have a subtler nature as you proceed upwards.

3) As the energy is transmuted, moving from one chakra to the next in the course of your inhaling, envision this energy as an elevator hoisting your consciousness from cogitating about material situations to grasping meaningfulness (the software) behind that which manifests at the existential level. As you exhale, capture emotions coming through you that appear endowed with

cosmic magnitude and are inspiring; then envision forms or landscapes, or even melodies, that manifest these concretely.

4) As you inhale, keep on shifting your sense of identity from being a physical body to being your etheric body, then to being your celestial body. Hold your breath and identify with being pure spirit. As you exhale, witness the way the features of your celestial being manifest right through your physical body, however hampered by the limitations attendant upon existential conditions.

The Sufi Vantage Point

It is usual to do these practices while identifying oneself with one's commonplace sense of identity. Starting from this vantage point, you may then extend your notion of yourself into vaster and vaster reaches, or turn deeper and deeper within, until you come up against a monolithic void. Or again, you could shift your sense of identity into subtler and still subtler aspects of yourself in the hope of reaching beyond yourself.

But let us now attempt to look at the Sufi perspective from precisely the complementary vantage point to the personal. Indeed, things looked at from different vantage points may look different, yet somehow we are able to extrapolate them; for example, the vision of each eye differs slightly as each eye has two dimensional vision, but the brain extrapolates them by translating the parallax between the two into a third dimension. David Bohm shows that if you were to film fish with two cameras, placed on either side of the aquarium, the motions on both films would appear totally different; yet one can sense compelling relationships between them. Extrapolating between two vantage points confers further dimensionality upon our consciousness. Likewise, grasping the congruence between two thoughts will trigger off the *aha!* leap of mental alacrity.

The consequent psychological yield is enormous. The Sufis call this vantage point, which is antipodal to our personal vantage point, the *divine point of view*. As we know, our concept of God is circumscribed within our capacity to encompass infinity, eternity, perfection and the undetermined, the software of the universe; and our capacity always proves inadequate. The Sufis endeavor to bring the divine viewpoint to light by experience rather than conceptualization.

According to the Sufis, our breath simply reflects the ebb and flow of the divine breath. Seen from the divine vantage point, the divine exhalation is an expression of the nostalgia to manifest and actuate the potentialities latent within the Divine Being. For example, celestial splendor is materialized as beauty; the divine harmony as orderliness, which begets power and majesty, and so forth.

Conversely, seen from the divine vantage point, the divine inhalation is an expression of the divine act whereby the gist of all that is gained by the existential condition is fed back into the divine software. We humans experience this in our need to free ourselves from involvement in order to find peace, or from conditioning in order to grasp meaningfulness.

For the Sufi Kalabadhi, as God exhales, God releases the potentialities latent in the Divine Being from the solitude of unknowing: the cloud of unknowing (*al-'ama*), the level that remains a mystery (*al-ghayb*) for humans, the treasury of the divine secrets (*sirr as-sirr*). As God inhales, God reabsorbs the quintessence of all that manifested in the existential state, by integrating it into the solitude of unity (*wahdat*).

Practices

1) Bearing the above in mind as you exhale, try to feel the divine nostalgia in your desire to involve yourself with life in the world: with people; in circumstances; in fact, in the whole drama of life with its joys and pains, its triumphs and its defeats and challenges.

As you inhale, give vent to your need for freedom: freedom from involvement, freedom from any form of compulsion, from conditioning, a need for peace and serenity.

2) As you shift your sense of identity while inhaling, turn your attention to the fact that the condition and attunement of your celestial bodies reflects upon the condition and attunement of your physical body. Then, as you exhale, turn your attention to the way the condition and attunement of your physical body and mind reflect upon the condition and attunement of your celestial bodies.

You will notice that it is the gist of that condition or attunement, and of the know-how gained in existence, which is incorporated on a higher level and distilled.

3) In the Sufi perspective, as you feel the divine impulse working through you, reabsorbing all things into unity, think of yourself as the perfume extracted from the flowers—the quintessence of the flowers. The contingent aspect of yourself is now discarded. You are experiencing resurrection. You will notice that you seem to be more and more impersonal, more and more amorphous; that is, space has lost its relevance. You also seem increasingly timeless, which means that the arrow of time has lost its significance.

Furthermore, you seem less and less limited, and more and more perfect, while realizing that this only applies to the higher levels of your being.

> *Divinity is human perfection and humanity is divine limitation.*[1]

Hazrat Inayat Khan

---

1 Inayat Khan, *The Complete Sayings of Hazrat Inayat Khan*, 19.

Chapter Six
Pranayama and Kasab

Yogis have devised a means of triggering off an outburst of energy in our electromagnetic field by learning how to polarize it right and left, bottom and top. This surfeit of energy is then applied to hoist consciousness into a transcendental state (*samadhi*), or turn inward.

It is known that energy, in the form of ions, is transported along three conduits made up of the bundles of nerves inside the spinal cord and along the two lateral trunks, all three being extensions of the brain. The spinal cord governs the functions of the central nervous system, whereas the lateral trunks form the two paravertebral sympathetic chains, and serve the autonomic nervous functions controlling the visceral functions of the body. The central (conscious) nervous functions are connected with the autonomic functions through a vast network of afferent-efferent fibers all along the spine.

Of course, one should not overlook the action of other currents of energy; for example, the aura, the chi force or the acupuncture meridians.

Yoga is founded on the assumption that, in principle, all autonomic functions can fall within the control of the will. At the physiological level, the secret would consist of facilitating the flow between the lateral trunks and the spinal cord. Nervous pathways are enhanced by repeated use; in learning, we are training both mind and body by wearing pathways in the brain and reprogramming the mind, enhancing memory by repetition.

The practice of *pranayama*, which is part of the overall training process formulated by Patanjali, consists in directing consciousness to the flow of energy, synchronized with the ebb and flow of breath, and thereby affecting it, and specifically, subjecting it to the will.

As we have seen in previous chapters, we can distinguish at least four directions taken by these currents: a) centrifugal-centripetal, b) ascending-descending, c) rotational (clockwise-counterclockwise), and d) spiraling (this last is a combination of the three previous ones).

By alternating between breathing through the left nostril and the right, one is segregating the lateral poles of the life field; then, by breathing through both nostrils simultaneously, the poles are being reconnected. By holding the breath after inhaling through one nostril, the energy of the left pole or the right pole is relayed upwards along the spinal cord, through the connecting pre- and postganglionic fibers, and enhancing this connection between the autonomic and the central nervous systems. Exhaling through a nostril after holding the breath enhances the impact of the central nervous system over the autonomic, by wearing a passage of ions along the connecting fibers.

Advanced Practices

To foster the connection between the central and autonomic nervous systems, Yoga methods enhance the connection between the hypothalamus and the pituitary gland. This is achieved by exercising pressure on the area of the palate lying just below the pituitary, by curling the tongue upwards and pressing it against the palate as you hold your breath; also, by crossing the eyes slightly while turning them upwards and concentrating on the location of the pituitary gland, called *bindu* in Yoga. Yogis train themselves to do this by concentrating for increasing lengths of time on the tip of the nose, then the bridge of the nose, then the middle of the forehead, then farther up backwards, concentrating on the top of the skull.

The retention of breath in the breathing practices adopted by Sufis is, in general, shorter than that recommended by Yogis or Tibetan Buddhists. This is because Yoga offers techniques that afford protection to the heart, liver, and pancreas against excessive pressure from overly distending the lungs.[1]

Yoga Method

Practices

Place the index finger of your right hand in the middle of your forehead (third eye), and rest the thumb of your right hand on your right nostril and the ring finger of your right hand on your left nostril.

1) Inhale through the left nostril while pressing your thumb;

2) hold your breath as you press your thumb and ring finger;

3) exhale through the right nostril as you press your ring finger;

4) inhale through the right nostril while pressing your ring finger;

5) hold your breath while pressing both fingers;

6) exhale through the right nostril while pressing your thumb.

1 The Yogic *bandhas* are intended to develop the muscles supporting the diaphragm and the larynx.

While holding your breath, curl your tongue upwards and press it against your palate, drawing it backwards without forcing. Also turn your eyeballs upward while converging them slightly.

In the Yoga method, you count four beats inhaling, sixteen beats holding the breath, and eight beats exhaling. A beat could be considered as one second. Being very still, one becomes aware of one's heartbeat and breathes in rhythm with the throbs of one's heart, which are normally somewhat faster than a second, more like seventy-two beats in a minute. As mentioned above, extreme caution is recommended to avoid exercising excessive pressure on vital body organs by distending the diaphragm.

Kasab, the Sufi Perspective on Pranayama

Principles

By and large, breathing exercises practiced by Sufis, called *pas-i anfas*, are associated with contemplation of the divine presence or of the divine names (the *dhikr*, or *wazifa*). Some of the methods adopted by the Sufi Order founded by Pir-o-Murshid Inayat Khan were probably derived from the osmosis that took place between Hindus and Muslims in India, where reciprocal influences were felt.[2]

The practice of *kasab* is very similar to that of pranayama, with the difference that one inhales through the left nostril and exhales through the right nostril three (or five, or ten) times; then one inhales through the right nostril and exhales through the left nostril the same number of times; then one inhales through both nostrils and exhales through both nostrils the same number of times.

The position prescribed for the hands is different: place the thumb of your right hand under your chin and rest the middle finger against your right nostril; then place the palm of your left hand on the back of the fingers of your right hand, resting the thumb of your left hand against your left nostril.

The timing is also different: the retention of breath is twice the number of beats of inhaling or exhaling. For example, inhale four, hold eight, exhale four; or five-ten-five, six-twelve-six, etc.

Sufism throws a whole new perspective upon the practice of pranayama. The reason for this is that pranayama represents a stage in Yoga that leads to samadhi by hoisting one's consciousness into a timeless state, riding the uplift of telluric energy as it is transmuted from one chakra to the next. Since Sufism validates what is gained in the existential state, the dervishes endeavor to explore the manner in which this timeless state flows into the process of becoming. Hence, one finds in Sufism a subtle analysis of the different

---

2 See Digby, "Encounters with Yogis in Indian Sufi Hagiography."

dimensions of time. This draws the attention of the meditator to the way the notion of time varies with the attunement in meditation.

Indeed, our commonplace notion of time proves itself to be totally inadequate. Present-day physicists recognize several dimensions of time.[3] These findings confirm the experience of some contemplatives.

As you meditate, at some point you will distinguish between at least two dimensions of time: a) the process of becoming, often described as the arrow of time; and b) a transcendental dimension. This latter dimension could be illustrated by noting that an event, which took place at the physical level at a given time and place, is extended in our memory. Or again, as you meditate, you derive the impression that, at some level of your being, you are eternal and unchanging; while at other levels you are changing, transient, and perishable. It may be helpful to illustrate this by a pendulum. The pendulum slows down as it approaches the end of its swing on one side, then on the other; and it seems to stop, as if it were suspended in space for a fraction of a second, before swinging back in the opposite direction.

In the same vein, as we hold our breath at the end of inhaling and before exhaling, we experience a state in which the process of becoming seems to be suspended. It is something like an apostrophe, a hiatus; for example, in a musical composition. It gives the impression of a break from the past, a new beginning, starting from scratch, a quantum leap. For the Sufis, time is ever-recurrent, rather than linear.

The Sufi contemplatives take advantage of this suspension to make a fresh start in their lives by finding some respite from the constraint of past patterns. Sufis clearly distinguish between the moment of time and the instant. In what we commonly call the moment of time, the past overlaps the future. For example, listening to music, the note that you heard a moment ago continues to live while you listen to the present one, and in some cases you can anticipate the note to come while listening to the present one.

What seems to be coming and going is really the result of becoming and manifestation.[4]

Abu'l-Hasan al-Hujwiri

But what emerges in the instant of time is perennial.

Whosoever, considering pre-eternity and post-eternity, is oblivious of what lies between these, simply proclaims the divine unity. And whosoever, dis-

---

3 That, psychologically, time seems to creep frustratingly slowly at times, or forge forward at a disconcerting pace at others, is a foregone conclusion; but in the findings of astrophysicists exploring black holes, there is some indication that time can be reversed. Logically then time can vary: slow down or accelerate.

4 Al-Hujwiri, *Kashf al-Mahjúb*, 369.

regarding pre- and post-eternity, considering what lies between these, simply observes the prescriptions of religion. Whosoever, however, bypasses both poles and what lies between them, grasps reality.[5]

Mansur al-Hallaj

In their meditations, the Sufis try to stalk the emergence of new dispensations of reality at their inception, thus applying the Islamic doctrine regarding the recurrence of Creation at each instant.

Commenting on the Qur'anic word, Ibn 'Arabi refers to the *renewal of the Creation by each breath.*[6]

What is more, that which is thus spirited into the existential state acquires perennity; it becomes adamant, like gold, if it is consolidated by the realization of the contemplative. According to the Sufis, there is no way in which what has been existentiated should return to the state of possibility.

When the owner of waqt *(the instant of time) comes into possession of* hal *(that is: it becomes a permanent state) he is no more subject to change, and is made steadfast in his state.*[7]

Abu'l-Hasan al-Hujwiri

Practices

1) As you inhale through your left nostril, ponder upon your life, which may seem like a film. The salient events will be highlighted, and an overall trend will become apparent.

2) As you hold your breath, reflect upon the fact that the past does continue to live, but is transformed. The seed you planted does not exist any more as a seed, but may have generated a harvest. The seeds of the plants thus generated may have mutated, but this only concerns the physical level. Actually, the occurrences at the physical level continue to live in our psyche. Here too, they are transmuted by repentance and our resolve. Otherwise, one could be damned forever.

There is no way in which, whatever compensation we might give for a hardship or injustice we inflicted upon a person, we can expect to be absolved. But, if having really done our very best, we decide not to repeat the action that we regret, it does affect the way the past lives in our psyche. And this is precisely where behavior that is psychologically motivated has its impact at

---

5 Massignon, Louis and P. Kraus. *Akhbār al-Hallāj, texte ancien relatif à la prédiction et au supplice du mystique musulman al-Hosayn b. Mansour al-Hallāj*, 78.

6 Ibn 'Arabi, *Les illuminations de La Mecque (Futuhat al-Makkiyah): textes choisis, présentés et traduits de l'arabe*, 89.

7 Al-Hujwiri, *Kashf al-Mahjúb*, 369.

existential levels. Therefore, we should not underestimate the importance of this realization to help us deal with our remorse. The Shaykhs have said, *Time is a cutting sword*, because time cuts the root of the future and the past, and obliterates care of yesterday and tomorrow from the heart.

You will find that a heartening realization dawns upon you: *I don't have to continue being the person or personality I have been so far—I am free!*

3) As you exhale, ponder upon how the future, as you had anticipated it, would now be relieved of a burden by your new way of looking at things. Project the way you could be. Realize that you carry within you the possibility of becoming a new person, and prefigure how it would affect circumstances. This is important because our future is considerably determined by our self-esteem.

4) As you inhale through the right nostril, consider your anticipation of the future. Our prognosis of the future is sometimes filled with hope, but we can never discount some foreboding. See to what extent your prefiguration of the future is influenced by your hope for a personal advantage, and to what extent it is motivated by your estimation of values, your pursuit of excellence, building a better world, or being of service. Give priority to your perceptions of covetousness, as this must inevitably reduce the options available to us. In addition, our fears about unanticipated hazards weigh upon our prefigurations.

5) As you hold your breath, ready yourself for those options for the future that you had not anticipated. You will find freedom from at least the constraint that you had imposed upon the possibilities for the future by your prefigurations of it.

6) As you exhale through your left nostril, see how the burden of the past living in your psyche is lightened by your liberated perspective on the future.

7) As you inhale through both nostrils, reflect upon the fact that in the process of becoming, both the causality generated in the past and the purposefulness governing the programming of your future condition you.

8) As you hold your breath, grasp the prevalence of the infinite, many-splendored potentialities of your higher self over the constraint of this existential conditioning. It is as though one is at the crossroads, where the vector of time, connecting transcendence to the process of becoming, intercepts the vector of becoming.

At this juncture, it looks as though one's personal will coincides with the divine will.

Waqt (the instant in time) is that whereby a man becomes independent of the past and the future, as, for an example, when an influence from God

descends into his soul and makes his heart collected, he has no memory of the
past and no thought about that which is about to come.[8]

Abu'l-Hasan al-Hujwiri

9) As you exhale, you feel the overwhelming thrust of the divine will com-
ing through you. You embody the quality of *Dhu'l-Jalal wa'l-Ikram*: the Lord
of Majesty and Splendor.

Let Thy wish become my desire.[9]

Hazrat Inayat Khan

---

8 Ibid., 367.
9 Inayat Khan, *The Complete Sayings*, 101.

Chapter Seven
Transmuting Energy
Kundalini

Energy Spiraling

The following is a more advanced form of pranayama. The advantage of this practice is that it combines the centripetal direction assumed by energy currents in the life field, with the ascending ones, and the centrifugal with the descending ones.

Let us take a further look at the life field. If, indeed, it is in some respects like a vortex, and since the center of a vortex is a vacuum, one may expect that energy rising or descending in one of the lateral channels of the spinal cord tends to be sucked into the central channel and will, consequently, spiral upwards or downwards, as the case might be. This would ensure the interconnections between the nerve transmissions in the lateral channels with the central channel, which is to say, between the autonomic and central nervous systems of the body and hence, between the unconscious and conscious functions of the psyche. Moreover, this allows access by the personal will to functions normally governed by the unconscious autonomic system, thus insuring an impact upon them.

These connections take place at those junctures where the spirals, which have a common axis, crisscross—precisely the location of the chakras. Moreover, emphasis is laid on the two ends: a point at the bottom of the spine, called by the Yogis *muladhara*, which means the root, and the point where the spirals culminate at a location in the brain, which the Yogis call *bindu*. This latter point corresponds to the point of junction where the pituitary gland is linked with the hypothalamus; this is perhaps the most important junction in the body, linking the central nervous system to the autonomic.

From the above, it is obvious that the configuration of these streams in the life field bear a close resemblance to the caduceus, the symbol utilized by the Greeks for medicine. The difference is that some meditators describe these as double-looping at each chakra;[1] otherwise, they would crisscross at the front of the second chakra, at the back of the solar plexus, at the front of the heart chakra, at the back of the throat center, and at the front of the third eye.

If, indeed, *the mind rides the wind,*[2] then the energy from the environment, including outer space, is transmuted as it closes in towards the center of the spinal cord; and at the same time, the energy is sublimated as it rises in the central axis. This creates the configuration of a parabolic double helix, shifting consciousness from the perception of reality experienced as *outside*, towards resonating with the inner lining of the same reality revealing itself *inside*. All the while, we snatch a grasp of the programming behind what manifests and occurs as facts or events.

Practices

1) As you inhale through the left nostril, you may observe the way that telluric (earth) energy flows from the bottom of the spine to the left, then forward, then right, etc.—clockwise, if seen from above—while being distilled as it rises. Feel the pull towards the vacuum in the center of the spine while at the same time it swirls upwards, culminating somewhere in the center of the brain.

2) Hold your breath, turning your eyeballs upwards while converging them slightly, and curl your tongue and press the tip end of the underside of your tongue against your palate. As we have seen, these are conditions favorable to recollecting having existed prior to our birth or conception; that is, prior to being involved in the existential state.

3) Exhale through the right nostril, swirling celestial energy, pure spirit, downwards and clockwise.

4) Now, as you inhale through the right nostril, you will be swirling the energy counterclockwise, both in the upwards direction and downwards. Follow the same principles as when inhaling though the left nostril, except that you will be swirling the energy counterclockwise. Your experience in holding your breath will be also identical as before. Do the same as you exhale, except that you will be spiraling downwards, counterclockwise.

5) Inhale through both nostrils. You will be swirling earth energy upwards in two concentric spirals, representing a polarity between the positive and receptive forces within you (left-handedness and right-handedness). While

---

1 For example, Lama Geshe Kelsang Gyatso, *The Clear Light of Bliss,* 21.
2 Ibid., 29.

being aware of the suction effect centered in the central axis, you will notice the way the spirals crisscross in the chakras.

6) As you hold your breath, attention is drawn to the way these currents merge in the brain, at the junction between the pituitary and hypothalamus. This is enhanced by turning your eyeballs upward, converging them slightly, and curling your tongue, pressing it against the palate.

As previously stated, holding the breath will rob you of one of the functions that provide you with a sense of the passage of time, favoring not just the memory of having existed prior to your birth or conception, but also of still being, at some level, the way you were before you were marked by the influence of your ancestral inheritance—that is, in your pristine state. There are several levels to this sense of identity, one being a kind of reminiscence of an angelic state accompanied by a sensing of what the Sufis call one's celestial bodies, and another being the awareness of being aware: pure intelligence beyond the act of consciousness.

7) Now as you exhale, it will appear as though a very fine kind of energy, (spirit), flows downwards in the central channel, bifurcating in the spirals as it descends.

These two branches then merge at the bottom of the spine as you start inhaling again.

In following chapters, we shall be encountering further applications of the principles governing the above practices: in the practices with light, and the connection between our mode of thinking and the energy level of our life field.

Tibetan Practices

Principles

The Tibetans attach much importance to reabsorbing the ambient energy into the void envisioned at the center of the spinal cord. Indeed, if our life field exhibits something like a vortex, then, as already mentioned, the core of the vortex (like a hurricane or a whirlpool) is a vacuum. Perhaps it may be helpful to represent what is commonly thought of as a void, as a latent state where potentialities are intermeshed, as in a wave interference pattern in which everything is everywhere and always.[3] In this way, by reabsorbing and transmuting the energy culled from outer space, energy can be recycled. It will have benefited by a process of extrapolation between all the dimensions of our being, rather than the short-circuiting that takes place when we simply react to an afferent impression.

---

3 The holomovement, according to David Bohm. See *Wholeness and the Implicate Order.*

Let us continue to bear in mind the noteworthy Tibetan slogan, *the mind rides the wind*. You are modulating your consciousness, and also the configuration of your thinking, according to the eight directions assumed by energy (four centripetal, four centrifugal). The left is the inheritance of the past; the right is the prospect offered by infinite potentialities latent in the universe (teleology); the bottom is telluric energy; and above is pure spirit. All four factors concur, are extrapolated and recycled in the void, and restructured through human creative incentive.

Tibetan breathing practices are designed to foster turning within, rather than enlisting the domination of the will mediated by the central nervous system and bypassing the unconscious.

Practices

1) Place the nail of your left thumb against the root of your left ring finger, and then make a fist and place it on the upper right side of your rib cage, under your right shoulder. Make the same kind of fist with your right hand, but extend your index finger. Press the index finger of your right hand on your left nostril while inhaling through your right nostril, and consciously draw the energy ingested from the right azimuth of the environment into the void in the center of that vortex, which is your life field, reached through the solar plexus.

2) Now move the index finger of your right hand to your right nostril. Exhale through the left nostril, while dispatching to the left the fresh energy that emerges from the void in the solar plexus but is radiated from the heart chakra. The solar plexus and the heart chakra are considered to be the two poles of the same center. The first is an inlet, and the other an outlet.

3) Proceed in the same manner with the left nostril as you press your index finger on the right nostril. As you inhale through the left nostril, you absorb and transmute afferent energy from the left into the solar plexus. As you exhale through the right nostril, radiate fresh energy emerging from the solar plexus, mediated through the heart chakra.

4) Next, place your right fist under your left shoulder, so that both arms are crossed like Osiris in the Egyptian papyri, while inhaling though both nostrils. While proceeding thus, you concentrate on the four winds: left, right, above, and below, which you mingle and absorb into the void reached through the solar plexus, and which are then transmuted as your attention is transferred from one chakra to the next in the ascent. As you exhale, broadcast the fresh energy emerging from your solar plexus and mediated through your heart center, to the four cardinal points.

A Further Tibetan Practice

Let us bear in mind that to foster a support system that favors realization, we need to transmute the energy field from gross energy (the life field) to subtle energy (the emanation body), then to very subtle energy (the enjoyment or celestial body). To this end, the energy field (the winds) is resorbed in the void in the center of the energy vortex; and then new energy is tapped from the solar plexus. This fresh dispensation of energy is envisioned as a fire blazing forth from unsounded depths. Now the contemplative concentrates on the *clear light of realization* enhanced by this outburst of very subtle energy.

In the previous breathing practice, we were reabsorbing the peripheral energy of our field into the center of the vortex, which is the spinal cord, and then mustering fresh energy from the void.

Your consciousness must follow suit. It must let itself be dissolved by the void, so that the clear light may emerge. The method consists in imagining your consciousness to be like a sparkling, phosphorescent, white drop exploring yourself from within, moving freely inside the complex network of channels within your body—and your subtle and celestial bodies.

Practices

1) First envision your consciousness as a searchlight within your heart center. Concentrate on the sound *hum*.[4] All about you is a baffling meshwork of eight bifurcations. As you cast your light through these channels, you will find that they get cleared and cleansed by the power of your light. However, you will be weary of venturing too far from the roundabout in your heart, where you feel more secure. It is your headquarters.

2) Now embolden yourself to venture up the central channel until you reach your throat center from within. Concentrate on the sound *om*. You will discover a still more baffling network of sixteen bifurcations. Imagine each to represent a different range of vibrations. Here your patience will be tested in the extreme, as you thrust your light down each of these, clearing the snarls responsible for short-circuiting and which engender confusion in the mind.

3) Further emboldened through having already practiced hoisting your consciousness by shifting your attention from one chakra to the next, you may now venture higher into the center of the crown chakra, the *bindu* in the pituitary gland. Concentrate on the sound *ham*.[5] The number of bifurcations is reportedly a mind-boggling thirty-two. In fact, it really seems infinite and

---

4 As in the Sufi dhikr, the sound *hu* (sometimes *hum*) is placed in the heart center..
5 Indeed, as the head is turned upwards in the Sufi dhikr, one intones *ha*.

intractable. Wherever you turn your searchlight, infinite avenues open up, triggering off an infinite plethora of thoughts.

4) You have now reached an interesting stage. Looking down and forward from inside your crown center through your third eye, you are able to reach into *outside* from within, escaping from the interlacing in the internal reticulation. However, if you wish to avoid slipping right back into the commonplace, illusive, sensorial perception scene, maintain that pinpoint flashlight of your consciousness, straddling the threshold between your forehead and the environment. You could fluctuate a little between inside and outside.

5) To return to the heart center, you will have to first reach up to the crown center, and then descend through the central channel. You will have a comfortable sense of finding yourself at home.

6) Now you venture into the solar plexus in order to spark the inner fire emerging from the void within. To consolidate your concentration, imagine the vowel *e* (the short *a* of the Tibetans).[6] Do not let the sixty-four bifurcations distract you overmuch. The key to stirring up the inner fire is to fan it by propelling the winds, mainly by dint of your attention cast upon them. We have already worked with the winds right and left in the solar plexus. Now we need to proceed in the same way with the upwind from the bottom of the spine, and the downwind from the top of the head.

7) To enhance the upward flow of energy rising in the spinal cord, contract the muscles of your lower body as you inhale, directing the energy from the bottom chakra into just below the solar plexus, where it is gathered and re-absorbed in the void and then replaced by the fresh emergent energy of the inner fire. Imagine your consciousness, in a similar way, to be dissolved in the void and reemerged anew.

8) Inhaling again, draw the winds from the upper body, particularly descending from the crown chakra, down through both lateral channels of the spinal cord and converging just above the solar plexus.

9) Now merge the upwind and downwind; the downwind, blasting against the upwind instead of descending below the solar plexus, will turn around upwards, hoisting your consciousness upwards. As this violent encounter arouses the inner fire to a blaze, harness the force thus unleashed to spur your consciousness into a breakthrough of awakening.

---

6 As in the Sufi dhikr, the vowel *e* (the short *a* of the Tibetans) is intoned or represented in the solar plexus.

PART TWO

WORKING WITH LIGHT

Introduction

If you are a sensitive person, motivated by an ideal of beauty and perfection, then light must be very meaningful to you. You will appreciate people who are radiant and bring light into the room and wherever else they go. They will help you to encourage your own radiance. You may be luminous yourself but wish to be more so. The word *illumination* will have a special significance for you, while you wish to understand more of what it actually implies. Perhaps you harbor some nebulous memory of having been a being of light prior to your birth, or to your conception. You may even sense the effulgence of your aura around you, but you may be discouraged in this awareness by those who argue that you are hallucinating. Imagination can play tricks upon one; on the other hand, it is imagination that triggers off the motion of one's limbs, and fashions symphonies, and materializes as computers.

Therefore, before you proceed with the following practices, it is good to gain conviction about what is really happening at the physical level. For this, a rudimentary, outdated knowledge about physics or physiology will not suffice. You will find it helpful and, as a matter of fact, exciting, to open the horizon of your mind to some of the current views in the new physics.

The atoms of the cells of our body function like those of crystals. Light can infiltrate between the atoms in a molecule; high frequency light can even infiltrate between the nucleus and the electrons of the atom.[1] Like the atoms

---

1 Physicists tell us that the spaces between the nucleus of an atom and its electrons, in comparison with the size of the nucleus itself, would be like an orange in a large concert hall. This representation of the fabric of our body will help us envision light infusing the body, not just surrounding it, as most people imagine the aura to do. Another salient feature is the perfect orderliness of the internal configuration of the crystal, which favors the passage of light. This orderliness is founded upon imponderable laws of cosmic resonance, evoking for Pythagoras the symphony of the spheres. See Murchie, *Music of the Spheres*. The orderliness of the configuration of our cells is much more complex, allowing for fluctuations, and thus presenting a marvelous support system for the evolution of intelligence in the human being.

of a crystal, those of the live cell fluoresce: they absorb light and emit light, and in certain cases they phosphoresce, that is, produce light by burning their own substance. The cells of the body avail themselves of this energy in the process of mitosis, in which the cells divide to multiply; and the cells actually sparkle as they divide, re-emitting some of the light they absorbed. Some electrons within the atoms that constitute our bodies avail themselves of light (which is a form of energy) to free themselves from the constraint of their orbital and jump to the next one, or, in some cases, even evade the pull of the internal atomic forces that hold the atom together, and escape into outer space as free electrons. When these atoms have expended all the energy available, any remainder is radiated into space as fluorescence. Light travels at a speed of 186,282 miles a second. It follows that the light of your aura will eventually hit a distant star, even though it forms a light-interference pattern with neighboring photons.

Since the brain is constituted of an intense concentration of nerve cells, the brain is lit up from inside. The optic nerves, being an extension of the brain, project the middle range frequencies of this light through the retina and cornea into space; but the high ultraviolet frequency passes through the skull and can be beamed through visualization.

While the phenomenon of fluorescence, called *bioluminescence* in physics, does account for at least some of the observable features of our aura, it would be simplistic to limit the aura to the more commonplace sensorial or measurable physical phenomena.[2] This dawns upon us when we shift our consciousness from its focus upon matter, and experience ourselves as etheric, that is, as a subtle body. We then envision ourselves as made of uncreated light, to use a term of Gregory of Nyssa; or as a celestial body, in the language of the early Mazdean Magi. There are unlimited frequencies of light beyond our visible range, but we tend to limit matter to whatever falls within our limited range. I will use the terms *subtle light* or *subtle body*, as they seem more appropriate than the term *uncreated light*.

A case in point, which opens new perspectives on this subject, is to be found in an experiments of Walter Chapell, a plant photographer who distinguished himself in photographing flowers in ultraviolet light. What might have appeared as the profile of the flowers as viewed in light in the visible range of light frequencies, appeared here like a sparkling aureole of sheer

---

2 The intensity of our human bioluminescence may now be measured with photo-electric cells. There is enough information that can reassure the student of these practices that we are not fantasizing as to their effects. Our cornea feature the properties of a lens, with the difference that they can alter their focus. See Motayama in White and Krippner, *Future Science: Life Energies and the Physics of Paranormal Phenomena*, 445f.

effulgence, and the texture of the flowers appears like gossamer, translucent, and even exposing other flowers that may be seen behind them. Here we encounter one more demonstration that the physical world is not the way it normally appears, since it may appear so different in a different light; there are many more demonstrations of this in physics. The significant breakthrough is that Walter Chapell contrived a way of illuminating the flowers with his own aura, and, lo and behold, was able to produce an identical effect! Even more significant is that when he was in a good mood, the corona of the flowers were like a beautiful array of diaphanous sparkling effulgence, and when he was in a bad mood, the flowers appeared to have spikes. Here we are in possession of one more demonstration of the mind-body axis. The flower read his mind through the message carried by the photon emission. Conversely, Walter Chapell learned something of the flower by actually seeing how the flower reacted to him, manifested as a tangible image: a communion in light. Walter Chapell was discovering himself through the plant's discovery of him.

Not only was he enthralled by the dance of light, flickering near the ultraviolet range, wrapping up petals and leaves with a gossamer aureole of scintillating effulgence, but also by discovering the interaction between the fluorescence of the plant and that of his own aura in a living dialogue. The plant told him something of itself in the language of light, whose meaning was translated into form, and it carried as much information as matched his own inner processes; we all are continually translating our thoughts and emotions into the configuration of our own aura. A comparison with x-raying is revealing. The x-ray will only show the image of the outer form, frozen in time-space, and not the energy field whose crystallization is the form; because the observer does not participate in the process.

How can we understand this?

Walter Chappell calls this looking actively instead of passively, which I like to paraphrase as the act of intelligence instead of the act of consciousness.

Obviously, this concerns an interactive process: the interaction of observer and observed in a dialogue of light. Since physicists have found that by watching an electron one interferes with the way the electron would behave otherwise, there are reasons to believe that, indeed, the electrons of the plant are interfered with by the photons of the observer. If so, we have a demonstration that, in healing, directing the light of the aura in a certain way to the patient could leave a lasting impact on the cells of the body of the patient.

Practices

The first step in the practices with light consists in *feeling* the radiance surrounding your body as a corona of light. That the body cells radiate light can now be ascertained in a laboratory. This radiance may equally be felt inside. This radiance is due to the fact that, as the inorganic or organic molecules of matter absorb light from the environment, their electrons use the energy of light to jump to the next orbital in the atomic structure; but no sooner have they expended the energy needed to free themselves from the constraint of their original position, then they fall back to where they were. Any energy remaining is re-emitted, being radiated in the environment. Note that this is not the same process as reflection. In the case of inorganic matter, it is called *fluorescence*; in the case of organic matter (our body) it is called *bioluminescence*.

You may enhance this process by the impact of mind over body. As you inhale, can you experience your body absorbing light from the environment and, ultimately, from the stars? And as you exhale, radiating light into the environment as matter, you are bombarding the stars and combining with their radiance, as light travels at the speed of 186,282 miles a second. But we are just talking about the generally accepted physical dimension of our aura.

Now, rather than identifying with your body absorbing and emitting light in the form of your aura, identify with your aura converging the light of the stars and then becoming intermeshed with the effulgence of the stars. Notice that your aura pulses in sync with your breathing. It seems to gather together as you inhale, and to disperse and radiate at the same time as you exhale. And of course, it does not have a boundary; so you may think that it is like an eddy in the ocean of light in the universe. The light of the stars gets interspersed in a wave interference pattern, but it maintains its particular frequency characteristics so that it never really gets lost: it gets dispersed in space but not lost. Rather than thinking of your body as being the hard core within which your aura is formed, think of the aura as being the template in which your body is being formed.

As you inhale, turn your attention within; in fact, imagine that your life field is a vortex. Imagine your solar plexus as the center of that vortex. The center of a vortex is a vacuum. Now hold your breath. Applying Dr. David Bohm's theory of the implicate order,[3] and also the current theories about white holes in space from which new energy emerges in the universe from subliminal universes, you may envision light in a state we might call all-pervading—maybe this is what is called the *light field*. As you exhale, imagine that you are now processing that light into radiant light, which accrues to the light that you emit by boomeranging back the light of the environment —as a matter of fact, the light of the stars. Whereas, in our ordinary perception of light, it radiates from a source located in a definable location in space, the mode of light we are now considering is spread out like radio waves.

3 See Bohm, *Wholeness and the Implicate Order.*

Lights are of two kinds: a light having no rays and radiant light.[4]

Muhyi ad-Din Ibn 'Arabi

According to Hazrat Inayat Khan, one draws on the inner light, which he calls *all-pervading*, and which is interspersed into a center. He illustrates this with the sun, which converges the light of the universe in a center and thence radiates it outwards.

The way you experience light through your senses is the way that light appears at the surface. If you step back, you can see that behind that there is a condition of light in which everything intersperses with everything else. Now think of yourself as a sun, which converges this inner light and radiates it, like light is radiated from a source in the explicate condition of the existential state.

Imagine that light emerges in your solar plexus, converges in your heart, and then radiates from your heart. Try to represent yourself as diffused, diaphanous, boundless light; and consider that the way the physical world looks is the way that things transpire as they break through at the surface.

In a further step, be aware of the beams of light that are projected by your glance. The brain absorbs light through the retina (also high frequency light through the skull); and since nerve cells absorb light most intensely, that light, threaded through the optic nerves and eventually the retina, radiates as your glance: as two beams of light that are cast forward in the dark, just like a searchlight or the head lamps of a car. The more you visualize this, the more effulgent those beams will become.

If you try to sense your whole aura in all its complexity, then you may become aware of some of its colors, which flicker and vary continually, according to your attunement. You can exercise an influence on the radiance of the different chakras simply by visualizing them, using the power of imagination. Colors are simply an indication of the frequency of the light waves.

We are endeavoring to affect orderliness in the sequence of colors by visualizing the color of each chakra in the sequence of the colors of the spectrum of light. In the course of inhaling, imagine your chakra at the bottom of the spine as being red; the second chakra as terracotta or vermillion; the solar plexus, orange; the heart chakra, gold; the throat center, green; sky blue in the eyes; your third eye, violet; and colorless light at the top of the head, sparkling with flashes of light of different hues. Now, as you hold your breath, you make a kind of quantum leap: cease to identify with your aura and discover yourself as being a luminous intelligence rather than an aura. Holding your breath, turn your eyeballs upwards, curl your tongue and press it against your palate. Your aura will now aver itself to be a support system,

4 Chittick, *The Sufi Path of Knowledge*, 217.

75

a scaffolding, while you consider that your real being is pure, luminous intelligence. As you exhale, cast the beam of luminous intelligence, with which you have identified, upon your aura. You may notice how the very awakening of that intelligence acts as a catalyst; it has an immediate effect upon your aura, which then bursts forth in an outburst of radiance. This is an apt illustration of the action of mind over body.

By transferring your attention from one chakra to the next up your spine, you will be arousing something like a flame originating at the bottom of the spine, which will serve as a support for the discovery of the light of your intelligence. This is a method applied to trigger illumination.

So far, we have considered our aura as a physical phenomenon, and the light of our glance to be a feature of our aura of physical light. However, at the stage we have now reached, it would be pertinent to posit a dimension of light that is not physical. What we know of the universe through our ordinary perception or through research in physics or biology, is but a mere intersection of the bounty of many-splendored reality.

As you inhale, turn your eyeballs upward, as though you were looking above your head; and then, as you exhale while concentrating on the beams of light of your eyes, you may feel that the light of your eyes seems to be an extension of your crown of light. In the same way, instead of your glance as a projection of the light of your brain, think of it as being an expression of your realization.

Withdraw your glance from being the witness of what is being perceived in the outer world, so that the inner reality may now transpire.

As for the light that has no rays, it is the light within which self-disclosure takes place without rays. Then its brightness does not go outside of itself, and the viewer perceives it with utmost clarity and lucidity.[5]

Muhyi ad-Din Ibn 'Arabi

Offset your glance so that you are not sensitive to the impressions of light coming from the physical world; but now, as you are blanking out the impressions of the physical world, the impressions of the light of the inner world are able to come through. It is as though they only become perceptible as they pass a threshold from the inner to the outer; just like the crocuses in the winter as they break through the surface of the snow, they are only visible when they make that leap from the unknown to the known.

But when meanings are embodied and become manifest in shapes and measures, they assume forms.[6]

Muhyi ad-Din Ibn 'Arabi

------

5 Chittick, *The Sufi Path of Knowledge,* 217.
6 Ibid., 354.

As you exhale, configure this light into a more tangible mode, into forms which thereby assume some kind of mode of expression, whereas in the inner state there is absolutely no form. You are not the spectator anymore of something other than yourself, but you are that which you are experiencing.

Turn your eyes upward and place your index fingers on the eyelids at the bottom of the aperture of the eyes so that you are not pressing on the cornea, which would be pressing on the retina. And think that you are really turning your eyes inside and withdrawing from the visual perception of the physical world. Hazrat Inayat Khan shows that when consciousness is deprived of the experience through the senses, then it turns within.

Now we're going to make a further step. Instead of concentrating on the inner light as you hold your breath, identify with being a pure luminous intelligence. Here lies the difference between turning within and turning upwards. Turning the eyes upwards favors one's attunement to what I call the transcendental dimension. Your glance is very different now, because you are illuminating it with a deep insight into the meaningfulness of life. It is as though that light were carrying meaningfulness. We have the capacity to raise our consciousness into the highest spheres

Through this self-disclosure (through all-pervading light), which makes the power of the eyes manifest and prefers them over rational faculties, God makes manifest the incapacity of rational faculties. And through His self-disclosure in radiant light, He makes manifest the incapacity of the eyes and the power of the rational faculties, preferring them over the eyes.[7]

Muhyi ad-Din Ibn 'Arabi

Now, instead of thinking of your glance as constituting two beams of physical light, think of them as being the light of your soul rather than the light of your body. Take your fingers away as you exhale. Instead of seeing through your physical eyes, try to perceive the physical world through the glance of your soul. It's like seeing without eyes. Think of your eyes simply as transducers of a deeper reality, which is what we mean by the soul; the light of intelligence is shone upon what one sees with the eyes—the light that sees upon the light that can be seen.

A light upon a light.[8]

Qur'an

Witnessing only takes place when two lights come together.[9]

Muhyi ad-Din Ibn 'Arabi

---

7 Ibid., 218.
8 XXIV: 35.
9 Chittick, *The Sufi Path of Knowledge*, 226.

By withdrawing our sense of identity from our human condition, we raise our consciousness to the higher spheres to discover our celestial nature, and even beyond that, the divinity of our being. The clue is thinking that your intelligence is the same as the divine intelligence; your consciousness is a focalization of it and therefore customized and personalized, but it is really absolutely boundless and universal. It is the intelligence of the universe. You may notice that your glance expresses this breakthrough of realization, this state of awakening that is erupting in your awareness.

It is not the light that one sees that is important, it is the way that this light awakens our realization that is important.[10]

Hazrat Inayat Khan

---

10 Inayat Khan, *Esoteric Papers.*

Chapter One
Working With the Aura

Practices

1) With closed eyes, imagine that you are looking into a bright light: the light of the sun, the limelight of a television studio, the head lamps of a car. If you love light, you will brave the hazard of being blinded by its effulgence because of the sheer joy of being flooded by its welcome glare.

The reason that you enjoy this communion with light is because it helps you become aware of the radiance of the light that you emit yourself: your aura.

2) Imagine your body to be of the nature of a crystal. The first feature of a crystal that strikes you is its transparency or translucency, as contrasted with our usual representation of the body as solid substance, and thus favoring the passage of light. Furthermore, the very sophisticated structuring of the cells, and the configuration of the atoms and subatomic particles within the cells, reflecting a cosmic harmony, determines a configuration of light frequencies in the aura whose complication defies our understanding. But there is a way of thinking or feeling your body into resonance with this harmony, so that the body feels wonderfully attuned, like a ballerina, savoring the effulgence of the aura.

3) Think of the way the pores of your skin open up when you sunbathe, welcoming the infiltration of the rays of the sun into your body. Proceed in a similar way with the cells of your body. As you inhale, visualize the rays of the light of the environment infiltrating deep into the ebullience of the cells of your body, and your cells ingesting particles from these rays. Hold your breath and visualize the cells being highly activated by this dispensation of energy in the form of light. As you exhale, visualize the cells radiating outward any surplus of light into the environment and, in fact, into outer space. You are radiant, like the sun, or a star.

4) Being now highly sensitized to light, try to sense the sparkling of the cells of your body. It will appear as a kaleidoscopic array of outbursts of luminous sparks. As a matter of fact, the more consciously you cast your attention upon this phenomenon, the more you will enhance this process within yourself.

Can you feel the joy of the cells, imbibing the light of the sun or the stars to free its atoms from a sclerosed order; exploring the infinite possibilities of a more sophisticated configuration at the service of our intelligence; and then, as it subsides, giving out its last supply of energy as light.

5) Now once more sense the corona of light that appears to be surrounding your body. It does not have a boundary, and seems to flash in rhythm with your breathing. As you inhale, it seems to contract, and as you exhale, to expand.

Advanced Practices

1) Instead of imagining yourself to be a body like a crystal, absorbing and emitting light, identify with your pulsing aura itself.

2) Visualize the starry sky: the planets, the stars, the galaxies, the cosmic rays. The universe is really an ocean of light, and your aura is like a wave or an outburst in that ocean of light.

Remember, it is the whole ocean that emerges in each wave; that is, the whole is involved in each part of itself.

As you inhale, the light of the whole ocean converges as your aura. As you exhale, your aura reaches out into the starry sky; in fact, each photon thereof travels through space at vertiginous speed and may well eventually hit a star. As you hold your breath between inhaling and exhaling, you identify with your aura, representing it as the template according to which your body was formed and is continually reformed.

3) At a more advanced stage, as you hold your breath, you will discover that the nature of the light at the center of your aura is of a different nature than at its surface. While the light of your aura radiates at the surface, towards the center it gets interspersed in a like manner to the way that we found energy inverted in the vacuum at the center of our magnetic field. Space being inverted, light is in the implicate order—it is all-pervading. What is more, a new, fresh dispensation of light now seems to emerge from the unsounded depths of your being, like a white hole in outer space. Since you did not originally converge it from the environment, you are not therefore simply boomeranging back into the environment: it is self-generated.

4) Scan your aura with your now sensitized consciousness. In a leisurely manner, scan each chakra. Note the feeling of each chakra and its particu-

lar color, starting from the bottom of the spine and moving upward; and also note the zone in your aura surrounding the chakra. The colors of your chakras will fluctuate, sometimes very quickly, according to your mood or your attunement. Conversely, the concentration on a particular color will evoke the desired energy conducive to getting yourself in resonance with the orderliness of the cosmos.

To achieve this, try to array the colors of your aura in the sequence of colors of the spectrum. The clue to doing this is to watch the way the particular type of energy you feel in one chakra tends to shift its frequency as it flows into the next one. You will find that when you concentrate on the lower chakras, the radiance of your aura is in the infrared or red frequency range; in the solar plexus, it is orange; and in the higher chakras, shifting from green, through blue to violet. The effect of this visualization is that the infrared radiance of your aura will automatically be transmuted into light in the visible spectrum, and eventually, ultraviolet. In the traditional schools this is referred to as transmuting fire into light. Your aura now appears as a spectrum of diaphanous hues, glistening like a rainbow.

Bottom chakra *muladhara*: red
Second chakra, *swadhisthana*: terracotta
Solar plexus chakra, *manipura*: orange
Heart chakra, *anahata*: golden
Throat chakra, *vishuddha*: green
Third eye chakra, *ajna*: violet
Crown chakra, *sahasrara*: colorless, multicolored

Pay attention to the corona surrounding each chakra.

5) Once you have become a little more familiar with the nature of each chakra, in one inhalation transfer your consciousness from the bottom of the spine to the crown chakra, while visualizing the colors.

With some practice, you will be thrilled by the intermeshing of the different colors emitted by the chakras as they dovetail. Note the glorious array of radiance above the head towards the end of the upwards sweep.

6) As you increase your ability, you will discover a yet further aspect in the radiance of your aura that is self-generated rather than boomeranged back from the effulgence of the environment: phosphorescence rather than fluorescence.[1] You will, with practice, develop the skill of enhancing this.

---

1 Here are some clues as to the difference between fluorescence and phosphorescence. The theory which physicists have come up with to account for the data arrived at in experiments with light is presented for convenience as a model. The electrons within the atomic structure appear to organize themselves in orbitals. The term *orbitals* must not be confused with the orbits of the planets, because in quantum physics one is talking of the probability of

7) This faculty culminates in being able to transmute the frequencies of light from the infrared range to the ultraviolet. This is a hermetic secret, hailing from the tradition of the Magi: transmuting fire into light.[2]

8) We have reached the stage where we may extend the sense of clarity and transparency, which we have gleaned from the aura, to the mind and to the emotions; by clarifying one's thoughts they become orderly, and the emotions become elegant and refined.

9) Holding your breath, imagine that you cross over a threshold into a totally different sphere of reality. You suddenly shift your sense of identity from being made of the fabric of light (your aura), to being a luminous intelligence: formless, colorless, not located in space or confined by time, and therefore, eternal.

Now your aura appears as a support system, or scaffolding, to serve your intelligence. You may scan it objectively without identification, as the Buddhists say, since it is a transient formation, while you experience yourself as permanent.

You will become increasingly aware of the sheer luminosity of your intelligence. Identify with it. One normally assumes that light is the object of perception rather than the perceiving subject, but the Sufis call this *the light that sees* rather than *the light that is seen*. This is what the Tibetans mean by *the clear light of bliss*. Now, as you exhale, you will notice the impact of the awakening of your intelligence upon your aura, which will glow incomparably more than before.

---

finding the electron at a mathematically harmonic discrete distance from the nucleus of the atom. When atoms are subject to light, the electrons manifest their absorption of that light by skipping away from their orbitals until they have exhausted the energy that they had absorbed, at which point they fall back into the orbital again; however, any leftover energy is radiated in what is called *flourescence*. This would account for the few seconds of afterglow in some crystals, after the light to which they had been subjected has been turned off. The reason why we see objects is because in part: a) they reflect light, b) they refract light, c) they re-emit the light. Therefore, any object that we see is fluorescing. In contrast, phosphorescence is exhibited by bodies whose cells, in the process of combustion, convert the fabric of their cells into radiance, mainly in the infrared frequency range. However, it extends into the visible range, as we have seen in the case of deep sea fish, fireflies, or certain bats.

2 See Kayvan in Rizvi, *Religious and Intellectual History of the Muslims in Akbar's Reign.*

Chapter Two
Working With the Glance

I emanated upon thee a force of love so that you might be fashioned according to my glance.[1]

Qur'an

Practices

1) Bearing in mind that the brain is intensely effulgent, as you exhale, concentrate on casting forward the two beams of light threaded along your optic nerves and projected forward by your retinas into the environment.

As you inhale, visualize the corona of sparkling diaphanous light, colorless although comprised of flickering flashes of multicolored light, which appears as a crown above your head.

As you exhale, concentrate intensely on the shafts of light cast forward from your eyes; imagine the headlights of a car, with beams that are blue. By concentrating intensely upon these beams, you will greatly enhance their intensity.

You will also find that the light of your eyes is clearly affected by your attunement, and reciprocally, your attunement is affected by your attention to light. If you entertain thoughts of despondency or resentment or guile, your efforts in the above exercise will yield disappointing results. Therefore, imagine that your thoughts and emotions are luminous. There is, indeed, a paradoxical connection between these psychological and physical phenomena.

2) Consciously and volitionally, cast these beams as far forward as you can into outer space. For this you will find it helpful to imagine the starry sky, or even practice this at nighttime, peering into the starry sky.

As you inhale, turn your eyes upwards. The beams will seem to merge into that focal center of the crown chakra called *bindu* in Yoga, which corresponds to the pituitary gland and flows upward, fanning out into the crown.

---

1 XX:39.

As you hold your breath, identify yourself with pure luminous intelligence. This will lead to a kind of samadhi state. Sustain it as long as possible, but without overly forcing it.

As you exhale, cast your eyes forward. The beams of light from your eyes will be greatly intensified. Converge them as you exhale, forming a spotlight at a distance of perhaps three feet, and then shifting it gradually forward in the course of the exhaling. With practice, you will become good at this and cast the spotlight right out into space.

3) Now proceed as above, except that you open your eyes as you exhale, at first just for a brief moment, and then increasingly, as you learn to avoid allowing your eyes to be forced into focus by the appearance of the environment. Keep your concentration by imagining that your eyes are lamps rather than organs of perception. By so doing, the focus of your eyes will automatically set themselves at infinity, so that the objects in your field of perception will appear blurred. If you apply mastery to keep your concentration, and avoid slipping into the usual focus by succumbing to your daily conditioning, you will find that the objects in the environment will appear translucent and will seem as though made of diaphanous light, while your aura seems to merge with them.

4) Shift your consciousness in such a way as to imagine that you have awakened from the perspective of what appeared as the physical world. To achieve this, think that it was just a perspective determined by the focus of your consciousness on a vantage point. Convince yourself that what appeared as matter was simply a construct or projection, like a hologram or the projection of forms on a celluloid film appearing as shades of light and shadow upon a screen.

You will now discover a transfigured world behind the overt one. The countenance of people will transpire through their apparent faces, and you will be aware of your own celestial countenance rather than identifying with your body. Furthermore, you will identify with your real nature rather than your personality, which now appears as a projection.

Advanced Practices: Working With the Third Eye

We will now begin to work with the third eye. As previously seen, some of the light within the brain is threaded along the optic nerves and has access to the environment through the apertures in the skull for the eyes; but the higher frequencies of light, i.e. ultraviolet, can traverse the skull. What is more, the pineal gland is highly light-sensitive, particularly to ultraviolet rays, and itself radiates high-frequency light beams.

1) Cast forward that beam of violet light. By converging your eyes, the beam will be funneled into a streamer oriented in the direction of your glance. This is what has traditionally been called the third eye. Now, as you exhale, imagine the spotlight as being blue, or imagine a blue sapphire. Moreover, visualize the beam of your third eye as violet, and as traversing the blue spotlight or the sapphire, cast at infinity.

2) Cast the violet beam of your third eye through the blue sapphire.

3) Maintaining yourself in this attunement and resisting any tendency of your glance to adjust to the perspective of the physical environment, if you open your eyes as you exhale, the physical world now appears multi-tiered. That is, you may perceive two superimposed layers, the physical and the celestial (or subtle), both translucent and interspersed, each allowing the other to transpire. Keep envisioning the image of the physical world as blue and that of the celestial counterpart as violet.

4) If you zoom your glance in the direction of a person, you may espy a countenance behind that person's face that will seem convincingly more real than what the physical features of the face convey. This countenance, according to the Sufis, gives a clue to the nature of our celestial being and thus reveals to us our true identity. Discovering your true face, it will become clear that it is being concealed by a mask, which is marked by the influences that have accrued in the course of your descent through the spheres, and in addition, through the osmosis with the existential environment on Planet Earth.

Chapter Three
Practices With the Sun

Advanced Practices

These practices should be prescribed only during a retreat, and only under reserve of the greatest caution. Discarding this warning may prove damaging to your eyes. The doctor's advice should be sought.

The following practices are to be undertaken starting approximately one hour before dawn, and then continued for some time after sunrise.

1) As a faint diaphanous light edges upon the horizon, wrapped in the rapture of the moment, proceed to do the following practices. Until the instant when the globe of the sun actually rises above the horizon, you may occasionally open your eyes and peer into the effulgence.

2) **Caution!** At the moment that the little speck of sun peaks over the horizon, surrounded by a plethora of apparently incandescent clouds, you will be filled with awe as its glow pours upon your body. Now take advantage of this moment to literally drink this light through your eyes and through every pore of your skin, while letting it permeate and percolate amongst the cells of your body. Within a short time it will be dangerous to expose your retinas to the glare of the sun. You could damage your retinas beyond repair within a few seconds. How surprising it is that rishis in the Himalayas and dervishes are able to peer into the sun for hours! The secret is in enhancing the intensity of the light emitted by your eyes, which acts as a shield.

To look into the sun, you must have eyes like the sun.[1]

Plotinus

You will, however, need protection. Be very aware of just how much brightness you can withstand as the sun gains in strength, occasionally closing

1 Plotinus, *Enneads*, First Ennead, Sixth Tractate, Section 9.

your eyelids, and eventually, keeping them closed. Quite a lot of light will filter through them.

3) There is a standard method to protect your eyes while they are open. It acts as a kind of eye-shield. Cup your hands around your eyes, making a frame, so that your glance is circumscribed by the frame.

a) Make a motion from left to right, then from right to left; and after that, up and down. Inevitably, for a short while during the swing, the rays of the sun will find their way inside your frame. You may adjust the rhythm of your swing according to how long you can withstand the glare in your frame; the quicker the rhythm, obviously, the shorter the exposure.

b) Next, rotate the frame clockwise, then counterclockwise. Keep the sun at the edge of that frame. It certainly is very difficult to maintain a motion of your hands as they revolve; consequently, sometimes the glare of the sun will spill into that frame. Always keep your eyeballs centered in the middle of the frame, offset from the sun. Thus you will be exposing the rim of your retinas to the sun, rather than the center.

Should you spot a black circle in the sky, it is a warning: a sign that you are over-stressing your retinas. Stop, and preferably, turn your back to the sun for a while. An alternative, if you have the luck of finding the right location, would be alternating between looking at the sun and looking at a lake. A simpler and lovely option would be rubbing your eyes with dew.[2]

4) When the sun's glare has become untenable, close your eyelids.

5) Adjust the stance of your head so that your forehead is at right angles to the sun. To be more precise, locate the point where the beam of your third eye traverses your forehead. Supposing your forehead were a planar surface, it has to be positioned in such a manner that the central ray of the sun hits that plane absolutely perpendicular to it, at that very spot.

6) Proceed in a likewise fashion, bowing your head, so that you feel the beam of the sun hitting your fontanelle.

7) Proceed in the same way with your heart chakra, pulling your shoulders back and extending your chest.

8) Now turn your back to the sun. Kneel, prostrating your body so that your forehead touches the ground. Feel the beam of the sun charging your muladhara chakra with its radiance.

---

2 Khwaja Mu'in ad-Din Chishti, the thirteenth century founder of the Chishti Sufi Order in Ajmer, India, used to perform this practice on the top of a hill and look into the lake from time to time to cool his glance. This is a very pleasant feeling. One may pick up dew from the earth with one's fingers and rub it on the eyes. This is also a practice of the rishi hermits in the Himalayas.

9) Lift your body up slightly so as to radiate your swadhisthana chakra.

10) Proceed likewise with your manipura chakra.

11) Now, as you inhale, let the power of the sun move up your spine, charging each chakra in turn, including the anahata chakra, the vishuddha chakra, the ajna chakra, and the sahasrara chakra.

Advanced Practices

1) Take stock of the situation in which you are sitting on Planet Earth, which is whirling around the sun, which itself is rotating in the galaxy, which itself is revolving in a cluster of galaxies. Now transfer your consciousness into that of the sun, viewing Earth from the perspective of the sun; and imagine what it would be like to be the sun. Understandably, when viewed from Earth, the sun appears as a globe of fire emitting light. But if you can envision what it would be like to be the sun, you would realize that it is a being endowed with intelligence, consciousness, will, thought, emotion, and identity, whose incandescence floods us with its radiance, and powers the life (the molecular-bodiness) on Planet Earth; and in addition, like us, has numberless sheaths of subtle or celestial matter. In fact, it is a real person, though huge when compared with the human being; and therefore it is considered by the Sufis to be an archangel called Prince Hurakhsh. It is amazing to envision the sun looking at you on Planet Earth, rather than the opposite.

2) Alternate between your vantage point and that of the sun. As you breathe in, imagine that you are looking at the sun; as you exhale, the sun is looking at you.

Chapter Four
Visualizations: Landscapes of the Soul

Perhaps our most cherished faculty is our creative imagination, which is our ability to translate our attunements and our grasp of meaningfulness into form. Reciprocally, we convert the forms that we perceive into meaning, and they trigger off emotions. Thus, creative imagination bridges the two poles of our being, and indeed of the universe: mind/body, or consciousness/energy, or software/hardware.

The fashioning of our being at all levels is a continuing process involving the entire universe, including all beings: the fabric of outer space, subatomic particles, cosmic rays, and of course, the incredibly smart software of the biosphere and of our psyches. Consequently, the trees and the flowers, the sun and the rain, the mountains and rivers, the forest or parks, the mighty cities, the works of art, architecture, music, arts, crafts and technologies—the yield of human ingenuity—the rituals of worship, dogma, customs and living standards, wars, conflicts, the human drama, the thoughts and opinions of people, acquaintances, and loved ones become organically incorporated into our beings at all levels. The world becomes us and is being processed through us in our diverse ways, becoming self-actuated in a novel style. The way in which all this bounty is, in some manner, integrated in a human being is perhaps one of the most surprising feats of the marvel of life. But admittedly, the degree to which so many heterogeneous factors are integrated in us generally falls far short of the mark. We have difficulty coping with the horn of plenty offered to us by life. The consequent, sometimes infuriating contradictions in our nature appear as one more demonstration of the smartness of the software behind our variegated configurations: it makes for that marvelous diversity of beings, which is on the increase as we evolve as a species.

Reciprocally, we have an impact upon the environment (in fact, the universe), both physical and social, with our being and its diversities and idiosyncracies.

Our creativity—our most wonderful gift—gives us a greater sense of fulfillment than simply being on the consumer side. Oftentimes, thoughts seem to emerge totally uncalled, *ex nihilo*; or emotions arise unaccountably. Was it because we did not see the connection with the circumstances that sparked them originally, because of the long period of incubation they incurred; or perhaps because that processing eluded our awareness in the deeper no-man's-land of the unconscious? In our thinking, we need to account for spontaneity rather than just conditioning, and likewise, in the universe as a whole; otherwise, nothing would ever change or progress.

Truly, we ingest the universe; yet it acts as a catalyst triggering off our creativity. Indeed, it is helpful to see ourselves the way we figure we could be, or to approximate a person who represents for us a role model. But we also need to project in our imagination our own idiosyncratic, prospective potentials. In addition, the landscapes that we encounter are not just as we have seen them, in some manner integrated in our psyche; but they do tell us something about our hidden selves, sometimes in a more relevant fashion than people can. Can you see the limpidity of a waterfall as an expression of the purity of your being, or the crackling of fire or thunder as honoring truth, or the cooing of the wind as your zest for freedom, or the majesty of the mountains as your sense of strife and courage, or the breakthrough of dawn as your sense of wonder?

Yet although these aspects of ourselves are enhanced by our experiencing them, we also have the faculty of imagining them. Here is some leeway for our fantasizing, and hence, our imagination. It is precisely in the imponderable, unpredictable dissimilitude between the photograph of a landscape and the painting of the same landscape that creativity can be detected. Here lies the critical edge that bespeaks our uniqueness. The difference in parallax tell of alternative space frames.[1]

The oftentimes gossamer-like quality ascribed to the physical fabric reflects the texture of our subtle bodies, while the very dissimilarity evidences our tacit assumption that the physical world is not the way it appears. Therefore, representing to ourselves landscapes, rather than perceiving them physically, adds a further dimension to our self-discovery; in fact, it reveals to us the features of our subtle, and even celestial, bodies. The same applies to imaginary scenarios rather than real life situations, which accounts for the powerful impact of fiction and theater on our psyche. But in the meditations that we describe here, we are not viewing paintings, or actually acting, or venturing into psychodrama, but letting the landscapes or scenarios emerge creatively from our unconscious and thus enrich our being.

---

1 See Gödel, *Paper On the Incompleteness Theorems*.

Consequently, these meditations, while enhancing our knowing, are particularly oriented towards doing. In bypassing the conscious volitional mind, we are able to foster dimensions of transformation that elude our understanding or will. We are truly marshaling our will, but in its deep unconscious springheads, where we customize the will of the universe in its bounty.

Imagination thrives in a state of reverie, somewhat suspended between day-consciousness and sleep in which the unconscious may be skirted. Rather than training the unconscious by autosuggestion imposed by our conscious will, we are actually encouraging the unconscious in its creativity, rather like a midwife, helping it to project to the surface of the psyche so as to enrich and transform it. What is more, by zooming upon the physical scene and the drama in our world from a transcendent vantage point, we are opening the door for the higher dimensions of our being to seep through into our personality, and eventually, to actuate themselves in our impact upon the environment within our handling of our problems.

Following are some proposed themes. It is good to start with prescribed norms; then, as you become more proficient, try improvising by inventing your own landscapes or scenarios. I recommend that you play music while visualizing these scenes. Suggestions of musical samplings that tend to convey something of the nature of these scenes are listed below.

The Lake in the Moonlight

Suggested music: Claude Debussy, *Clair de Lune*

Imagine that you are wandering leisurely alongside a tranquil lake, so relieved to have escaped from the humdrum turmoil of life in our modern societies. The atmosphere is windless, nebulous, sedate, eerie under the diaphanous glow of the full moon. The sheer sight of the stars peering through evanescent clouds confers a sense of immensity to the environment. The turbulence in your mind and emotions is becalmed, so you cannot resist the quiescence enveloping you. A sigh of relief infuses your being. It is drizzling. Watching the eddies formed by each drop of water as it impinges upon the surface of the lake, and observing the way they fan out, merging with adjacent ones, you lose yourself in their elaborate wave interference patterns as they merge and compose, dancing in covert collusion, glistening under the dazzling eye of the mystic full moon.

Drops of Light Sparkling on a Pool of Light

Suggested music: Johann Sebastian Bach, Prelude and Fugue in D Minor

Now imagine a less realistic scene, a phantasmagoria of the mind, reminiscent of subliminal worlds touched upon in a state of reverie. Instead of drops of water, there are drops of light. And the surface is in the likeness of a pellucid, opalescent layer of sheer stratified or laminated light. Once more each discrete drop of light, hurtling upon the luminescent surface, fans out into scintillating eddies of pure effulgence. As you shunt your thoughts into that meaningful encounter, you notice, perhaps more than before, the tacit connivance between the particles in which the universe explodes, and which is written into the universal programming. The sheer flashing of light sparkling, rather like a moiré fabric shimmering in the sunlight, or a kaleidoscope flickering as you shake it, sparks your spirit with delight! In all of this, you recognize the likeness of your intelligence when it is aroused, alive, and sprightly.

There is yet a further development: in addition to absorbing the environment and inviting it to catalyze our creativity, we rear and foster its growth in us.

If a pebble thrown into the sea puts the water in action, one hardly stops to think to what extent the vibrations act upon the sea....It takes in everything and it brings it up; it rears and allows it to grow.[2]

Hazrat Inayat Khan

Supposing that our implicit intelligence is represented by the surface, and that the intelligence of the universe, manifesting itself through the forms of the world, is represented by the drops spurring our intelligence, our intelligence is thereby awakened. But what is more, it processes the intelligence of the universe, having an impact upon it and raising it to foster its growth. Imagine the eddies intermeshed within the wave interference pattern, flourishing in profusion and increasingly beautiful: divine intelligence growing in and through us.

You discover this phenomenon in yourself; interconnections being formed interrelate you with people, becoming increasingly beautiful and fulfilling as you resonate with their idiosyncratic beings and learn to appreciate their gift to you.

The Phantasm of the Kaleidoscope

Suggested music: Igor Stravinski: *The Firebird*

You want to take a break from your humdrum existence in a virtual world of pure, though exhilarating, phantasm. Peering through a kaleidoscope sparks a whole venture in worlds of light. Imagine, most realistically, spirals of light extending and closing in on you, beams of light like a beacon at sea, random flashes and sparks bursting forth like fireworks, sometimes in symmetrical formations, sometimes in multicolored patterns of the most

2 Inayat Khan, *The Music of Life*, 178.

exquisite hues. Give yourself over to this enthralling effulgence until you feel a spillover in your clothes, in your aura, in your eyes. Imagine that you are a firecracker exploding in innumerable sparks and colors, shapes and patterns, and then diffracting within a landscape of light.

Instead of sitting and enjoying the scene, you can step into this world of light, forging forward towards a horizon of light getting brighter and more magnificent as you advance. Now it seems as though you were soaring above the clouds just at that moment when the sun rises above the luminescent tufts of the windblown clouds, spreading its glow upon the surface that you are scudding over, as though strapped to a hang glider. The sheer ecstasy of buoyancy, of being part of this volatile skyscape!

But to make the next step, you have to abandon your identity and realize that you are a being of light, of like nature to the scene. If you have the courage, you will discover worlds of light beyond worlds of light, familiar though forgotten landscapes of light of pure splendor. Presently, you identify yourself with sheaths of light of increasing subtlety enfolding you, reminiscent of the celestial spheres. There seem to be several levels.

Now your perspective seems to shift suddenly, as in a quantum leap, and you realize that these are the blueprints of the forms of the world sketched in light. Their architectonics seem like the structure of temples of light inhabited by beings of light. Are these the intensive meditations of someone who has been intoxicated by light? Yet there must be some reality to it, because you can observe its effect upon you. As you gaze in the mirror, you cannot believe what you see: you are transformed beyond recognition, radiant, glowing. And if you offset your glance, you will discover, behind the features of your face, a countenance so beautiful that you cannot believe it is you; and you think it is an angel revealing itself to you.

Celestial Skyscapes

Suggested music: Tomás Luis de Victoria, *Vespro della Beate Virgine*

Now you are in an attunement that is conducive to getting to know more about this celestial counterpart of your own being. The key to this is to once more avail yourself of your imagining faculty, to represent to yourself faces of angels. If your attunement is close, they will seem very real indeed, but of a gossamer-like texture and immaculate, like a porcelain doll. You will have to discount any conditioning from the romanticized pictures that some artists have made of angels. You need to allow yourself to be transfigured by your exaltation at your communion with light.

Thanks to having followed your imagination, you have discovered the celestial reality behind your physical sheath.

The Mountain Scene

Suggested music: Ludwig van Beethoven, first *Coriolan Overture*, then the Sixth Symphony

You have been laboriously working your way up the meandering lacework of uphill footpaths, threaded through the dense pine forest of the foothills until the trees appeared smaller and more sparsely distributed. Lo and behold, at last, there is a clearing. Yet it is only when whiffs of breeze melt away the mist for a brief instant that you discern the austere rock formations above your head, and the rivulets of limpid water flowing generously. The valley is blanketed by dense fog through which, however, some of the lights of the city below transpire hazily in patches.

Now for the vigorous scramble aloft, braving the abyss looming abruptly below the sharp and slippery rocks. You need to wait for a relatively secure ledge before you venture to look up into the sky. The clouds, racing in violent winds, reflect an array of incredibly vivid colors: bright orange, red, vermillion, green, sepia, brown and a silver gray, continually changing in their diverse formations.

This is the world of light of your dreams! You have a sense of déjá vu: *This is the world to which I belong!*

The glow of one corner of the sky is growing to incandescence faster than you estimated. While you were hoisting yourself up to the next ledge, having miscalculated your timing, the golden disc of the sun explodes out of the profile of a boulder, first as a tiny spark; and then growing rapidly into a fiery luminary, now shrouded by a black cloud, now again bursting forth in full force, riveting you to your precarious foothold. But this is a being! Could it be the body of an archangel, you fantasize? The sun is upon you with its overwhelming presence, wrapping you in its warmth and effulgence.

Freedom from the valley, the freedom of the peaks—communion with the sky. It took this mastery over the fear of the abyss, this discipline over your human reflexes, to taste this freedom which was always there, waiting to be released. Mastery, courage, overcoming, and enterprise beget freedom.

By this time, the mist in the valley has melted, pushing past you in gusts of wind. There is a roar of thunder across large stretches of space in the valley, whose gloom is recurrently broken by flashes of lightning. All the while, the sky above is blue, except for a magnificent rainbow crowning aloft the storm that looms below, offering you a grandstand scene of that marvel of nature when everything breaks loose: a thunderstorm.

Of course, you are reliving the paradoxical admixture in yourself of a need to let your anger burst forth and yet find serenity in freedom—and exulting over the splendor enfolding your very being.

Renewal in the Life Cycle

Suggested music: Claude Debussy, *La cathedrale engloutie*

Back down in the valley as winter sets in, how inebriating it is to savor the musty scent of the earth sodden with abundant rainfall. Your attention is drawn towards all that impending life, grinding to a halt or poised in waiting underground: the hibernation of hedgehogs and badgers and umpteen other little creatures, and the germination taking place in the seeds in anticipation of the breakthrough of spring. Turning ponderously upon yourself, you recognize yourself in this teeming wellspring of life. One needs to step back in life before stepping forward—to lie low. It is not really escaping from the unceasing challenges, but anticipating action by fostering a renewal of life; for life is not just cyclic, but ever-recurrently renewed. For this one has to sometimes skim rock bottom.

You are touching upon the root of your being. You will notice that, likened to the earth, it is profuse in its generosity, unrelenting in its benevolence in reabsorbing our pollution and recycling it into something beautiful. Only a small fraction of its bounty normally flowers in our personality, and we have to plunge deep into these springheads of our being to haul it to the surface—in rapt contemplation. In the silence within, new ideas surface unpredictably, and fresh resolve, a new zest to respond to life's calling, as though as you lie underground as a seed in incubation. The sun beckons upon you with its flares to emerge from your lethargy and dance the round of life. You stretch, your being unfurls restored, recharged, reinstated, re-enchanted.

The Human Drama in War

Suggested music: Ludwig van Beethoven, *Eighth Symphony*

Now you will need to thread your sense of identity into that of a soldier going into the devastated zones of modern warfare, unarmed while being shot at, transporting supplies of food for the innocent victims of an oppression stirred by hatred and sadism. Amongst the heaps of maimed corpses, you hear the groans of humans desperately clinging to life, begging to be rescued. You think of life at home, not always so easygoing, albeit a sinecure in comparison with this. But then you think of the heartless opulence of the uncaring. A shot hits your leg; you spot the offender. He is a dedicated hero; it was his last chance to aim at you, whom he had mistaken for the enemy, before dying of his excruciating wounds. Would you stagger towards him to disarm him, arms up, declaring yourself as friend rather than foe? Would you dress his wounds while incurring the risk of being shot at again? Would you?

But there is a worse case: you are being tortured by a sadistic brute in a concentration camp. You filter into his psyche and see his rancor, his heart full of hatred for having been beaten up by his drunken stepfather. Besides, he has been brainwashed as a youth against the enemy, portrayed as his ruthless stepfather. Can you forgive him? Some people have done just this.

We can unlock dramatic transformation by discovering slumbering aspects of ourselves in other ourselves. We carry compassion deep in the roots of our being. It gets buried by our resentment for having been abused, but it is still there. The drama of life at its most terrifying calls for our best. See if you can uncover that mercy deep down in your soul!

Chapter Five
Unveiling Spheres of Light

The foregoing attunements and practices were intended as steps leading to illumination. At the point we have now reached, we are making the ultimate attempt to attain our cherished aspiration.

The very concept of illumination can be a cliché paraded by aspiring spiritualists. It would be futile to attempt to have the slightest idea as to what one means by illumination, unless one actually achieves it; and then it would be even more obvious how inadequate our syntax and language is to describe it. Perfunctorily though, we imagine that it would imply that one would grasp meaningfulness where others cannot see it, and consequently, one would be radiant and sport a sparkling eye. Actually identifying oneself with a luminous intelligence, rather than simply envisioning oneself as an aura of light, has an impact upon one's sense of meaningfulness. This is why realization and illumination are often confused with each other: they are the two sides of the same coin.

What are the clues leading to it?

The methods advocated by the Sufis challenge all our commonplace assumptions. Basically, we need to reverse our vantage point and try to envision how things would look from the antipodal vantage point. The dervish strives to snatch a glimpse of the divine perspective. Doing this, you will have the impression of awakening beyond your usual focus, into other dimensions.

Consequently, the practices advocated aim at challenging our sense of being a physical being, of having a form, of being located in space, of being involved in the process of becoming, even of identifying ourselves with the physical fabric of our aura, and in general, of being an incarnated, existentiated being. The clue consists in (1) starting by identifying with one's physical aura; (2) then discovering ourselves as always having been, prior to our birth or conception, a being of non-physical effulgence; (3) then making the shift to identifying ourselves with our intelligence, envisioned as luminous.

Following are some of the methods used by the Sufis. As these constitute some of the most advanced practices, it is not advised here to undertake these unless one is a highly skilled meditator. Discounting this warning, you run the risk of spacing out and finding yourself unable to meet your worldly responsibilities.

Advanced Practices

1) It is extremely helpful at this stage to meditate at night, particularly if you can see the stars. First imagine that behind the physical scene there is a world of light, and beyond that world, worlds of subtle light in infinite regress.[1]

2) As you look at the stars, realize that just as the whole ocean emerges as each wave, so it is the worlds of light that emerge to our view as the stars. It is as though the unfathomable reality behind the universe is squeezed within the capacity of each star to convey some of its glory.

Beyond the stars are stars in which there is no combust, nor sinister aspect, stars moving in other heavens, not the seven heavens known to all.[2]

Jalal ad-Din Rumi

When you learn from the writings of the ancient Sages that there exists a world possessed of dimensions and extent other than the pleroma of Intelligences and the world governed by the Souls of the spheres, and that in it, there are cities beyond numbers among which the Prophet mentioned Jabalqa and Jabarsa, do not hasten to proclaim it a lie, for there are pilgrims of the spirit who come to see it with their own eyes, and in it find their heart's desire.[3]

Shihab ad-Din Suhrawardi

Therefore, the universe seems made of formations within this symphony of light. Moreover, these formations seem to emerge and fade back into the totality like waves in an ocean of light.

3) Envision yourself to be such an evanescent formation. Grasping the likeness of the fabric of your aura with that of the stars, if you feel endowed with the spirit of a dervish, you may feel like eluding the monotony of sitting still by whirling.[4]

---

1 Hildegarde of Bingen refers to her visions of worlds of ever subtler light. See *Liber divinum operum.*

2 Nicholson, *Selected Poems from the Divani Shamsi Tabriz*, 8.

3 Corbin, *Spiritual Body and Celestial Earth*, 118.

4 As Mawlana Jalal ad-Din Rumi, the thirteenth century mystical poet and founder of the Mawlawi (Mevlevi) Order of the Whirling Dervishes, taught his disciples to do.

O dawn, break through! the atoms dance
Souls enraptured in ecstasy dance,
I could whisper to you where the dance leads;
All the atoms in the air and of the desert,
Be assured are caught in divine madness.
Every atom, whether happy or miserable
Is enamored with the sun of which naught can be said.[5]

Jalal ad-Din Rumi

Mentally drop your body and enjoy the freedom of gravityless motion in space. If you identify with your aura, the spirals of light your aura emits would indubitably form an ever-extending sphere of spiraling light. You are revolving like a star in the choreography of the heavens.

5) Now sit back, but whirl your aura. Since it does not have a boundary, the whole fabric of light of the universe is drawn into this swirl—amongst an infinite number of swirls—in the boundless vastness of space. Participating as a being of light in the choreography of the heavens, by swirling the fabric of the celestial light, of which the stars are just a temporary expression, you are building a temple of celestial light.

6) Bear in mind that our notion of light, and of matter generally, is limited by our range of perception; and as you inhale, identify yourself with the area of your aura beyond the visible range of light frequencies—as ultraviolet. Imagine yourself now to be made of a very subtle volatile fabric, like gossamer, and reminisce about having been thus prior to your landing on Planet Earth at the instant of conception. This will give you a feeling of what could be the nature of the fabric of the celestial spheres.

7) Envisioning yourself as fashioned in the fabric of this subtle light, apply some of the principles encountered when fashioning your physical aura into a temple. Now fashion your celestial light into a temple.

The temple of light that you built has now been transfigured into a further temple of subtler light, which appears to adumbrate the temple of physical light. You will find it difficult, however, to envision this temple, since it does not seem to have a form but a countenance.

It appears as a glorious luminous reality of pure splendor. At this stage, you will find yourself immersed in worlds of light, the like of which cannot be described in physical terms. We are led here to infer that there are several superimposed layers of matter, and consequently, light in increasing degrees of subtlety, finely woven.

---

5 Rumi, *Ruba'iyat* 702 and 306, my own English translation.

8) The clue to this attunement is to be found in shifting your sense of identity. As you identify with subtle matter, you discover the corresponding degree of subtlety in the celestial spheres.

To the wanderers who knock at the gates of the lofty halls of (light).., the angels of God come to welcome them, drawing them towards the orient of light.[6]

Shihab ad-Din Suhrawardi

9) You will also need to shift your emotional attunement. Feel the nostalgia driving you into the deep springheads of your being. Nostalgia and bewonderment are modes of psychic energy that can spark a shift in your sense of identity. Bear in mind that beauty, in its many-splendored manifestations, is a projection in the spacio-temporal grid that we impose upon reality by the limitation of our mind's capacity to encompass infinite dimensions of space and time: that deeper, formless reality that is pure splendor. According to the Sufis, to grasp this splendor, one needs not only to drop one's body identity as a shroud, but even one's physical aura.

10) As a preliminary step, first enjoy the freedom of the gravityless motion in space. Imagine yourself as light passing through outer space without any resistance (except being deflected by the gravity pull). Then imagine that you are formless.

Immediately, space has lost its significance in your perspective. You will have hoisted yourself into the sphere which the Sufis call *jabarut*. Now you will understand why the temple of celestial light is without form. The temple of celestial light cannot brook the limitations in our thinking incurred by our mental representation of our physical body. The field of the mind needs to extend to the scale of the choreography of the heavens, yet beyond the physical sphere. If you do this, you will experience the freedom and delight of being a being of light at a cosmic scale.

11) If you now make an effort to extricate yourself from not only your existential perspective, but even your dream perspective where there are still forms, and awaken in deep sleep, then you will find yourself gaining access to the consciousness of luminous beings.

All these are illuminations which rise over the human soul when it is master of its body. Then they are reflected on the bodily habitation. These photisms mark a halfway stage at which some stop. Sometimes these Lights carry them

---

6 Corbin, *Oeuvres philosophiques et mystiques de Shihabaddin Yahya Sohrawardi*, 56, my own English translation.

in such a way that they walk on the waters and glide through the air. It may be that they ascend to Heaven, but in a body that is their subtle body.[7]

Shihab ad-Din Suhrawardi

12) Focus your consciousness to imagine that you have awakened from the perspective of what appeared as the physical world, realizing that it was just a perspective determined by the focus of your consciousness in a vantage point, and that what appeared as matter was simply a construct or projection, like a hologram.

13) Think of the stars or, better still, the galaxies as the mere actualization of the unseen, covert, implicate light of the universe. Consequently, your consciousness reaches beyond our commonplace representation of what we mean by the physical universe, into the perspective of the celestial spheres.

The light of dawn rises on the soul in such a way that part of the victorial realities emanating from the constellations and from the Angels who are their theurgies predominates in them.[8]

Shihab ad-Din Suhrawardi

At some point, the Sufis experience something more specific than simply this immersion into the ocean of light, subjacent to the apparent light of the starry firmament. They ascribe it to the fact that not only do we participate at some level in the effulgence of the heavenly spheres, but we discover ourselves to be the light that sees rather than the light that can be seen. The stars are not considered just globes of luminous, physical light manifesting a deeper subjacent orb of light, but are seen as archangels endowed with a luminous consciousness.

14) If you shift your memory from the transient to the transcendental dimension of time, you will suddenly realize that your intelligence is of the same nature as that of the archangels whose bodies are the stars, and ultimately, of the whole universe. The Sufis call this *luminous intelligence*.

15) Envision your celestial body as being a support system for that intelligence. Inasmuch as that celestial body may be looked upon as a temple of celestial light, you may represent this luminous intelligence as descending upon it.

A light upon a light.[9]

Qur'an

---

7 Corbin, *Spiritual Body and Celestial Earth*, 126.
8 Ibid., 125.
9 XXIV:35.

16) The clue to this breakthrough is in shaking off the memory of your existential perspective. In so doing, the memory of the universe stored in your deep memory will emerge. You will find that you will reminisce viewpoints giving a sense of meaningfulness at a cosmic scale, rather than recounting occurrences.

17) If you now focus on a star, you will realize that its appearance as seen from Planet Earth is just the way that the consciousness or intelligence of that being, which is a star, is configured at the existential level. You are experiencing how the spheres of celestial light appear from the vantage point of the archangels. Indeed, in this perspective, the stars appear as the epiphany of beings: a glowing extension or projection in the physical universe.

18) You will now discover a kind of kinship with these celestial beings, realizing that this is what you are, essentially and eternally; and that in this dimension of your being, you have inherited your celestial nature from them. This is where you have the deep roots of your being.

18) Lie on your back.

a) Holding your breath, think of yourself as a being of celestial light. Envision your aura as a limited manifestation of your true being.

b) Concentrate on the beams projected from your eyes as the actualization in space of the celestial light that you really are.

20) Now open your eyes, and look through your third eye. You will encounter a maze of evanescent, elusive, nebulous forms. They convey archetypal symbols whose objective seems to be to reveal a paradoxical meaning to you that you need to decode.

Are there any further steps?

21) Discover that we not only need to fashion the temple, but also fulfill our human role in the temple, as priest, as knight, as hermit, as devotee, as musician, as verger, as sweeper, and many more.

PART THREE

WORKING WITH SOUND AND MANTRAM

Introduction: Sound

Principles

Some things can only be understood and appreciated by those who have experienced them personally. The mystical experience of sound is one of these. One would have to experience personally the effect of uninterruptedly repeating words—which, even though in a foreign language, are pregnant with meaning—until the mind abandons its commonplace linear thinking and becomes receptive to a totally unforeseen, archetypal understanding, which seems to be revealed from the far corners of the universe. When this is done for hours daily and for weeks, in a cave or cell, one has the impression of having awakened, from one's complacent accommodation to the limitations of our day-to-day conditioning. The emotion accompanying this breakthrough defies description.

The repetition of mantrams (in Sufism called wazifa, plural *waza'if*) often appears as the staple food among the practices of meditation schools. This is because it associates a sound pattern with an archetype of the unconscious, thus establishing and reinforcing a conditioned reflex. Indeed, the common ground of the human unconscious—called the collective unconscious by C. G. Jung—exhibits basic principles upon which our human psyche is built. This actually forms the seedbed, nurturing the seeds of the values we pursue and the qualities that we unfurl in our personality. In the unconscious, they are stored holistically; in the conscious area of the psyche, they are personalized, customized as idiosyncracies. The unconscious thinks holistically; that is, in our deep unconscious we share the springhead of the psyches of all humans, and indeed, of what we might call the psyche of the universe. The conscious psyche understands reasons; for example, *I need to develop such or such a quality to be better able to deal with this or that problem*. However, the unconscious does not brook the limitations of human reason, but is endowed with an ability to grasp what our mind merely surmises, of a quality far beyond our mental representations; for example, infinity, perfection, etc.

Like the buds of a plant, qualities are continually burgeoning at the threshold of the unconscious in a bid to blossom forth in our personality. They are, paradoxically, obstructed by our lack of faith in our capabilities, by their being enshrouded in the unconscious, and by the way we limit ourselves to our totally inadequate self-image. If we bypass our mental constructs, mind games, and categorizations, the unconscious potentials can be aroused by imagery and sound. This is why the creative imagination is so important in unfolding our personality, evoking the hidden artist in us.

That which our ears perceive as sound is really the way fluctuations of energy may manifest as pulsations in the environmental air, triggered off, for example, by our vocal cords or a loudspeaker. These form basic wave interference patterns, which our brains extrapolate as sounds, and which we have been trained since childhood to associate with meaning. What is more, we only perceive a fraction of the intricate complex of sounds that our brains process for us, just as we could never explain all that we imply behind what we say.

Sound (*shabd* in Sanskrit, *sawt-i sarmadi* in Sufi terminology) then, is the way that an energy wave may affect the air. Sound is a more primary reality than light, since it is wavelike, rather than both particle-like and wavelike. We are talking of a field that is spread out in space, rather than a particle that is located in space. Therefore, it tends to affect our consciousness by modulating it to sense the deep underpinning or the springhead of life, the implicate order, discovered in the vacuum within even more intensely than in light, which one experiences more readily as external.[1]

The sound wave interference pattern produced by all the objects in the universe—for example, the wood of the trees, the burbling of water, the hissing of the wind, the vibrational patterns of the planets and stars and molecules and atoms—may well be considered as the holistic language of the universe.

There is some cryptic relationship between the signature tune of an object, for example, a bell, and the geometrical pattern of its molecules. According to Pythagoras, mathematical equations are translated in the universe into harmonic structures. One may posit that the reality behind matter is its code,

---

1 "The concept of second quanticization takes the point of view that the field is primary and has the particles as 'resonances' or 'quanticized oscillations' or excitations of that field. The vacuum state or state of implicit reality is perturbed by the available energy becoming realized as a particle or physical presence. The vacuum state is akin to the concept of emptiness in Tibetan Buddhism, where all that is possible exists waiting for the fluctuation in space-time which will bring it into manifestation." Dr. Raqib Ickovits.

a patterning of energy frequencies, which may very well be considered to constitute the language of the universe.

And He gave to Adam knowledge over all things, then presented them to the angels. Then He said: "Tell me the names of those if you are right."[2]

Qur'an

The one who possesses the code has the recipe of creativity that can then be applied to creativity at the personality level.

Traditionally, sound, which is actually vibration, stands as more primary than light.

In the beginning was the word.[3]

St. John

Sound is associated with the code of the hologram that is the universe. The code is the matrix, the basic reality according to Shabistari:

The elements which are below the heavens serve in their appointed place ever united together. From them is born the threefold Kingdom of Nature...[4]

We could call this a complex of frequencies. For our senses to become aware of this code, it needs to be actuated into a hologram, which is a reality fashioned in the fabric of the particle aspect of light. For the Sufis, our intelligence, beamed in consciousness and parallel with the wavelike aspect of light, not only reveals the code by transfixing the hologram with our inherent sense of meaningfulness, but also unfurls its potentialities. In the practice of the *dhikr*, the Sufis work with both sound and light.

Indeed, in the chapters on light we caution about the reductionism involved in restricting light to what we or our instruments record as light within the range of the frequencies available to us.

In the first part of the Sufi practice of the *dhikr of light*, you fashion a hologram in the fabric of your aura, within the energy field of your magnetic field, by swirling. In the *intoned dhikr*, you fashion a hologram of sound within the energy field of the vibrational patterns behind the sounds, in addition to the light hologram—actually you are swirling or churning a sound wave interference pattern. In the second part of the dhikr, you are x-raying the hologram, as a composition both of sounds and colors, with the light of your third eye, in which the frequency configurations match our innate sense of meaningfulness.

---

2 II:31.
3 John 1:1.
4 Shabistari, *The Secret Rose Garden of Sa'd ud Din Mahmud Shabistari.*

We will be fostering the use of both sound and a laser-like light as a vehicle to penetrate and illuminate these worlds, and to bring life to the worlds behind the scenes by properly illuminating the hologram and your relatedness to it, all tied up together by the vehicle of light and its harmonics.[5]

---

5 "What is key here, and necessary to decipher the hologram, is the correct laser frequency, which was initially used to record the hologram and now is needed to view the Fourier transformation of the hologram to bring it into regular three dimensional perspective." Dr. Raqib Ickovits

Chapter One
The Mantram

To discover experientially the effect of the different frequencies of energy experienced as sound, and actuate this effect in our bodies and psyche, we need to start by earmarking basic vowels produced by our vocal cords, and by endeavoring to direct the vibrations thus produced into those centers in the body that resonate optimally with the specific frequencies of these vibrations. In our esoteric traditions, the appropriate centers are found to be the plexuses of the autonomic nervous system, which the Yogis call *chakras* and the Sufis the *lata'if* (subtle centers). These represent a subtle chemistry of the constituents of nerve cells in general, and in particular, their intricate interconnectedness. We can imagine what would be the effect of the impact of sound vibrations upon the body cells, particularly in these highly sensitive areas. There has been some scientific research in this field, indicating that the interrelationship between molecular patterns can be modified into a more complex conformation. Moreover, we could account for the impact of the vibrational frequencies upon our emotional attunement and mode of thinking, and conversely, the impact of our attunement and thinking upon the molecular conformation of the body cells.

It is as though for each type of energy of our electromagnetic field, ranging, for example, from high voltage-low amperage to low voltage-high amperage, there is a corresponding mode of thinking, ranging from projecting images to grasping significance. Each new insight affects not only the circuits in the brain, but also the entire nervous system, which is an extension of the brain, as well as the nuclei of the body cells and, eventually, the environment.[1]

Each chakra is connected with an endocrine gland. Bombarding the cells of those plexuses of the body with vibration will trigger off the secretion of the specific hormones of the corresponding endocrine glands, monitoring not only body functions but also emotions and the thoughts connected

1 See Bohm, *Unfolding Meaning*, 95.

with them. We must remember the Tibetan adage that the body constitutes a wonderful medium to foster illumination, providing one transforms it.

While our modern languages are conventional to a high degree, in contrast, the older languages, which were elaborated by civilizations that were steeped in the unconscious, convey sounds based upon a harmonic code behind phenomena. We can hear this in nature, for example, or encounter it in scientific inquiry. If certain sound frequencies correspond with parallel archetypal thoughts or qualities, one recipe to develop our human potentials involves invoking these latent forces through the corresponding sound frequencies.

A pertinent example would be the Atlantean word *asatar*. As stands for water, *at* fire, and *ar* earth; so *asatar* signifies Planet Earth: a planet of earth, water and fire.

The Hindu mantram may be broken down into the basic vowels: *e* intoned in the solar plexus, *a* intoned in the heart chakra, *o* intoned in the wheel of fire (a Tibetan chakra), *u* in the throat chakra; the *i* in the third eye is an overtone, and the *m* broadcasts the sounds into outer space. In Sufism, the wazifa *Haqq* (the truth) triggers off a traumatic effect upon the heart chakra, whereas *Quddus* (the Holy Spirit) exercises a life-dispensing effect arising out of the throat chakra. The *i* in 'Alim (a sense of meaningfulness) is a strident sound placed in the third eye, which fosters sharp perspicacity, crystal clear insight. The *e* of *illa 'Llahu* (here the *i* is pronounced as a cross between an *i* and an *e*), sounded in the solar plexus, touches upon the vacuum in the center of the vortex of the human electromagnetic field, unleashing latent potentialities.

Practices

1) Intone and repeat the vowel *a*, placing it in the location of the cardiac plexus: the anahata chakra in Sanskrit. Consider the nerve tissue of the cardiac plexus as the surface of a gong, which you strike with a controlled thud. After the moment of impact, let the vibrations subside, then pick up where you left off and escalate the vibrations in a short crescendo, as you might do in playing the violin or cello.

2) Proceed similarly with the vowel *u* in the area between the larynx and the pharynx. This is the anterior part of the vishuddha chakra in Sanskrit and the *latifa ruhiya* in Sufi terminology; the posterior root is in the recess situated at the bottom back of the skull, at the juncture with the spinal cord, and called the atlas. Shift your focus from the pituitary gland to the pineal by deflecting the sound *oo* into *u* (as in French).

3) Proceed similarly with the vowel *i* located in the pituitary gland and corresponding to the point called *bindu* in Sanskrit: the nexus of the sahasrara

chakra, *latifa haqqiya* in Sufi terminology. However, we need to bear in mind that there is an axis connecting this center with the pineal gland, which is popularly known as the third eye: the ajna chakra of Yoga and the *latifa khafiya* of Sufism. While doing this, turn your eyeballs upwards, converging them slightly. Also curl your tongue backwards so that it titillates the palate like the reed of a clarinet.

4) The sound *e* intoned in the solar plexus (the short *e* of the Tibetans) is more difficult to bring into resonance, because it sounds very dull until one masters the art of striking that deep center, called manipura chakra in Sanskrit and *latifa qalbiya* in Sufism, which sucks one into a void. It actually is best produced by harnessing the thrust of the rotational movement of the upper trunk of the body in the Sufi dhikr into a powerful thump in the first vowel of the formula *illa 'Llahu*. Dervishes practicing this almost continually manage at times to generate a sound like a low sounding gong with higher overtones. The awakening of this center confers a very great power.

5) Pause after three or four repetitions and listen to the echo that you have generated in the surrounding space, which echoes back to you. In fact, it is not simply a reflection of the sound broadcast by your voice, but expresses something of the nature of the environment, like a radar beam.

6) At a further stage, listen and see if you can hear and produce overtones. To do this, many techniques may be offered. Increase the thrust of your exhalation while tightening your lips. Try to bring the pitch of your intonation up very slightly, but gradually. Draw your cheeks in. Curl your tongue back as you would do if you were pronouncing *j* or *kh*, while drawing it upwards, pinching the flow of air in your mouth while escalating the pressure. Keep shifting from one vowel to the next, as in the mantram *aum*, which is really *a-ou-u* with overtones of *i*, then finishing with *m*. Listening to these overtones lures your auditive faculty beyond its normal range towards higher frequency areas. Curiously, with increased sensitivity, the threshold between your usual auditive range and the supersonic shifts. Traditionally, the overtones produced by the foregoing techniques are considered to constitute a ladder conducting consciousness into areas where matter is rarified, which esoteric lore calls the *celestial spheres*.

Chapter Two
The Sufi Dhikr

The Sufi prepares himself by his exercises of Dhikr and Fikr to make his heart capable of producing that resonance that may be caused on earth or descend from heaven. When the centers of the body and faculties of the mind are prepared to produce that resonance, then they respond to every sound , and every time the bell is rung, it has its echo in the heart of the mystic, and every center of his being begins to think of God and to feel God.[1]

Hazrat Inayat Khan

Personal Experience

My endeavor can, of course, only be formulated in terms of my personal cogitations and soul-searchings in the perspectives of the Sufi tradition, with cross references to Qur'anic verses; also in the context of kindred spiritual traditions; and in addition, the rendering of my father, Hazrat Inayat Khan, which was couched in the current idiom that can be understood, particularly in the West, by adepts who are not familiar with Arabic or Farsi terminology.

Preparatory Steps

To prelude the practice of the dhikr, I perform breathing practices based upon utterances of dervishes that were referred to by Kalabadhi.[2] I take the liberty to paraphrase his quote: *As God exhales, He projects His Being in a vision in which He contemplates Himself.*

I can see that my need for freedom reflects my participation in the divine freedom, because it would not be possible to extract the gist of the know-how gained in existence without rejecting the contingent support system in the existential realm. And I can see that my need to involve myself in life, to achieve, to build a better environment, is my way of customizing the divine

---

1 Inayat Khan, *Esoteric Papers.*
2 See *Kalabadhi: Traité du Soufisme.*

nostalgia to manifest and actuate the bounty of divine potentialities in real life.

The Practice of the Dhikr

1) Kneeling, as you exhale, rotate your head and upper trunk clockwise as follows: head turned towards the zenith, left shoulder, left knee, the nadir, right knee, right shoulder, back to the zenith; then turn the head downwards, concentrating first on the solar plexus, then the cardiac plexus.

2) Shift your sense of identity from being a body to being an electromagnetic field, then to being your aura of light, and then to being a composition of sound. As your magnetic field rotates, you will first become aware of churning the Earth's geomagnetic field. Then you will become aware of your aura in its paradoxical connection with the ocean of light, studded by stars. Churning the audiosphere of the universe, traditionally called the *akashic field*, is even more startling.

3) You will feel like a centrifuge. Notice two motions in your life field, one centrifugal, the other centripetal, both occurring simultaneously; the grosser elements of your being seem to be pushed outwards into the environment, while the elements and impressions coming from the environment appear to be processed and transmuted inside into an uncanny, rarefied mode.[3]

4) While turning your attention to the periphery, you will feel boundless, like a vortex without a boundary.

5) As you inhale, tip your head downwards, also your upper trunk. Since circumambulating a center has the effect of drawing one's attention to that center, you will feel sucked into the void in your solar plexus. This, however, proves to be the seedbed of your being, wherein lie the inexhaustible potentialities of the universe, incorporated in your own psyche as qualities awaiting actuation.

6) Now, while continuing to inhale, raise your head from facing the solar plexus to facing the heart chakra. You will notice that a formation seems to be taking place within the vortex. You will realize that you are both a vortex and a transient entity bounded by a permeable membrane. Hazrat Inayat Khan compared us with a wave in the ocean—a temporary formation within the whole, which Arthur Koestler called a sub-whole.[4]

7) Now, while holding your breath and concentrating upon the crown chakra without, however, lifting your head, identify yourself with pure luminous

---

3 See Bohm, *Unfolding Meaning*, 86.
4 Ibid., 7.

intelligence, pure spirit and cosmic nostalgia—the transcendent trinity—while x-raying the hologram with the violet and ultraviolet beam of your third eye.

8) At this stage, we can add the words of the dhikr: *la ilaha illa 'Llahu.*

a) As you repeat *la ilaha*, your all-encompassing mental grasp of the bounty and majesty of the universe exercises an impact on, not only the cells of your brain, but those of the plexuses of your autonomic system, thereby affecting the configuration of the sound wave interference pattern—a sound hologram which you are fashioning.

b) As you repeat *illa 'Llah*, mentally imagine that you are transmuting the sound wave interference pattern into an energy wave interference pattern (the sawt-i sarmadi of the Sufis). Draw attention to the way the sound pattern affects your thinking.

c) As you repeat *hu*, you are investing the hologram, which we have called the cosmic dimension of our being, with this transcendental dimension, awakening those dormant potentialities by illuminating them with the beam of intelligence, quickening them with the catalyst that we call spirit, and luring them into manifestation by the prospect of the fascination of existence.

Nasut
At the Outset, While Still Identifying With One's Body

When I say *la ilaha*, which is a negation of any notion of otherness than God, my natural impulse is to think that the extinction (*fana*) of my notion of myself, as a discrete entity, will be followed by a reinstatement (*baqa*) of the One and Only Being in my awareness: God consciousness. There may even be some kind of self-annihilating, or even self-defeating, instinct in the human psyche that may surface at moments of despair, compensated by a need to merge in the whole, eschewing the tyranny of the ego. But I am warned again by Ibn 'Arabi:

Many make a ceasing of existence and the ceasing of that, a condition for attaining the knowledge of God, but this is an error....not He entering into thee nor thou entering into Him nor thou proceeding from Him nor Him proceeding from thou.[5]

Repeating *la ilaha*, whirling my head while circumambulating my heart center, I grasp the universe globally in its immensity, myself inherently part of it. I can look upon this body as being made of the fabric of the stars.

---

5 Ibn 'Arabi, *Whoso Knoweth Himself,* Weir, T.H. trans.

I muse upon the millions of light years that it has taken for this stardust to transmute itself into the complex biological configuration of these body cells which, in my perfunctory thinking, I identify with as my body. Indeed, consciousness slumbering in the Big Bang has burst forth with dramatic alacrity in this corporeal underpinning as it awakens.

Every atom, every object, every condition and every living being has a moment of awakening. Sometimes this is a gradual awakening and sometimes it is sudden.[6]

Hazrat Inayat Khan

As I whirl my head around my solar plexus, swirling this luminous stardust, so marvelously kneaded and transmuted through the aeons of time into these intelligent body cells, participating in the choreography of the galaxies, I remind myself that the configuration of these cells bespeaks of a cosmic meaning that molds them recurrently, as I awaken to that meaning.

I remind myself that, for Sufism, the existential realm is not illusion, but a projection of a formless reality in which God conveys clues as to that which transpires behind that which appears.

Therefore, I try to imagine that I am participating in the vision that God has of the Divine Self. God reveals God's own Self to the potentialities of the Divine Being by projecting the shadow of God.

The world is related to God as the shadow to the person....From the perspective of His Unity the shadow is God; and from the perspective of multiplicity, it is of the nature of the world....Know whereby you are God and whereby you are not God.[7]

Muhyi ad-Din Ibn 'Arabi

In Sufism, there are the signs (ayat) whereby God discloses the divine Self to God, through me and to me.

We shall show them our signs at the horizons and in themselves.[8]

Qur'an

A sign is a signal giving a clue as to what it stands for, like a signpost. The Sufis posit that what appears is only that which transpires from behind that which appears.

Since my head describes a circle, I rotate my vision; consequently, the diversity within the unity manifests to my view, and I think I understand what is meant by *wahdaniat* (unicity) instead of *wahdat*, (unity). It is only when I

6 Inayat Khan, *Esoteric Papers*.
7 Ibn 'Arabi, *Études Traditionelles* , Valsan trans. Jan./Feb.1951; *Fusus al Hikam*, Chap. 9.
8 XLI:53.

say *hu* suspending the head movement, that I grasp some sense of absolute oneness (*ahadiat*).

Khayal
The Mode of Thinking When Identifying With the Body

I come to the conclusion that when I am declaring *la ilaha*, I am not really annihilating myself but what I think I am; and this applies to the notion that I entertain of my physical body and to the universe, and by the same token, to my self-image and my assessment of my social problems. Hence the *la*, which is a negation, applies to my personal projections upon the universe. This illustrates more significantly what the dhikr requires me to overcome.

An interesting parallel is found here with Yoga. The first step (*nirvitarka samadhi*) leading to awakening (*asamprajnata samadhi*) in Patanjali's *Yoga Sutras* consists in cleansing one's picture of the world from one's personal projections: that is, what it means to one, and consequently, one's assessment of one's problems.

No sooner I question whether I am really the spectator of what I am experiencing, than I espy the divine Spectator behind my consciousness, and now envision my consciousness as the focalization of the divine consciousness.

He is not only the Perceiver but also that through which He perceives.[9]

Muhyi ad-Din Ibn 'Arabi

Ajsam
Identifying With the Subtle Bodies: Life Field or Physical Aura

As I intone *illa*, orienting my head towards my solar plexus, I am lured deeper within. Downplaying the consciousness of my physical body, I feel as though I were made of a fine texture of the nature of gossamer. Maybe I am sensing my life field or electromagnetic field. I distinguish several layers. Paradoxically, that which I discover behind one veil avers itself, in turn, to be a veil.

Sufi metaphysics (*tasawwuf*) teaches me to distinguish several layers to whatever erupts behind the apparent (*zahir*), which is the shroud (*hijab*). I espy, behind the profile of my face, the countenance that transpires through the cells of my face. It evidences a deeper reality (*batin*), the etheric template, more cosmic, more enduring—that which this illusive reality reveals (*tajalliat*).

Whither you turn, there is the Face of God.[10]

Qur'an

---

9 Ibn 'Arabi, *Whoso Knoweth Himself*, Weir, T.H. trans.
10 II:115.

This would mean that behind all faces, the Face of God is hidden: that God is hidden within God's own Creation. I feel God's face trying to transpire though my countenance. It is my identification with my self-image that stands in the way.

At this point, turning within has lost its spacial connotations, because I have lost my sense of space.

As any vestige of a sense of bodiness has absconded, I have lost the feel of the gravity pull of the planet. Since, as I intone *illa*, I cease whirling as I keep turning deeper within, I reach into the void at the epicenter of my being: my solar plexus.

The foundation of khalwa *(seclusion) is* al-khala, *the void.*[11]

There is no doubt that it is my desire for freedom that leads to me to turning within. However much as I long to find freedom from my involvement in the world, in order to awaken beyond the commonplace perspective and look for a retreat as an opportunity to secure this, I remind myself of Shaykh Muhyi ad-Din Ibn 'Arabi's warning:

Some people enter into a retreat (khalwa) because they are wary of society and oppressed by the experience of the world or even of their families, seeking solace in the tranquillity of a retreat; others look for a retreat to be in euphoric state. These motivations are counterproductive.[12]

Muhyi ad-Din Ibn 'Arabi

In fact, the freedom (*vairagya* for the sannyasin) sought by the retreatant evidences a personal wish; whereas in the perspective of Sufism, our personal longing for freedom is always looked upon as the customizing of the divine freedom.

Therefore, in what I presume to be my need for freedom, I am actually reflecting the divine independence from God's own Creation.

I am aware of the immaculate state at the core of my being. It acts as a mirror, simply reflecting impressions from the physical environment and also from my psyche, which now seems external to me. The core of my being never seems tarnished or defiled by my guilt.

In Persian, the mind is called a mirror. Everything in front of the mirror appears in it, but when this is taken away, the mirror is clear.[13]

Hazrat Inayat Khan

---

11 Ibn 'Arabi, *Études Traditionelles*, Valsan trans. March/April 1969 No. 412.
12 Ibid.
13 Inayat Khan, *The Sufi Message* series, *Healing; Mental Purification, the Mind World*, 147.

Here lies the divine grace (*Rahman* and *Rahim*). But I have to merit that grace by repenting and making a pledge never to repeat the mistake. The pledge marks a hiatus, an apostrophe in the process of becoming, intercepting the chain of causal conditioning—the law. To paraphrase al-Hujwiri: *Waqt (the instant of time) is like a sharp sword that cuts the guilt of the past and the expectations for the future.*[14]

A whiff of what it would be like to be liberated from the conditioning of the past and the feedforward of the destiny that one's own limited self build out of inadequacy, flutters over my consciousness.

Mithal

Having proclaimed *illa* as I turn towards my solar plexus, I plunge deeper within, edging upon what seems like an abyss where all that I am familiar with is turned inside out.

I make a point of noticing how my thinking has altered. Instead of reflecting upon the impressions imported from outside, thoughts seem to surface from inside, impromptu, unaccountably, and creatively; whereas when my head was describing the circle saying *la ilaha*, I was thinking of the universe, such as I perfunctorily interpret my ordinary perception of it,

Should the flimsiest impression from outside reach me in this depth of my being, it appears different since I have now witnessed reality backstage.

The one who tunes himself not only to the external, but to the inner being, and to the essence of all things, gets an insight into the essence of the whole being; and therefore he can to the same extent, find and enjoy even in the seed the fragrance and beauty which delight him in the rose.[15]

Hazrat Inayat Khan

At the level in which I am now immersed (mithal), I learn to project the image of my soul upon my view of the universe, rather than projecting my psyche.

So what the soul shows to itself...is precisely its own image: the Earth it projects, the Earth of Hurqalya, is the phenomenon of the Earth in its pure state, since it directly reflects the Image premeditated by the soul.[16]

Henry Corbin

It is all an expression of that aspect of God that is meant by divinity (*uluhiyat*), through which God discovers God's own Self by revealing the Divine Self:

---

14 Al-Hujwiri, *Kashf al-Mahjúb*.
15 Inayat Khan, *The Music of Life*, 75.
16 Corbin, *Spiritual Body and Celestial Earth*, 76.

He brought the cosmos into existence upon His own Form. Hence it is a mirror within which He sees His own Form.[17]

Muhyi ad-Din Ibn ʿArabi

The elation, and therefore peace, that I experience, reflects my freedom from the relatively delusional memory of my commonplace assessment of circumstances that I was carrying in my psyche, so that I am open to new meanings.

However, while not being aware of one's reminiscences of the phenomenal world, this experience may unconsciously trigger off spontaneous thoughts that ought not to be confused by reacting to them, or trying to interpret them with one's commonplace mind (the khayal mind).

Bearing in mind that meaning alters not just the brain circuits but the body in general, one is transmuting one's bodiness by grasping a further level of meaning.[18]

According to Mazdaism, *it is by this projection of its own Image, that the soul [is] effecting the transmutation of the material Earth.*[19]

Applying the principle of trying to see things from the antipodal point of view to my own—the divine point of view—I realize that while the scene and the scenario of the world could serve as clues as to a deeper reality (a device whereby God reveals some hint as to God's nature), God is revealing incomparably more of God's own Being in the unfurling of the divine nature as my personality, albeit restricted by the very limitations I wreak upon this process by my own self-image. Interestingly, these spontaneous thoughts that sometimes coalesce into images are clues as to how God is trying to manifest through me and as me.

In the burgeoning core of my being, the seedbed out of which I am recurrently reborn, a mystery reveals itself, which Ibn ʿArabi had pointed out: I know God through the knowledge that God has of God's own self through me.

You know yourself with another knowledge, different from that which you had when you knew your Lord by the knowledge that you had of yourself, for now you know Him, and it is through Him that you know yourself.[20]

Muhyi ad-Din Ibn ʿArabi

Actually, you now know yourself through the knowledge that God has of God's Self through you.

---

17 Chittick, *The Sufi Path of Knowledge*, 297.
18 See Bohm, *Unfolding Meaning*, 95.
19 Corbin, *Spiritual Body and Celestial Earth*, 14.
20 Corbin, *Creative Imagination in the Sufism of Ibn ʿArabi*, 133.

I realize that at this level, I am now privy to a totally different way of thinking than my ordinary thinking; what I was seeking to experience in the world, I am discovering in myself.

To achieve this, I need to let go of any hint of spatial form, so that my evanescent thoughts and emotional attunements may configure themselves in what the Sufis recognize as non-spatial forms, which have their existence in the realm of metaphor—*'alam al-mithal.*

These forms are compared by Shihab ad-Din Suhrawardi to the forms suspended in a mirror that have no substance; therefore they have their existence in our mind's imaginative faculty.

Forms seen in mirrors, just like imaginative forms, are not imprinted materially either on the mirror or on the imagination. No, they are "bodies in suspension".... *They certainly have places where they appear...but they are not materially contained within them.*[21]

Shihab ad-Din Suhrawardi

It is only thanks to my having lost my self-image that these thoughts can flash upon my mind. They are simply the kaleidoscopic appearances (*tajalli*) of the divine attributes (*sifat*) which I project into illusive thoughts and then strive to embody.

As they gel into ephemeral subtle forms, I realize that I am amongst the clues that my understanding is searching for. This *I am* that I come to grasp is the seed of my personality, which is seeking to unfurl within my personality. Yet Sufi metaphysics (*tasawwuf*) teaches one not to confuse the divinity (*uluhiyat*) of God with the reality (haqq) of God or the essence (*dhat* or *'ayn*) of God.

No man has a right to claim divinity as long as he is conscious of his limited self.[22] *...But at the same time it is in man that divinity is awakened, that God is awakened, that God can be seen.*[23]

Hazrat Inayat Khan

To distinguish creative thoughts from fantasies, Henry Corbin calls these *imaginal* (imaginative) rather than *imaginary*:

If there were not within us that same power of imagination, which is not imagination in the profane sense of "fantasy" but the active imagination quwwat al-khayal *or imaginatrix, none of what we show ourselves would be manifest.*[24]

21 Corbin, *Spiritual Body and Celestial Earth. 127.*
22 Inayat Khan, *Song of the Prophets*, 128.
23 Inayat Khan, *The Sufi Message* series, *The Path of Initiation*,16.
24 Corbin, *Creative Imagination in the Sufism of Ibn 'Arabi*, 187.

But the curious feature I discover here is that by projecting my form before my imagination, I discover it. The reason for this is that my imagination is an extension of the divine imagination, which creates the world by projecting it in forms. But the only guarantee as to their authenticity requires a catharsis, freeing one from the bias inflicted upon our intellect by our ego.

The surface of human intelligence is the intellect; when it is turned outside in, it becomes the source of all revelation.[25]

Hazrat Inayat Khan

Malakut

As I turn my head upward, moving from facing the solar plexus to facing my heart, intoning '*Llah*, my aspiration for that paramount value so meaningful to me, the sublime, hoists me into higher planes. I recall the utterances of my predecessors to help me attune to the celestial sphere—the sphere of *malakut*.

Souls which have become conscious of the angelic spheres...hear the calling of that sphere.[26]

Hazrat Inayat Khan

The movement of the body contributes towards this upliftment. I remind myself of the Sufi precept: *always try to envision how things would look from the divine point of view.*

But this requires of me to let go of my attachment to my dependence upon the earth, and even to the subtle level discovered when turned within. It is my need for freedom that gives me the power to let go.

I have a sense of having extricated myself from my existential underpinning and transcending it. My consciousness seems to be deflected away from the familiar space-time framework, yet there is no displacement of my body in space; rather it appears as though I keep shifting my sense of identity.

It is a matter of realizing that one can exist without the body, and of downplaying my human identity and highlighting my celestial identity, which is buried in deep unconscious memory.

How can this be achieved? It is helpful to retrieve the memory of one's state prior to one's birth, while one needs to remind oneself that although one may not ordinarily be conscious of it, one's being straddles all the planes.

The key is shifting your identity from being a transient, perishable personality and body, to identifying yourself with the level of your being that gives you a sense of perennity, of always having been, and being at present what

---

25 Inayat Khan, *The Complete Sayings of Hazrat Inayat Khan*, 142.
26 Ibid., 198.

one was prior to one's birth, albeit one's bodiness and psyche have accrued to one on earth.

The Sufi therefore practices the process by which he is able to touch that part of life in himself which is not subject to death.[27]

Hazrat Inayat Khan

This requires one to shift one's sense of the substantiality of the body to the gossamer quality of the subtle body, to the effulgence of the aura and then, from the effulgence of the aura, to being an effigy woven in the fabric of diaphanous, non-physical light.

Performing the dhikr at night is extremely inspiring if you think of physical light as the secondary effect of an imperceptible effulgence. If you simply remind yourself of your celestial being, cast in the fabric of celestial light prior to your birth, it will appear to you immature, like a beautiful child: innocent but not wise. But if you can grasp it now, while it still maintains its pristine immaculate state despite being imprinted with the shadows of the earth, it has gained maturity and wisdom. You will find that it fluctuates according to your thoughts, and particularly, your emotional attunements, which weave it into recurrently new patterns. Consequently, we do exercise some impact upon its construction. We can even model it according to our specific ideas as to how we wish to be, but only while we are attuned to the celestial level.

The countenance of this effigy of uncreated light, which you now identify with, strikes you as being so splendid that if you were to allow yourself to slip back into your ordinary consciousness, it would be difficult to believe that it is you; however, you will recall that it undoubtedly did bear a resemblance to your physical face—but clarified, sublimated, transfigured.

Know that there is no form in the lower world without a likeness (mithl) *in the higher world. The forms of the higher world preserve the existence of their likenesses in the lower worlds. Between the two worlds there are tenuities which extend from each form to its likeness....These are like ladders for the angels, while the meanings which descend in these tenuities are like angels.*[28]

Muhyi ad-Din Ibn 'Arabi

But our sense of human limitation has difficulty in countenancing this. To avoid your very understandable skepticism leading you to infer that it is a hallucination prompted by wishful thinking, remind yourself once more of the Sufi precept: *try to reverse your personal vantage point and see things from the divine perspective.* Imagine that God is trying to discover God's own per-

27 Inayat Khan, *The Sufi Message* series, *The Alchemy of Happiness*, 272.
28 Chittick, *The Sufi Path of Knowledge*, 406.

fection in our imperfection; God's own splendor that transpires in forms, however distorted; God's own love in a distressed, maybe sardonic heart. Imagine that rather than being a polished mirror, you are like the surface of a lake rippled by a zephyr.

And imagine that your celestial effigy is working at transforming your human frame to match it; but it requires your facilitation through your being conscious of this process, and to this end, discovering your celestial being.

It is one's glorification that raises one from one plane to another, not one's will. But the key of letting this happen is to let go of one's attachment to the earth and then to the next plane.

I cannot trigger off this shift with my will. This is where the prayerful attunement of the dhikr avers its efficacy. As I lift my head, proclaiming *'Llah*, I am exalted by my very act of glorification.

Our soul is blessed with the impression of the glory of God whenever our lips praise Him....I reach Thee before my feet can reach Thy dwelling place; and I see Thee before mine eyes can reach Thy spheres.[29]

Hazrat Inayat Khan

Paradoxically however, according to the Sufis our celestial counterpart is embryonic in its original state and only gains maturity through the earthly experience.

Think of yourself as always having been a being constructed in the fabric of a nonphysical light.

Commenting on Ibn 'Arabi, Henry Corbin shows prayer as a colloquy (*munajat*), an intimate dialogue shared between Him who shows Himself (*mutajalli*) and him to whom it is shown (*mutajalla lahu*):

A psalmody in two alternating voices, one human, the other divine...The prayer of God aspiring to issue forth from His unknownness and to be known... in [the prayer of man] and through it the form of God becomes visible...to the active imagination which projects before it... the image, whose receptacle is the worshipper's being in the measure of its capacity.[30]

Henry Corbin

Have Me present to your heart, I shall have you present to myself.[31]

Qur'an

According to Ibn 'Arabi:

29 Inayat Khan, *The Complete Sayings of Hazrat Inayat Khan*, 235, 163.
30 Corbin, *Creative Imagination in the Sufism of Ibn 'Arabi*, 249, 248.
31 Ibid., 250.

Prayer, because it is an intimate dialogue...must open out into contempla-tive vision...First, the faithful must place himself in the company of His God and converse with Him. In an intermediate moment, the orant, the faithful in prayer, must imagine His God as present in his Qibla, that is, facing him. Finally, in a third moment, the faithful must attain to intuitive vision or visualization, contemplating his God in the subtile center which is the heart..[32]

The first phase is the action of the faithful toward or upon his Lord. The divine response is: *Now my faithful makes me present to Himself. Now my faithful makes of me the Glorified One.*

The second phrase is a reciprocal action between the Lord and His faithful. The divine response is: *Now there is a sharing in common between myself and my faithful; my faithful sings my praise. Now he exalts My glory and puts his trust in Me.*

The third is an action of the Lord upon His faithful. The divine response is: *To my faithful belongs what he asks.[33]*

My glorification carries me beyond my notion of myself. Yet while any vestige of personal identity lingers, I engage in a dialogue between what I imagine to be my celestial counterpart and God as *other* and too lofty to reach, albeit giving evidence of hearing my prayer as I imagine God's response when repeating *hu.*

When we are face to face, Beloved, I do not know whether to call Thee me, or me Thee. I see myself when Thou art not before me; when I see Thee my self is lost to view. I consider it good fortune when Thou art alone with me; but when I am not there at all, I think it the greatest blessing.[34]

Hazrat Inayat Khan

It is only when, by dint of the power of exultation through glorification any remnant of self-identify has evaporated, that the realization dawns that it is God who exults in ecstasy when discovering the many-splendored bounty latent in the Divine Being, by projecting it into existence—which is in me, as in all life.

Jabarut

At this point, the two *ll*s of the word *Allah* serve as wings bearing you aloft. Linger upon these, soaring ponderously in the realm of pure thought, discovering how your thinking has changed because it no more rests upon

---

32 Ibid., 250–251.
33 Ibn ʿArabi, *The Seals of Wisdom*, 200–201.
34 Inayat Khan, *The Complete Sayings of Hazrat Inayat Khan*, 60.

perceptual experience, or your interpretation thereof, or upon your personal creative imagination.

In the Arabic alphabet, the letter *l* is represented by the arc of a circle. In its Qur'anic metaphoric allusions, it refers to the bow, whereas *a* is represented by the arrow. It is these two *l*s of the word *Allah* that figure in the Qur'anic version of the *mi'raj*, or ascent of the Prophet into the heavenly spheres.

So he was the measure of two bows or closer.[35]

Qur'an

The distance between the bow and the arrow, *gab*, served as a yard stick amongst the Bedouins. *Between them is the measure of a bow,* is a proverb indicating closeness. The same measure between two bows indicates being in sync, as in the *mi'raj* between the Prophet and God. For the *dhakir* (the one performing the dhikr) the two *l*s represent the perfect reciprocated conjunction between the heavenly counterpart of the dhakir (at the malakut level) with the dhakir's divine legacy or archetypal treasure-house (at the *lahut* level).

How does one operate the transition from one's more personal, malakut effigy, to the impersonal springhead of one's being (lahut)? So far, the only clue we had to the Reality behind the existential was through the signs, the pug marks, either in the perceived world or in our own personality. Then we tried to reverse our vantage point to grasp how God could discover God's own archetype exemplified, however ineptly, by us. We are referring to a shift in perspective extant at a higher level of thinking, which Hazrat Inayat Khan calls the thinking of the soul rather than of the mind.

The one who lives in his mind, is conscious of the mind; the one who lives in his soul is conscious of the soul.[36]

Hazrat Inayat Khan

At this level, our ordinary picture of the existential world seems like a hoax. One's perspective has shifted dramatically, but it is in the notion of being the subject—the spectator—that the shift in one's sense of identity is most dramatic.

It is God contemplating Himself in this contemplation of the mystic directed toward His Witness [Shahid].[37]

Henry Corbin

---

35 LIII:9.
36 Inayat Khan, *The Complete Sayings of Hazrat Inayat Khan*, 200.
37 Corbin, *The Man of Light in Iranian Sufism*, 92.

Now having reversed our vantage point, we need to grasp God's knowledge of Divine Self in the very principle of Divine Being, irrespective of the way it manifests itself through that bountiful device that is the existential world, which is beyond existence. At an advanced stage one learns to grasp God as God is in God's own Self, rather than the knowledge gleaned of God, either through the signs in the phenomenal world or those exemplified in one's own nature, or through creative imagination.

You will notice at first that there are no more images with profiles. However, although you have lost a sense of spatial form, still you will have the feeling of being endowed with a countenance that reflects your lofty attunement.

Let alone emancipating oneself from reliance upon one's commonplace thinking (khayal), one dismisses even creative imagination (mithal) as an inadequate mental device to convey more excellent levels of meaningfulness.

This mode of thinking, which the Sufis call the divine thinking, can obviously not be acquired by willing it. It is revealed to you in the measure of your having obliterated even the memory of the physical and psychological environment, which now seems to orbit in the twilight of your consciousness as, lifting your head, you spring over the hiatus between the two *Is*.

It is as though when you question your knowing and dismiss it, your thinking has emancipated itself from the limitations of knowing and becomes all-encompassing, where everything is seen in the context of everything else; also, your thinking seems to foreshadow existential reality in a paramount way, just as your intention presides over your deeds. The light that sees dawns upon the horizon of your knowing.

Al-Hallaj clearly dismisses the arguments of the mind at this stage:

Henceforth there are no more explanations between Thou and me, no proofs, no miracles are needed anymore to support my conviction. The proof is His, from Him, toward Him, in Him. It is the testimony of the truth—a self-explanatory knowledge.[38]

The power of this thinking will shatter your understanding, repudiating and bypassing the very reason it used to rest upon.

Exaltation comes by touching the reason of reasons and by realizing the essence of wisdom.[39]

Hazrat Inayat Khan

---

38 Massignon, *La passion d'al-Hosayn-ibn-Mansour al-Hallaj*, 72.
39 Inayat Khan, *The Sufi Message* series, *Healing, Mental Purification, the Mind World*, 118.

Lahut

Before proceeding further, let us first recapitulate:

In a first step (khayal), we were:

(i)   extending our sense of bodiness spatially;

(ii) expanding the outreach of our consciousness;

(iii) reconnoitering our realm of responsibility.

In a second step (mithal):

(i)   As we turn within, our notion of space is convoluted. Consequently, we grasped the implicate order of light and sound.

(ii) The advance of the arrow of becoming seems suspended. At the instant of time, metaphorically, the horizontal vector of time is intercepted by a vertical one, introducing a new dispensation.

(iii) Verbal expression avers itself to be inadequate and even deceptive in comparison to the meaningfulness behind it.

(iv) Rather than interpret events accruing from outside, we learn to project emotions and thoughts emerging spontaneously from within, creatively, into forms.

In a third step: (jabarut: the two wings, two throws of the arrow):

(i)   One probes immensity irrespective of space.

(iii) Bereft of perceiving physical events, and having ceased to interpret experience in the existential realm, and also having ceased to be aware of one's personality, one's consciousness is reabsorbed in its ground, which is pure intelligence.

(iv) Consequently, one's thinking deploys its inherent sense of meaningfulness in an infinite context defying logical inference.

In a fourth step: (lahut)

(i)   One discovers the bounty of one's inheritance in the realm of personal idiosyncrasies.

(ii) One discerns these same attributes in fellow beings and events.

(iii) In the light of these, one espies the divine intention behind events.

(iv) One touches upon the powerful emotions that impel the universe: the divine nostalgia, *'ishq.*

Now the *I*s have led me to what appears as the springhead behind the scene of the world, and also behind that facade that is my personality. It avers itself to be the divine nature customized in my personality as me. I now identify with

127

the seed of my personality, rather than the plant that unfurls only a modicum of the bounty of the seed.

As we know, perhaps the main thrust in Hazrat Inayat Khan's teaching is gaining awareness of one's divine inheritance, which he calls the seed of our personality. In Sufism it is called *lahutiyat*.

The seed, which is the origin of the flower and the fruit, is also the result of the flower and the fruit. Therefore man is the miniature of the personality of God; God is the seed from which the personality comes. Man, in the flowering of his personality, expresses the personality of God.[40]

Hazrat Inayat Khan

You may think of yourself as a plant in which only a little bounty latent in the seed is manifest. Yet in you the seed that caused the whole existence— God—is to be found.

When this has been done, we discover the bounty of what the Sufis call the *divine names, asma ilahi*. For the Sufis, the word *names* (the sound of the wazifa)[41] carries a particular significance, because we are talking of the divine language. Each object has its specific signature tune; each object is the configuration of a composition of vibrations, which we perceive as sound. We try to reproduce these sounds in our mantras or waza'if.

The Sufis distinguish different kinds of signs, ayat, through which God reveals something of the Divine Self by means of clues. The first sign, in 'alam an-nasut, was through the forms of the world; the second, in ajsam, was by dint of that which transpires, through our nature, of the divine nature.

Now, at the lahut level, after passing though the jabarut state where we forego our conscious act to give vent to the divine point of view, the divine nature is revealed directly, notwithstanding any signs that might have been culled in our personality.

We remember that the forms of the world and the idiosyncrasies of our personality were signs, clues as to the formless Reality. Now that any vestige of forms has faded away, it is the divine attributes, which the Sufis call *His Names*, the archetypes of which our idiosyncrasies are the exemplars, that reveal themselves.

Is it possible, realistic, to see things from the divine vantage point? Let us remember that we are describing here a very advanced level that can only be reached after experiencing the previous ones leading up to it. It is that transit that we need to look into. At some point, Ibn 'Arabi said that one only knows the archetype through the exemplar.[42] What meaning does *roundness* have

40 Inayat Khan, *The Sufi Message* series, *The Unity of Religious Ideals*, 70.
41 In Hinduism: *nama rupa*.
42 See Chittick, *The Sufi Path of Knowledge*, 84.

for us, if not through round objects? Our minds extrapolate between the experience we have of the round objects. Somehow when we see a round object, what is common between all the round objects we have previously perceived is subsumed; and that is what we mean by the archetype. The question is: could we have any notion of roundness without having experienced round objects? It may well be that it is just because roundness is written into the ROM[43] of the software of our minds that we recognize roundness in objects. But how can we reach it? What do the divine attributes mean to us? This is the complementary way of grasping the attribute in the divine mind.

Such is the significance of a method used by an early church father, Tauler, which proved invaluable to Martin Luther. It is called *significatio passiva*.

> *In the presence of the Psalm verse* in justitia tua, libera me *(may Thy attribute of Justice liberate me), he experienced a movement of revolt and despair. What can there be in common between this attribute of justice and my deliverance? And such was his state until the young theologian Martin Luther perceived in a sudden flash... that this attribute must be understood in its* significatio passiva, *that is to say: "Thy justice whereby we are made into just men, Thy holiness whereby we are hallowed..." Similarly in the mystic theosophy of Ibn 'Arabi, the divine attributes are qualifications that we impute to the Divine Essence...as we experience it in ourselves.*[44]

Henry Corbin

To grasp the divine archetypes, Martin Luther was extrapolating between the two poles of the same reality, the archetype and the exemplar, which is what one does at the malakut level.

This realization establishes a new mode of relationship between God and the creature or sentient being, which are the two poles of the same reality of the nature of the relationship between the lord and the vassal, originating in Iranian chivalry, *futuwwat*.

> *The divinity seeks for a being whose God it is. The divine sovereignty has a secret, and that is thou.*[45]

Sahl Tustari

Our recognition of our office of representing the divine Lordship, by facilitating God's manifesting divine qualities or *sifat*, established God's sovereignty.

However, if one has reached the perspective of the lahut level, one proceeds more radically. One captures directly the seeds of those qualities we inherit,

---

43 Read Only Memory (ROM) is a data storage device.
44 Corbin, *Creative Imagination in the Sufism of Ibn 'Arabi*, 300.
45 Ibid., 123.

irrespective of what we have made of them in our personality; thus, in the *tawhid* level, one will be able to customize them in one's personality in a new dispensation while disintegrating one's previous personality rather than adapting it, which could be a compromise.

There is no way in which we can gain a clue to the divine magnificence vested in our divine inheritance, or even of what it is, unless we reverse our vantage point and look at things from the divine point of view. This is, indeed, the main objective of Sufism. To achieve this, one needs to let go of one's personal self-image, which is an outgrowth of what one really is. If we cease identifying with it, it will dissolve and give way to a fresh dispensation from that seed which is our divine inheritance.

At this level, we are overwhelmed by the inexhaustible bounty of possibilities, of which so little ever materializes at the existential level. Sometimes this is called by the Sufis *the level of possibilities, imkan*. Buddha refers to this level in the *arupa* meditations: meditations beyond form, which he encountered on the way to illumination. In Islam, it is the treasury.

There is no thing whose treasuries are not with Us.[46]

Qur'an

The first of these Treasuries is the world of the divine Imperative, the world where to be is eternally in the imperative—"Be! and it is." (Qr 2:111). Every being proceeds from this existence-giving Imperative. The second Treasury is the world of Intelligence, which is the world of the materia consubstantialis, *for the* materia prima *of beings and things was created first, and afterwards their form. The third Treasury is the world of the soul, the place where the forms of beings and things are 'situated.'*[47]

Abu'l-Qasim Khan Ibrahimi

For clarity sake, let us recall that at the ajsam level we were facilitating the unfurling of the potentials of our being, in the process of becoming. But here at the lahut level, since our notion of time as an arrow has collapsed, we are experiencing conditions that favor our being aware of the immortal dimension of our being. The Sufis refer to a causal chain different than Laplacian determinism; they are talking of what one might call a horizontal chain of cause and effect.

When one says that the Truth most glorious comprehends all beings, the meaning is that He comprehends them as a cause comprehends its consequences, not that He is a whole containing them as His parts...[48]

Nur ad-Din 'Abd ar-Rahman Jami

---

46 XV:21.
47 Corbin, *Spiritual Body and Celestial Earth*, 254.
48 Jami, *Lawa'ih*, Vol.XVI, Flash XIX.

In our meditations, if we can let go of our personal identity and reverse our consciousness, so that instead of looking for God as the object of our cognizance, we try to open ourselves to the divine revelation of God's own vision in pre-eternity (*azaliyat*); then irrespective of ourselves in our temporary state, we will find ourselves in sync with the following perspective of al-Hallaj, who left an unforgettable testimony of what was revealed to him in a meditation.

In His Self He contemplated in His pre-eternity (azaliyat) all the invisible.... This is the original state in the absence of all creatures, of all qualities...Then He entertained a dialogue through a thought, by means of all His thoughts. He conversed with Himself. Then He contemplated Himself in the attribute of love, because in its essence, the essence of all essences is love. Then He contemplated in His attribute of love all the other attributes of His Being. Then He glorified Himself in Himself... He looked into pre-eternity and created a picture. This picture is His picture, the picture of His essence. And when God beholds anything, He creates His picture in it for all eternity....Then He saluted it and congratulated it for its splendid countenance.[49]

Mansur al-Hallaj

Hahut

As I pronounce the *h* of the word *Allah* not only the experience of the world and my self-awareness fade away, but even the memory of these.

The *h* of *Allah* represents the shift from my sense of being the subject, the Knower, to the takeover of God as the Knower, the Supereminent Subject. But where there is a knowing subject, even if singular, it follows that there is a known. This is dichotomy, and consequently we are still at the level of duality; whereas when the *h* is transformed into the *hu*, I am hoisted beyond multiplicity into unity.

Let us summarize the steps we have been following. In my ascent, I first integrated the objects or thoughts experienced in the world into a vision of the universe as one being; then I shifted my notion of being the knowing subject, *shahid*, to the One and only Witness. And now, as I bypass the *al*'s and *la*'s and *ll*'s of my recitation by intonating the *h* of *Allah*, I reach into the *hu*. It is only accessed beyond the existential realm.

The letter h is the symbol of something that is absent.[50]*...It stands for the state of non-manifestation of the pure essence.*[51]

Muhyi ad-Din Ibn 'Arabi

---

49 Massignon, *The Passion of al-Hallāj,* Vol. III, 113.
50 Ibn 'Arabi, *Études Traditionelles,* Valsan, trans. May /June 1961, No 365, 149.
51 Ibid., June 1948, No 268, 154.

Paradoxically, even the void in which I thought I lost myself in the *illa* opens the way to the ultimate reality. But I cannot experience it: it is self-revealing

Now the perspective of the qualities at the lahut level fade, as I pull myself away from even the slightest trace, of even the seeds, of the existential state.

I realize that since any sense of being the observer is vanishing, the only way in which cognizance can take place at this level is by dint of the fact that my mind is homologous to the mind of the universe, albeit customized and thereby less effective (on the holographic model). Any remnant of my sense of individual identity limits the vastness and splendor of the thinking of the universe, which is shattering my faltering mind.

In Yoga, one would say:

Intellect (buddhi), having accomplished its mission, withdraws.[52]

Mircea Eliade

What is more, one cannot say that one is experiencing fana, because one is not conscious of being the experiencing subject. This is called *fana al fana*. One is not aware of not being aware.

To be conscious of annihilation is incompatible with annihilation.[53]

Nur ad-Din 'Abd ar-Rahman Jami

But something in the depths of one's being spells a kind of premonition of death. It is the *asamprajnata samadhi* of Yoga, *parat param*: beyond the beyond. The word *fana* assumes its apparently irrevocable meaning. Later, upon reflection, I understand al-Hallaj; at the supreme moment, hanging on the cross after the most atrocious tortures, there was no more *I am* left whereby to recite the *shahada: La ilaha illa 'Llahu.*[54] There is a contradiction in affirming the divine unity if one is aware of oneself as the one affirming it. Therefore, at this pinnacle of the mystic's acid test, at the collapse of any remnant of one's sense of *I-ness*, any human affirmation is handed over to the supreme and ultimate divine unifying act. His last words were:

It suffices if God alone unifies the mystic in His Unity (wahid-wajid).[55]

Here lies the difference between Yoga and Sufism. It is mind-shattering to hear that this crucial and last sentence of al-Hallaj was the answer to the

---

52 Eliade, *Yoga, Immortality and Freedom*, 93.
53 Jami, *Lawa'ih*, Flash IX.
54 The shahada is the Islamic profession of faith in the divine Unity.
55 Massignon, *La passion d'al-Hosayn-ibn-Mansour al-Hallaj*, Vol. I, 603.

impudent question asked him by his erstwhile presumptive friend Shibli, while al-Hallaj hung bleeding and agonizing on the cross: *What is Sufism?* Instead of trying to reach beyond the edge of their consciousness by isolating themselves from the existential realm, the Sufi mystics lend themselves to the divine action, which resorbs them in the Oneness of His being.

I see myself when Thou art not before me; when I see Thee my self is lost to view. I consider it good fortune when Thou art alone with me, but when I am not there at all, I think it the greatest blessing.[56]

Hazrat Inayat Khan

The subtlety of the language used by the Sufis makes it possible to distinguish different aspects of God. The word *Allah* originated from the word *luh*, which means *the One whom I make into the worshipped one—Allah—by my glorification*. But God cannot be limited by this aspect of God's own being, which requires the antinomy of the worshipper and the worshipped one that I bring forth by my worshipping God. Nor can it be restricted to that aspect called *rabb* whereby, through my manifesting the divine qualities invested in my nature, I confer upon God a mode of existence in and as me. For the awakened one, the ultimate reality (Haqq), bypassing any dichotomy, takes precedence over these aspects of God. This is the reason for the dervish's *Haqq la ilaha illa 'Llahu.*[57] Whatever we countenance and ascribe to the universe as we whirl our head is only the projection or the shadow of that aspect of God that is denoted as *Haqq*. Therefore the dervish's dhikr is: *Haqq la ilaha illa 'Llahu.*

Hence al-Hallaj's famous exclamation: *Ana'l Haqq* (I am the Truth).

A zephyr of perplexity may trouble your spirit. The dervishes evoke this uncanny divine emotion encountered by the *dhakir*, called *hayrat*, ecstasy— or perhaps *beyond ecstasy*—sometimes called the *consternation of intelligence*.

This cannot be known by reason, nor conceived by thought, only he who has attained divine intuition savors the pure taste of this total revelation which one calls the "divine unveiling"; and this is the object of the perplexity hayrah of the perfect amongst the initiated.[58]

'Abd al-Karim al-Jili

Be not surprised if God Himself is perplexed![59]

Hazrat Inayat Khan

---

56 Inayat Khan, *The Complete Sayings of Hazrat Inayat Khan*, 60.
57 *Truth! No God but God.*
58 Al-Jili, *De l'Homme Universel*, 42.
59 Inayat Khan, *Esoteric Papers*.

Tawhid

We stumble upon the crowning enigma at the critical turning point, which we encounter as we confront the implications of the awakening attained beyond the existential level, when facing real life situations—again, without losing sight of that transcendent awakening.

For the Sufis, in the ascetic reclusion one would be missing out on the opportunity that life offers, whereby God reveals the Divine Being in the measure of our capacity to countenance the clues covertly intimated through the existential realm.

We are witnessing a radical reversal of perspective; granted our objective is to awaken beyond the limited commonplace personal vantage point, but what point could there be in one's incorporation in the fabric of the universe if one alienates oneself from it? One would be missing out on the purpose of life altogether.

The man who shuts himself away from all men, however highly evolved he may be spiritually, will not be free in the higher spheres....The man conscious of his duties and obligations to his friends is more righteous than he who sits alone in solitude.[60]

Hazrat Inayat Khan

I trigger off the transit into life by espying distant echoes of a remote inflow of what one might call *know-how*, featuring the way in which the distillate of existential experiences—wisdom—is being fed back at this lofty level into the programming of the universe; otherwise, whatever is gained by experience, by the interaction between the fragments of the One Being, would be lost, which wouldn't make sense.

These elusive impressions serve as the chain linking me to an anchor beyond my reach in the world. But I do not wish to loose my perspective, the awakening gained in the ascent.

I distinguish two stages leading to awakening in life:

(i) *Hu* manifests as *Allah* so long as I abstain from trying to experience what is happening, but simply exult in glorification.

(ii) I regain my sense of being the spectator, and then I can only address God as *Thou, anta.*[61]

As I intone *hu*, I become aware of the transformation operated by the way the realization I attained in the state of hahut transforms my whole being at all levels, including the configuration of my subtle bodies, and then of

---

60 Inayat Khan, *The Complete Sayings of Hazrat Inayat Khan*, 218, 206.
61 See Ibn 'Arabi, *Études Traditionelles*, Valsan, trans. Oct./Nov. 1948, No 271, 343.

the material body, starting with my celestial shroud and concretizing in the descent towards manifestation.

Now the challenge consists in maintaining the divine point of view while recovering one's personal identity.

While there is no way in which we can discover the ultimate reality of Haqq, which is the ultimate condition of God, we may be invited to participate in the divine vision whereby God sees that reality projected in the mirror of the universe as in the reflection of the Divine Being that constitutes our personalities. To accede to this mode of cognizance, we need to serve as a mirror, to abstain from interposing our reason or our act of consciousness, but rather simply allow our understanding to be transfigured by this unfamiliar way of looking at things.

Paradoxically, this ineffable reality may be revealed within, in the existential perspective rather than beyond existence, which is what is sought in the Yogic samadhis. And therefore, for al-Hallaj, the Sufi dervish must abstain from self-isolation; and then, absorbed in the divine unity, the dervish is co-opted by the divine unifying operation, to be integrated in the divinity of God: *infirad*, rather than *tajrid* or *tafrid*.

Louis Gardet defines tajrid as isolation from any objective input, and tafrid as retraction of one's self from any act (operated by the self). In contrast, al-Hallaj advocates *infirad*, the passive mode of the verbal form.

It is God who elects him and draws him into His state of isolation, that he may participate in the mystery [of the divine solitude].[62]

Louis Gardet

Therefore, rather than loosing myself, I can now see myself inextricably intermeshed in the Total Being of which I am clearly an integral element. It is a shattering, and at the same time, overwhelming experience.

At this point, as we intonate *Huwwa*, turning our head towards our heart, we are invited to extrapolate between all the perspectives encountered in the course of the whole recitation of the dhikr. This would mean (i) expanding the outreach of our vantage point; (ii) seeing the *outside* from *inside*; (iii) in addition to hoisting one's consciousness *beyond the beyond*, (iv) now to partake in an overview of the way things appear on earth. This represents a kind of tour de force, challenging all the views we have encountered so far. In fact, it could be defined as stereoscopic consciousness: being able to extrapolate between the perception vouchsafed through our personal vantage point and the transcendental one.

---

62 Gardet, *Expériences mystiques en terre non-chrétiennes,* 135–136.

How can this be achieved? It is a matter of keeping constantly in mind one's connection with the totality of which one is a part, while acknowledging that one has gained some kind of relative autonomy as a visitor on Planet Earth.

True exaltation of the spirit resides in the fact that it has come to earth and has realized there its spiritual existence.[63]

Hazrat Inayat Khan

Moreover, one needs to continually keep oneself highly attuned by offsetting one's consciousness so as to grasp the splendor that is striving to transpire behind the sometimes offensive appearance of things.

Note that as we hoisted our concentration from *la ilaha* to *illa*, we shifted our awareness from the perceptual and interpretive mode, to grasping the emergence of the world and ourselves from the implicate order; then, when we hoisted our consciousness from *illa* to *'Llah*, we shifted from the world of metaphor to thoughts bereft of any form or image whatsoever. Now, as we intonate *hu*, we descend into the realm of configurations and matter. Our intelligence discovers itself by awakening in the atoms of the cells of our bodies.

Let us now see how this attunement and perspective is going to affect our daily lives. Passing though the stages of the dhikr, we have not only been discovering unfamiliar perspectives, beaming new light upon our problems, but awakening dormant faculties. The shift in outlook triggers off transformation. Let us now consciously awaken the umpteen faculties governing the programming of the whole universe, which lies dormant in ourselves.

Realization needs to be backed up by doing.

In order to gain God consciousness, the first condition is to make God a reality, so that He no longer is an imagination.[64]

Hazrat Inayat Khan

The clue consists in experiencing God discovering God's own Self as you.

How is higher consciousness attained? By closing our eyes to our limited self and by opening our heart to the God who is all perfection, who is in heaven and on earth, within and without, who is visible, audible, perceptible, intelligible and yet beyond man's comprehension.[65]

Hazrat Inayat Khan

---

63 Inayat Khan, *The Sufi Message* series, *The Alchemy of Happiness*, 242.
64 Inayat Khan, *The Sufi Message* series, *The Way of Illumination*, 145.
65 Inayat Khan, *Esoteric Papers*.

The Sufi's task is to be instrumental to God's purpose in the very creation of the world. Here lies the secret of the Hadith Qudsi that lies at the basis of all Sufism: *I was hidden treasure...*

God knows Himself by His manifestation. Manifestation is the self of God, but a self that is limited, a self which makes Him know that He is perfect when He compares His own Being with the limited self which we call nature. Therefore the purpose of the whole Creation is the realization that God Himself gains by discovering His own Perfection though His manifestation.[66]

Hazrat Inayat Khan.

The key is, rather than thinking of God as other, discovering the various levels of Godness in yourself.

How do we reconcile this with the thought which we came across, and which led us to the hahut or samadhi state: *How do we work through the ties with the life of the world?* Having loosened these ties, we are able to reconcile what would seem to be irreconcilable: to involve ourselves with unconditional love with all beings, while not being dependent upon attachment or gain.

Here lies the enigma:

He who arrives at the state of indifference without experiencing interest in life is incomplete and apt to be tempted by interest at any moment; but he who arrives at the state of indifference by going through interest really attains the blessed state.[67]

Hazrat Inayat Khan

---

66 Inayat Khan, *The Complete Sayings of Hazrat Inayat Khan*, 194.
67 Inayat Khan, *The Complete Sayings of Hazrat Inayat Khan*, 231.

PART FOUR

MODULATING CONSCIOUSNESS

Introduction

The Mind-Energy Connection

There is geometry in the humming of the strings;
there is music in the spacing of the spheres.

Pythagoras

The pilot of our being is our mind-brain, which extends throughout our body to our whole nervous system, right into the nucleus of each cell. It needs a wide scope of understanding and stimulation to reach a state of fulfillment.

Imagine, it took fifteen billion years of the cataclysmic convulsions in the birth pangs of umpteen cosmic galaxies to fashion the hundred million trillions of atomic particles constituting the fabric of our bodies, and to coordinate them to the point that they may, in their cooperation, offer a support system to the mind of the universe—what we call the mind of God, customized into what we call our thinking. The fabric of our bodies, which serves us as the underpinning of our thinking, existed as stardust out of the original chaos fourteen billion years ago, and is the fruit of the cosmic gestation of the universe.

As we have seen, the fabric that embodies our thinking, particularly the brain and nervous cells, was on its way to being formed even in the original chaos, in the form of millions of billions of electrons and quarks. One thousandth of a second after the Big Bang, the quarks formed their building blocks: protons and neutrons.

Millions of years later, the fabric of our bodies found itself in the galaxies, which gave birth to stars in which the nuclei of the atoms of our bodies were incubated. It was only after the enormously long lifespan of one of these stars, at its death in a frantic explosion many thousand million years before the birth of the sun, that the particles of the our body cells were projected as stardust into the chilling cold of interstellar space; after which they could be incubated in the furnace of our sun, the nuclear, cosmic alchemical athanor where protons and neutrons combined to form the nuclei of the atoms, of which the molecules of our bodies are built. Thus it is not surprising that if we "think big," we realize that we are discovering the universe right in our body.

In our psyche we experience the incredible antinomy between celestial harmony, the precarious grace of well-being, and the terror of cataclysmic disrupture; and this seems so meaningless to our understanding in our ordeals and catastrophes and psychic collapse. How can we reasonably account for the fact that things that were going so well may suddenly fall apart in a senseless and seemingly unnecessary fiasco? The cosmic order breaks down to restructure itself. But, from our personal perspective, this seems counter-productive. There is so much pain involved: imagine the tortures inflicted on innocent victims, not just in concentration camps, but simply though disease and death. It seems as though the body of the Divine Being disintegrates at the jagged ends.

If we look at the positive side, by what tour de force of cosmic ingenuity did these molecules, having discovered their identity eons ago—feeding themselves from the environment, dividing, proliferating, transmitting their heredity—connive to reconnoiter kindred molecules. Bypassing those immediately adjacent, they find freedom from the constraint of their conditioning by cooperating with others, limiting their prerogatives, and thus building up information, not just about their kind but about the intention motivating them. Do we not recognize ourselves in this, albeit at a larger scale?

Imagine what it has taken for the grouping and cooperation of these molecules constituting our bodies, after making the quantum leap from the inorganic to the organic, to make possible the formation of our body cells, and to conspire together to form a biological organism as a whole; and then what it took for these organisms to evolve through the vegetable and animal stages to the point of the emergence of what we call human. And then again, what it has taken for the Neanderthal man to evolve to the stage you are in. Let us bear in mind that we are only at a transitional stage in the evolution of the human species, which keeps evolving further with, however, a lot of misfits, accidents, spoliation, and decadence.

The very structure of the fabric of our body cells and organs, and the organization of body functions that illustrate laws of harmonic resonance,[1]

---

1 Pythagoras's theory of the music of the spheres is illustrated by the harmonic intervals of the seven notes of the scale, harmonics, the nodes of oscillation of pendulums, the nodal lines of atomic patterns, the intervals between the shells of an atom, the seven octaves of the Periodic Table of elements, Bode's law and Balmer's ladder, the Mendeleev table of particles, the Trojan Asteroids, the wave ratios that govern sea waves, dunes, tides, etc.. The corrobo-

bear the stamp of the thinking of the universe. This thinking evolves as its material support system becomes more elaborate; and reciprocally, the support system perfects itself as it evolves, just as our brain (and body, for that matter) develops latent faculties as our thinking brightens, and we exult in our grasp of meaningfulness. Our thinking perfects itself as our brain, and its extension as the nervous system, is activated. Yes, even the nuclei of our body cells are endowed with a degree of pragmatic understanding, greatly enhanced by their cooperation.

By virtue of our tacit covenant with the universe of which we are a part, the cosmic mind, called the mind of God and delegated by our minds, gains vistas, which, while latent in the cosmic mind, are only actuated through our free will and incentive. Thus our grasp of our fealty to the intention of the divine sovereignty, at the scale of cosmic chivalry (*futuwwat*), confers upon us suzerainty over the domain of responsibility assigned to us in order to insure order. By so doing, we foster the mutation of the software of the universe, fluctuating it by our personal incentive.

Since the divine mind, or mind of the universe, is the matrix of our mind, it can never be the object of our cognizance; yet, we can invite more of its bounty to percolate as our thinking. To do this, we need to eradicate the mental restrictions we impose upon our thinking by our very notion of ourselves as a fraction of the totality, and by the same token, as other than God, which is the very principle of the Islamic shahada:

Thou art not thou: thou art He, without thou.[2]

Muhyi ad-Din Ibn 'Arabi

This way of thinking evidences our having faild, in our commonplace thinking, to make the step in the evolution of human thought marked by the holistic paradigm, and even beyond this, to realize that while the fraction of a hologram functions like the whole hologram, it functions less effectively. But it acquires a uniqueness, which makes for variety and cooperation in the interest of the whole, and which would not occur if everything were undifferentiated.

The functioning of our minds is illustrated most pertinently by the DNA. Each cell organizes the fabric of the environment absorbed in its tissue, on the model of the blueprint of the universe that ensures that the cells differentiate in order to cooperate in the interest of the whole body. Similarly,

---

ration of so many observations lead to the inference that matter conforms in principle to a certain orderliness, whose harmonic resonance is evidenced in music, rings of Saturn and the nodes of the Trojan Asteroids.

2 Ibn 'Arabi, *Whoso Knoweth Himself*, T.H. Weir trans.

every human psyche is formatted by the software of the cosmos; but it customizes the principles governing that software in its own unique way, and thus processes the environment differently from its neighbor. The complex structure of our body serves as the support system for that very intelligence configured in the cosmic blueprint, by turning certain genes on and others off. Even so, although our minds potentially carry the mind of the universe, they are diversified, and thereby restricted by their vantage points and their specializations.

As Karl Pribram shows, the brain functions jointly as a hologram and as a network of circuits.[3] May I add: ensuring both the transpersonal and the personal dimensions of our motivations? The more transpersonal, the more the holistic mode of our thinking prevails over our personal opinion. This is what is meant in mysticism by *awakening to God consciousness*. It is as though one were releasing one's personal constraints to one's understanding of meaningfulness or, more precisely, giving up one's personal interpretation of situations and problems, which is precisely what is meant by *maya*.

The exhilarating aspect of the whole marvel, of which we are a contributing part, is that the springheads behind its superb alacrity is sheer excitement! The brain needs stimulation, the mind needs the joy of discovering ideas, the psyche needs ecstasy.

Dr. Alfred Tomatis, a physiologist, found that our brain requires three billion stimuli a day to keep awake. These include, of course, light and sound, smell, taste and tactile impressions. These sensorial stimuli are translated by the brain as energy pulses, stimulating the mitosis of nerve cells. We know that our body cells, particularly our nerve cells, absorb light from the environment that catalyzes their powerhouse, freeing their electrons from their initial constraint for a split second of a degree of freedom; and this also happens when they pick up and communicate sound messages. Hence the importance of music as fuel for our brain, and also of our communication with the physical environment, which is nothing less than a communion of light between the light fluoresced by the environmental objects, the sun and the stars, and the light thrust by our brain through the optic nerves and retinas into the environment.

Contemplate the degree of excellence attained when the extraordinary variety of frequency resonances of the already complex, atomic configurations of vocal cords, guts, wood and metals, which constitute musical instruments—already reflecting the orderliness of the blueprint of the universe—is further configured by the mind of God when funneled into the human mind, as in our symphonies and choruses; or when the latticework of the internal fabric

---

3 See Pribam, *Brain and Behavior*.

of stones and glass and ceramic are assembled into a statue or cathedral; or the gossamer film of paints, which in many ways are of the nature of liquid crystals, already so splendid in themselves, is blended into a painting. Paint, like sound, is a noble expression of the software of the universe, which does not need to be fashioned to copy perceived objects like the paintings of old, or like Beethoven's description of a thunderstorm in the Sixth Symphony, or Honneger's imitation of a train puffing along. The form of a flower or the countenance of a human face figure at the prow of the evolution of divine thought, configured as form. However, the soul-searchings, aspirations, misgivings, compassion, and wit erupting in human emotions described, for example, by Brahms, dramatize the mutations incurred by the Divine Being in the existential condition. This represents progress compared to the sounds of nature at the mineral or plant level, sometimes depicted in the dehumanized austerity or exuberance of some modern music. When these media of expression are fashioned to express our creative thinking, they enrich the software of the universe. Our thinking, which customizes the divine thinking, having projected itself into matter that already carries the hallmark of thinking at the cosmic level, is recycled into the cosmic thinking. And what of the delight to our minds and emotions when carried beyond the trite commonplace by the inspiration of poets rearranging the divine thinking in unexpected ways; we discover new horizons of meaningfulness, evidencing the splendor seeking to transpire through the appearance of things. Our mind-brains feast at the banquet offered by the creative geniuses who have conceived our great civilizations, and we are enriched and transformed thereby.

But what of the light that we ourselves awaken, probably as phosphorescence, by our visualizations?[4] And can we imagine the delight of composers improvising musical themes emerging from inside, projecting an inner mandala in an audible structure? Think of a toccata and fugue of Bach, or a prelude of Chopin, or a sonata of Brahms! Most of us have that uncanny ability as we hum randomly, yet it gains incomparably in excellence when cultivated. According to Hazrat Inayat Khan, as we turn within in meditation, we discover our ability of awakening the sound of the universe[5]—the audiosphere—even written right into the fabric of our body cells, which carry not only the memory of the sonic outbursts accompanying the birth and demise of the nebulae (whose stardust has coagulated into the atomic fabric of our body cells), but also the present resonance of the subatomic structures of our

---

4 This has been demonstrated by Dr. Motayama's experiments with meditators in light-proof cells equipped with photoelectric sensors. See White and Stanley Krippner, *Future Science.*

5 Inayat Khan, *The Music of Life*, 3.

cells, which are affected by our psychological attunements. What a miracle is the human skill of translating this ubiquitous symphony of the spheres into music meaningful to humans!

Hazrat Inayat Khan further points out the way to arouse the light within that flares like a flame.[6] The ebullient incandescence that burst out of the cataclysmic conflagration of the Big Bang is stored in the very fabric of our bodies and released as phosphorescence, whereby we transform the atomic structure of our body cells into light—a capacity found in the glowworm and firefly, and which we also possess, and which can be released by appropriate visualizations.

It is not just the energy of stimuli that charges the powerhouse of our brains, but the meaningfulness of the universal blueprint conveyed by these stimuli, triggered off by the configuration of the atomic structure of the environment and of our very flesh. Our minds can grasp this because they are modeled on the mind of the universe. Therefore, Hazrat Inayat Khan adds: it is not light or sound that spells awakening, but the vistas that they trigger off in our intelligence.[7] Every *Aha!* moment triggers off a peak experience—a tidal wave of delight. The springhead of the whole phantasmagoria that we perceive as the universe, the divine nostalgia, spills over into our psychological attunements as we discover the intention behind it all, which is written right into our own deep motivations. This only happens when we reach beyond our limited thinking, our limited vantage point, and limited self-image. Imagine: our psyche is garnished with our misassessments of the physical and psychological environment.

Consider the impact upon the brain cells, and by the same token, upon the whole body, of our mind's ability to reach beyond its middle range and our emotions into the many-splendored shimmering gamuts of cosmic ecstasy. This is precisely what we achieve in our meditation skills, in samadhi practices, Vipassana, Kabbalah, the theology of Aquinas, and the Sufi dhikr.

Exploring the levels of our thinking, we find that at a basic level, our minds reconnoiter facts. At a higher level, our minds try to grasp relationships or interactions between these. At a still higher level, our minds capture meaningfulness, sometimes irrespective of the facts, or catalyzed by the facts.

A major aspect of meditation consists in learning how to think beyond the commonplace syllogism. In *Tertium Organum*, P. D. Ouspensky announced the advent of a super-logic, surpassing the simple syllogism: *All men are mortal; Socrates is a man; ergo, Socrates is mortal.*

Our ordinary logic helps us to gauge only the relations existing in the phenomenal world....We must come to the conclusion that separateness and combination are

6 Inayat Khan, *Esoteric Papers.*
7 Inayat Khan, *The Music of Life*, 32.

146

not opposites in the real world, but exist together and at the same time without contradicting each other.[8]

Peter D. Ouspensky

Our objective is to explore the many-tiered levels of mental functions, which are discovered in carrying the mind beyond its middle range activities in meditation. And further, we propose to harness energy to serve as an underpinning for our mind. May we add a Pegasus to hoist consciousness into farther reaches of realization? However, it is good to bear in mind that Pegasus could not reach Mount Olympus, but could only take his rider, Bellerophon, so far, after which Bellerophon had to soar aloft alone. The wind typifies here the energy of our magnetic field, monitored by our breath.

A correspondence between different modes of energy and the correlated levels of thinking have been observed by meditators.

By identifying with our subtle energy, we awaken our subtle mind. To achieve this, we need to disidentify with our gross energy field, i.e., the ordinary electromagnetic field; and this will bring our gross mind into disarray.

The Tibetans distinguish between a) the *gross mind* that interprets phenomena and events; b) the *subtle mind* (the creative mind) that projects its understanding into images; for example, in our day or night dreaming; and 3) the *very subtle mind* that carries within itself an inherent sense of meaningfulness without depending upon the feedback of experience for understanding.[9]

The commonplace mode of knowing, or *najat*, which Suhrawardi calls *speculative knowledge*,[10] (the activity of the gross mind according to the Tibetans), is discounted by Sufi mystics as totally inadequate.

When man arrives at God-knowledge from self-knowledge, he makes God as small as his little self; but when he comes to self-knowledge through the knowledge of God, he becomes as large as God.[11]

Hazrat Inayat Khan

---

8 Ouspensky, *Tertium Organum*, 106.
9 See Gyatso, *The Clear Light of Bliss*, 97.
10 Corbin, *Suhrawardi d'Alep*, 29.
11 Inayat Khan, *The Complete Sayings of Hazrat Inayat Khan*, 150.

Chapter One
The Cosmic Dimension

Understandably, we are all in search of our identity. We now know that our individuality is both a fraction of the universe, and also a focal point in which the totality of the universe converges and meshes. Furthermore, it radiates, impacting not just the physical and psychic environment at an infinite scale, but upgrading the very software of the universe. Consequently, our realization of what we mean by our individuality enriches that very individuality. It does this by opening doors that remain closed if we simply cloister ourselves in our reductionistic notion of ourselves, thereby dismissing and obstructing the larger resourcefulness of our being. By some puzzling paradox challenging to our middle-range thinking, we are also a fraction in the sense that we do not just converge the totality but also process it (just like our digestive system and our body cells) by rejecting that which is too incompatible, and transubstantiating it to match our idiosyncrasies. By the way, these idiosyncrasies incorporate more and more richness, and adapt themselves to the environment through osmosis. To act on the environment instead of just assimilating it, we impose our own code upon the information or structures ingested.[1] Moreover, we need to account for a further dimension, the transcendental dimension: our understanding, our realization, our sense of meaningfulness.

Let us take a further look at this whole question with regard to our objectives in meditation. Our objective is to evolve, to progress, to arrive at a greater understanding and realization. We expect the meditation practices to furnish us with clues as to how to achieve this. We have now reached the point where it has become clear that, to enrich ourselves, we need to do at the human scale just exactly what our body cells are doing: cooperate with all the others. To coordinate with others, we need to specialize, to find our idiosyncratic niche. But for this niche to enrich us, it needs to be relevant to all the others. If

1 Just like the enzymes of the pancreas, duodenum or liver, or the RNA.

we segregate ourselves in the fantasies of our personal idiosyncrasies without networking with others, we remain inbred and can never be part of "where things are at," and thereby fulfill a purpose in life.

Conversely, the only way in which we can synthesize the environment by which we nurture ourselves, and which is now being digested, is in terms of what it means to us—from our personal and limited perspective. Hence, we do not just converge the universe like a focal point, but also impact it with the uniqueness of our particular psychic code.

What this actually implies surpasses the wildest flights of our imagination and is threatening to our commonplace sense of identity.

Extending Our Sense Of Identity

In the light of the foregoing, it is clear that it is not sufficient to embrace wider fields of reality; for example, encompassing the stars by modulating consciousness in its cosmic dimension. We need to simultaneously enhance our sense of identity, including our psyche in its cosmic dimension. To this end, our commonplace sense of bodiness will prove frustrating, because one normally envisions one's body as being skin-bound.

This is why we need to shift our sense of identity upwards, including our subtle and celestial bodies while extending our identity cosmically. Our electromagnetic field is indeed an aspect of our body that assumes much more of the aspect of a vortex than what one simplistically ascribes to bodiness. As for the aura, as we have seen, it extends into the starry sky and is part of the light of the galactic luminescence.

You will find that as you expand your consciousness, the line of demarcation between yourself and other-than-yourself advances progressively like a galloping tide; and it also merges with the environment like an eddy within a wave interference pattern.

As we expand our consciousness in its cosmic dimension, we give vent to our sense of infinity. Not only do we encompass ever wider horizons, but our sense of identity also expands and resonates with ever wider fields of reality, including the celestial spheres. And what is more, our sense of meaningfulness sharpens, so that we cannot suffice ourselves with the field of the middle range mind; and therefore, we beam our perspective with a transcendent realization.

The very notion of the Big Bang baffles our innate sense of meaningfulness. Instead of satisfying our need to understand, it exasperates our understanding. It incites us to ask the inevitable question: *What existed prior to the Big Bang?* or *What caused or initiated the Big Bang in the first place?* Obviously, when faced with a dead end, the mind is pressed to take the antipodal point of view, or accept to be stymied. The mind's faculties do not need to put up with the limitation incurred by the personal vantage point. No sooner do we elude that constraint by realizing that its purview is the effect of conditioning, then whole new horizons open up for our understanding.

In the course of efforts to try to expand the mind, each meditator reaches a point, which varies according to the degree of realization of that person, at which the mind falters. This explains why certain perspectives articulated by contemplatives in the esoteric literature do not make sense to most people. One realizes the powerlessness of the middle range mind to interpret data.

If you understand that reality only becomes known to us when it squeezes into its focalization within the capacity of our minds, like the plethora of impressions of a landscape passing though a key hole, or the numerous frequencies of a radio network in the atmosphere being brought into focus by the radio, then you cease being frustrated at not being able to grasp meaningfulness. But every now and again, shift your perspective into the divine mode, while dismissing the commonplace perspective as misleading though only relatively valid.

If, at our human scale, we realize the degree to which we limit the information we cull from our experience of the universe to what seems relevant to us, we can well imagine the paramountcy of the underlying intelligence subtending its the structures and functions.

Methods

We are now going to apply the method we adopted in modulating our life-field[2] to alternatively expand our consciousness, and conversely, turn it within in the introspective mode. Applying the skill thus achieved, we can tap the latent potentialities lying in wait in the deeper strata of our psyche, and actuate them in our personality.

We could also apply this to extending the field of our thoughts to thinking at a cosmic scale. Alternately, we could learn to probe into the deeper thoughts implied behind our ratiocinations and rationalizations.

We will, in addition, apply this technique to try and capture something of that oceanic euphoria to which some mystics bear testimony. In contrast to this, we can then shift from this emotional attunement, which we might call cosmic, to the opposite, enjoying a sense of detachment, independence, liberation, and serenity.

Practices

1) As you exhale, expand your consciousness so that you have the impression that your consciousness is all-encompassing. Your consciousness seems now to be the consciousness of the universe, the cosmic observer watching

---

2 See Part One, Chapter Four, "Breath Directed Centrifugally Versus Centripetally."

what you thought was yourself. The Buddha described his experience thus: the personal notion of consciousness is carried over into cosmic consciousness, without any break in continuity, and consequently, no break in memory.

2) You may enjoy letting go of yourself, knowing that by so doing you will not lose yourself irretrievably. You will notice that as you expand, you also disperse. The condition for change and, therefore, improvement, is to flow with that law of the universe outlined by alchemists: everything needs to break down, fall apart, and dissolve before it can be reformed in a new con-figuration. This will give you a sense of freedom from your self-image, from your opinions, from being bogged down in your personal emotions.

3) While enjoying this sense of vastness, you may be afraid of losing yourself. This is very understandable; it is due to the compulsiveness of the most basic of all instincts: self-preservation. The realization that we could not even lose ourselves if we tried, should give you some reassurance.

As we have seen, the eddies caused by gravel thrown on the surface of a lake intersect with each other in a wave interference pattern, so that while one has lost sight of the individual eddies, yet one can retrieve them unscathed.[3]

One of the aims of the ascetics is overcoming fear. When the fear of the unknown is overcome, you become an adept on the spiritual path. However, as stated earlier, do not overstress yourself. Just stay at the edge of your capacity.

4) The thought that will help you, which we have come across in the General Introduction,[4] is the reconciliation of the model of the vortex with that of the cell endowed with a permeable boundary.

5) Now, as you inhale, concentrate on the way that the consciousness of the universe gets focalized into your personal conscious focus.

If a wide panorama gets focalized through a convex lens, its features are going to be squeezed into a small surface, and much of the detail will get lost.[5] On the other hand, if you scan a narrow stretch with a concave lens, you will discern more detail. The beauty of alternating consciousness in this way is that one learns to extrapolate between long-sightedness and short-sightedness—both being complementary to each other.

---

3 An illustration of a wave interference pattern would be as follows: if you should drop gravel on a lake, each particle will form eddies that will extend further and further. These eddies will compose to form what in physics is called a wave interference pattern. Looking at this wave interference pattern, one cannot detect the individual eddies; but if two wave fronts cross one another, they will be able to extricate themselves from their composition unscathed. In the same way, these eddies that elude detection can be extricated unscathed This is known in physics as the Fourier analysis.

4 Preamble, Chapter Three, "Introduction to Meditation."

5 This varies with the resolution.

6) Having modulated your consciousness, now proceed in the same way with your thoughts.

7) Likewise with your emotions.

8) Likewise with your identity, and also with your psyche.

Chapter Two
Turning Within

It is ordinarily taken for granted that meditation consists in turning within and lending oneself to elusive and evanescent internal musings and ponderous soul-searchings. This is a symptom of the unrelenting human excursions into the far reaches of the mind. The meditator is spurred by the expectation of discovering, in the hidden depths of the psyche, solutions to the paradoxical riddles we ponderously grapple with, albeit inadequately, using the ordinary performance of our minds.

Humanity as a whole has participated in the factual explorations of outer space by our astronauts, and also in the mental inquiry into outer space by our astrophysicists, which is popularized in the media. A few are privy to the exploration of outreaches of the mind through meditators, availing themselves of the know-how of their predecessors but carrying that assignment yet further, thanks to the new paradigms in our way of thinking in this day and age.

Should we venture beyond the wall of mystery unprepared, we find ourselves dumbfounded and shattered, and often confused, unable to extrapolate between the profusion of bounty flooding the skylight of our mind. The human mind is yet in its developmental stage and still has a long way to go until it grasps the thinking of the universe, which is, however, enfolded in our own mind.

Our programming protects us from realizations that our minds would fail to encompass, by blanking out the large areas of the psyche that we call the unconscious; for example, the veil offered by sleep, which shields our minds, is a protection. Yet flimsy clues regarding wider dimensions of realization and evidencing the software behind the existential scenario, sometimes trickle through, particularly when one is precariously poised upon the threshold between the diurnal waking condition and sleep with dreams. This is precisely what occurs as we turn within in meditation,

Even though the data crossing over into the area of our psyche that is illuminated by the spotlight of consciousness, are scarce and equivocal, they constitute for the psychotherapist an invaluable mine of resourcefulness. Equally so for the one bent on exploring the secrets behind, not just our personal thinking, but the thinking of the universe. When intruded upon, the subliminal area of our psyche, evasive as it is, in certain conditions will yield cryptic clues to some of its secrets, providing we know how to decipher its code. This has been utilized by psychotherapists to gather clues about their patients through the reminiscences of their dreams, which are trickling across the border from the unconscious. Advaita Vedanta provides an extremely elaborate parallel between sleep and clearly defined stages in meditation.

The difficulty encountered by the uninitiated is that the mode of thinking of the unconscious is totally different from the commonplace rational modes, which we have been conditioned to rely upon by our standard educational curricula. While in the usual mode, we think of ourselves as the subject or observer, and consider either our perceptions, or thoughts, or feelings, or self-image as the objects of our experience, envisioned as discrete entities in meditation, or rather, contemplation; then we switch to a totally different mode whereby everything intersperses everything else, including one's thoughts, even one's self-image, and what is more, one's consciousness, and ultimately, one's sense of identity. It is not surprising, therefore, that people get lost in this unintelligible miasma; and quite understandably, the accounts given of it by mystics and poets seem totally ambiguous.

Reverting to this mode is not without hazard, because unless properly understood, it offers an escape from the glare of the everyday scenario, which may prove to some unbearably painful. Therefore, it provides a psychological opiate from dealing with reality, and consequently, can make the amateur otherworldly. It tends to worsen the psychological dysfunction of persons whose psyche is in a precarious state in a crisis or is, in general, borderline. In some cases people with a bad self-image enjoy the sense of personal annihilation. Unless one can handle the antinomy between the ensuing sense of the annihilation of one's notion of oneself, together with the euphoria of discovering the bounty of one's being, one will be nonplussed, confused and overstressed.

This is why psychotherapists contrive to build a person's personal identity, rather than let it disassociate; it is also why psychotherapists accuse spiritual groups of the spiritual bypass, of making people high and unable to deal with their problems. I would equally call attention to the danger of the psychological bypass—underestimating people's need to get in touch with their soul; that is, prodding deeper than the areas generally explored in the party line of acceptable professionalism. In fact, people entertaining lofty values are desperately in search of the sacred, and naturally seek it within. Notwithstanding, there is a place for escape, a need to occasionally give ourselves a break—a sabbatical. It may well aver itself to be more efficient to bypass the less important issues and to prioritize the more meaningful ones. We tend to spend more time dealing with urgent things rather than important ones. Unless one balances adaptability to the social environment with adapting the social environment to one's sense of purpose, one fails to be creative or to affirm oneself, and one lingers in mediocrity.

Doubtlessly, turning within is an art and a skill that requires a lot of know-how and training. Unless one knows how to make sense of that inner world, one incurs the risk, when turning within, of discounting the very purpose of life that is actuated in the existential world; and one finds oneself ineffective in life.

We are, therefore, deeply beholden to the hermits, monks, nuns, and mystics who have pioneered in exploring the remote outposts of the mind—whatever their religious background, which must, of necessity, affect their orientation. The ultimate laboratory is the mind when stretched beyond its ordinary limits.

Is there any way of describing the internal mode of thinking? This is tantamount to transposing several totally incompatible modes of thinking into one another. Rarely do the contemplatives attempt to do this except evasively or idyllically, in poetry, music or art. It is most often their pupils who venture in this area, without having tasted of the contemplatives' experience.

On the other hand, the scientific mind is trained in devising models, taking for granted that the model could in no way describe the reality. The map is not the territory.

They have developed a language of symbols that convey cryptically encoded messages to each other's idiom-programmed minds, in the paradoxical intricacies of mathcmatics that thc layman trusts that they understand mutually; although to witness their basic disagreements, one sometimes wonders whether they always do.

However, if that remark may be countenanced without my dismissal, I certainly value the help provided to us by Dr. David Bohm's model of the implicate order. An eminent physicist, he has developed an extremely lucid model for thinkers, whatever their expertise; and it is most particularly helpful for meditators to make some sense of what happens to their minds as they turn within. In fact, he is applying the holistic paradigm that revolutionized science in our time, helping people to more generally grasp meaning.

The model that is most likely to help us understand what happens to our minds as we meditate, turning within, or in our sleep, is Bohm's implicate order as opposed to the explicate order.[1]

In the diurnal perspective illustrated by the explicate mode, our commonplace intelligence earmarks waves in the sea. It takes the mystic or the scientist to see that it is the whole sea that emerges as each wave. This puts our commonplace ideas about causality totally in jeopardy. According to Bohm, a wave is not the sequel to the wave preceding it, but each wave is projected out of the whole sea and interjected back into the sea; and it is the whole sea that is projected in the next wave. Another example: the sounds we hear from the radio, are just the way our radio extrapolates the immense variety of interspersed radio waves, which extend in space as an interwoven web (a wave interference pattern), in a manner such that our intelligence is able to make sense of it. A lens functions in a like manner, by focusing a large panorama to make it more accessible; however, this reduces much detail that conveys more than our intelligence could extrapolate. Our eyes function in rather the same way. So does our brain. Contrasting with this, in the state experienced by the meditator turning within, or in the dream state, thoughts are so fine-woven (in Greek, *implicate* means fine woven) that one cannot distinguish them; but one gains an overall sense of meaning implied behind the variety of thoughts. However, to explain that meaning, one would have to project one's mind back into the explicate state, whereby the meaning would be reduced—which is precisely what we have to come to terms with when we deem our verbal expressions inadequate.

A readily understandable illustration of this would be contrasting the way things look when swimming at the surface of a lake, where one perceives clearly distinct water lilies; or swimming under water, in which case one sees a network of roots emerging at the surface as distinct water lilies.

To cooperate, we need to be in touch more and more with others. Indeed, we are so programmed that our consciousness has the faculty of expanding and contracting, or concentrating, just as our sight can extend its field of vision to a vast panorama, or converge upon a letter in a book. By expanding, our consciousness exhibits its cosmic dimension; and by contracting, it focalizes whatever it has encompassed and converges it in a focal point.

The cells of our body could not satisfy themselves in their effort to get in touch with other, for example, distant cells, but just through information mediated through neighbors, and then through their neighbors, etc. They must be able to do this through a hotline, bypassing all intermediaries. If you try to figure this out schematically, you discover that this cannot be done in

---

1 See Bohm, *Wholeness and the Implicate Order.*

a two-dimensional diagram, nor by the same token, in a three-dimensional diagram; we would have to proceed in infinite regress, and consequently, infer that space is infinitely dimensional. Since our intelligence cannot ordinarily extrapolate between more than three dimensions, reality is reduced in our grasp to a model of what it is. Imagine—we take this to be reality! We would have to imagine a situation in which each point in the universe would be spatially contingent with each other point. David Bohm illustrates this in his theory of the implicate order by a sheet of paper that could, in theory, be crumpled to the point where each point is in contact with every other.[2]

It is helpful to discern this two-way motion of our minds which David Bohm calls the *holomovement*.[3]

To train yourself to do this intentionally in meditation, while poised at the threshold, keep on reminding yourself that what you see is only the tip of the iceberg. If you persist, you will get used to espying how things would look if viewed from within.

Under cover of sleep, the mind digests the diurnal impressions, breaking them down rather like our liver breaks down the amino acid chains. The unconscious then builds up new thought patterns, just like the way the RNA builds new amino acid chains in keeping with the template of the RNA. Then our psyche projects these nascent thought-forms, which are intended to enrich our conscious psyche if they are able to cross the barrier between unconscious and conscious.

Granted that should we venture to peer into the phantasmagoria of our dream world, or the state of reverie when poised between the diurnal state and the dream state, we will find that thoughts are blurred. But if we capture the nascent thought patterns as they try to break the barrier into real life, then we access an enormous and invaluable pool of resourcefulness, revealing a new meaning to our problems or personal development, or inspiring us in our creativity.

There is still a further dimension to turning within, as in the dream process. As we cast the light of our awareness and intelligence upon the nebulous regions of our unconscious psyche during sleep, at first we cannot make sense of the paradoxical thought-wave interference pattern opening to our view. Our natural tendency is to blank out, or at best, to find our understanding stunned and our will stymied. With determination and by repeated exercise, we can train our mind by stretching our intelligence beyond its normal frontiers. Our mind now switches to its implicate mode, which is precisely what we mean by intuition. Should we wish to remain poised on the threshold as we meditate, we learn to toggle between this mode and the explicate mode.

---

2 See Bohm, *Unfolding Meaning*, 12.
3 Ibid., 12–13.

There is a further factor to help us gauge ourselves in all our dimensions and understand our purposefulness and meaningfulness. We need to beam this complex information-field by our paramount sense of meaningfulness, in order to cohere it. But instead of envisioning that we have several elements that need to be synthesized, we need to look at it the other way round: it is the meaningfulness of the whole that discovers itself by organizing itself in the parts, and thus coheres the meaningfulness culled by the parts.

In matter, life unfolds, discovers, realizes the consciousness that has been, so to speak, buried in it for thousands of years.[4]

Hazrat Inayat Khan

This could be illustrated by a holograph. In every part of that construct of light that is the holograph, the light-wave patterns of every feature of the original object are interspersed with those of every other feature. Our eyes and brains could not make sense of this wave interference pattern. But when a laser beam, a beam of coherent light of the same frequency as the original beam, is thrust across the holograph, it extrapolates between the enormous variety of waves in a coherent way that makes sense to our perceptual faculty.[5]

Let us remember that understanding is the act that coheres thoughts, just like the laser beam. David Bohm calls this dimension of reality the *super-implicate order*.[6] We now understand the role of the coherent light of our intelligence as it projects into the nebulous region of the unconscious. It coheres the paradoxical wave interference pattern of our mind, in its implicate format, into an understandable sense of meaningfulness; but it fails to account for the many-splendored richness lying in wait in our psyche. This evidences the action of this further dimension of our mind, which is described in this manual as the transcendental dimension, the super-implicate order.

If you apply this model, the enfoldment is now seen on two levels: first, an enfolded order of the vacuum with ripples on it that unfold; and second, a super-information field of the whole universe—a super-implicate order which organizes the first level into various structures.

4 Inayat Khan, *The Sufi Message* series, *Sufi Teachings*, 317.
5 This is how Dr. David Bohm describes Dennis Gabor's invention: Light from a laser falls upon a half-silvered mirror. Part of the waves reflect and part of them come straight though and fall on the object The waves that strike the object are scattered off it, and they eventually reach the original beam that was reflected in the mirror and start to interfere with it, producing a pattern of two waves superimposed....It may be invisible, or it may look like a vague indescribable pattern. But if you send a similar laser light through it, it will produce waves that are similar to the waves that were coming off the object; and if you place your eye in the right spot, you will get an image of the object that will appear behind the holograph and be three-dimensional.
6 See Weber, *Dialogues with Scientists and Sages*, 330.

Indeed, as we practice Yoga Nidra,[7] we find that by zooming the beam of our consciousness upon nebulous thoughts and emotions, we actually extricate them from their concealed condition and capture them unfurling, as the focus of our consciousness shifts from the implicate order into the explicate.

The Sufis teach their students to actively cast the light of their intelligence (*nur-i ʿaql*), the light that sees instead of the light that is seen, upon problems, rather than to simply witness them passively by the act of consciousness. The Tibetans call this light *the clear light of the very subtle mind*. They distinguish this light from that of the subtle mind, the creative mind, and the gross mind that interprets data.

Interestingly, not only does the beam of our intelligence cohere interwoven thoughts, but it acts creatively in making these thoughts functional at the existential level.

[The glance of the seer] opens, unlocks, and unfolds things. It also possesses the power of seeking and finding....As it falls upon a thing, it makes that thing as it wants to make it. This is not actual creating; but it is awakening that particular quality which was perhaps asleep.[8]

Hazrat Inayat Khan

Practices

Skills are taught in various esoteric traditions to train ourselves to learn how to turn within and maintain ourselves at that threshold between the diurnal scene and the inverted state. At that juncture, the door is open between the perceptions of reality manifesting at the physical level, and the unbridled effusion of imagination, ranging from the fanciful to the congruent. You will find some rare milestones in the carefully guarded practice of Yoga Nidra.

In Buddhism the adept needs to free the self from the illusion of the appearance of the world, in order to foster the construction of the *illusory body*.[9]

Sufi practices teach the adepts to eschew the commonplace view in order to grasp things from within.

God placed within each thing—and the soul of man is one of the things—a manifest dimension (zahir) and a non-manifest dimension (batin). Through the manifest dimension, man perceives things which are called "entities"; and through the non-manifest dimension (batin), he perceives things which are called "knowledge."[10]

Muhyi ad-Din Ibn ʿArabi

---

7 See Mishra, *The Yoga Sutras*, 50.
8 Inayat Khan, *The Sufi Message* series, *The Gathas*, 54.
9 See Gyatso, *The Clear Light of Bliss*, 190. seq.
10 Chittick, *The Sufi Path of Knowledge*, 218.

1) In that twilight of the spotlight of consciousness, discern the difference between the incoming impressions hailing from your memory of perceptions or interpretations thereof, and the freewheeling of your creative imagination. At first they seem to blur, but, with concentration, you can distinguish them.

2) Offset your consciousness from its usual focus. You will find that the environment overlaps with the psyche, most times in an ambiguous fashion. This is because our psyche is holistically implicated in the whole existential realm at all levels, including the physical.[11]

When reminiscences of the physical or psychological environment loose their compulsive impact upon our awareness and get assimilated by the psyche, their outer appearance seems deluding. This accounts for the theories of maya, and is precisely what makes for the dream perspective. This will prove useful to you in practicing turning within. If you maintain this thought, you will find that the appearance of the outer scene looses its grip on your consciousness; but you will discern that which transpires behind that which appears. Superimposed upon these, elusive vestiges of sensorial perceptions or the mental constructs they trigger off, tend to linger in the twilight while your hidden thoughts get highlighted.

3) You will then discover several tiers in the unconscious. The layers targeted by psychotherapists, urging their patient to get in touch with their personal emotions, is still superficial compared with the deeper strata of the unconscious psyche, where one encounters the impersonal springheads of one's personal emotions. The Sufis call this deep-seated nostalgia driving the universe, *'ishq Allah.*

4) Avoid turning the spotlight of your consciousness towards the overt impressions. In this subliminal perspective try to zoom upon that which transpires behind that which appears, by calling upon a deeper layer of your psyche. This discovery of the mystics is borne out, in our day and age, by those physicists who are at the prow of the advance of scientific thinking. In fact, the idea of enfoldment is an ancient idea. It was known in the East a long time ago.

5) Recall that while in the diurnal state, you reacted to the challenges impacting you from outside. Now in the inverted state, the imaginings that emerge from inside prevail upon those lingering in your psyche in the after-glow of the reminiscences of the outside scene.

6) With accrued perspicacity, you will notice that impressions from the environment, processed under cover of your unconscious, act as catalysts orienting your imaginings.

11 See Bohm, *Unfolding Meaning,* 21.

These are conditions that favor creativity. If composers simply describe the environment without conveying how they feel perceiving it, they fail to convey that precious emergent psychic content of all masterpieces, which resonates with kindred feelings that we were unable to sense without the extra prompt.

7) Maintain yourself on the threshold and toggle between, on one hand, the diurnal state where you clearly distinguish between your consciousness as the spectator and the object of your awareness (either the physical world or your psyche or thoughts); and on the other hand, the dream state in which spontaneous imaginings flow from your unconscious, unawares.

8) You will notice that by spotlighting your random thoughts, you slip back into the diurnal subject/object format and loose the spontaneity of emergent thoughts.

9) Furthermore, to tune into a state of reverie, you will have to loosen your identity in the flow of thoughts
According to Yoga, in *nirvecara samadhi* consciousness espouses the forms of the emergent thoughts of the subtle creative mind,[12] manifesting the nature of the timeless essence of our being (*purusha*).

10) A further step to switching off from the diurnal perspective is taking for granted that not only the physical world is not what it appears to be, but your self-image is not your true identity.

11) Realize that the forms assumed by your imaginings are not your imaginings but only projections thereof—the tip of the iceberg. Consequently, let the forms emerge out of the flow without trying to spotlight them; but while this occurs, try to remain aware of their trace in your remote diurnal memory.

12) When you have become used to toggling between the two perspectives, you reach a point where you are capable of countenancing a double-exposure: your creative ideas gel so that they may be communicated to others while you stay in contact with their source; and what is more, they enrich your conscious psyche with their resources.

Perception may separate him from many things which he would perceive if not for this obstruction.[13]

Muhyi ad-Din Ibn 'Arabi

13) Consider the forms of the physical world to be of the same nature as the reality inside appears when projected to the surface. This could best be

12 See Eliade, *Yoga, Immortality and Freedom.* 76–78.
13 Chittick, *The Sufi Path of Knowledge*, 218.

illustrated by imagining that a plant is just the way that its DNA manifests at the surface, but that this manifestation is secondary and derivative, its reality being the DNA.[14]

14) At this point, to keep maintaining yourself at the threshold, you have to keep reminding yourself of this thought, which is taken for granted: *mind and matter are not separate realities.*

15) To achieve this, train yourself by repeated autosuggestion prior to going to sleep; it needs to be drummed into one's mind until it is taken for granted.

For the Tibetans, as one falls to sleep, one shifts from the activity of the gross faculty of the mind, which is based upon the input from outside, to the activity of the subtle faculty of the mind, which grasps meaning without resting upon perception. Simultaneously, one shifts from identifying with the gross mind riding the gross wind (energy), to the subtle mind riding the subtle wind (actually one's subtle bodies); and even further, from the subtle mind riding the subtle wind, to the very subtle mind riding the very subtle wind.

16) As you begin to become more familiar with the lie of the land of the dream world, you will distinguish in your state of reverie, in addition to the factors and levels we have examined so far: (i) the simple regurgitation, digestion and storage of inputted impressions; (ii) the aspirations, nostalgia, and repressed emotions trying to make themselves known by crossing the barrier (or censorship) between the covert and overt zones of the psyche; (iii) out-of-body travel; (iv) uncanny impressions of the heavenly spheres, and even communication with celestial beings or people's minds (one distinguishes different levels of bodiness and mindness that spark prenatal memories, which one ascribes to celestial spheres); (v) the spontaneous creative thoughts that appear as inspirational.

17) To switch over from the diurnal state into the inverted state, disidentify with your body, now considered perfunctorily as a shroud, and feel yourself as an effigy of subtle unstable fabric—like gossamer.

18) To balance yourself on the threshold, maintain a remote memory of the profile of your body, while superimposing upon it the countenance of your dream body. You will notice a correspondence between these—in a kind of double-exposure. It becomes clear that one's subtle bodies arise out of the configurations of one's very thinking, and that a grasp of meaningfulness or a strong emotion, in turn, affects the formative processes active within physical matter.

---

14 See Bohm, *Unfolding Meaning*, 15.

The Sufis teach their pupils to mold the features of their subtle bodies in the shapes that are expressive of their emotional attunements or paramount thoughts. The Tibetans do this by imagining that their subtle bodies are those of the deity of their choice.[15]

The Sufis proceed likewise, but by highlighting a particular divine quality (*sifa*), reinforced by repeating the name (*ism-i ilahi*) corresponding to that quality, and imagining the form that this quality would assume as it manifests through them in their personality, and consequently, marks their very countenance The Sufis distinguish between various subtle bodies and the corresponding spheres highlighted as one shifts from one stage to the next. As you become more conversant with these nebulous regions, you will learn to distinguish between a state in which you feel like an ethereal, elusive body called *jism-i latif* (the body of resurrection or the illusory body of the Tibetans); from a state in which your body seems to be hewn in the fabric of light, corresponding to the celestial sphere, *malakut* (the emanation body of the Tibetans); and from a state in which you have lost any sense of form, *jabarut*, which Buddha calls being of pure splendor (corresponding to the enjoyment body of the Tibetans); to the infinitely transcendental levels, in Sufism called *lahut* and *hahut*, which correspond to the Truth body of the Tibetans.[16]

19) To shift your body identity from one level to another, envision each body as the underpinning of energy serving your mind as your mental functions shift from one level to another. Remind yourself of weaving the Ariadnian thread of consciousness over the threshold, straddling several levels. The rationale behind this consists in grasping how, somehow, the different bodies intersperse rather than fan out in different locations in space, as in astral projection.

20) To achieve this, compare the feel of the kind of energy you sense at the periphery of your being, as compared with the kind of energy you feel as you close into the center. Think of your energy field as a vortex, and realize that the center thereof, which corresponds with your solar plexus, is a vacuum.

21) Now you will notice that, while on one hand the grosser energy tends to get scattered at the periphery in a centrifugal action, on the other hand, some measure of energy gets sublimated (the alchemists say distilled) as it gets sucked into the center.

22) In addition, while you turn outside, it is the grosser functions of your mind that are active, whereas as you turn within, it is the subtle mind, the creative mind, that takes over. To maintain yourself at the threshold, rather

---

15 See Gyatso, *The Clear Light of Bliss*, 104.
16 See Part Five, Chapter One, "Exploring the Spheres."

than dismissing the memory of your gross mind, unmask the hoax of your commonplace thinking, thereby correcting your assessment of situations.

23) If you identify with your aura, you will find that the further you turn within, the subtler is the nature of the light, until you reach what Hazrat Inayat Khan calls the *all-pervading light*. This term avers itself to be eminently appropriate, since in the implicate order, everything intersperses with the light wave interference pattern of the stars. That is the reason why, in the inverted state, one cannot spot a location from which light radiates.

24) Venturing to anticipate the next step, the transcendent state, as you move up from one sphere to the other in Yoga Nidra, your sense of being the spectator will become increasingly impersonal; and if a believer, you will attribute it to God as the Supreme Spectator. Here lies the key to shift, as you meditate, from this introverted state into the transcendental dimension.

Let us bear in mind that the further our minds stretch, the further the horizon of the unknown recedes. Besides, one is only allowed to know that which one needs to know. So the divine secret that our will tries to grasp, forever remains inviolate.

O secret so subtle that it escapes the perception of all living beings.[17]

Mansur al-Hallaj

---

17 Massignon, *Akhbār al-Hallāj*, 111.

Chapter Three
Transcendence

Of course, most thoughtful people cherish the aspiration to understand the meaning of their lives, the issue in the challenge of their circumstances, why things happen the way they do—ultimately, meaningfulness in general.

It would be a truism to say that our inability to attain this objective is due not only to the limit in our mind's ability to extrapolate data input, but also to encompass our mind's own inherent, yet virtual, sense of meaningfulness. In short, we are mostly utilizing a meager range of our mind's capacity—the middle range. There is also no doubt that our mental functions are monitored by the setting of our consciousness, and can be extended by modulating our consciousness. This is why we started by modulating consciousness on the fluctuation of our breath. Then we explored the way our mental functions could be modulated by fluctuating energy. Now we are exploring how to inflect mental functions by fluctuating consciousness.

By so doing, we discover unchartered reaches of the mind and learn to distinguish different modes of thinking; however, knowledge is only totally fulfilling when it is transforming. By altering consciousness, we alter our state of being. This is the reason why the Yogic samadhi[1] is considered to be a state[2]: the kind of cognizance gained results from the state.

This state makes possible the self-revelation of the Self Purusha, by virtue of an act that does not constitute an experience.[3]

Mircea Eliade

What do we mean by *modes of thinking* or *kinds of cognizance*? Normally, our minds digest experience by forming mental categories. These mental clichés are then sorted out and pigeonholed. The mind performs this task

1 The ultimate objective of Jnana Yoga is a state of consciousness in which one transcends the existential experience.
2 See Eliade, *Yoga, Immortality and Freedom*, 79.
3 Ibid., 79.

precisely on the model adopted by the program manager of a computer, or better still, on the model of the basic mental functions elicited by artificial intelligence.[4] This sorting out is easier when categories can be clearly differentiated, as exemplified by the *or* of artificial intelligence. It is more difficult for our commonplace mind to grasp the *and*; for example, that it is never the same water that runs under a bridge, and yet we call it a river. Our notion *river* is really a continuity in change. Another example that may prove even more difficult for the mind to grasp, would be that light can be both wavelike and particlelike. St. Augustine called this *conjunctio oppositorum*, and in modern science it is called *complementarity*. More difficult still for the mind, is to grasp conjunctions in phenomena; for example, a concatenation where more than one cause clicks.[5]

Sufis such as Sahl Tustari highlight, amongst the many-tiered levels of our thinking, three levels: (i) *'aql*, intellectual knowledge; (ii) *'ilm*, acquired knowledge; and (iii) *ma'rifat*, revealed knowledge.

Junaid Baghdadi distinguishes between: (i) the knowledge acquired by interpreting the signs that are vouchsafed by God in our experience of the world; (ii) a further knowledge acquired by espying the way things and events look from the divine vantage point; (iii) the knowledge that God reveals to the mystic of God's own Self.[6]

A parallel with the Yogic methods helps the student to elucidate the views expressed by the Sufi mystics in their ecstatic musings. The Yogic methods present an incisive exploration of mental functions, thereby disclosing the extent to which we let ourselves be fooled by our mind games.

According to Patanjali,[7] the Yogic method aims at freeing the mind of the meditator from the hoaxes of illusion and imagination, which becloud our direct grasp of reality.[8] Let us bear in mind that knowledge is based upon the interface and intermeshing between our innate sense of meaningfulness and experience.

Wisdom is born out of the meeting of the knowledge of the heavens and the knowledge of the earth.[9]

Hazrat Inayat Khan

---

4 Incidentally, this bears a striking similarity with the Sephirotic Tree of Kabbalah.
5 An example of this is found in the algorithm. See Penrose, *The Emperor's Mind*.
6 See Abdel-Kader, *The Life, Personality and Writings of al-Junayd*, 96.
7 Patanjali, *Yoga Philosophy of Patañjali*, 89, 94. Patanjali describes not only the methodology, but also the experiential states in the practices of Yogic meditation.
8 Things are not the way they look. The gross mind assesses phenomena from its vantage point and within its middle range, and therefore, gets caught in illusion. The subtle mind, which translates the sense of meaningfulness of the very subtle mind by projecting it in the act of imagination, gets itself equally caught in the phantasmagoria of these imaginings.
9 Inayat Khan, *Esoteric Papers*.

These do not come together easily since, while our inherent sense of meaningfulness is all-encompassing and of an archetypal nature, our commonplace thinking is limited by the fact that the consciousness of the universe is focalized in the human being, and therefore, limited in its compass of understanding.

There is no doubt that our experience catalyses our innate sense of meaningfulness, but we get overwhelmed and befuddled by the plethora of impressions to which we are exposed in our lives. Basically, our minds are programmed after the model of the functioning of our sight.

Like those of an eagle, our eyes are programmed to zoom upon a moving object. But in this mode, the object acts simply as a signal drawing our attention. Consequently, our perception of it remains perfunctory. To know the object, which may be considered as a sample of the basic reality that is the universe, we need to still our eyes. This will result in our minds stilling themselves.

Therefore, the methods applied in Yoga instruct the meditator to start practicing by reducing the field of experience of the physical world, by narrowing down the beam of consciousness. This is called *one-pointedness*, *ekagrata*.

We encounter the same principle in the Qur'an where Prophet Muhammad's journey in the celestial spheres is described: *his sight did not rove.*[10]

Since our attention to thoughts is spurred by emotional springheads (some being unconscious), during meditation, Yoga recommends indifference towards sensory impressions; the recollection of painful events or even attachment to joyful experience, acts compulsively upon the orientation of the flow of our thoughts, robbing our will of its control of our thoughts. This is called *pratyahara*.[11]

In this context, it may be well to bear in mind the Sufi view. According to Ibn 'Arabi, by cloistering oneself from the world, one may miss out on the divine revelation which is being offered by life itself.[12]

By freeing the mind from impromptu and wistful fluctuations, and by narrowing its field and pacifying its emotional turbulence and sensory yearnings, we may now practice concentration—in Sufism, *muraqaba*; in Yoga, *dharana*.

Practice

Select an object from the mantelpiece (for example, a vase, or a flower), or pinpoint a star at night. Keep your glance riveted to that object, grasped as a

10 Qur'an LIII:17.
11 According to Patanjali, the clue to destroying the gross mind is renunciation. However, this is bypassing attachment by severing contacts with the world, instead of dealing with the attachment.
12 See Ibn 'Arabi, *Études Traditionelles*, Valsan trans. March/April 1969, No. 412.

unit, without scanning its different features or parts. Maintain your concentration for at least twenty minutes without wavering.[13]

When you now extend your field of vision to the environment, you will notice a striking contrast between the object and the environment. The object will appear clearly standing out in contrast with the environment, as floating in the air.

Principle

When we look at an object, our sensorial functions are not the only ones involved; a whole network of mental activities interpose themselves between the purely sensory experience and our grasp of the object. These are the veils which the Sufi Abu Yazid Bastami yearned to tear asunder. Suhrawardi distinguishes between two modes of cognizance: that knowledge which does not change, because its object is indestructible; and that knowledge that changes, since its object is transient.[14]

Mental clichés are defined by the names that we tag onto things as labels, *nama*, idioms and syntax, which Yoga looks into and unmasks.

Moreover, for Yoga, the physical world (or occurrences) are not the only object of our musings; thoughts themselves are the objects of our thinking. This is why both sensory impressions and the fluctuations of the psyche, *chitta*, are batched together as *prakriti*, matter.[15]

Sufi Method

For the Sufis, God is the ultimate subject behind our assumption of being the subject experiencing, and God is the ultimate object behind what we assume to be the object of our experiencing.

In our perceptions of the world, we only grasp the traces (ayat) of the reality that is God, which vouchsafe to us some clue as to the nature of that reality that is God. And in our representation of our own self-image, we are only picking up the traces of the divine nature invested in the very idiosyncrasies of our personality, which give us a clue as to the nature of God. Both serve as objects through which we seek to experience reality, and which we confuse with reality. The Yogis point out that we erroneously take just these clues to be that reality, and consequently, guard us against the illusion, maya, which entraps our minds.

---

13 This parallels the concentration taught in the Muslim prayers, on the model of the one-pointedness of Prophet Mohammad's glance during his vision of the *mi'raj*.

14 See Corbin, *Spiritual Body and Celestial Earth*, 78.

15 This is contrary to Cartesian philosophy, which discriminates between matter that is extended in space, and thought that is not. Yoga's antinomy is based upon time: both matter and thought are transient; it is only spirit, *purusha*, that is imperishable and eternal.

Conversely, we think that we are the subject experiencing the world. Our *I* is a derivation from the paramount divine *I*. Something is gained by the divine Spectator experiencing through our eyes. However, since it is the divine Spectator adumbrating our consciousness who is experiencing, the Spectator cannot be the object of our experience.

In addition to availing ourselves of the clues as to the nature of God's Being, since our consciousness is of the same nature as the divine consciousness, we may be vouchsafed a fleeting glimpse of the way things look from the divine point of view. Indeed, we can shift the focus of our consciousness to the antipodal vantage point.

Chapter Four
A Comparison Between the Advanced Stages of Dhikr and Samadhi

In the following pages, we shall attempt a comparison between the stages of the advanced practice of the dhikr by the Sufis, and the stages of the practice of samadhi, as described by Patanjali in his *Yoga Sutras*.

1. Annihilation of the Subject in the Object
Fana bi'l-madhkur 'an al-dhakir

Since we ordinarily think of God as the object that we wish to know, and since we project the psychological constructs of our psyche upon our experience of the reality that transpires through that which appears, the first step in the dhikr consists in eliminating our personal interpretations of reality so as to hand ourselves over, unreservedly, to that reality objectively. Instantly, our representations of objects and events whereby we interpret the physical world evaporate, allowing its bounty to transpire in the measure to which the distortion, caused by the mediation of our mind games, recedes. For the Sufis, there is a further stage whereby you see all things from the divine point of view.

As we have seen, Sufis describe the ultimate state of human realization as that where God reveals the Divine Self, regardless of any clues as to God's nature, and regardless of God's experience of the Divine Self as projected in the cosmos.

We find the very same viewpoint in Yoga. Since there is a sense of meaningfulness inherent within the depth of our transient nature, the Self, *purusha*, can never be the object of the grasp of our minds, *bodhi*; but it reveals itself when we have removed the obstacles in our very thinking.

This will, therefore, be our objective. To achieve it we will need to strip systematically, one by one, the sheaths beclouding the ultimate realization

170

which we are pursuing.[1] To see things from the divine point of view, we need to eschew taking the clues to be reality.

Yoga Method

The Yogis concentrate particularly on wiping away those clues mediating as a bridge between the two poles of the subject-object dichotomy in our experiencing, so as to touch upon the deeper reality manifesting as the subject and the object. Our interpretation of those signals is fraught with self-deception, wishful thinking, one-sidedness, mental associations recalling past experiences, and sometimes bigotry. Therefore, to outwit these, we need to x-ray our mental functions and unmask our mental constructs.

Thought grasps the form of the object directly without the help of categories or imagination....There is a real coincidence between knowledge of the object and the object of knowledge. [2]

Mircea Eliade

Freed from the separate notions of meditation, object of meditation and meditating, subject the transformation of the object [the world] into knowledge-possession.[3]

Vijnana Bhikshu

Here lies the realm of psychology proper. Patanjali and Vyasa certainly throw some light on this, but there is no denying that their methods bypass this mental bridge rather than dealing with it.

Contemplation
Mushahada in Sufism, Dhyana in Yoga

Indeed, while in the act of concentration, the presence of the subject, the object, and the act of cognizance are clearly felt; at the next stage, contemplation (*dhyana*), the meditating subject grasps the object directly, dismissing all mental activities associated with it. To illustrate this, let us bear in mind that we generally grapple with our concepts of our problems rather than our problems.

The Sufis maintain that the real object lies beyond the ayat, the signals, and this object is Reality, God. The Yogis in dhyana are clearly foraging below the nebulous smoke screen emitted by the mind, in an effort to touch upon this reality, *swarupa* (sui generis).

---

1 See Pribham or Weber. We never experience the reality of the physical world, but our brains extrapolate between signals, which our minds interpret.
2 Eliade, *Yoga, Immortality, and Freedom*, 77.
3 Bhikshu, *Yogasara-Sangraha*.

Having achieved this, the contemplative is instructed to take the steps in turn, leading to the ultimate realization or awakening, However, we need to be clear that awakening is dependent upon personal transformation. We enrich ourselves by ingesting the universe at all levels, but that nutrient is usually distorted by our deceptive interpretation of it. In the example of digestion, we need to break down the ingredients and rebuild them in keeping with our biological code. A faulty replication can prove fatal. Our understanding would aptly illustrate the role of the enzymes. It is vital to clarify our thinking.

In our ordinary state, we assume that we are the subject experiencing an object or grasping a thought. We do not normally notice that between our consciousness (the subject) and the physical world or our psyche (the object), we interpose a whole network of mental constructs and emotional attunements, which adorn the object in its nakedness with our subjectivity. Actually, the object is just the way the ultimate reality becomes known to us through a form and a substance.

By stripping both the physical scene (the object) and our notion of ourselves (the subject) of our mental projections, both subject and object recognize their mutual identity in their basic reality, as they resonate in their interfacing. Hence the equation: *Tat twam asi*, and its equivalent, *ana'l-Haqq*.[4]

In the method elaborated by Patanjali's *Yoga Sutras*, we start by concentrating on a physical object, then strip the object of these subjective projections. Then we emancipate our sense of identity from our self-image by dissolving the way it projects in a form. Finally, we discover our true identity as impersonal, which is what we mean by God.

In the advanced dhikr, we follow identical steps: (i) as we rotate our trunk around our solar plexus, saying or thinking *la ilaha*, we dissolve the appearance of the physical world; (ii) as our head turns toward the solar plexus saying or thinking *illa*, we dissolve our notion of ourselves; (iii) as we say or think *'Llah*, we realize that the basic reality behind both the object and subject is God; (iv) and as we hold our breath, saying or thinking *hu*, we discover our identity with that reality.

In the practice of the dhikr, the Sufis outline seven steps which can be paralleled with those described by Patanjali and Vyasa in their Yoga sutras.[5]

From the Sufi point of view, that which accrues to God's awareness through the mediation of our consciousness, can be distorted by our limited appraisal of reality. If we clear our notion of ourselves as the spectator, which stands <u>in the way, we</u> participate in an incomparably more authentic perspective

4 Thou art That (*Tat twam asi*), and I am the Truth/God (*ana'l-Haqq*).
5 See Part Three, Chapter Three, "The Sufi Dhikr."

of the universe in which God discovers the Divine Self. Immediately, our mental constructs, that is, our perfunctory representations of objects and events whereby we interpreted the physical world, evaporate, allowing its bounty and splendor to transpire increasingly. The universe, now stripped of our sensorial, space-time representation of it, emerges in all its reality. Consequently, we discover a splendor far beyond anything that we may have ever imagined or assumed was the physical universe.

For the wise, nothing appears as a "discrete entity," but everything is seen as the face of reality.[6]

Muhyi ad-Din Ibn 'Arabi

In the course of whirling the head, the concentration of the dhakir is drawn further and further away from the solar plexus representing the self, and reaches out into glorious layers of that reality beyond that which appeared at first, as in the form of the objects of the dhakir's perception.

This vision is not just informative, but transforming; the mind of the adept restructures itself to encompass this bounty and splendor. However, since that reality remains concealed behind that which manifests it, we will have to take further steps.

Yoga: Savitarka Samadhi

To outwit our self-deceptions, we need to unmask the conditioning of our minds that proceeds by the association process. Here lies the realm of psychology proper.

Patanjali and Vyasa certainly throw some light on these mental constructs, which we interpose between reality and our experience of reality. In fact, the *Yoga Sutras of Patanjali* constitute an incisive inquiry into the misconstruction of the reality of a situation, which is distorted by the projections of the psyche.[7]

A correspondence could be drawn between the first stage in the dhikr and *savitarka samadhi*.

A good example of unmasking an optical illusion is to be found in Shankaracharya's Advaita Vedanta. One sees in daylight that what appeared at night as a snake was actually a rope. Having destroyed the misassessed mental constructs projected upon experience by the subject, the mind can now configure itself purely on the model of the object beyond its appearance.

This is called in Yoga *pratyaksa*, direct perception.

---

6 Ibn 'Arabi, *Études Traditionelles, Valsan, trans.* 6. 1952, 186.
7 See Mishra, *Yoga Sutras*, 165.

2. Annihilation of the Object in the Subject
Fana bi'l-dhakir 'an al-madhkur

According to the Sufis, the bounty and splendor that opens up to our view accrues to the divine vision. Thus we participate in the vision whereby God discovers God's own embodiment as the existentiated universe. By extending the divine consciousness, our consciousness is enriched by a spectacle bespeaking a bounty of reality surpassing anything we realized so far. The subject absorbs the object. Thus it is held that God becomes increasingly present in the dhakir. But this requires the dhakir to eschew thinking of God as *other*.

> *Know that thou art not thou; thou art He, without thou, not He entering into thee, nor thou entering into Him, nor He proceeding forth form thee, nor thou proceeding forth from Him....Thou art He without one of these limitations.*[8]
> Muhyi ad-Din Ibn 'Arabi

Bowing one's head towards the heart after whirling the head and facing the solar plexus, reinforces the thought of incorporating God as the object.

A correspondence could be posited here with the second stage in samadhi: *nirvitarka samadhi*

Yoga: Nirvitarka Samadhi

> Citta *becomes* nirvitarka *after the memory ceases to function, that is, after verbal or logical associations cease; at the moment when the object is empty of name and meaning; when thought reflects itself directly, by adopting the form of the object and shining solely with the object in itself.*[9]
> Vyasa

The mode of thinking corresponding to this level of identity is what the Sufis call *ajsam* and in Yoga is called *nirvitarka samadhi*.

(i) Our thinking is likewise fragmented in discrete thoughts: categories of reason, syllogistic logic. We are using static words, nouns like *thoughts*, instead of dynamic words, verbs like *thinking; feelings* instead of *feeling;* an *act* instead of *action;* an *event* or *occurrence* instead of *processing*, etc.

(ii) Our thinking is biased by our personal vantage point as the spectator.

(iii) We can simply discern the consequence of our past actions and those of others, upon ourselves and our circumstances at present: causality.

(iv) Our motivation is selfish: pursuit of material gain, possessions, dominating others, recognition, appreciation, being loved rather than loving.

---

8 Ibn 'Arabi, *Whoso Knoweth Himself*, T.H. Weir, trans.
9 Eliade, *Yoga, Immortality and Freedom*, 81–82.

(v) We fail to see from another person's point of view, or sense or validate another's grievances.

(vi) We entertain resentment for people's abuses wreaked upon us, which generates a wish for revenge, intolerance, unkindness, violence and cruelty, with its trail of suffering, misery, crime, the terror of murder, the sheer insanity of the mass destruction of life, and the wanton vandalism in war by pillaging and ransacking the fruits of the achievements of great civilizations.

Having cleared the distortion created by the misassessment of the mind's interpretation of what is experienced, we can now incorporate our corrected grasp of reality into our psyche.

It is thought that becomes the given object.[10]

Patanjali

3) Annihilation of the Act in the Object

At this stage, the dhakir is so absorbed in God's revelation of divine splendor and bounty in the marvel of the universe, and God's consciousness illuminating the dhakir's consciousness, that there is no awareness of repeating the dhikr. Should we achieve this, contemplating through God's eyes the reality that transpires through the universe as the object experienced, we discover the divine act fashioning all objects, sparking all phenomena. At an advanced stage, one sees in everything the mark of God.

When meanings are embodied and become manifest in shapes, and measures they assume forms, since witnessing takes place through sight....Know that there is no form in the lower world without a likeness in the higher world. The forms in the higher world preserve the existence of their likenesses in the lower worlds.[11]

Muhyi ad-Din Ibn 'Arabi

Instead of being entrapped in our thinking in the present, representing objects as static, a cross section of the universe, we envision reality dynamically. We are touching upon the eternal dimension of that which appears as evanescent. The consequence is that instead of contemplating the fruit in its completion (that is, as the physical universe), we discover the process leading to that finished work.

The one who tunes himself not only to the external, but to the inner being and to the essence of all things, gets an insight into the essence of the whole being

---

10 Lindquist, *Die Methoden des Yoga*, 118, 144.
11 Chittick, *The Sufi Path of Knowledge*, 354, 406.

and, therefore, he can to the same extent find and enjoy even in the seed, the fragrance and beauty which delight him in the rose.[12]

Hazrat Inayat Khan

This could be illustrated by a musicologist discovering the pattern of themes and rhythms and modulations in the scales in an étude of Chopin, or an architect reading the blueprints of a building. This is tantamount to grasping the divine architectonics manifesting as the universe.

Consequently, a transfigured world subjacent to the apparent world, reveals itself to us. Sufis refer to this level of reality as the celestial earth, *Hurqalya*. It gives the impression of being of the nature of gossamer, diaphanous and fine-woven. It is as though one were capturing reality on its way to its emergence, confinement, defilement and perishable condition within the existential state.

Here again, correspondence could be seen with the third step in the samadhi practices: *savicara samadhi*.

Yoga: Savicara Samadhi

Thought no longer stops at the exterior aspect of material objects.[13]

Mircea Eliade

As we x-ray what we commonly imagine to be matter more profoundly, we see that the deeper reality (subtle matter, *tanmatra),* masked by the appearance, is its code *(rupa),* a template.[14]

One unearths deep strata of the unconscious (what we imply behind what we explain) that unfold in our thoughts. The code governing the physical order evidences cosmic programming, cosmic thinking. Even the subtle under-pinnings of the object are grasped beyond their unfoldment in time. Looked upon in the process of becoming, a river can be envisioned as a continuity in change; but a river could be considered as a reality, regardless of the evanescence of its substance. Likewise, our body is for us a reality, regardless of the fact that it is only momentarily the same cells that form it.[15]

4) Annihilation of the Object in the Act
Fana bi'l-dhikr 'an al-Madhkur'

Since the dhakir has lost the sense of being the actor in the act of the dhikr, it is God who reveals the divine Self as the one repeating the dhikr through the dhakir. These were al-Hallaj's dying words:

---

12 Inayat Khan, *The Music of Life,* 75.

13 Eliade, *Yoga, Immortality and Freedom,* 82.

14 In our experience, the electromagnetic field (of the body or of the environmental objects) constitutes a deeper level of reality, an underpinning. If we probe deeper, we reach a still deeper level which we have referred to as the *scalar field.* See Mishra, *Yoga Sutras,* 177.

15 See Bohm, *Unfolding Meaning,* 12.

What is important for the worshipper of God is that He should reduce Him to Unity.[16]

This saying is interpreted as meaning: *It is good enough if it is God who repeats the dhikr.*

This then corresponds, in the repetition of the dhikr, to the stage where the dhakir repeats the word *hu*, or holds the breath while thinking of the divine creative act in the dhakir's own self.

Once more, we may see here a correspondence with the fourth step in the samadhi practices: *nirvecara samadhi*.

Yoga: Nirvecara Samadhi

In nirvecara, our minds take on the nature of the eternal substrate that unfolds, not only in matter, but also in our psyche, or the psyche of others, or the psyche of universe in general.[17]

Thought then becomes one with these infinitesimal nucleuses of energy which constitute the true foundation of the physical universe. It is a real descent into the very essence of the physical world; not only into qualified and individual phenomena.[18]

Mircea Eliade

5) Annihilation of the Act in the Subject
Fana bi'l-dhakir 'an al-dhikr

At this stage, rather than highlighting the thought that God is the One repeating the dhikr through divine mediation, the dhakir begins to grasp the divine intelligence coming through the dhakir's own intelligence; the dhakir begins to grasp the knowledge that God acquires by discovering the Divine Self in God's very manifestation and actuation of God as us.

Man realizes his perfection in God, and God realizes His perfection in man.[19]

In matter, life unfolds, discovers, realizes the consciousness which has been so to speak buried in it of thousands of years.[20]

Hazrat Inayat Khan

By losing our notion of being the spectator, the mental constructs that we project upon the divine Spectator evaporate gradually, and are replaced by a grasp of the divine thinking behind the universe at the archetypal level.

16 Massignon, *Akhbār al-Hallāj*, 71.
17 See Mishra, *Yoga Sutras*, 215, 218.
18 Eliade, *Yoga, Immortality and Freedom*, 83.
19 Inayat Khan, *The Sufi Message* series, *The Way of Illumination*, 29.
20 Inayat Khan, *The Sufi Message* series, *Sufi Teachings*, 317.

At this point, we reach the initiating seminal wellspring of being, which the Sufis ascribe to the sphere of *lahut*, beyond the existential realm—a potential world lying in wait, where the seeds of all possible things await their chance of manifesting to view.

We are bordering on a virtual world, the realm of all possibilities.

In respect of Himself, He is independent of the worlds, (Qur'an III, 96) but in respect of the most beautiful names which demand the cosmos because of its possibility, in order for their effects to become manifest within it, He demands the existence of the cosmos.[21]

Muhyi ad-Din Ibn 'Arabi

At this stage in the repetition of the dhikr, according to Shihab ad-Din Suhrawardi, the *hu* of the shahada becomes *ana* (I am).

In this condition, the Sufis identifying with the subject, God, share in the divine bliss, *'ishq Allah ma'bud Allah*, which they see as the paramount springhead behind the whole of the process of existence: life as the fulfillment of the divine love for splendor.

Yoga: Anandanugata and Asmitanugata Samadhi

Anandanugata: *When abandoning all perception, even that of "subtle realities," one experiences the happiness of the eternal luminosity and consciousness of Self that belong to* sattva.

Asmitanugata: *The intellect,* buddhi, *completely isolated from the external world reflects only the Self.*[22]

Mircea Eliade

Far from countenancing what is commonly experienced as the physical world, or even the subtle infrastructure, *tanmatra*, and subjacent to what our senses grasp, our mind reaches an archetypal level of thinking. It is a though one were touching upon the principles, the software behind everything appearing at the surface as its exemplification; for example, roundness instead of round objects, humanity instead of a person, compassion instead of a compassionate person or acts of compassion, and so on. At this stage in samadhi, the only content of consciousness encompassed by the meditator is of an archetypal dimension. It is as though one were backstage of life.

Clues to the archetypal level of the thinking of the universe are to be found in us in the form of both *anandanugata samadhi* and *asmitanugata samadhi*, transcendental knowledge and ecstasy, both faces of the same coin: the ecstasy of knowing and the knowledge accruing from an aesthetic sense of el-

---

21 Chittick, *The Sufi Path of Knowledge*, 41.
22 Eliade, *Yoga, Immortality and Freedom*, 84.

egance. At this juncture, not only does the Yogi experience an oceanic bliss, but sees the whole universe as an expression of the divine bliss. *Ananda* and *asmita* are often brought in tandem, because asmita represents the psychic inner lining of existence, our psyche; there is no more concern about the physical world as outside, but rather as inside.

At this stage, the physical order is seen in Yoga as replicating the domain of the psyche. One unearths deeper strata of the unconscious that unfold our thoughts: that which we imply behind what we explain.

6) Annihilation of the Knower in the Act of Knowing
Fana bi'l-dhikr 'an al-dhakir

We are no longer discussing the mode of knowledge acquired by God by discovering those aspects of the Divine Self that have arisen out of the act of manifestation (therefore resting upon the feedback of experience), but of the knowledge that God has of the principles of Divine Being in all eternity, which knowledge is inherent in our intuition. In philosophic terms, it is called *proto-critic*: the premises upon which our judgments about existential phenomena must necessarily be based.

If we think of God as the Spectator, we are still positing the dichotomy between the knower and the known; we are still thinking in terms of duality.

The principles upon which this thinking is based is totally different from speculative, syllogistic thinking, in that it is free from the subject-object dichotomy. Having annihilated the notion of God, both as the object cognized and as the knowing subject, the subject-object dichotomy vanishes; and all that remains is the notion of the divine act of *knowing by becoming* and *becoming by knowing*.

Somehow the thought of God as the Spectator involves, perhaps unwittingly, our own notion of ourselves as the medium of the divine subject, even if we assume that we have eluded it.

We have already, in the first step, attempted to dissolve the focus of consciousness to peer deeper into the nature of reality manifesting as the universe, and to allow the divine Spectator to come through unimpaired (or less impaired). Later, we encountered the divine act behind the divine subject, which gave us insight into a deeper layer of reality manifested as the universe. At the present stage, we access the divine thinking itself.[23]

We realize that it is God who is revealing God's own Divine Self in our thinking. How much greater the Knower than the knowledge!

However, al-Hallaj warns against the danger of isolating oneself from the existential realm:

---

23 See Gardet, *Expériences mystiques en terre non-chrétiennes*, 136.

The first step leading towards tawhid, *unification, is to give* tafrid, *isolation. Then God elects you to be isolated in his Unity.*[24]

Mansur al-Hallaj

It is only when we have given up any personal intervention by a volitional act that this level of knowledge is revealed:

Yoga: Nirbija Samadhi

We have reached the stage of *nirbija samadhi*: without seed, beyond the archetypes.

*Nothing remains but the unconscious impressions (*samskara*), and at a certain moment even these imperceptible* samskaras *are consumed, whereupon true stasis "without seed" (*nirbija samadhi*) ensues.*[25]

Mircea Eliade

7) The Annihilation of the Act of Annihilation
Fana al-fana

Even the act of knowing is surpassed. This stage is marked by the shift from experience to being.

A state is reached in which one has the impression that one sees the world inside-out. It is as though a veil had been lifted from one's eyes.

When the unreality of life pushes against my heart, its door opens to the reality.[26]

Hazrat Inayat Khan

Yoga: Asamprajnata Samadhi

*Fixed in samadhi, consciousness (*citta*) can now have direct revelation of the Self (*purusha*).*[27]

Mircea Eliade

Bereft of its content, consciousness, *bodhi* now gets absorbed into its ground, *purusha* (commonly translated by the word *Self*).

All consciousness vanishes, the entire series of mental functions are blocked... During this stasis, there is no other trace of the mind Chitta save the impressions Samskara left behind by its past functioning; if these impressions were not present there would be no possibility of returning to consciousness.[28]

Vijnana Bhikshu

---

24 Ibid.
25 Eliade, *Yoga, Immortality and Freedom*, 91.
26 Inayat Khan, *The Complete Sayings of Hazrat Inayat Khan*, 163.
27 Eliade, *Yoga, Immortality and Freedom*, 83.
28 Bhikshu, *Yogasara-Sangraha*, 14.

The paradox here is that with all the detachment and isolation that paved the way, the practictioner, now assimilated with *purusha*, sounds the depths of *prakrit* rather than bypassing or disregarding it, as is so often assumed.

The prakritilayas...pierce the cosmic egg and pass through all the envelopes... down to the primordial Ground, prakrti *in its non-manifested mode...Consciousness is saturated with a direct and total intuition of being.*[29]

Mircea Eliade

For Patanjali, since we are not talking here about experience, we may not consider this as acquiring knowledge, but rather attaining a *state*. It is not just awakening, but replenishing one's being with its potentialities, and therefore, modifying one's existential condition.

When the mind, *bodhi*, is resorbed in the divine mind, *purusha*, the object, now stripped of all our commonplace representations, has transfigured the subject.

This is called *parat param*, beyond the beyond.

---

29 Eliade, *Yoga, Immortality and Freedom*, 92–93.

Chapter Five
Self-Transcendence

The key to self-transcendence is segregating your notion of being the observer from your identification with the psyche; most commonly, we confuse the two or lump them together. Then, in a further step, you shift from identification with what you believe to be your consciousness, which is just the personal focus of the cosmic consciousness, to identifying with the cosmic consciousness.

Self-transcendence consists in:

a) watching those aspects of yourself that you normally identify with, such as your body, mind, thoughts, even emotions or personality, objectively, without identification;

b) watching events in their context objectively, while trying to grasp the software behind the hardware, to use an analogy.

Your body now seems to be a transient formation, unconnected with your will or being. Likewise, as you observe the way the mind functions, you can unmask the hoax of mind games and detect the inadequacy of the middle range mode of your commonplace thinking. What is more, the extent to which you get caught in the bind of your personal emotions also strikes you profoundly. Your personality appears to be inherited, and therefore, as something you need to bear with, rather than identify with.

This analysis leads to great clarity, since we usually confuse that aspect of ourselves that is the observer, with our psyche. Distinguishing these proves most useful to psychotherapists in their efforts to alleviate the despair of patients, by teaching them to identify with the observing self, while pointing out that it is the psyche that is distressed, not the observer.

The steps leading to this are outlined by Buddha in the practices of *satipathana*, as follows:

a) observe the body without identifying with the body; think of it as an ephemeral formation molded by nature, irrespective of you;

b) proceed similarly with the mind;

c) proceed similarly with the personality, which is inherited from your ancestors in the forward march of the evolutionary process;

d) then shift your sense of being a personal observer to denying *I-ness* to the observer, thereby allowing consciousness to extend beyond the point where it is functioning as a personal consciousness. It becomes clear that the picture of the world, as observed through the personal vantage point of consciousness, is misleading and deluding. Ultimately, it is the personal focal center of consciousness that is observed.

This has far-reaching consequences, because we see that the physical world is not the way it appears. Consequently, we grasp a deeper stratum of reality that, according to Sufis, transpires behind that which appears. More importantly, it becomes evident that our problems are not what we assessed them to be; and we may grasp the issues behind the facts and circumstances. This could alleviate a great deal of suffering, much of which is due to our faulty evaluation of our problems.

In Buddhism, at the completion of the four stages in satipathana, you observe that which you tend to identify with your own consciousness in the act of observing an object or a scene, or assessing an event or a problem. The clue to this operation is that you keep shifting your sense of identity back and further back, until your sense of *I-ness* has melted away and merged into an impersonal consciousness. Sufis teach that at this stage you are able to envision your personal consciousness as a focalization of consciousness at a cosmic scale; for example, the consciousness of the universe, which they call *divine consciousness*. Conversely, your vantage point merges with the consciousness of the universe. Thus, one may extend one's notion of oneself as the observer, which one had erroneously confined to one's personal vantage point, to the all-encompassing dimension of consciousness, which is the consciousness of the universe. The consequence is that in the awakened state, the objects, scenes, and events you remember having perceived in the scenario of life through the personal vantage point, now appear as they would through a lens: as a distortion of the way they are viewed from the impersonal, all-encompassing vantage point. However, it is more like the lens of an automatic camera, since it can shift its focus at will from a discrete unit to infinity.

Like the cornea and lens of the eye, consciousness adapts itself to the way objects appear, but this can be offset. The focus of consciousness now appears unstable, since it adapts itself to the objects. Eventually, one realizes that the observer was not the individual pole of one's being, but transpersonal. Therefore, both Buddhism and Sufism deny *I-ness* to what we assumed was the observer.

Chapter Six
A Comparison Between Buddhism and Sufism

At a time when Buddhism has gained so much acceptance in the public eye, and Sufism increasingly intrigues the serious amateurs in quest of the unknown, an inquiry into their differences and similarities seems called for. Hence the following study, which is simply a cursory attempt.

Shall we contrive to consider that which at first seemed contradictory, as complementary? Moreover, dare we, in the all-encompassing trend of our day and age, extrapolate between these apparently antipodal views, in an integrated picture?

The Concept Of God

At this point, we urgently need to confront the apparently intractable differences between the Sufi's continual reference to God, and the Buddhist undogmatic attitude towards the notion of God. However, probing deeper, if we look into the insights gained by the mystics, rather than basing our judgment on belief systems, the differences tend to be bridged more easily.

In his scruple for not affirming anything on the strength of belief, Buddha was wary of the popular anthropomorphic projections paraded as God in his time—as indeed Buddhism is wary of in our time.

Of course, Sufism recognizes our anthropomorphic projections upon what we ascribe to God:

Since we know Him by ourselves and of ourselves, we attribute to Him all that we attribute to ourselves.[1]

Muhyi ad-Din Ibn ʿArabi

On the other hand, Sufism always elicits the counterproposition to any proposition, by the permutation of the terms. Seen from the antipodal point of view, the counterpart is:

---

1 Ibn ʿArabi, *Whoso Knoweth Himself*, T.H. Weir, trans.

Since the form in which He discloses Himself in a faith is the form of that faith, the theophany takes the dimension of the receptacle that receives it, the receptacle in which He discloses Himself.... That is why there are many different faiths. To each believer, the Divine Being is He who is disclosed to him in the form of his faith.[2]

Henry Corbin

Should one have a problem with the anthropomorphic connotations of the word *God*, since this is the term used, one could call it what we mean by reality, both known or unknown. Do we mean that which lies behind the physical cosmos? Shall we say: the software behind the hardware of the universe? or do we include the hardware? or do we mean that which transcends all human notions?

Should we strip that ambivalent idiomatic term *God* of its anthropomorphic semantics, we would be depriving ourselves of the wide range of *realness* ascribed to that term.

In Sufism, the term *God* is looked upon as the antipodal pole of an antinomy, in which what we consider to be our personal self is the opposite pole. Without this pole, our personal dimension would not make sense; precisely as in mathematics, the notion of the unit implicitly presupposes infinity, and infinity presupposes the notion of the unit. Mathematics would not be possible without seeing the connection between the unit and infinity.

For Hazrat Inayat Khan, the concept of God, upon which belief may be grounded, is an unreliable yet indispensable stepping stone.

He is not wrong who makes God in his imagination, the God of all beauty, free from ugliness; the God of all the best qualities, free from all evil; for by that imagination he is drawn nearer and nearer every moment of his life to that Divine Ideal which is the seeking of his soul.[3]

Hazrat Inayat Khan

The Antinomy
Reality Seen As Transcendent Or Immanent

In his retreat under the Bodhi tree where he attained illumination, the Buddha found refuge in the *non-become*, marking a clear cleft between the transcendent and immanent.[4]

Buddha seems to dismiss the relevance of the existential condition to the eternal to attain illumination: *Everything is transient and nothing endures.*[5]

2 Corbin, *Creative Imagination in the Sufism of Ibn ʿArabi*, 197.
3 Inayat Khan, *Song of the Prophets*, 97.
4 See Majjhima Nikaya II, 32; Samyutta Nikaya ll, 28.
5 Carus, *Gospel of the Buddha*, 2.

185

We find in Sufism the need to awaken beyond the existential, transient condition and also the need to awaken in life.

All the holy beings of the world have becomes so by freeing the soul, its freedom being the only object there is in life.[6]

Hazrat Inayat Khan

And then, we reach the opposite:

O Thou who art absent there, we have found Thee here. Thou art nonexistent as Essence, existent in Thy person.[7]

'Abd al-Karim al-Jili

The Sufis try to grasp the link between these two dimensions of our being, and as a matter of fact, of the Divine Being, pulling us in two directions: the need for involvement and the need for freedom.

The soul manifests in this world in order that it may experience the different phases of manifestation, and yet may not lose its way...but may attain to its original freedom in addition to the experience and knowledge it has gained in the world.[8]

Hazrat Inayat Khan

For the Sufis, all that we know of that reality we call *God* is through clues. So that, in their view, there must be some relationship between that intangible reality and its means of manifestation, which is of a transient nature.

It is only at a very high level that Sufis describe the state of human realization in which God reveals the Divine Self, regardless of any clues as to God's divine nature, and regardless of God's experience of the Divine Self as projected in the cosmos. Sufism acknowledges modes of knowledge that do not rest upon experience. By shifting the notion of the personal self, a meaningfulness may be revealed to the contemplative, which he could not acquire by his personal volition.

The difference between these perspectives could be accounted for by the contrast between the activity of consciousness, which experiences reality in the space-time existential state, and the act of intelligence, the ground of consciousness that is endowed with an inherent proto-critic knowledge of the software of the universe, not subject to the duality of subject versus object, which is found in the activities of consciousness.

Consciousness must always be conscious of something. When consciousness is not conscious of anything, it is pure intelligence.[9]

6 Inayat Khan, *The Sufi Message* series, *The Sufi Message of Spiritual Liberty*, 237.
7 Al-Jili, *De l'Homme Universel.*
8 Inayat Khan, *The Sufi Message* series, *The Way of Illumination*, 150.
9 Inayat Khan, *The Sufi Message* series, *Philosophy, Psychology and Mysticism*, 69.

If the soul could see independently of mind and body, it would see infinitely more.[10]

Hazrat Inayat Khan

Buddha ascribes this perspective, rarely reached by a contemplative, to the plane beyond existence attained through the practice of the *Jhana*.

As a result, in Sufism one's logical understanding is continually taxed by what seems like blatant contradictions. To add enigma to paradox, one could entertain two complementary (though at first sight contradictory) views:

God can only be known by the synthesis of antinomic affirmations.[11]

Abu Sa'id al-Kharraz

It is at its transcendent level of thinking, as Buddhism confirms, that the mind can overcome these contradictions that aver themselves to be conceptual.[12]

Nostalgia Versus Desire

Surveying the links in the causal chain (*pattica samuppada*) leading to the suffering attendant upon existential conditions, Buddha infers that it is due to craving (*asava*), normally rendered by desire, that begets ignorance; whereas liberation from attachment to contact of the world sparks realization and enlightenment.

Both Buddhism and Sufism see desire as the prime mover leading towards existence. But desire is considered pejorative in Buddhism, while liberation from the existential state is coveted.[13]

Sufism paradoxically embraces both detachment and involvement. On one hand:

The real proof of one's progress in the spiritual path can be realized by testing in every situation in life how indifferent one is.[14]

Hazrat Inayat Khan

And then the absolute opposite:

He who arrives at the state of indifference without experiencing interest in life is incomplete and apt to be tempted by interest at any moment; but he who arrives at the state of indifference by going through interest really attains the blessed state.[15]

Hazrat Inayat Khan

---

10 Inayat Khan, *The Sufi Message* series, *Sacred Readings*, 52.
11 Ibn 'Arabi, *Whoso Knoweth Himself*, T.H. Weir, trans.
12 See Carus, *Gospel of the Buddha*, 3, 5.
13 See Davids, *Dialogues of the Buddha*, Part I, 84.
14 Inayat Khan, *Esoteric Papers*.
15 Inayat Khan, *The Sufi Message* series, *The Sufi Message of Spiritual Liberty*, 27.

How can one reconcile these two objectives, which are pulling one in opposite directions?

Interest also gives great power. The whole of manifestation is a phenomenon of interest....The whole Creation and all that is in it are the products of the Creator's interest....The power of indifference is a greater one still....Because although motive has a power, yet at the same time motive limits power...yet it is motive that gives man the power to accomplish things.[16]

Hazrat Inayat Khan

The very foundation of Sufism, based upon the famous Hadith Qudsi, earmarks love (*hubb*) as the motivation behind the great achievements of our civilizations. Hence the existential state is looked upon as the fulfilment of the purpose of life.

Manifestation is the self of God; but a self which is limited...which makes Him know that He is perfect when He compares His own Being with this limited self which we call nature....The purpose of the whole of Creation is fulfilled in the attainment of that perfection which is for a human being to attain.[17]

Hazrat Inayat Khan

For the Sufis, realization in life is attained by fulfilling the purpose of life, which is actuating the splendor behind the existential level in building a beautiful world of beautiful people. In the course of accomplishment, new horizons of meaningfulness reveal themselves.

Admittedly, once involved in the rat race, one tends to forget one's initial motivations and gets inveigled in the vicious circle: greed—unkindness—ignorance.

Buddha lived as a recluse and founded a monastic order. Christ said of his disciples that they were in the world but not of the world.[18] For Ibn 'Arabi, by cloistering oneself from the world, one misses out on the divine revelation; because if one can espy what transpires behind what appears, one will, at least at the first stage, earmark signs (ayat) in the existential realm thatgive clues to the intention behind the human drama—and in a second step, clues as to the perfection of the divine archetypal attributes exemplified, albeit imperfectly, in our very human nature. The exemplar gives a clue as to the archetype. Therefore, the key is to see clearly the relationship between the two poles of this dichotomy.

For the Sufis, as in Advaita Vedanta, reality includes both its paramount eternal ground and its unfurling in the transient, existential condition of

---

16 Inayat Khan, *The Sufi Message* series, *The Alchemy of Happiness*, 176–177.
17 Inayat Khan, *The Complete Sayings of Hazrat Inayat Khan*, 194, 204.
18 John 15:19.

becoming and unbecoming in their interrelationship. In Sufism, when considering our contingent ego, it is always envisioned with reference to this antipodal pole of our being. There is no cleavage, and hence, no duality, although these apparently contradictory propositions are sometimes reconciled in an antinomy:

Understand whereby you are He and whereby you are other than He.[19]

Muhyi ad-Din Ibn 'Arabi

Levels Of Experience, Spheres Of Reality

Conceptualization is the first step. Mysticism starts with experience.

The God who is intelligible to man is made by man himself, but what is beyond his intelligence is the reality.[20]

Hazrat Inayat Khan

Looking from a loftier vantage point, all the aforesaid depends upon the level at which one's thinking is operating. To make ultimate sense, one would need to explore these various levels of our thinking and reconnoiter, in particular, those levels of thinking that are bereft of the notion of the personal *I* of our middle range, spacio-temporal windows, through which we try to scan reality. This is precisely what is meant by enlightenment, and where the conjunctions between Buddhist and Sufi views, though not identical, are remarkable and gratifying.

Both Tibetan Buddhism and Sufism distinguish several levels of thinking. The similarity (though not identity) is striking. For each body that one identifies with, a corresponding mode of thinking exists. In the Tibetan saying, *the mind rides the wind*, the wind typifies levels of energy, and matter is energy.

We are talking about various levels of reality evidencing one's insight. Depending upon one's perspective, one could posit degrees of *Godness*, ranging from an impersonal absolute to an all-encompassing view of God as the Being of which the universe is the body. For our intellect, these two extremes designated in Buddhism as *the non-become* and *the become,* are designated in Sufism by *haqq* and *khalq*.[21]

Reconciliating The Irreconcilables

Is it possible to extrapolate between these two perspectives?

The Sufi dervishes bear testimony, in lofty flights of their souls, to planes or spheres beyond the existential sphere, where an infinite plethora of possibilities

19 Corbin, *Creative Imagination in the Sufism of Ibn 'Arabi*, 192.
20 Inayat Khan, *The Complete Sayings of Hazrat Inayat Khan*, 11.
21 *Truth* and the *created world*.

(*imkan*) lie dormant. While eternal in the principles of their nature, these virtual archetypes of what is experienced on earth, project themselves in the existential mode, which is transient. Moreover, there is an ever-recurrent flow from the inexhaustible pool of all possibilities into the existential realm. The non-manifest slumbers in the virtuality of possibility.

There is no thing whose treasuries are not with Us.[22]

Qur'an

The treasuries of the things...are only the possibilities of the things, nothing else, since the things have no existence in their entities. On the contrary, they possess immutability....For in the state of their nonexistence, the things are witnessed by God.[23]

Muhyi ad-Din Ibn 'Arabi

The crucial issue is whatever interaction these two poles of the antinomy might entertain.

In matter, life unfolds, discovers, realizes the consciousness which has been, so to speak, buried in it for thousands of years.[24]

Hazrat Inayat Khan

It is in the manifest realm that it becomes a reality.

For possibility is a prayer, a call to the Necessary Being who at every instant recreates the cosmos in a new form.[25]

Muhyi ad-Din Ibn 'Arabi

According to al-Hallaj, God, envisioned as Reality beyond the existential state, in the solitude of oneness beyond multiplicity, projected God's own Self by dint of form (although intrinsically formless) in order to acquire a subsidiary, supererogatory mode of knowledge, which accrued to the knowledge of the principles of Divine Being that God embodies eternally, presumably adding further sense to this primeval, paramount knowledge.

For the Sufis, beyond the existential condition all possibility lies in wait as the undertone of the universe; these virtualities are released in the existential condition, out of love rather than necessity.

God does not need the world.[26]

Qur'an

---

22 XV:21.
23 Chittick, *The Sufi Path of Knowledge*, 87.
24 Inayat Khan, *The Sufi Message* series, *Sufi Teachings*, 317.
25 Chittick, *The Sufi Path of Knowledge*, 19.
26 III:96.

He created them to enable them to enjoy existence, to free them from the constraint of the void.[27]

Muhyi ad-Din Ibn 'Arabi

The Feedback

The converse question is whether there is a feedback from the state of becoming, which is the condition of the existential universe, into what Buddha calls the *non-become*. If our eternal dimension cannot be subject to change, how can it be affected by what is gained by the miracle of existence, in terms of cosmic know-how? And if not, then what purpose could the whole phenomenon of existence have—particularly to us?

Both Buddhism and Sufism agree that simply unclutching the permanent aspect of our being from the perishable is not going to affect that component of one's being that is not subject to change: the permanent component.

This not become does not become through the ceasing of this that ceases.[28]

The Buddha

It is gratifying to find precisely the same thought amongst the Sufis:

Most of those who seek God make ceasing of existence, and ceasing of that ceasing of ceasing, a condition for the knowledge of God; and that is an error and a clear oversight. It is not their existence that ceases, but their ignorance.[29]

Muhyi ad-Din Ibn 'Arabi

It is also heartening to point out the concurrence between the notion of *nirupadhi* and also nirvana in Buddhism, which both connote the destruction of the entity of craving that is attached to the personal notion of the self, and fana in Sufism, which means the annihilation of the notion of the personal self. However, we need to bear in mind that in Sufism fana is always accompanied by baqa, as a correlative that stands for our dimension of perennity that is not subject to transiency, and hence endures all-abidingly.

The same is found in Buddhism: downplaying the perishable features of one's being needs to be compensated by highlighting one's sense of eternity. By so doing, the transcendent pole of one's being can impact the contingent.[30]

One needs to distinguish between the recurrent recycling of life from the nucleus of one's being, like the stump of a tree that has been felled and starts regrowing again, and where a transformation has taken place at the

---

27 Ibn 'Arabi, *Whoso Knoweth Himself*, T.H. Weir, trans..
28 See Davids, *Dialogues of the Buddha*, Part III, *Dīgha Nikāya*.
29 Ibn 'Arabi, *Whoso Knoweth Himself*, T.H. Weir, trans.
30 See Davids, *Dialogues of the Buddha, Part III*, 221.

transcendental level of one's being. The ability to mutate is where, through one's realization, potentialities which were recessive in one's genetic code are released, pervading one's being.

It would be inadequate to try to illustrate this by distinguishing between a continuity in change as, for example, a river where it is never the same water that runs under the bridge but where there is some constancy in the river and what could be depicted as the point upon which a pendulum is suspended, which remains unchanged while the other pole is moving to and fro. Rather, it could be illustrated by distinguishing between the stump of a tree that can grow again by recycling it, and the genetic code of the tree that could mutate.

We are talking of a level which Buddha referred to as the ultimate *arupa jhana*: the cessation of the determined, a level transcending Laplacian causality, and therefore, not subjected to causality. Interestingly, Speiser refers to it:

It is an initial state which is not governed by mechanistic law, but is the precondition of law, the chance substrate upon which it is built.[31]

Andreas Speiser

The Sufis posit a vector of causality proceeding downwards (vertically, as one might plot it) from the transcendent level of reality to the transient, which once more corroborates the Buddhist view of conditioned genesis, the causal chain triggering off existence. But in addition, the Sufis posit a feedback from the experience of the existential state to the transcendent or, shall we say, near-transcendent state.

Indeed, life would not make sense if nothing were gained by it. There must be a feedback flow from the existential realm reaching, in infinite regress, into the eternal ground, the non-become; this is evidenced by the phenomenon whereby the quintessence of know-how gained by experience survives the transiency of becoming in our memory.

That which is conditioned by finitude will become the absolute.[32]

Nur ad-Din 'Abd ar-Rahman Jami

Could the answer to the riddle be that there is a gradual transit from becoming to eternity, as there is from eternity to becoming?

Both Buddhism and Sufism refer to many-tiered intermediary spheres, or planes, spanning the gulf between the non-become—*Huwwa* (He, not present)—and the earthly sphere, each corresponding with a level of awareness and a mode of thinking.

---

31 Speiser, *Über die Freiheit*, 41.
32 Jami, *Lawa'ih*, 59.

By passing wholly beyond such a sphere of consciousness, he enters into and abides in that rapt ecstasy which is a consciousness of the infinitude of consciousness itself. By passing wholly beyond such a spheres of consciousness, he enters into and abides in that rapt ecstasy which regards consciousness itself as nothing whatever, a sphere of nothingness. By passing wholly beyond such a sphere, he enters into, and abides in that rapt consciousness which neither is, nor yet is not to be called conscious. By passing wholly beyond such a sphere, he enters into and abides in a state of unconsicounsess, wherein awareness and feeling cease.[33]

The Buddha

Embodying States Of Realization

Moreover, we need to account for the opposite: one's descent as erstwhile celestial beings, in such a manner that we may become instrumental to the transformation of the fabric of this world, by configuring it according to the celestial mode. It is a matter of entering states of consciousness corporeal.

With his heart thus serene, made pure, translucent, cultured, devoid of evil, supple, ready to act, firm and imperturbable, he applies and bends down his mind to the calling up of a mental image. He calls up fom this body another body, having form, made of mind, having all (his own body's) limbs and parts.[34]

The Buddha

Techniques leading to achieving this have been developed, particularly in Tibetan Buddhism. The sources for these are to be found in Vajradhara's teachings contained in the *Guhyasamaja Tantra,* and also in Nagarjuna; and practical exercises are outlined in Geshe Kelsang Gyatso's *The Clear Light of Bliss.*

Practices of a kindred nature are to be found in Indian alchemy, which is called *Rasayana,* and is a product of Tantra.

Like the Alchemist, the yogin effects transformations in "substance."[35]

Mircea Eliade

Recollecting the genesis of the cosmic, formative processes that fashioned the Yogin since their inception, irrespective of his will, he recaptures each step and recreates himself anew volitionally.

What returns in reality is matter in a certain form, but this form is precisely the work of the individual person.[36]

Ahmad al-Ahsa'i

---

33 Davids, *Dialogues of the Buddha, Part III,* 242–243.
34 Davids, *Dialogues of the Buddha, Part I,* 87–88.
35 Eliade, *Yoga, Immortality and Freedom,* 274.
36 Corbin, *Spiritual Body and Celestial Earth,* 219.

Our subtle and celestial bodies serve as intermediary links between the non-become and the become, cross pollinating between the celestial influences adumbrating them and the spillover from earthly conditions, including the wisdom acquired by mastering the challenges wreaked upon us by our human problems.

Hazrat Inayat Khan distinguishes two kinds of angels: those who, incarnating as humans, invest us with the innocence, glory and sacredness of the heavens; and those who, having incarnated, feed back something of the wisdom and sovereignty acquired on earth in their upward journey.

It is the work of the souls who return from the earth to communicate with the earth very often, and it is such angels who are generally known to man. Angels who have never manifested as men on earth, only experience life on earth by the medium of other minds and bodies which, by their evolution, come closer to the angelic heavens.[37]

Hazrat Inayat Khan

And some being or other, because his span of years has passed, or because his merit has exhausted, deceases from the world of radiance and comes to life in the abode of the Brahmas.[38]

The Buddha

This interaction from the eternal level of our being to the existential, and from the existential to the eternal is mediated by our celestial effigy. This effigy is also matured by imprinting it with the know-how gained by earthly experience.

The transient realm, rather than being an illusion, is a projection of the eternal and formless reality behind it. What seemed illusion avers itself to be what it is all about—it is here and now that what lies latent as sheer possibilities becomes real.

Application

The key to self-transcendence is segregating your notion of being the observer from your identification with the psyche; most commonly, we confuse these two or lump them together. Then, in a further step, you extend your consciousness beyond its ordinary purview, thus shifting your sense of being the personal observer to countenancing all things from an impersonal vantage point.

Looked at from the Sufi view, it is difficult to keep oneself from jumping to the conclusion that this is what Buddha refers to when he says that consciousness has been carried beyond the point where it is a personal consciousness.

---

37 Inayat Khan, *The Sufi Message* series, *The Way of Illumination*, 122.
38 Davids, *Dialogues of the Buddha, Part I*, 26.

It is a setting of consciousness which the Sufis ascribe to the divine consciousness, which takes over when we cease to identify with our notion of our personal self.

Taking a modern view, I would put it thus: if we think of the cosmos as a composite being, and ourselves as holistically integrated in this being, then we can infer that our consciousness is the focalization of the consciousness of the cosmos. Furthermore, we have the ability to reverse this by ceasing to identify with our notion of our personal self. Should we do this, since consciousness cannot operate anymore from a personal vantage, a wider dimension, subliminally latent behind our personal focus of consciousness, emerges and takes over, giving us a sense of awakening. Indeed, what we mean by awakening is always a sudden shift from one perspective to another. At that point, inasmuch as one identifies with being the observer, one identifies with cosmic consciousness, which is at least one of the dimensions of what the Sufis call divine consciousness.

Practicing satipathana, which I am now calling self-transcendence: a) you watch those aspects of yourself that you normally identify with—such as your body, mind, even your emotions or personality—objectively, without identifying with them; b) you watch events in their context, objectively, while trying to grasp the software behind the hardware (to use an analogy).

Practices

To understand the following study, it is necessary to clarify as follows: It is possible to distinguish three stages in the Buddhist practices: i) the four satipathana practices, ii) followed by the *vipassana jhanas* (applying the insights gained by the satipathanas), iii) followed by the *arupa jhanas* (focusing consciousness into transcendental levels).

In the satipathana practices, we are unmasking the hoax of our personal perspectives as we view the body, mind, personality, and consciousness. In the vipassana jhanas, we discover how the world looks when consciousness has freed itself from its limited vantage point; then how thoughts appear from this cosmic perspective, and so forth. In the arupa jhanas, levels of reality beyond the existential level are discovered.

Let us examine these methods, paralleling them with Sufism.

I. Matter

Buddhist Method: First Stage in Satipathana

1) Consider your body as a transient formation, irrespective of your conscious or volitional participation, without identifying with it. That is, as a function of the impersonal forces of the world.

2) Realize that in our usual thinking, in our use of the word *I*, we unwittingly are not clear as to whether we mean our personality, our body, or whether we mean the observer and willer. Clearly distinguish between that part of you that functions as the observer and those aspects, like the body, mind and personality, that may be observed.

3) At a first stage, abstain from ascribing *I-ness* to the observed, whether body, mind, emotion, or personality, considered as perishable underpinnings produced by the universe irrespective of your person. Start by considering your body, made of cells, bone, muscle, nerve tissue, mucous, hair, and organs such as the liver, the heart, the intestines; and then consider the molecules, atoms, and electrons within these. You will conclude that it is difficult to ascribe a sense of *I-ness* to these.

4) In the next step—but not before completing the previous stages—deny *I-ness* to the observer that you thought you were.

Sufi Method

1) Realize that however inadequate and illusory your notion of yourself is, your involvement with the very actuation of the reality underlying it is important, since by dint of your involvement with it and through experience, that reality has accrued to you and has proven enriching. It has become part of you. In like manner, although the principles behind all existential reality are already virtually present in the divine mind, something is gained by the divine mind by experiencing what accrues to it by the actuation of these principles, thanks to existential conditions. Indeed, let yourself wonder at the miracle of life, making itself known by existentiating itself, sparkling and proliferating at the surface as if by magic.

2) Consequently, discounting your body as not being you would not honor that aspect of you that has accrued through your involvement with the fabric of the universe. You will discover that, indeed, you can observe your body and mind and personality while identifying with them, although admittedly, it is easier to observe them if you dismiss them as other than you. This requires stretching your thinking from the commonplace mode, which thinks in discrete categories, to the mode in which the mind is able to extrapolate between external and internal impressions and reconcile the irreconcilables, or have a concurrence of the incongruent.

Furthermore, while the ascetic cultivates aloofness and detachment, the Sufi dervishes, who may spend years of austerity in a cell or in a desert fastness, ultimately find their seat in the marketplace instead of the cave, having developed the ability to see, in the moving scenario of life, the fulfillment of the divine nostalgia ('ishq Allah) for the manifestation of the non-manifest. R. A. Nicholson reports how, as a young man, the Sufi dervish Abi'l-Khayr said: *I had a cell in which I sat, and sitting there, I was enamored of passing away from myself."*[39]

Whereas decades later he is quoted as saying:

The true saint goes in and out amongst the people, and eats and sleeps with them, and buys and sells in the market, and marries and takes part in social intercourse, and never forgets God for a single moment.[40]

3) Even though the manifest reveals but a sliver of the reality behind it, try to earmark the clues to this reality in the physical world or in your body. Granted, the reality behind it is concealed—Sufis use the word *veiled*—but:

The very veil that conceals it reveals that which transpires through that which appears.

Farid ad-Din 'Attar

That reality is envisioned as the divine splendor, and the veil as the beauty in which splendor is endeavoring to manifest.

4) As I have previously mentioned, there is some concurrence between the Buddhist and Sufi methods at the level of the vipassana jhanas. The Sufi view, however, rather than simply asserting that the negative assessment of what we identify ourselves with is misconstrued, affirms that both the observer and the observed are projections of an underlying, single reality, traditionally called *God*. Ponder upon this thought.

Dismissing body, mind, etc. as *other than me* is evading the issue, since body, mind, feeling, personality, or the outside world are all ultimately expressions, or spin-offs, of the One and Only Being.

The difference that ensues from this positive attitude regarding these manifestations of an underlying reality, is that you will try to unfurl the potentialities that lie in wait in the seedbed of your personality. Admittedly, in this respect there is a greater similarity between Sufism and Mahayana Buddhism, particularly Tibetan Buddhism, which works with the construction of the subtle bodies in order to render spiritual states corporeal, than with Theravada Buddhism.

5) In the perspective of Sufism, see the way that which appears as your consciousness, and also your body, etc. is inscribed in the totality of being in a holistic way. While that which you believe to be your consciousness is the focalization of the divine consciousness, it is also interdependent with that

---

39 Nicholson, *Studies in Islamic Mysticism*, 16.
40 Ibid., 25.

which you believe to be your body—which is inextricably interrelated with the fabric of the universe, like the constituents of a hologram. See how the divine consciousness, through its focalization in that which you believe to be your consciousness, entertains a different relationship with your body than the one it entertains with other physical objects, which are considered as being outside your body. Hence, you cannot dismiss it as *other*.

6) Flip your consciousness in the complementary perspective to the usual one. In the divine perspective, it will look as though God incarnates, thus fulfilling the divine nostalgia to manifest and actuate the many-splendored potentialities longing for expression; for example, God's qualities manifesting as the idiosyncrasies of your personality.

The servant is the hearing and seeing of the Real.[41]

Muhyi ad-Din Ibn 'Arabi

7) To accomplish this fully, discard your body image and envision the cells and molecules of the physical fabric of your body as they would appear if illuminated by the light of your glance. Imagine your glance as luminous and as the extension of the divine glance.

Buddhism and the Vipassana Jhanas

The next step: How does the world at large, including your body, appear when consciousness has outreached its focalization in a personal vantage point? This is to be found in the vipassana jhanas.

First Vipassana Jhana

1) In the first jhana, while still using the crutch of perception and representation (in Yoga, sarvitarca and savicara), caution yourself by this thought: this is the way it appears within the constraint imposed by the focalization of consciousness, due to my notion of myself as an individual.

The breakthrough is sparked when you realize that while you considered the personal focal center of your consciousness as the observer, it is now that which is observed.

You will notice that we have been systematically shifting our sense of identity back and further back, from being a body, or a mind, or a personality, until our sense of *I-ness* has melted away and merged into an impersonal consciousness; our vantage point has merged with the consciousness of the universe.

The consequence is that in the awakened state, the objects, scenes, and events you remember having perceived in the scenario of life, through the

---

41 Chittick, *The Sufi Path of Knowledge*, 329.

personal vantage point, now appear as they would through a lens; that is, as a distortion of the way they are viewed from the impersonal, all-encompassing vantage point. However, it is more like the lens of an automatic camera, since it can shift its focus at will from a discrete unit to infinity.

Moreover, like the cornea and lens of the eye, consciousness adapts itself to the way objects appear; but it can be offset. The focus of consciousness now appears unstable, since it adapts itself to the objects. Sufi contemplatives try to sense the divine consciousness adumbrating and overshadowing one's personal consciousness. Ultimately, both Buddhism and Sufism deny *I-ness* to what we assumed to be the observer.

This has far-reaching consequences, because we can see for ourselves that the physical world is not the way it appears. Consequently, we grasp a deeper stratum of reality, which according to Sufis, transpires behind that which appears. More importantly, it becomes evident that our problems are not what we assessed them to be; and we may grasp the issues behind facts and circumstances. This could alleviate a great deal of suffering, much of which is due to our faulty evaluation of our problems.

This analysis leads to great clarity, since we usually confuse the aspect of ourselves that is the observer, with our psyche. Distinguishing these proves most useful to psychotherapists in their efforts to alleviate the despair of patients, by teaching them to identify with the observing self, while pointing out that it is the psyche that is distressed, not the observer.

If indeed, the map is not the territory, then it is possible to reach the bare reality. To do this, you must not be sidetracked by a) the sensorial-perceptual neural mechanism, which mediates between, on the one hand, the peripheral impressions of sound waves or light particles impinging upon the eardrum, retinas, neurotransmitters and brain circuits (savitarka); and on the other hand, mental constructs; or b) by the interpretations and association processes which we tag onto the data communicated by the senses. If you can be so watchful as to grasp that these are not the reality, but simply the transmitters of that reality, then you will touch upon the *that-ness* (*tat*) that our senses perceive as matter.

This indeed corroborates what physicists encounter when they find that if they are to obtain a clearer grasp of the phenomena observed, they are required to abandon one assumption after another: (i) that particles are located in space; (ii) that phenomena are caused in the time sequences that we represent as becoming; (iii) that particles can be observed as they would be if not observed. The attribute of emptiness, which Buddhists append to what we commonly and unquestionably ascribe to physical reality, does not mean that there is no matrix behind what appears; for example, in Tibetan

Buddhism, when one realizes the emptiness that is the illusory nature of the apparent light, the clear light emerges.

This view tallies completely with the Sufi view, according to which the manifest is made of innumerable veils concealing the non-manifest, undefinable reality behind it. The light which we perceive, the light that is seen, is only the epiphany, the appearance, of the light that sees. At a critical point, the antinomy of subject-object disappears.

If you go to infinite depths of matter, you may reach something very close to what you see in the depth of the mind.

The method advocated by the Buddha in the arupa jhanas (the contemplations beyond form) as leading to grasping emptiness, consists in imagining a forest, then just the land without the trees, then the space without the land. This is again borne out by quantum physics, where waves and particles are the unfolding, explicate mode of the field, and space is landscaped by the emergence of mass from pure energy.

Sufi View

In the view of the Sufis, how would matter appear when freed from our conceptual representations of it—from the divine perspective?

When your soul has been purified and its mirror has been polished, do not consider the world to receive in it the picture of the world, but turn your soul towards the dignity of the Essence in its purity, in the perspective of the cognizance that it has of itself.[42]

Vision is not preceded by knowledge of the object of the vision, while witnessing is preceded by a knowledge of the witnessed.[43]

Muhyi ad-Din Ibn 'Arabi

As previously mentioned, for the Sufis, it would appear like a holographic projection of a formless, yet meaningful, reality that can never be the object of our perception or cognizance; albeit the mystic may have flashes of the divine vision.

For the Sufi Mahmud Shabistari, the physical world is like the reflection in a mirror.

Not being is the mirror; the world the reflection; and man is as the reflected eyes of the Unseen person. In that eye, His eye sees His own eye.[44]

Mahmud Shabistari

In the light of the present viewpoint, this may be better illustrated as a hologram. A hologram is not an illusion; it is a real replica of the original

---

42 Ibn 'Arabi, *Études Traditionelles*, trans. Valsan, 1952 Mai-June, 129.
43 Chittick, *The Sufi Path of Knowledge*, 227.
44 Shabistari, *Gulshan-i Raz*.

object constructed in the fabric of light, and having its existence in space-time. But it is not the original object. The analogy with the hologram, however, breaks down here, because in the Sufi view, the original does not have form, and only acquires it when projected.

Practices

1) Liberate your consciousness from the stress imposed upon it by the commonplace appearance of things, which forces your glance in a definite focus. Offset your glance from its usual perspective by casting it at infinity.

2) Try to x-ray your usual perception by thinking of your glance as casting the light of your intelligence upon it, so as to highlight that which lies behind it; the light of your intelligence is the divine intelligence, but focalized rather than being at the receptive end of the impressions. How does physical reality appear? Do you find yourself in a transfigured world? Do you espy, as the Sufis say, that which transpires behind that which appears?

3) Consider yourself as conjoining both the eternal, transcendent dimension that is coextensive and isomorphic with God, and the transient existential aspect of your being. Think of it as a pendulum, where one pole remains unchanged while the other moves in space-time.

4) Consider your body as an aspect of the Being of God that has accrued to the way you were prior to your conception, and which carries the inheritance of your ancestors right back into the early beginnings of the evolutionary process. This represents a stage moving toward the fulfillment of the divine purpose.

5) Represent clearly to yourself the following: *One of the aspects of myself that I observe in my meditations in the mode of self-transcendence, and which is also endowed with a sense of* I-ness, *namely, my body, started as a mineral, then became a vegetable, then became an animal, then became a human. I will continue in the heavenly spheres.*

6) Consider in the same way those features of your body that configure some of the qualities of your eternal being, which the Sufis call our divine inheritance, mediated through your subtle bodies.

7) Furthermore, consider those aspects of your body that reflect the environment, both physical and cultural, and therefore, have accrued to you on Planet Earth. Moreover, consider that although a transient formation, the body is a continuity in change; the electrons, protons, and photons continue to live indefinitely and are interconnected in a non-local way, though interspersed within the wave interference pattern of the universe. This is what Sufis and Christians call resurrection.

8) Instead of simply dismissing your personal assessment of physical matter or circumstances as illusory, try to grasp how matter and events would appear from the divine perspective. In this view, rather than being a hoax, the hardware of the universe avers itself to be the very purpose of the software.

Rather than thinking of matter as simply solid stuff (substance), physicists never cease to be amazed at the discovery of the extraordinarily smart congruence of the planning behind phenomena and structures found in the universe, and even more so, at the elegance in the configuration of the atoms. As a biologist, your heart would leap at the discovery of the way that the conformation and functioning of the body cells evidences not only intelligence, but a will to serve the community of body cells. This present-day view corroborates that held by the Buddha, who considered the body to be made of cyclic elements that will return to the earth, or more precisely, survive in the universe. We see this particularly as we learn that the electrons and protons of the body continue to live indefinitely, each storing a few bytes of memory and networking these non-locally in a way that is different from communicating information mutually, which would be impossible owing to the constraint of the speed of light. Therefore, the specter of the putrefaction of the body can be considered as a pragmatic method to arouse aversion for attachment to the body, rather than as a philosophical statement.

II. Thoughts

Buddhist Method: 2nd Stage in Satipathana

Watch your thoughts objectively. Catch them as they arise or recede, often provoked by a process of association but more generally conditioned by our upbringing. Consider the mind as a formation programmed by the universe, just like the body, irrespective of any *I-ness* whatsoever. It is a support system, but it is not you.

Sufi Method

Granted, many of our thoughts are predictable and therefore conditioned by a programming outside our control, irrespective of our will or initiative. However, for the Sufis, these thoughts are the divine thoughts, albeit limited by the human scope within which we constrain them, often distort them, and even defile them. Rather than dismiss them as conditioned, Sufis try to espy the divine intention behind them, which is revealed in the measure to which one downplays one's personal bias or wishful thinking. Here the concurrence with the Buddhist satipathana avers itself in the need to bypass the personal perspective. In fact, in the corresponding vipassana jhana, when consciousness (in the nirvecara state according to Patanjali) is able to sustain itself without resting upon thought (sarvicara), there is an awakening, *bojjhanga*, in which consciousness is pervaded by bodhi, a transcendental mode of knowledge. This would seem to correspond to the experience which the Sufis describe as bypassing the personal dimension of thought and having a vivid sense of awareness, which they ascribe to the divine revelation.

We have seen that creative thought, unpredictable as it might seem, can be catalyzed by events of psychological syndromes. According to Tibetan Buddhism, creative thoughts fall into the category of the activities of the subtle mind, which projects the urge of expressing the ineffable in tangible forms. Being mere projections, these are obviously derivative, and consequently secondary; and they could prove illusory if one took them to be the ultimate reality of which they are mere expressions. In the view of the Sufis, one creates an inadequate assessment of the mind by limiting it to the portion of it that emerges at the personal level like the tip of an iceberg, discarding its cosmic extension, which is coextensive with the mind of the universe.

In their musings in a state of reverie, Suhrawardi, Avicenna, and Ibn 'Arabi, among many Sufi mystics, explore the world of metaphor behind the thinking of our conceptual minds.

Practices

Consider your thoughts. Differentiate between:

1) thoughts that may be ascribed to your psyche's regurgitation of impressions accruing from the environment;

2) thoughts that represent your psyche's reacting to thoughts communicated to you from other people;

3) those thoughts in which you reflect your own soul-searchings, and sometimes reverie—notice whether new vistas emerge;

4) those thoughts which seem to arise purely spontaneously, or are perhaps triggered off by covert impressions or preoccupations but cannot simply be considered to be reactions to these. These are ascribed by Tibetan Buddhists to the subtle mind; our psyche is programmed to project inner feelings and thoughts into forms, images, landscapes. Such imaginary landscapes confer concreteness upon these spontaneous musings of our soul. While these musings seem random, they are triggered off by strong human emotions, or sometimes, a nostalgia for values beyond the usual human range.

5) You cannot truly own your thoughts. Sufis call them the divine thoughts. You will notice that they are archetypal rather than factual. Sufis ascribe them to the world of metaphor (*'alam al-mithal*).

6) At the extreme limit, you may feel that a sudden insight is revealed to you that you could not possibly have figured out. Notice that it is not articulated in the form of thoughts, but is a sudden awakening to a sense of

intense meaningfulness, accompanied by an intense, ecstatic sensitivity to sheer beauty.

Buddhism: 2nd Vipassana Jhana

How do one's thoughts appear to one, and how does the thinking of others, the thinking behind existential phenomena, appear when consciousness has spilled over the boundaries of the personal vantage point? This occurs in Buddhism at the stage corresponding to the second jhana: one grasps meaningfulness everywhere, directly and at a cosmic scale, while eschewing any tendency to restrict one's thinking within the limits of one's mental constructs. More precisely, one rests one's cognizance neither upon the perception nor upon the representation of forms or events.

By passing wholly beyond all consciousness of material qualities, by the dying out of the awareness of sensory reactions, by the unheeding of any awareness of difference, he enters into and abides in that rapt ecstasy which is a consciousness of infinite space.[45]

The Buddha

The knowledge thus acquired is of a transcendental nature; in Buddhism it is called *panna*, and in Sufism, *ma'rifat*.

Sufi Method

For the Sufis, there is indeed an a priori sense of meaningfulness called *transcendental knowledge*, which is written into the software of our thinking, like the ROM of a computer, and buried in deep memory in our psyche. The Sufi mystics testify to its being revealed or released, by dint of the divine operation, to the measure of one's ability to encompass its vastness, complexity, and subtlety. Sufis contrast the knowledge that God possesses of the principle of God's own being, with a further knowledge that God acquires through its exemplification in the existential realm. We humans participate holistically in this second mode of knowledge, whereas the first mode is revealed, albeit exceptionally and only as a flash, to the mystic in rare moments of exaltation.

This first mode of knowledge is ascribed to the act of intelligence, and the second to the act of consciousness. Intelligence is considered by Hazrat Inayat Khan to be the ground out of which consciousness emerges in the presence of an object. Intelligence becomes consciousness when faced with an object.

Consciousness must always be conscious of something. When consciousness is not conscious of anything, it is pure intelligence.[46]

Hazrat Inayat Khan

---

45 Davids, *Dialogues of the Buddha*, Part III, 242.
46 Inayat Khan, *The Sufi Message* series, *Philosphy, Psychology and Mysticism*, 69.

Consciousness depends upon its content, corroborating the Buddha, just as the flame is combustible. When there is no perception nor representation, consciousness recedes back into its ground; the act of intelligence takes over.

Practices

1) Take heed of the fact that, caught up in the flow of everyday life, you had let yourself be caught up in a personal vantage point, which like a lens, presents the scenario of life within a certain bent. Not only has your glance been coerced into focus by the way objects reflect or fluoresce light in the middle range, but how easily you were caught in the commonplace thinking that is taken for granted by most people. Now you will begin to see how people are caught in their perspective, and consequently, the extent to which most people suffer, albeit unwittingly, from being low-key—just as you yourself may well have slipped into being off-guard prior to this awakening.

2) If you achieve this, your mind, freed from its conceptual underpinning, can enjoy an unmediated grasp of the programming behind phenomena and occurrences. Indeed, if the physical world exhibits the features of a holograph, then the thinking behind it is holistic. This requires stretching your thinking from the commonplace mode, which thinks in discrete categories, to the mode in which the mind is able to extrapolate, to reconcile the irreconcilables, or grasp the concurrence of the incongruent.

3) If you manage to hoist yourself to an impersonal level of thinking, you will be awed by the discovery of the fact that your thinking seems to have become both all-encompassing, cosmic, and in addition, transcendent. This is due to the fact that the human mind is isomorphic (of identical nature) with the divine mind. But, of course, the more you fraction a hologram, each part, though behaving functionally like the total hologram, does so less effectively. However, it does not behave as though it were just a discrete part or fraction of the totality. This would tally with the holistic view, according to which everything is seen as interrelated in an undivided wholeness.

> *You are plurality transformed into Unity,*
> *And Unity passing into plurality.*
> *This mystery is understood when man*
> *Leaves the part and merges in the Whole.*[47]

Mahmud Shabistari

> *You will know nothing of God except that which comes from Him and which He brings into existence within you.*[48]

Muhyi ad-Din Ibn 'Arabi

---

47 Shabistari, *The Secret Rosegarden of Sa-'d ud Din Mahmud Shabistari.*
48 Chittick, *The Sufi Path of Knowledge*, 341.

However, let us bear in mind that even though our perception is constrained by our conditioning, and our thinking hackneyed, yet the know-how thus gained, although relative, is valuable. Indeed, our objective in awakening to the program behind the occurrences is also to extrapolate between the knowledge gained by the feedback of experience, with a kind of intuitive insight that reveals itself to us as we awaken.

4) Imagine that you are flying in a helicopter over the streets of New York, rather than walking in the streets. You would miss a lot of detail of the shops, etc. but grasp the overall lay of the land by which the streets are interrelated; therefore, one needs to extrapolate between both perspectives. Similarly view your problems in their context as relevant to adjoining problems, rather than confine them to your assessment, which is limited to your arbitrary delineation of the boundaries of the problem; and at the same time, bear in mind the vital issues: that which is enacted in the problem.

5) To grasp these issues, you will need to change your perspective by disidentifying with your self-image as the one involved in the problem. For this, offsetting your consciousness from its usual vantage point will not suffice. You will need to shift your personal sense of identity into identifying with your being in its cosmic and transcendent dimensions, since the seedbed of your personality is incomparably more bountiful than what comes through in your personality.

6) To achieve this, you will need to relax to the point where an impersonal will takes over from your personal will.

7) Meditating thus, you will be able to recognize that even though your problems are very real, they only make sense as functions of the programming behind them and the values behind the issues they enact. Instead of simply dismissing your personal assessment of things as illusory, endeavor to grasp the programming. Rather than being a hoax, the hardware of the universe now emerges as the very purpose of the software.

8) If you are prepared to step further afield, you will realize that the evolutionary process can proceed further in your being, spurred by the awakening attained in meditation. One can attain a monumental stature in one's realization. One can see one's past, one can anticipate the future and prepare for the future. One is deciphering the code of the universe because one is that code oneself.

III. Emotion

Buddhist Method: 3rd Stage in Satipathana

Watch your feelings without identifying with them. Watch how they arise, escalate, fade away and are replaced by new feelings. Watch how pleasant, neutral and unpleasant feelings are associated with perception (see the role of form), with covetousness, craving; gauge the bond between the central stump of your being that is the life of your life, and its existential setting, involvement in its underpinning, the contact of subject and object.[49]

There can be no doubt as to the number of cases of psychological distress that are due to the frustration of one's desires, particularly concupiscence, although there are, of course, a number of other causes of distress, such as abuse, illness, etc.

Sufi View

That eschewing desire would free one of the disappointments which beget pain is a foregone conclusion. This is the way of the ascetic, and the Buddha was an ascetic founder of an ascetic order. The very principle upon which asceticism is founded is called in India, *vairagya*, detachment. This would prove an anesthetic to preserve one from pain. But would it not alienate one from the fulfillment enjoyed by involvement in life, with all its hopes and disappointments, its challenges and hard lessons, its bewonderment and soul-searching, its fervor and misgivings, its zeal and its toll, its passion and compassion, its stress, distress, joy, and despair?

One would miss out on the sense of attainment gained by the venture of commitment to one's fellow beings, struggling in the drama of life, sharing similar fates, subject to the same dangers, trying to live up to their values; struggling for self-esteem, the confrontation with iniquity, the solidarity with those who are victims of their erring; the humility stemming from repentance, the pride of steadfastness, the discovery of sacredness amongst the poor in spirit, upholding belief in an ultimate meaningfulness and goodness despite proof of the contrary. Moreover, one would lose the privilege of sharing all that has been gained by the bounty of our civilizations: the legacy of our temples, palaces, cathedrals, symphonies, technology, inventions, our inroads into the sub-atomic and outer space, medicine, our social institutions, the inexorable advance of our understanding in wresting the intelligence behind the marvel of our universe, and our chance of contributing further to our pioneering and creative spirit by putting ourselves on the line!

Indeed, how could we avail the universe of the bounty lying in wait in the deep strata of our being, unless we put it to the test of the tune, rhythm, consonances and dissonances of the symphony of life?

The concurrence with Buddhism comes to light when one sees how easily one gets oneself involved in the proverbial tempest in a teacup. Furthermore, we react, rather than acting out of an awareness of the ideals of our deeper

---

49 See Davids, *Dialogues of the Buddha, Part III*, 216.

self. Perhaps the clue is in the discrimination between the quest for joy and the quest for felicity. The Sufi dervishes do practice *rida*, equanimity, which is often paralleled with the Buddhist *samatha vipassana*, imperturbability; *adab*, nobility in emotional sensitivity; and also *akhlaq Allah*, the divine manner, as the conditions conducive to manifesting 'ishq Allah, divine love.

The difference lies in the fact that the Sufis unfailingly ascribe emotions to their source, divine emotion; and they consider that the divine emotion is constrained, defiled and distorted at the scale of the individual. One is always seeing, experiencing, feeling things from the diametrically opposite vantage point to one's own. But is this not what Buddhists do when consciousness is no longer the consciousness of an *I*? Or where the Buddha refers to uncoupling the central aspect of one's being, illustrated by the stump of the tree, from the samsaric aspect of one's being, illustrated by that part of the tree that appears above the ground?

According to the Sufis, the emotion that one limits within the confines of the scope of one's consciousness, is the personal dimension of what is divine emotion at a cosmic scale. The mystic encompasses this overwhelming emotion when carried beyond the self by divine ecstasy.

Divinity is the exaltation of the human soul.[50]

Hazrat Inayat Khan

Buddhism: 3rd Vipassana Jhana

The Buddha points out that as one reaches further awakening, one develops an enhanced sensitivity to the quality of emotion enlisted, eschewing vulgar emotions, and fostering sublime and noble emotions. Emotions become more and more noble as consciousness becomes increasingly cosmic. And the demeanor and way of behaving and handling circumstances reflect this sublimation of emotions in the adept.

At this stage, since one's joy is not dependent upon favorable circumstances anymore, one has freed oneself from the suffering resulting from unfavorable circumstances; and one is not constrained by one's personal likes or prejudices. According to the Buddha, this is the destruction, or in some cases, catharsis of even the residue of the manias. An untrammeled felicity arises spontaneously from deeper impersonal roots of one's being, protected by one's detachment and imperturbability. The Buddha testifies to feeling this sense of beatitude even in the body. Evidence that Buddhism does not prescribe an escape from real life into a samadhi state, nor discard the body, is to be found in the emphasis in making one's realization or attunement corporeal:

50 Inayat Khan, *The Complete Sayings of Hazrat Inayat Khan*, 170.

And his very body does he so pervade and infuse, drench, permeate and suf-fuse with the joy and ease born of the serenity of concentration, that there is no spot in his whole frame which is not suffused therewith.[51]

The Buddha

To illustrate the difference between joy and felicity: information is built up at the cost of energy, whereas transcendental knowledge is vouchsafed as a grace. Just so, joy is built by the work of creating favorable circumstances, which, whether physical or psychic, require a lot of painstaking care and may collapse in the storms to which we humans are exposed; whereas felicity, which requires no mortgage in the world, is vouchsafed to those who make no demands upon people or circumstances, but prepare themselves to receive the illumination of the clear light of bliss.

This condition is attained by dint of a paradoxical combination of unruffled coolheadedness, which results from having attained freedom within oneself and a higher liberty, and unconditional love, with which one irradiates all sentient beings, starting with those close to one, then further and further, until one embraces the whole world up to its confines.

The Brahma Viharas

1) No doubt, the condition for the outreach of unconditional love is an unwavering endurance regarding people's treatment of you, so as to neutralize your inborn conditioning that makes for resentment, which can develop into hatred. As a consequence, the love that springs from acquired inner freedom bursts forth as an irresistible disarming power, which neutralizes the hostility in beings who suddenly find themselves discovering this self-same cosmic love in the depths of their own being.

2) At a further stage, love manifests as compassion, which must not be confused with pity, since it springs forth spontaneously from the liberated being rather than being a reaction when confronted with suffering, which is the case with pity.

3) The felicity that is aroused by this gift of oneself, merging into those who seemed other than oneself while one was still caught in self-identification, is then communicated to them as an antidote to their suffering.

4) Finally, that which started at the satipathana stage as a protective strategy against the manias, proves to be the ultimate positive power: serenity that gains ground as it spreads like an undaunted, restorative, ever-widening eddy in a perturbed world, reaching human beings from inside.

---

51 Davids, *Dialogues of the Buddha, Part I*, 85.

Sufi Practices

1) Try to encompass the emotion that became the universe, that manifested as a flower or a crystal or a falcon or a deer. Imagine an emotion manifesting as a being, like the emotion of a composer manifesting as a symphony.

Think of some of the succulents in the desert that might take many years to build up enough sugar to be able to burst forth as a flower. Suddenly, within a few hours, the plant has succeeded in manifesting its impending glory in a plethora of colors in the form of a flower. And a few hours after that, the petals fall and the plant has died. A perfect example of a moment of glory! Then the seed remains, and the perfume is diffused in the atmosphere. Can you imagine the nostalgia of that plant to express the splendor that was invested in it, and the limitations within which it could express that splendor? It can't move very much, bound by its roots, and the only way it can express that splendor is by colors and by shapes. Within its own species, that form has been elaborated over eons of time. You feel that nostalgia towards manifestation overcoming all the constraints and obstacles in order to break through in a moment of glory.

2) Now honor your intuition that behind all this, there is great splendor; and that you are born out of the divine nostalgia to manifest that splendor in as many ways as possible; and you are one of the ways. Accept the divinity of your being, manifesting as the beauty of your personality. Be wary of a sense of false humility that can prove self-denigrating and self-defeating.

3) In the light of the Sufi view that the existential world is the materialization of the divine emotion, can you feel the emotion that has become your being as emotion at the cosmic scale?

IV. Personality and Its Processes

Buddhist Method: 4th Stage of Satipathana

1) Observe your personality without identification, as though it could be the personality of another person. It will now appear to you as a compound of idiosyncrasies inherited from the psyche of your ancestors, hailing right back into the elementary psyches of primitive species. If you limit your identity to being the observer, this composition of idiosyncrasies is a transient formation, fortuitously offered to you by the universe, irrespective of your *I* in the same way as your body and your mind. It is obviously conditioned, and therefore, left to its own devices it will display primitive behavior.

2) This way of looking at things is useful in dealing with pain. See the pain that comes through identification and attachment. If it is your personality that is distressed, by disidentifying with that personality, you will build a buffer between you and that which is distressed; and thus you will not be

involved in the pain. This is the Buddhist *samatha vipassana*: unshakable calm gained by non-attachment to the self-image.

3) You cannot control this personality and its processes if you identify with it, but by adopting this attitude, you may watch it objectively, work with it, console and admonish it.

Sufi Method

For the Sufis, our personality does not simply inherit from our ancestors, but also features our divine inheritance. Or, if you prefer an alternate terminology: if indeed the universe is of the nature of a hologram, every fragment potentially carries the software of the totality, yet somewhat diminished. The ancestral heredity is one factor in the cosmic inheritance that we carry.

Practices

1) We observed awakening to the divine investiture gently stirring in the flower. Now, giving vent to the splendor invested in your being by raising your emotion to a high attunement, and by spurring your intelligence to beat its records by manifesting and actuating it, be aware of the divine nostalgia that beckons you into becoming the fulfillment of the divine purpose.

2) Therefore, instead of thinking of yourself as a person, think of yourself as the fulfillment of the divine purpose. Or let us say you are one of the stages moving towards that fulfillment; for example, Leonardo da Vinci would draw a number of different sketches before making the final picture. So think of yourself, in your present condition, as one of the sketches leading up to the perfect picture whereby God finds fulfillment of God's own Being.

3) Try to earmark the qualities that are attempting to come through at the personality level, like power, compassion, truthfulness, etc. These did not appear so distinctly in the mineral, nor in the plant, although sometimes one begins to observe some features of compassion or humor in the animal. It then becomes clear that as evolution advances, these qualities, whose archetypes one may grasp at a lofty level of meditation, are able to manifest and actuate themselves increasingly as evolution marches forward.

Buddhism: 4th Vipassana Jhana

How does one's personality, or the personalities of others, appear when consciousness has been carried beyond the point where it is functioning as an individual vantage point?

1) Disengage the central principle of your being, as illustrated by the stump of a tree, from the existential outgrowth of your being, by standing apart from it and observing it objectively and dispassionately, bereft of the emotions aroused by identifying with it.

2) Realize that your psyche or personality are not located in space or constrained in time. You could be anywhere or nowhere. Besides, you are not limited by your individual idiosyncrasies.

Sufi Method

1) A Sufi would say that we are invested with the infinite, many-splendored, bountiful qualities that manifest in the whole universe.

Even as you can only experience the consciousness of the crystal by imagining what it would be like to be a crystal, or a flower by imagining what it would be like to be a flower, experience the feeling of the universe by imagining what it would be like to be the universe, by discovering yourself *in* the universe, and then *as* the universe.

2) We have, in the earlier stages of this meditation, come to value what a privilege it is to be human and to be evolving as a human being towards the next step in the evolutionary march, which may be seen as awakening into the higher levels of our being—that is, of the universe.

3) Behind your wishes, your involvement in existence, your creativity, and your appreciation of the value of the bounty of the universe, discover the divine nostalgia to manifest and actuate a vision of splendor. This occurs through inexhaustible fleeting formations, constructions, and phenomena. While normally actuated in the form of our motivations, it not only becomes restricted by the narrowness of our scope when constrained within our personal consciousness, but is distorted by any greed or unkindness.

V. The Transit Beyond Consciousness

Buddhist Method

As we have seen, the breakthrough marking the passage between the satipathana practices and the vipassana jhanas takes place when consciousness has been carried beyond the boundaries of the personal vantage point, circumscribed by our notion of ourselves as discrete individuals.

1) Watch your consciousness watching an object. Clearly we have been withdrawing our sense of identity further and further back from all those aspects of ourselves with which we identified: body, feelings, personality, and now, from the personal vantage point of consciousness. We have seen that in Buddhism our personal consciousness is likened to a flame that can only maintain itself if there is something combustible. This means identification with perception and conception; being transient and perishable, it cannot be *I*. What this means is that our sense of being the knower or witness extends to an impersonal dimension of which, according to the Sufis, our consciousness is a focalization.

2) When one achieves this, it becomes clear that to perform the satipathana practices, one needed from the start to overcome one's identification with being the personal observer. It seems that we could have proceeded by an alternative method by first disidentifying with the personal observer and then with the observed: body, mind, personality, etc. However, our body and personal identity would have stood in the way. Therefore, let us consider the stages of satipathana as preparatory, leading up to the great breakthrough at the fourth stage.

Sufi Method

This is where Buddhism and Sufism concur. For the Sufi, we can never be the observer; it is God who is the Witness. What we may think is our *I* is simply the extension of the divine *I* as the ultimate witness. Since Buddhism does not posit the existence of God, or even the consciousness of the universe as a whole, one cannot, in the language of Buddhism, assume that our consciousness is a focalization of the cosmic consciousness, as Sufis do. More precisely, in some Sufi views, the personal vantage point of our consciousness is the focalization of the divine perspective. For others, it is only the reflection of the divine *I*.

Buddhist View: 4th Vipassana Jhana

How does consciousness appear when it has been freed from its constraint? One reaches a deeper zone of one's being, more permanent, like the stump of a tree which, having been hacked down, could manifest in a form different from its previous configuration.

Having disengaged this central principle of yourself from its existential projection by dismissing the supports of consciousness, (*vitakka*, perception and *viccara*, conception), having carried consciousness beyond the purview of the personal focal point of consciousness, the memory of the cosmic dimension of one's being reemerges.

Proceeding thus, you will find yourself at the threshold between day consciousness and sleep; skirting the unconscious, you will be naturally carried beyond normal consciousness into prenatal and pre-conceptual states.

The Buddha refers to heavens of pure forms; he even refers to conversing with gods or angels,[52] recognizing the celestial sphere to which they belong and the corresponding jhana state.[53]

It will be tempting to try this; however, be careful not to let yourself confuse the genuine experience with projected apparitions.

---

52 See Carus, *Gospel of the Buddha*, 168.
53 See Davids, *Dialogues of the Buddha, Part III*, 242–243.

Sufi View

As we have seen, the Sufi view is a complementary view to the Buddhist one described above, since Sufis considers their consciousness as focalizing or mirroring the divine consciousness, and therefore, at the passive end of the divine act of cognizance.

In God's descent from the solitude of unknowing, God, (i) in a first emanation (*fayd aqdas*) discovers God's Self in the essence behind the reflection. (ii) At the second stage (*fayd muqaddas*), God reveals God's Self through beings who exemplify this essence, which manifests when qualified by archetypal attributes. (iii) In a further descent, those qualities assume forms in beings.

If you set your consciousness so that it mirrors the consciousness that God has of God's Self through you, then you will follow that reflection in the opposite direction.

1) Discover, through and in the form of your body and the forms of the world, a clue to the archetype of what it is the exemplar—namely, the form that God assumes in and through you. Think that the divine imagination coming through as your imagination is continually translating the divine emotion, diversifying as the cosmic principles into progressively evolving formations in your celestial bodies, and solidifying in your physical body. See how the same applies to the forms of the world you perceive as outside, including that which transpires through them.

2) See, in the idiosyncrasies of your personality, the clue as to which divine attributes are invested in you, of which your personality is an exemplar. Infer the same regarding the personalities of fellow beings or the qualities configuring matter. Your inherent sense of analogy will enlist your ability to transpose the forms back into their archetypes (*ta'wil*).

3) This will lead you into recalling your angelic counterpart: not only the sublime, celestial environment, but your celestial countenance.

4) Let your consciousness mirror the divine consciousness. In this perspective, discover the divine consciousness discovering itself as the spectator. You will realize that the Divine Being can only become the spectator by projecting God as your consciousness and actuating God's Being as the object of God's own discovery in the form of your body and the idiosyncrasies of your personality. And reciprocally, you can only know God by the way God manifests as you.

He who knows himself, knows his Lord.[54]

Prophet Muhammad

---

54 Hadith.

One may recognize here four steps:

1) First imagine that you are the observer, and what you observe is just the projection of a reality that can never be the object of your observation, because it is beyond form and is really the meaningfulness latent in the subjective pole of our being. The only clue to this reality is that it consists, at one level, of the archetypes of what you are experiencing, so that you are experiencing the exemplars of it.

2) As a further step, grasp the intention (or the Intentioner) behind occurrences, which is delegated, and hence, shared in your will by the grace of free will. Therefore, insofar as that intention is customized in your intention, you become aware of it.

3) Envision your consciousness as mirroring the divine consciousness, considered as the antipodal pole of your consciousness at infinity, watching this projection of that reality; whereas in your personal vantage point, you would take the picture to be the reality. By mirroring this view, it will now strike you as the complementary view to your personal one. You will now realize that reality is discovering itself through your discovery of it, through yourself.

4) However, there is a still further mode of knowledge: the knowledge that God has of the principle of Divine Being, regardless of the cognizance acquired by discovering what accrues when the metaphors are actuated in existence, which is a secondary or derived mode of cognizance. According to the Sufis, God enjoys the option of existing or not existing.

God is independent of the worlds.[55]

Qur'an

This realization figures as the fourth awakening in the arupa jhanas of Buddhism.

The knowledge that God acquires of God's own Self as an essence ('ayn) in all eternity, can never be grasped by the human pole of the antinomy of consciousness. Nor can it be captured by the act of mirroring, as described earlier. But according to al-Hallaj, an-Niffari and other Sufis, a flash of it may be revealed when least expected, in an instant of time; but it resists any effort on the part of the mystic to hold or possess it.

Sufis call it the secret of secrets (*sirr as-sirr*) and the mystery (*al-ghayb*) encountered when one is faced with the dilemma of intelligence and the concatenation of events. For this, one needs to discard all one's acquired knowledge. Yet paradoxically, one has to acquire the kind of knowledge that

---

55 III: 97.

can be acquired, before dismissing it as inadequate; otherwise, one could not know how to discard it. As Hazrat Inayat Khan says, one's conception of God is a stepping stone toward the experience of God.[56]

One needed to first build and then destroy the idol whose purpose has been fulfilled.

As we awaken, we explore levels of the universe unthought of before: beyond the physical realm, the celestial planes, the subtle bodies.

Instead of simply offsetting consciousness from the physical plane, Sufis try to view the physical world from the perspective of the celestial planes.

The next level above the physical at which they can be captured, is the plane of metaphor (*'alam al-mithal*), the level at which we discover the archetypes, of which physical reality is the exemplification. At this level, by the act of creative imagination, we grasp the primordial image.

The world of Idea-Images, the world of apparitional forms and of bodies in the subtle state...the intermediary between the world of pure spiritual realities, the world of Mystery, and the visible sensible world.[57]

Henry Corbin

Professor Corbin points out that attaching too much importance to sensory reality will obstruct our ability to grasp the archetypes behind it. No sooner does one touch upon this level of realization, than things begin to reveal their meaning.

We must remember that in Sufism, the usual perspective is reversed; everything is envisioned as it might be seen from the divine point of view. This sudden reversal of perspective can seem to be puzzling and paradoxical.

You will know nothing of God except that which comes from Him and which He brings into existence within you, either as inspiration or the unveiling of a self-disclosure.[58]

Muhyi ad-Din Ibn 'Arabi

We have, through the stages of this meditation, come to value what a privilege it is to be evolving as a human being toward the next step in the evolutionary march: awakening into the consciousness of the universe.

Spiritual attainment is to be conscious of the Perfect One, who is formed in the heart.[59]

Hazrat Inayat Khan

---

56 Inayat Khan, *Song of the Prophets*, 81.
57 Corbin, *Creative Imagination in the Sufism of Ibn 'Arabi*, 217.
58 Chittick, *The Sufi Path of Knowledge*, 341.
59 Inayat Khan, *The Complete Sayings of Hazrat Inayat Khan*, 67.

Chapter Six
Kabbalah

The Sephirotic Tree

At first glance, a meditator would be inclined to consider the Sephirotic Tree of the Kabbalah as a convenient mapping of states experienced in meditation. It might also provide a topography of the psychological area covered by meditators, plotting pathways that could prove useful. However, upon actually practicing it, the meditator discovers that Kabbalah represents the nostalgia of the Jewish mystic for the living and transforming presence of God—the same God as in the theology of the Talmud, but brought closer by the sheer power of mystical love, and experienced by a judicious manipulation of the human mind carried beyond its limits.

The origin of the Kabbalah is attributed to the inspiration and power of a prophetic figure in Judaism, Simeon bar Yochaii, known as the Holy Lamp. Kabbalah runs as a cryptic, and not always approved tradition, through the Middle Ages in Palestine, and then Spain. It attained its ultimate flowering in another prophetic figure, Abulafia, in the thirteenth century, a disciple of the famous Jewish philosopher, Moses Maimonides, whom he quotes as saying: *The only cognizance is the divine revelation in the course of mystic ecstasy, intentionally provoked.*

In its middle range, the mind grasps the more obvious connections between data; this occurs as the mind grows from one thought to another by the psychological process of association of ideas. However, by stretching the mind, says Abulafia, the soul jumps (*delug*) from one zone of associations to another, and thus it is hoisted from one sphere of thought to another, widening the field of consciousness until it reaches an infinite dimension and discovers its affinity with the divine.

Rather than thinking of ecstasy as a state that can be reached by dint of human effort,[1] Maimonides held the Sufi view that as the mystic exults in

---

1 In Latin *ex stasis* means *beyond the usual state.*

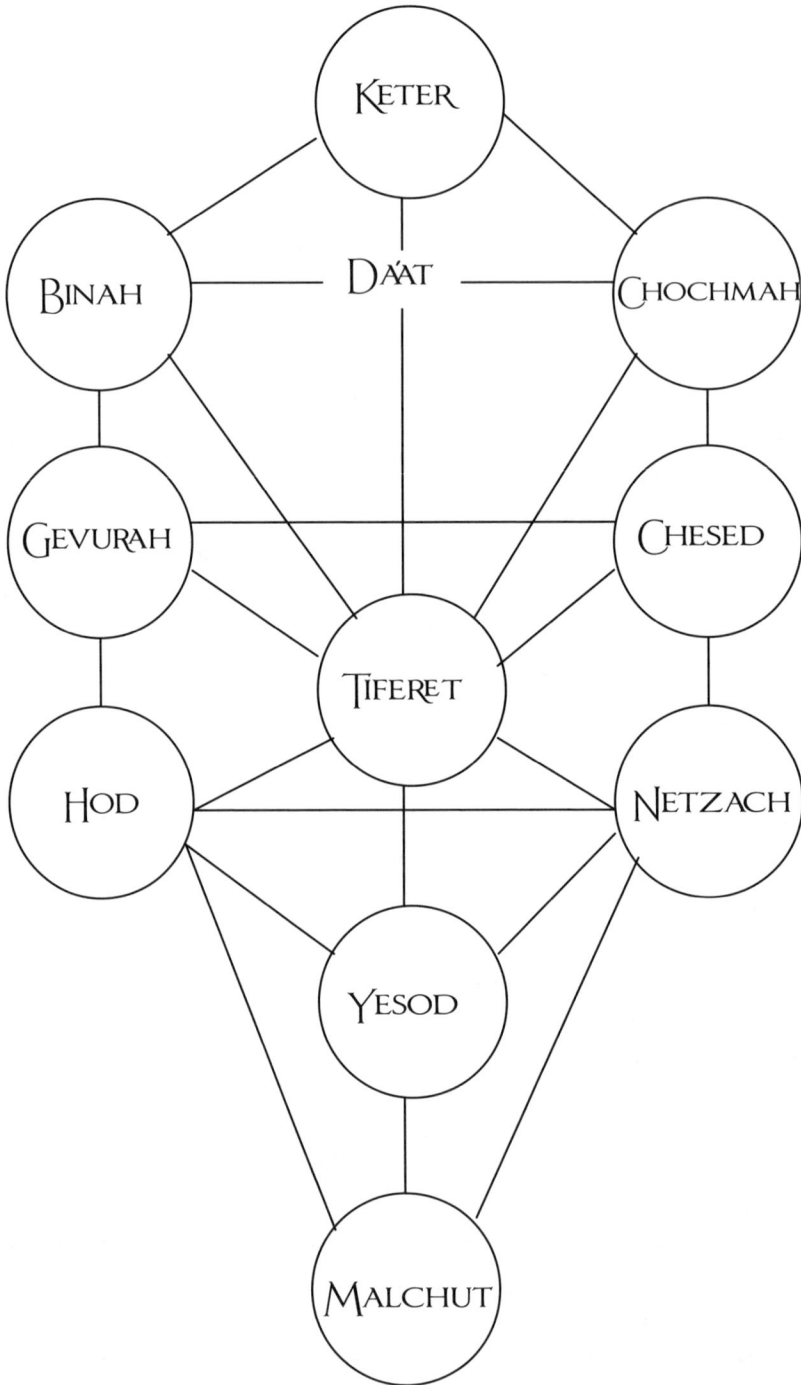

The Sephirotic Tree

love for God, the mystic discovers that one is just reciprocating God's love for oneself. In this passive state, the mind is able to respond to what Avicenna (Ibn Sina) defined as the *intellectus agens*, a hypostasis of God as pure intelligence.

Since the intelligence organizing the universe configures our language, and more especially, the very letters of the alphabet, by penetrating into the meanings conveyed by these letters, the mind is able to hoist itself above its usual field of understanding. Thus in the esoteric science of *tserouf*, the Kabbalists combine and permute these letters, grasping a connection between *sephar*, the number (or an alphabetical letter considered as a cypher, as in physics, for example); *sipour*, discursive logic; and *sephor*, the written word (according to the *Sepher Yetzira*).

For the mind to soar, the thoughts upon which it rides need to be made more and more abstract, increasingly devoid of their physical implications, which are secondary effects. The principle is to transcend the letter by the spirit. This progressive technique enables the mind to free itself from its infrastructure, just as a composer may defy the more harmonious consonances by transiting into dissonances that challenge the ears, the mind, and even the soul, beyond comfortable complacency.

Both Simeon bar Yochaii and Abulafia suffered persecution. Sixty-eight years after the Roman legions under Emperor Titus had destroyed the temple at Jerusalem in the year 70 CE, and forbidden the Jews to observe their religious rituals, Simeon, known for his stalwart refusal to compromise, was sent as ambassador to Rome to plead for the right of the Jews to celebrate their rituals. According to the chronicles, a miracle saved his life: he gained the favour of Emperor Antonin by exorcising his daughter. However, the governor later condemned Simeon to death. He and his son Eleazar sought refuge in a cave near Safed in Palestine, and to avoid detection, spent the whole day buried in the sand up to their necks. It is said that it was in these conditions that the *Zohar, the Book of Splendor*, was conceived; but it was not before the end of the thirteenth century that it was put together by the hand of Moses de Leon, and only published three centuries later.

Abulafia attempted to have an audience with Pope Nicholas III, who condemned him to be burned alive. Undaunted, Abulafia traveled to Rome, and at the very moment that he crossed through the city walls, the pope died suddenly.

The word *Kabbalah* owes its etymology to the root KBL, which means *to receive*. It contrasts with the Torah, the written law conferred upon Moses on Mount Sinai. Kabbalah is the oral message, *Kibbel*, that he received. Consequently, it benefits by having a margin of interpretation. A parallel between the

Islamic *shari'a* and the mystical *ta'wil* interpretation of the Qur'an is quite striking.

The long-standing interface between Islam and Judaism deserves our attention. During the flowering of Kabbalah in the eleventh and twelfth centuries, Kabbalists and Hassidim frequented the *khanaqas* of the Sufi mystics of Baghdad. Bahya ibn Paquda's *Duties of the Heart* bears the unmistakable imprint of the Sufi exhortations of the time, although he has reservations about the self-annihilation found amongst some Sufi ascetics.[2] While the Crusaders were besieging Jerusalem, a large number of Jews fled to Cairo, fostering a Jewish-Sufi movement; they were, no doubt, encouraged by the progressive philosophy of Moses Maimonides, and even more so, by the influence of his son, Abraham Maimonides, whose attachment to Sufis is known. The Jewish Sufis found in Sufism, a restoration of practices that had been prevalent in Israel in former times.[3] Abraham Maimonides is quoted as having said, in reference to the Sufis: *The latter imitate the Prophets (of Israel) and walk in their footsteps.*[4] But it was in the *Al-Maqalat al-Hawdiya* (*The Treatise of the Pool*), authored by 'Obadyah b. Abraham b. Moses Maimonides, the grandson of the renowned philosopher, that deep familiarity with precepts reserved only for Sufi initiates evidences an initiatic affiliation with a Sufi order. The treatise describes, in true Sufi vein, the *maqamat*, the stages in the journey of the Sufi initiate, rather on the lines of 'Abdallah Ansari's *Kitab at-Tamkin fisharh Manāzil as-sa'irin* (*Book of Waystations for the Wayfarers*).

While this Jewish Sufi movement was flourishing in Egypt, the structure of the Sephirotic Tree was being formulated in Spain by Moses b. Nachman, Ezra b. Salomon, Isaac the Blind, and Gikatilla. Reference to the Tree of Life, which gave rise to the Sephirotic Tree, first surfaced in the Kabbalist school of Narbonne, in Southern France, in the eleventh century, in a controversial book called *Bahir*. There can be no doubt that the Kabbalists were seeking to cohere the intangible, perennial Jewish mystical thought into guidelines for those in search of a method for their meditations. The tour de force they attempted was tantamount to illuminating their intuition with the grasp that our understanding proves unable to fathom.

First let us familiarize ourselves with the significance and attunements of the Sephirot with respect to our experience of the corresponding state in meditation. For the theoretical and traditional background of these, we refer the reader to a number of excellent books listed in the Selected Bibliography.

---

2 Another example of this interest is to be found in Isaac Albalag's translation of al-Ghazali's *Maqasid al-falasifa*.

3 See Maimonides, *The Treatise of the Pool.*

4 Ibid., 4.

The following interpretations must necessarily be subjective and personal, since they are based on experience.

The following is a classical rendering of the mysterious Tree, but its interpretation varies by wide margins. There are also several ways of using it as a wayfarer's guide: (i) we could starting from *Keter* and zigzag down; (ii) we could start with *Malchut* and zigzag upwards, which makes more sense; (iii) we could bypass the bifurcations and move up in a straight line; (iv) alternately, we could move down in a straight line; or, what I advocate personally, we could descend along the left branch and rise along the right branch, while bearing in mind the central trunk throughout the process.

If we consider the Sephirotic Tree as depicting guidelines for the contemplative, then let us envision a tree upside-down. The root is divine transcendence; the trunk is flanked with branches bifurcating right and left, representing a basic antinomy of bounty and restriction until we reach the culmination, which represents the existential realm Malchut—divine immanence. The junctures in the Tree feature the stages in the descent, from the initial stage of all-potentiality, into their actuation in real-life situations.

We can identify five phases in this descent, which correspond with our experience in meditation.

i) Of course, the pristine splendor of the heavens lies beyond our reach in the *Ein-Sof*, the ineffable void, the immaterial palace in which God remains eternally unattainable; albeit, it is out of this non-being that all being emerges. Yet at the outset, the mark of the oneness presiding over all multiplicity or becoming prevails at the root of the Tree: the state, or sephira, called *Keter*.

(ii) Realization, or capturing a sense of meaningfulness. The intention motivating the existential state, this level is called *Atzilut*, emanation, because intelligence in the creature is an extension of the divine intelligence, and therefore, not *other than God*, which is sometimes considered in theology to be the status of Creation.

(iii) The orderliness or harmony of the universe. For the Sufis this embodies the divine nostalgia for excellence in our dedication to safeguard order against entropy. The term *Briyah* is used here, since it is considered that the order of the universe is a secondary reality.

(iv) Actuating this springhead of life, guided by our sense of aesthetics and reason, to build a beautiful world. The term *Yetzirah* applied here signifies the formative process whereby the order of the universe is gelled into forms that give clues as to the nature of that order, including the forms of all living beings, all living things;

(v) The actuality reflecting all the above within the limitation of existential conditions (in Kabbalah, *tsimtsum*), constricting circumstances whereby the possible is actuated. Here the word *Assiyah* is used to mark the action and the transformation that the existential state gives rise to.

The above principles unfurl into ten archetypes, called *Sephirot*, which are all aspects dedicated to the One and only Being.

Keter: signifying the crown, is experienced in the state of awakening when one grasps the unity, or the unifying principle, behind the many-splendored bounty in the multiplicity that is actuated at the existential level, which seems remote in the perspective of the contemplative.

Chochmah: the divine intelligence, of which we become aware when we realize that if we have any understanding of the universe, it is because we think the way the universe thinks. This is, as we have seen, an inborn inherent knowledge, not based upon experience. But we match the feedback of experience with this archetypal built-in substratum, just like the ROM of computer software matches the RAM.[5] The quality ascribed to this sephira is intuition.

Binah: our intelligence becomes focalized in our consciousness when we perceive and interpret an object, or assess a situation. In this manner, the divine intelligence functioning in the creature becomes constricted (*tsimtsum*). However, according to the Sufis, the mode of cognizance gained by this focalization of the one intelligence into infinite focal centers of consciousness, accrues to the divine mind. The quality ascribed to this sephira is insight, acuity.

Da'at: the mysterious, occult principle and juncture, not always acknowledged as a sephira, is the link between cognizance and sovereignty. Therefore, while Chochmah and Binah converge in Da'at, to which omniscience is ascribed, it is the key to the antinomy *Chesed-Gevurah*, representing sovereignty as a guarantee to safeguard the harmony governing the universe against chaos or entropy. Da'at embodies the prestigious congruence presiding eternally over all phenomena. The reason for its having been kept secret is that whosoever has reached it enjoys a spiritual power that could be abused unless the contemplative has the vocation of a consecrated knight. This is experienced by the contemplative when in sync with this harmony; any aberration is considered as the necessary dissolution of all formations to ensure that the harmony be dynamic rather than static. Since Da'at extrapolates between Chochmah and Binah, thus including the experiential mode of knowledge, it denotes a radical landmark transiting into Atzilut, where

5 Read Only Memory (ROM) and Random Access Memory (RAM).

knowledge is vouchsafed by sovereignty (in Chesed and Gevurah); thus it never figures on the Tree where Kether is highlighted. The quality ascribed to this sephira is supremacy.

Chesed or *Gedula*: represents the power of love that prevails over compulsion and manifests as grace. For the Sufis, it is at this stage that the contemplative's heart feels the divine nostalgia, the cosmic springhead behind all created things. The quality ascribed to this sephira is magnanimity, compassion.

Gevurah or *Din*: power, the deployment of energy to ensure the actuation of the divine programming. At this stage, the contemplative discovers the role of discipline, of rigor, of fortitude working in the very mechanism of the universe, and perceived in oneself as though invested with power, invested with the onus of ensuring the government of the world. The quality ascribed to this sephira is mastery.

Tiferet: Here we encounter a further principle in the descent: affirming sacredness in the midst of the profanity that ensues from the abuse of free-will in life. Tiferet has often been described as the sanctuary in the Holy of Holies of the Temple. It marks a transition, a threshold between the sacred and the profane, the divine and the human. In the course of our ascent through the sephirotic pathways, this is where we encounter a test: only if we are willing to make some sacrifice of our personal greed or worldliness do we have access into the higher sephirot. In the course of our descent along the labyrinth of pathways, we are sworn to recollect our covenant with God as we enter the battle of life.

Of course, in the descent, at the level of Yetzirah it is the objective (teleology) that determines the antinomy, namely the crystallization of these principles in form. Hence *Netzach*, *Hod* and *Yesod* form an inverted triangle: it is the confluence of emotion and reason that makes for creativity.

Netzach: represents the splendor of the heavenly spheres reflected in our quest for beauty in form or structure, aesthetics, glorification, the triumph of excellence over mediocrity. The quality ascribed to this sephira is beauty.

Hod: represents the cohering impact of reason and logic upon all formative processes, the mathematical laws presiding over the configuration of matter—the symphony of the spheres. There is something sacrosanct about these laws which reflect the divine programming; it fills the one discovering them with awe. The quality ascribed to this sephira is wisdom—sophia, the wisdom of the earth.

Yesod: is the template, the seminal etheric mold, not only determining the forms of the world, but insuring their perennity, and at the same time, uniqueness, by replication or reproduction. The contemplative realizes that it is one's own idiosyncratic originality that constitutes the objective of the whole process of existentiation; because, thanks to diversification, the constituents of the whole may cooperate by completing each other in the interest of enriching the whole. The quality ascribed to this sephira is creativity.

Malchut: All the above principles are manifested and actuated in the existential state. It is the realm whereby the unknown, virtual God becomes the King of the Universe, the King of Kings whose sovereignty is vouchsafed by our fealty or suzerainty. The quality is loyalty, fealty.

Practices

1) The journey commences by reinstating your allegiance to the sovereignty of what may be called the spiritual government of the world. In the Jewish tradition, it is a recollection of the covenant made between God and Moses on Mount Sinai, sealed in the lightning and thunder; or of Abraham with God, sealed by the rainbow. In Islam, the Covenant sealed in eternity, *Azaliyat*, links all humans to God in a pledge of allegiance, which establishes the relative autonomy of humanity. At this stage, gauge the balance between your destiny or conditioning, and your free will.

2) At the next step, corresponding to Yesod, identify with your etheric body, which survives the dissolution of your physical body, like the river that survives the transiency of the water; or information that survives the collapse of its energetic underpinning.

3) Now in the station of Hod, try to grasp the programming behind matter. This is where the paradigms of present-day physics could lend themselves as meditation themes, conveying a sense of the extraordinary ingenuity of the software behind all physical phenomena. You may sense the same in the very functioning of the cells of your body.

4) At the next stage, Netzach, you will gauge what physicists call the *elegance* (rather than the ingenuity), not only in the somatic structures, but the very organization of physical functions that strike you as aesthetically beautiful. This cannot be assessed by your intellect, but by your emotions. It will, therefore, spark a sense of exaltation at the discovery of the emotion at a cosmic scale that has gelled into these functions and forms. You will be participating in an act of glorification.

5) The very act of glorification will convey to you a sense of the sacred. You may even visualize this as access to the Holy of Holies, represented by Tiferet, and honor your need for the sacred. But you will realize that for this to be an authentic and transforming experience, you will have to make a pledge, which does, of necessity, entail a sacrifice. It will occur to you that

religious ceremonies are endeavoring to enact precisely what is happening to you experientially.

6) It is only after having taken this test, considered as an initiation, and having undergone a marked transformation, that you will feel ready to fulfill the covenant with which you commenced your inner journey: namely, to qualify as a vice-regent or knight to take action in insuring the orderliness of the realm within your jurisdiction in your life's circumstances. You will discover the very dilemma facing all those in a position of authority: the balance between severity and magnanimity—Gevurah and Chesed. Paradoxically, while it is at the station of Assiyah (Malchut) that action is ascribed, you will find that to be able to act appropriately you need to attune to Gevurah and Chesed, and thus become aware of the investiture of sovereignty sealed at the level of Da'at.

7) Now comes the moment when it occurs to you to what extent it is your realization that is the key to your action, beyond any power you may wield. You will gauge the difference between your intuition, Chochmah, and the know-how gained by experience, Binah. Beyond this antinomy, you sense an awakening into access to the divine intention behind all occurrences: Keter. It will defy your reason and sense of justice.

8) Consequently, you will have to cleave to the flashes of divine revelation in the dark night of your understanding, and even deeper, into the night of unknowing, where your sense of identity is shattered in the discovery of the unity behind all multiplicity.

9) Now, having familiarized yourself with these different stations, descend through the sephirot on the left side, one by one, experiencing the way the divine perfection is constricted in your being as you focus increasingly upon the existential sphere. Having become aware of your incarnate style, and having renewed your covenant, ascend up the sephirot of the right side and experience the liberating effect, the cosmic dimension gained in your self-image, and finally, the transcendence.

10) Having mastered these stages, descend in a straight line through the trunk of the Tree, and see how your realization will confer upon you authority; and your allegiance to the sacred value behind the profane will make you creative, and thus free you from conditioning and confer a sense of mean-ingfulness and fulfillment to your life.

The Hekhalot

The discovery within yourself of the divine aspects symbolized by the sephirot will entrench you introspectively unless, while you attune to one aspect or another, you echo the condition of heavenly beings immersed in the condition you are now experiencing. Therefore, a parallel is sometimes drawn between the Kabbalah and the Hekhalot which describes the heavenly spheres as envisioned in the Jewish angelology. On deeper observation, a correspondence transpires between the sephirot (with the exception of the three sephirot reaching to Atzilut) and the heavenly spheres.

The seventh heavenly sphere, called *Araboth*, corresponding to the sephira Chesed, is described as a realm of pure vibration. Each new born soul creates an eddy on the surface of this ocean of vibration, which spreads throughout the whole expanse of space. This sphere is presided over by the Ancient of Days, whose name is *Yah*, and who rides in the cloud of unknowing, and is watched over by the four *Hayoth* referred to by Ezekiel, representing cardinal principles that were later reflected in the Christian evangelists. The archetypal seminal seeds of all things pervade this sphere.

But at the sixth sphere, called *Makhon*, is found the treasury[6] where these values are assigned. Therefore, this sphere is paralleled with the sephira Gevurah or Din, where cosmic principles are solidified by dint of rigor, of law. The particular attunement of this sphere conveys a sense of immaculate rigidity. The vibrations of the seventh sphere are fossilized into crystals. The divine sovereignty that governs the world is safeguarded at this level mainly by four archangels: Mikhael, Gabriel, Raphael and Oriel.

At the fifth sphere, called *Maon* (abode), corresponding to Tiferet, the primeval vibrations break into luminous effulgence, sparkling flashes of colors. This sphere is presided over by four Cherubim, archangels of light. The impression is of a cosmic celebration. A distinction is made here between those denizens of this heavenly sphere, the angels who chant in a chorus of adoration at night, and the souls of resurrected humans, who chant during the day in consort with those humans who are still incarnated.

The fourth sphere, called *Zebul*, which is a manifestation of the divine ascent symbolized by the sephira Netzach, is a place of reckoning on the Day of Judgement, presided over by archangel Mikhael chairing a celestial tribunal, and inhabited by Seraphim, the angels of fire described by Isaiah and Ezekiel. A mitigating grace is personified here by Isaac who, having accepted to be sacrificed, intercedes for those who have suffered abuse or martyrdom.

The third sphere, characterized by the *Shehaqim*, mists of grace, is seen as a manifestation of Hod: divine intelligence configuring the code of the universe. Its inhabitants are epitomized by the four *Ophanim*, the celestial wheels of the chariot described by Ezekiel. At this point the throne becomes the chariot: the *Merkabah*. The Ophanim represent the untold spirals of

---

6 Compare with the treasury in Sufism.

energy whose eddies interpenetrate, in a cosmic wave interference pattern in outer space.

The second sphere, called *Raqiya*, corresponds to Yesod, the cosmic template or morphogenetic field, where people are invested upon their descent with their talents, and carry their merits upon their ascent. This sphere is inhabited by the *Galganim*. At this stage the Ophanim have materialized further into intangible beings, crystallizing as the galaxies.

The first sphere, corresponding to Malkuth, configurating the existential realm, is typified by being a veil, *velum*, enshrouding reality. Here the divine transcendence infuses the world with its spirit, *Shekina*; and this spirit pierces the veil, insuring a communication between heaven and earth. A distinction is made between the luminous *Saphira* and the nebulous *Lebanah*, the two faces of this veil, representing respectively, the astral and etheric spheres.

By attunement and awakening beyond the veil of illusion, in full cognizance of the topography of states and the pathways linking these, as in a labyrinth, the contemplative can rise up from the confining perspective of Malchut into the heavenly spheres, and incorporate these into the contemplative's own being.

Part Five

Clues to Subtle and Celestial Levels

Chapter One
Exploring the Spheres

We are bound for heaven, who has a mind to sight-seeing? We have been in heaven, we have been friends with the angels. Thither, sire, let us return, for that is our country. We are even higher than heaven and more than the angels. Why pass we not beyond these twain?[1]

Jalal ad-Din Rumi

How is higher consciousness attained? By closing our eyes to our limited self and by opening our heart to the God who is all perfection...the God who is in all, yet beyond man's perception.[2]

Hazrat Inayat Khan

Let us explore, in the light of Sufism, those unfamiliar levels of our being of which we are sometimes nebulously aware, and those zones of reality that we normally relegate to a kind of no man's land. Bear in mind that the celestial planes are not somewhere else or up there; rather, it is the same as the way the mind cannot be located in space; for example, as the brain.

However, in the case of the etheric body, one may envision it to be interspersed within the atoms and cells of the body, just as an eddy may be interspersed with other eddies in a wave interference pattern.

As you perform the following practices, your attention is drawn to the correspondence between your subtle counterpart and the spheres at which they function.

Also, you may recognize the difference between those spheres considered as the heavens, Hurqalya,[3] and the corresponding subtle earth. The Tibetan adage, *the mind rides the wind*, is highly relevant in our work. For every level of energy, you will recognize a mode of thinking. For example, the sphere of

1 Rumi, *Selected Poems from the Divani Shamsi Tabriz*, 33.
2 Inayat Khan, *Esoteric Papers*.
3 See Corbin, *Spiritual Body, Celestial Earth*, 79.

231

metaphor, mithal, is the heaven of the astral plane of subtle matter, ajsam; and the sphere of splendor, jabarut, is considered to be the heaven of the celestial plane; and the sphere of pure intelligence, hahut, is the heaven of the plane of archetypes, lahut. You will also notice that while at the lower levels we sport a form, as we proceed upwards our subtle attire does not have a profile, and therefore, becomes more a countenance, or effigy; and ultimately, all that remains is an insubstantial, flimsy imponderable that conveys an elusive impression of the code of what materializes as the configuration of our being.

While performing the practices with the life field,[4] you may have also sensed the difference between the levels of energy of your life-field. We offered a perfunctory clue: opposing high-voltage/low amperage with low-voltage/high-amperage. But the gradations are more subtle and little known. The kind of energy sensed at the ajsam level is finer than the one at nasut; and the one at the malakut level is again finer than the one felt at ajsam; and the one at lahut is most elusive, yet basic[5] and overriding, which we may call the energy of orderliness against entropy.

If the life energy of the body may be likened to a vortex, with the grosser energy being found at the periphery and the subtler at the center, by concentrating upon the center we plug into the functions of the subtle, or even the very subtle, mind.

Also, prior to doing the practices, your attention is drawn to the difference between your thinking while being aware of the physical world,[6] that is, the mode of thinking of the speculative mind (the gross mind of the Tibetans), with your thinking at the level of ajsam (the subtle mind according to the Tibetans) when conscious of your subtle body at the ajsam sphere; and again, your thinking at the level of jabarut (the very subtle mind) when conscious of your celestial body at the malakut sphere; and ultimately, at the level of hahut (which could be called your supermind) when sustained by that basic underpinning that is the wellspring of your personality, your divine inheritance, at the lahut sphere.

You will also notice that to awaken from one sphere to the next, you will need to offset your consciousness from its focus by questioning the reality of the way things appear at that level, and awaken to the next sphere. We have endeavored in the following to define the differences between these spheres. Our work will thus consist of a series of awakenings from one sphere to the next.

---

4 See Part One, Chapter Three, "Sensing the Life Field."
5 Like the gravitational force in physics as opposed to the electromagnetic.
6 Some Sufi metaphysicians insert a level between nasut and ajsam called *khayal*, the speculative mind.

Every atom, every object, every condition and every living being has a time of
awakening. Sometimes this is a gradual awakening and sometimes it is sudden.[7]

Hazrat Inayat Khan

In your ordinary consciousness, your sense of identity was delineated as a
discrete entity based upon *me-or not-me*; and while doing the meditations
in the cosmic dimension, you envisioned yourself as a vortex without
boundary. Now think of yourself as a many-tiered reality, extending to all
spheres, transcendent, cosmic and immanent—like an inverted cone whose
apex is isolated, but whose base is coextensive with that of all the other cones
composing the universe.

'Alam an-Nasut: The Physical Sphere

As you sit to meditate, you will, of course, start by being aware of your
body and the physical environment. As we have seen,[8] the only way to shift
your sense of identity into the subtle levels of your being, consists in first ques-
tioning that physical matter is what you ordinarily think it is, and secondly
by the same token, that the fabric of your body is not what you might have
imagined. Think that this commonplace representation is the consequence
of our conditioning. This is the negative, agnostic outlook. A more positive
approach would be to think of this fabric as physicists are now trying to
convey it, by producing models challenging our understanding. According
to Islam, instead of postulating that matter is maya, it is considered as a system
of clues signaling a reality, of which it is just the signpost.

We shall show him our signs on the horizon of his being.[9]

Qur'an

Envision the body as an invaluable underpinning for our realization,
fashioned out of that very fabric, albeit highly upgraded over eons of time.[10]
Avoid thinking of it as a garment that you have donned and will cast aside
at death, but rather ponder upon the extraordinary way in which your body
cells incorporate your thoughts and consciousness. Moreover, keep remind-
ing yourself that somehow its quintessential template,[11] your subtle body, is
non-substantial, and therefore, not subjected to the disintegration of what
we call matter.

This body is the reality of the human being which without increase or decrease
survives in the tomb after the body of flesh made of terrestrial elements...have

---

7 Inayat Khan, *The Sufi Message* series, *Sufi Teachings*, 318.
8 See Part Four, Chapter Three, "Transcendence."
9 XLI:53.
10 See Reeves, *Poussières d'étoiles.*
11 See Becker and Selden, *The Body Electric.*

been separated from it and dissolved....This is the body in which humans are resurrected. [12]

Ahmad al-Ahsa'i

Incidently, a parallel with Dr. Rupert Sheldrake's theory of the morphogenetic field comes inevitably to mind.[13]

'Alam al-Khayal: The Reflexive Mind

The very gist of Avicenna's fundamental theory is that man attains insight into meaningfulness from the divine mind that confers form to material beings. Therefore, to obtain insight into meaningfulness, do not obstruct the gift from above by excessive attachment to the perceptual reality.[14]

In the initial stages of meditation, you will find yourself cogitating the ordinary way—the way we have been conditioned. The difference encountered at the khayal level resides in the fact that you have totally lost sight of the physical world; but you simply remember it, the way it appeared at the nasut level.

Granted that our commonplace thinking is limited, to reach into higher levels of awareness you will have to earmark the features in our commonplace thinking that are inadequate, so as to devalidate it.

Practices

1) Ascertain that, in the measure that your thinking refers to your personal focus of consciousness, the personal bias is inevitable.

2) Check the difference between those thoughts that are interpretations of current or past experience, and those thoughts that are creative—that denote your impact on the environment (speculative thoughts).

3) Draw your attention to the fact that our very language betrays our tendency to shrink dynamic thinking into static thoughts. There is no such thing as thoughts. They are simply abstracts of our thinking process. They evidence the way we ordinarily limit our thinking. Thinking is dynamic, thoughts are static. A thought is a cross-section of thinking. Reality is dynamic, and we are limiting it by thinking statically; this is indicated by our language, which articulates semantics.

4) Note that our conceptualization is based upon discrete concepts. We have difficulty in reconciling irreconcilables; for example that we can be mortal and immortal at the same time. In artificial intelligence, both *and* and *or* need to be accounted for. But in our simplistic thinking, we understand *or*, but have difficult in grasping *and*.

---

12 Corbin, *Spiritual Body, Celestial Earth*, 184–185.
13 See Sheldrake, *A New Science of Life.*
14 See Avicenna, *Kitab al-'Isharat wa'l-Tanbihat.*

5) Our minds in their ordinary functions have difficulty grasping what we imply; a lot of things are taken for granted behind what we affirm.[15] These assumptions stand in the way of our mind's reaching higher levels of thinking.

6) Moreover, our minds in the middle range ordinarily account for events by postulating that they are caused (by past inference); and our mind has difficulty in grasping that each event involves the totality, and even more difficulty in grasping spontaneous recurrent generation.

7) Letting go of your previous perspective, you will come to a further level of thought beyond the middle range. Consequently, you will develop a far greater perspicacity; this state has often been called *lucid dreaming*.

8) You are aware that the objects of your cognition are your thoughts, rather than physical objects, although the impressions which you are regurgitating refer to physical objects or events. Alternatively, if your thoughts are creative, you will imagine physical objects of your own fashioning; and you will visualize landscapes or situations, scenarios. When we reach the mithal level, we will be able to gauge the differences in the levels of mental function.

'Alam al-Ajsam: The Level Of The Subtle Template

To shift your identity from the physical level to one step upwards, imagine that you are awakening out of the perspective of physical reality. Cling to the notion of being an energy field rather than substantial. We have already learned to do this.[16]

You will find yourself in a state called reverie, somehow vacillating at the threshold between day consciousness and sleep, yet straddling both in a paradoxical way. You have not lost sight of the physical world altogether, as in sleep; yet it seems nebulous, its objects appear transparent, like gossamer, and surrounded by an eerie halo—and your body also.

Your basic sense of identity has shifted suddenly beyond recognition. Remember Chen Fu's metaphor:

Last night I dreamt that I was a butterfly and this morning I was not sure whether 1 was a man who had dreamt that he was a butterfly or a butterfly that is dreaming that it is a man.

All the while, however, you will notice that your etheric body is interspersed with the cells of your physical body while, by the same token, structuring them, like the magnetic field within the molecules of the magnet.

Pondering upon this, your imagination eludes your will and idles unaccountably.

---

15 The implicit in psychology parallels the implicate in physics. See Part Two, Chapter Four, "Visualizations."

16 See Part One, Chapter Three, "Sensing the Life Field."

You will experience a wonderful sense of freedom from dependence upon your physical body, and in fact, from the need of the existential state to survive. It will occur to you that you are anticipating life after life.

The soul manifesting as a body has diminished its power considerably, even to the extent that it is not capable of imagining for one moment the great power, life and light it has in itself. Once the soul realizes itself by becoming independent of the body that surrounds it, the soul naturally begins to see in itself the being of the spirit.[17]

Hazrat Inayat Khan

'Alam al-Mithal: The Level Of Metaphor

Professor Henry Corbin defines this plane as the intermediate world, or plane of being, specifically corresponding to the meditative function of the imagination, as:

The luminous world of Idea-Images, of apparitional figures....Here all the essential realities of being are manifested in real Images.[18]

Henry Corbin

To capture this state, proceed as when about to go to sleep, by turning away from the more overt peripheral impressions striking consciousness through the senses, and allowing your thoughts to idle ponderously in a state beyond reverie enshrouded in a spell of silence, while echoes of the turbulence of the universe reach you as from afar. Then withdraw from the thoughts by which you tend to interpret these (the gross mind of the Buddhists), or from the cognitions on thoughts encountered in conversations or readings. Indeed, to capture emerging creative thoughts, you need to free your mind from the constraint of the more forceful and commonplace ones. The clue consists in devalidating these ponderous thoughts as being deceptive, because limited by our personal bias. Consequently, one comes upon a psychological emptiness, from which a new awareness will arise.

You become aware of this level of your being when you awaken from the limitations of the middle range operations of your mind, and begin to grasp meaningfulness without the support of the perception of a physical event, or relying upon your interpretation of situation; for example, your personal problems.

To hoist yourself to the sphere of metaphor, you need to imagine in order to experience. This a radical change of tack. To experience, you are passive, on the receiving side; to be creative, you are on the active side. We are here at the crossroads between both.

---

17 Inayat Khan, *The Sufi Message* series, *Philosophy, Psychology and Mysticism*, 69.
18 Corbin, *Creative Imagination in the Sufism of Ibn 'Arabi*, 190.

The clue to doing this is to offset consciousness. You do not perceive the environment (sensory perceptions) but remember it. You also remember the psychological environment (circumstances) just as we recall a dream when awakening, except that here we are awakening the other way around.

You will find that you have not only lost sight of the physical world, but you can see how your subtle body is simply an effigy reflecting, on one hand, the configuration of your physical body, and on the other hand, the metaphors of your higher mind. It translates your realization, rather than your experience, into a template. You find yourself in touch with that stratum of your dreaming where thoughts are creative, rather than just regurgitating the input from the environment.

Every experience on the physical or astral plane is just a dream before the soul. It is ignorance when it takes this experience to be real.[19]

Hazrat Inayat Khan

The clue to offsetting consciousness in the dream state from simple input processing, lies in acquiescing once more to the proposition that you are a different person from the self-image that you have identified with so far. This is the secret of lucid dreaming.

You will find yourself at the crossroads between planes because, while processing the input from the existential plane, you are somehow prioritizing impressions that seem to emerge spontaneously, apparently randomly, highlighting the feedforward of our inventiveness over the feedback of experience. The input from outside acts as a catalyst releasing latent creative ideas. If the forms of the world reveal meaning, it is because they serve as expressions of a language that articulates that meaning.

You will relish in fantasies, sometimes fictitious, random phantasmagoria. These do illustrate our creative faculty of improvising, maybe even of processing, the collective unconscious of humanity in a tangible way; but to avoid having them elude control and lead to whimsical chimera (virtual reality), you will need to somehow extrapolate them with hard existential reality.

How may I know Thee since Thou art hidden? yet how could I fail to know Thee since Thou are that which appears in all things, which makes Thee known to me.[20]

Everything manifest in the cosmos is an imaginal engendered form that conforms to a divine form.[21]

Muhyi ad-Din Ibn 'Arabi

19 Inayat Khan, *The Sufi Message* series, *The Sufi Message of Spiritual Liberty*, 237.
20 Ibn 'Arabi, *Études Traditionelles*, Valsan, trans. Sept. 1949, 251.
21 Chittick, *The Sufi Path of Knowledge*, 362.

Keep imagining how things could be, instead of observing the way things are.

This is the plane from which artists, musicians, and other creative beings derive inspiration. If you expand your consciousness while hoisting it, as we have learned to do, you will realize that your thoughts are imbued with a self-organizing faculty; and thus they customize the self-organizing thrust of the universe as a whole, in its evolutionary advance.

For example, you will be concerned with the architecture or basic geometric configurations behind forms, rather than the perceived; and the issues enacted behind events, rather than just recollecting the events.

Practices

1) Form: Concentrate on a mandala, or square, circle, triangle, cross, cube, cone, sphere, spiral, spin, vortex, or bow and arrow.

2) Music: Reflect upon a musical scale rather than the individual notes; or a syncopated rhythm, rather than its applications; a sarabande, a passacaglia, a chaconne, etc. Transpose a theme in another scale. Improvise a harmonic progression.

3) Archetypes: Instead of the landscapes we visualized earlier, contemplate symbols like the father or mother archetype, or the virgin, or the old wise man, or the child, or the wizard, or the villain, or the hero versus the traitor.

'Alam al-Malakut: The Celestial Sphere

To hoist yourself higher, you will need to once more shift your sense of identity further. Now that your thinking has reconnected with its cosmic and transcendent matrix, you will gauge the formative processes unfurling in the architectonics of your body and your mental constructs as secondary, derivative effluxes of a more fundamental reality to which you belong: your celestial being.

Since the active imagination is itself a psycho-spiritual power belonging to the world of the Malakut, all the forms arising from it are of the same nature as itself; these forms are independent of external sensory realities....The imaginative forms are not merely creations of the Imagination, but that they are a creation of the Creator of the imagination....The Imaginative Forms are also things that He brings down from the Treasuries.[22]

Ahmad al-Ahsa'i

Muse ponderously upon your state prior to your birth—actually, prior to your conception. You will grasp a sense of timelessness if and when you

---

22 Corbin, *Spiritual Body, Celestial Earth*, 211–212.

recall your pristine, celestial state; you realize that you are still now a celestial being, with all the underpinnings we have encountered so far that have accrued to your real being in the course of time.

The Sufi, therefore, practices the process by which he is able to touch that part of life in himself which is not subject to death.[23]

Hazrat Inayat Khan

To retrieve the memory of your pristine condition, you will need to avail yourself of all the quintessential sensitivity of which you are endowed in your soul; gird yourself with the nobility of your divine legacy. To this end, cleanse yourself of dusky thoughts and emotions, like hatred or guile; and entertain luminous thoughts and sublime emotions, a kind of spring cleaning of emotions. You will notice that you will be developing a sparkle in your mind, alacrity in your heart, and that your consciousness has become sprightly and alert. The Sufis refer to a condition in which the soul perceives a nonphysical reality, which is considered to be the state of the archangels.

You have already highlighted your subtle body by downplaying your body consciousness; you have extended your thinking beyond the personal middle range and identified with your creative mind-world, as opposed to the insubstantial fabric of your subtle body. Now you need to discount any assumption of being even etheric, though, somehow, you feel as though you were fashioned of the fabric of a supernal effulgence unknown on earth. Nor do you seem to sport any kind of profile, even a halo; nor are you located in space. Therefore, it could not be considered as a body, however subtle, but rather as what we commonly understand by the soul, although Ahsa'i calls it the astral body.[24] It serves as an intermediary between the archetypal world, lahut, and the intermediary world, ajsam, communicating something of the nature of our archetypal soul belonging to the lahut sphere, to our etheric body in the sphere of ajsam. But in turn, according to Ahsa'i, it eventually disappears at the time of resurrection, recycling the experience gained on earth back into the treasuries, the sphere of lahut.[25]

What "returns" in reality is matter in a certain form, but this form is precisely the work of the individual person....For in truth, Form is the configuration of matter; therefore it is the configuration of the thing "which returns," it is not the thing itself.[26]

Ahmad al-Ahsa'i

23 Inayat Khan, *The Sufi Message* series, *The Alchemy of Happiness*, 272.
24 Ahsa'i describes our malakut effigy as an underpinning for the paramount core of our being.
25 See Ahsa'i in Corbin, *Spiritual Body and Celestial Earth*, 219–220.
26 Ibid., 219–220.

Yet the semblance of a face will surreptitiously dawn upon you. It transpires through the countenance of your subtle body suddenly, but merely as an ineffable impression transcending form: a nebulous effigy. You just know: *this is my real being, whereas my physical form and even that of my subtle body was a mask.* This is illustrated by the picture of Dorian Gray.

A further discovery may well confuse you. You will notice that, unlike your subtle double, the image is multi-tiered; it features an ubiquitous admixture in which several forms are intermeshed.[27] You will be intrigued to earmark the immaculate condition of your celestial being, somehow interspersed with its defilement. Yet surprisingly, it remains unscathed by the distortions contracted through the spillover of earthly impressions, as the voice of Caruso that can be retrieved out of its distortions from the bad recordings of the time.

Be sensitive enough to feel life and its beauty and to appreciate it, but at the same time to consider that one's soul is divine, and that all else is foreign to it.[28]
Hazrat Inayat Khan

In the context of alchemy, Ahsa'i describes the work we can effect upon our celestial body, clearing it from the defilement incurred by the earthly condition.

This incandescent glass is homologous to the astral body which accompanied the Spirit at the time of the exitus, *when the latter departs from its elementary material body....If the Elixir of whiteness, "the philosopher's chemical," be projected unto this fine glass, then it becomes a crystal which flames in sunlight... If this sparkling crystal is melted once again, and the white Elixir is again projected onto it, lo and behold, it becomes diamond. It is still glass and yet no, it is something other....homologous to the Resurrection Body.*[29]
Ahmad al-Ahsa'i

Understandably, every level of our being must interconnect with every other, both upwards and downwards. Since it acts as a go-between, it needs to extrapolate between very different impressions.

When these bodies, such as you see them in our world, have been completely purified of accidents foreign to them, the way of being those who were below rejoin the way of those who are above. Then the spiritual bodies perceive of and by themselves the spiritual realities of the Jabarut as well as the pure suprasensory forms of the Malakut....For their bodies to be spiritualized, to

27 Like a wave interference pattern in which several eddies permeate and suffuse each other.
28 Inayat Khan, *The Sufi Message* Series, *The Alchemy of Happiness*, 85.
29 Corbin, *Spiritual Body and Celestial Earth*, 201.

become spirits, they only have to will it; on the other hand, for their spirits to be embodied, to become bodies, they have only to wish for it. [30]

Ahmad al-Ahsa'i

To retrieve this memory, you must attune yourself to a combination of a state of great serenity together with allowing yourself the enthusiasm of thinking of something sublime, such as the luminous eyes of a baby, or celestial music in a cathedral, or a mountain scene with an effulgent, multicolored sky at dawn. This will resonate with your sense of the immaculate nature of your true being. Also, you need to believe that behind whatever appears is a reality incomparably more beautiful, including your own countenance.

Imagine a holographic slide in which two similar yet different images are superimposed, one blue and the other violet. You can toggle from one to the other. By dint of your willpower and creative imagination, you can correct and reverse the distortions in the blue one to approximate the violet, while honoring the maturity evidenced in the blue one. You are able to confirm that you can ally wisdom with innocence.

Having captured a hunch of the nature, and even the features, of your angelic being, can you see how the attunement of the celestial spheres tends to configure your psyche, and even your body—at least the expression of your face and your deportment?

Let yourself be carried into a dream in a dream, beyond sleep with dreams in forms and images. If you seize this moment to represent to yourself angels, or masters, saints, and prophets in their transfigured state, you will feel inspired. Ibn 'Arabi refers to heavenly encounters with the spirits of earlier prophets and saints.[31] When functioning at this level, one does establish a communication with these beings.

'Alam al-Jabarut: The Sphere Of Pure Splendor

It will seem difficult for you to imagine that you could hoist yourself still further aloft into the unknown. We are touching upon the domain of the sacred, resonating with the cosmic emotion out of which beauty is born—pure splendor. Can you sense that the nostalgia for the epiphany of beauty and majesty, at the existential level, is the springhead motivating this whole process of manifestation, of which you are a part? Our nostalgia for beauty, whether of nature, art, beings, or actions, calls upon a resonance at this lofty level of our being.

You will find that you cannot reach further upwards by an effort of your will or understanding, but simply by dint of a very high emotion, glorifica-

---

30 Ibid., 208.
31 See Chittick, *The Sufi Path of Knowledge*, 221.

tion, by imagining that you are participating in the cosmic celebration in the heavens. Here we discover the relevance of prayer, in addition to meditation. Allow yourself to be aroused by the emotion that moves the universe; feel it in you as it stirs your soul in its very depth. You are discovering your true being; in the quintessence of your being, you are pure splendor.

Since for every level of energy there is a corresponding mode of thinking, you will need to shift to what the Tibetans call the very subtle mind, instead of the subtle mind. You will remember that the subtle mind projects ideas into forms, whereas, at the level of the very subtle mind, there are no forms. The very subtle mind thinks in a holistic mode rather than an assemblage of discrete thoughts.

For the wise, nothing appears as a discrete entity, but everything is seen.[32]
Muhyi ad-Din Ibn ʿArabi

This becomes more understandable when we realize that our imagination customizes the thinking of the universe more authentically at this level than at ajsam, where it has lost the personal vantage point, and therefore, serves as a transducer to relevant experience. At the malakut level, you might have gleaned remote echoes of the semblance of inspiring beings, but in your present state (the jabarut level), deeply moved by the magnificence of their beings, you will sense their attunement, which becomes more and more real to you.

At the level of ajsam, we were trying to grasp that which transpires behind what appears as physical reality. These are considered by the Sufis as the signs through which God reveals divine intention. But at the level we are touching upon, a further dimension of knowing is operative.

There is a further perspective: you discover in your consciousness the act of the divine consciousness whereby God discovers Himself through your discovery of Him.

Muhyi ad-Din Ibn ʿArabi

At the level of malakut, you still identified yourself with your individuality, although at that level it was not couched in a fabric, however subtle, nor configured into a form, or located in space, or even limited by transiency. But you still had the sense of touching upon the quintessence of your individuality beyond time and space, and the existential state in general, which is considered to characterize the state of the archangels rather than the angels.

The clue to reach the jabarut level is to lose your sense of somatic, and even noetic, individuality. But it would be fruitless to contrive to annihilate your

---

32 Ibn ʿArabi, *Études Traditionelles*, Valsan, trans. Nr 287 June 1952, 184.

sense of individuality by an act of your individual will. This accounts for the guidelines given by the Sufi mystics. According to al-Hallaj, you have to give up trying to annihilate your ego in the practice of the dhikr.

You will distinguish two complementary actions: your act of glorification, which calls for the divine operation upon you, or rather facilitates it; and the divine operation. The Sufis go further and say that our glorification is simply our response to the divine act of love; God is always considered as initiating, and man as responding.

'Alam al-Lahut: The Sphere Of The Archetypes

To reach this level, you will need to grasp the seedbed of the idiosyncrasies out of which your personality unfurls, which is what the Sufis call your divine inheritance.

The seed comes last after the life of the trunk, branch, fruit and flower; and as the seed is sufficient and capable of producing another plant, so man is the product of all planes, spiritual and material. And yet in him alone shines forth that primal intelligence that caused the whole, the seed of existence: God.[33]

Hazrat Inayat Khan

What the Sufis call divine could be illustrated as the blasthema state of the embryo where the cells are not yet differentiated. That diversification is achieved by a smart device of nature: many of the genes remain recessive, while only a few are active (dominant), yet paradoxically, all are present in each cell.

You discover a world of archetypes, and can see that what you thought was the existential world is made up of the exemplars of these archetypes. And now you are immersed in these archetypes. These are the secret treasures in the Qur'anic verses.

There is not a thing, but with us are the treasures of it; and we do not send it down but in known measure.[34]

In fact, your personality is just an exemplar of your real being, which is of the nature of an archetype—the seed out of which your personality unfurled.

In him is awakened that spirit by which the whole universe was created.[35]

Hazrat Inayat Khan

This is the level that we attune to when repeating our waza'if. The only way to have any sense of the archetype of the idiosyncrasies of our personality

33 Inayat Khan, *Esoteric Papers*.
34 XV:21.
35 Inayat Khan, *The Sufi Message* series, *Healing, Mental Purification, The Mind World*, 120.

is by reversing our vantage point, and trying to imagine how things would look from the divine point of view.

ʿAlam al-Hahut: The Paramount Sphere

To trigger off the quantum leap from the existential state to the meaningfulness or programming beyond, you will need to eschew all activities of your consciousness. When voided of experience, you will find that your consciousness will be absorbed into its ground, which is the act of intelligence:

Moreover, while the consciousness of the totality is focalized in your consciousness, the intelligence of the totality cannot be subdivided.

You will need to suspend any activities of your mind, whether of the gross mind, speculative mind at the khayal level; or the subtle, creative mind at the ajsam level; or the very subtle mind or sublime mind at the jabarut level; or the supermind at the hahut level. The inherent knowing of the supermind, culled by intelligence rather than consciousness, is considered by the Sufis to be revealed rather than acquired. Since at this level you have lost your personal identity, you cannot grasp it with your will.

Lo, for I to myself am unknown.[36]

Jalal ad-Din Rumi

You will not only be oblivious of the world, but your thoughts will seem to have evaporated, also your emotions; you have lost your personal identity. Not only have you lost sight of your subtle and celestial bodies, and of course, your physical body, but you have lost sight of the very seedbed of your personality belonging to the sphere of archetypes. Hence, you have lost any sense of multiplicity.

I have circled awhile with the nine Fathers in each heaven, For years I have revolved with the stars in their signs. I was invisible for awhile; I was dwelling with Him, I was on the day when Names were not.[37]

Jalal ad-Din Rumi

This level lies beyond the horizon of understanding in infinite regress, *beyond the beyond,* as the Upanishads say. The shock of awakening will consternate your mind and reverberate at all levels of your being. At this pinnacle of your being, you will have the feeling of merging into the Reality beyond the actuality of the existential state. Granted that the world is a hologram, now the original picture behind the hologram is revealed to you. Or rather, you discover that at the pinnacle of your being you are coextensive and

---

36 Rumi, *Selected Poems from the Divani Shamsi Tabriz,*177.
37 Ibid., 182.

isomorphic with this original picture. But here our semantics fail us, because the words *I* or *me* or *you* have lost their meaning as the hallmark of individuality. Here we appreciate the importance of preserving our reference to the transcendent dimension of God beyond the immanent, which theology has always maintained, whether Islamic, Christian, Jewish, Zoroastrian, or Hindu.

There is a stage at which, by touching a particular phase of existence, one feels raised above the limitations of life, and is given that power and peace and freedom, that light and life, which belongs to the source of all beings. In other words, in that moment of supreme exaltation, one is not only united with the source of all beings, but dissolved in it, for the source is one's self.[38]

Hazrat Inayat Khan

In the absence of any vestige of existential awareness, you find yourself more aware than ever, but of meaningfulness, of what the Sufis call the divine intention; you are suddenly awake beyond life, beyond the beyond. You are experiencing what one experiences in deep sleep. The reason why we cannot normally recollect it in day consciousness is because its mode of thinking cannot fit into the constraint of our middle range mind, which rejects it. In the state of awakening, the conscious mind realizes that it is a subsidiary of the supermind, a sub-whole.

Here thought overreaches the procedure whereby it distinguishes the thinker and the thought, the subject and the object. The supermind is self-generating.

This is the key:

As the eyes cannot see themselves, so it is with the soul. It is sight itself. The moment it closes its eyes to all it sees, its own light makes it manifest to its own view.[39]

Hazrat Inayat Khan

You will recall that at the physical level, 1+1 in infinite regress = infinity; seen from the personal vantage point, you are a fraction of the totality. But at the top level, 1= infinity. This is why, at the limit of mystical experience, the mystic says: *I am God.* Since the commonplace mind cannot countenance this, which seems like a preposterous claim, those articulating such a realization have been martyred in the past, like Jesus and al-Hallaj; while today they may be committed to a psychiatric clinic. The difficulty is in extrapolating this state with the commonplace diurnal state. Those who achieve this are illuminated.

38 Inayat Khan, *The Sufi Message* series, *Healing, Mental Purification, The Mind World*, 115.
39 Inayat Khan, *The Sufi Message* series, *The Smiling Forehead*, 181.

I am the One I love, and the One I love has become me. We are two spirits in one body.[40]

Mansur al-Hallaj

A Note of Caution: You are warned against the danger of overstressing your capacity in undertaking the practices relative to the higher planes, particularly this last one. The danger is in losing your sense of existence and being unable to recontact it.

I am the Wine of the Holy Sacrament; my very being is intoxication. Those who drink of my cup and yet keep sober will certainly be illuminated; but those who do not assimilate it, will be beside themselves and exposed to the ridicule of the world.[41]

Hazrat Inayat Khan

Summary

Let us review the steps we have taken; incidentally, you may have noticed that the spheres alternated between somatic and noetic.

(i) To identify with our subtle body, we first discounted sensorial impressions, but remembered them while still interpreting them with our speculative mind.

(ii) To identify with the level of our mind that we called *metaphor*, we then allowed our memory of the physical world to evaporate, and we projected creative thoughts upon data ingested from the environment.

(iii) To identify with our celestial being, we discounted our sense of transiency and carried our memory back, so as to grasp the matrix of our being, which is a continuity in change, and which remains immaculate within its defilement.

(iv) To identify with pure splendor, we had to abandon any residue of personal identity and exult in glorification.

(v) To identify with the archetypal seeds of our personality, which we call our divine inheritance, we needed to discover the way the divine programming is actuated in us, by reversing our vantage point.

The following is an attempt at establishing, to the best of my judgment, a table of correspondences between some of the major angelologies in the esoteric teachings of world religions.

---

40 Al-Hallaj, *Diwan*, 93.
41 Inayat Khan, *The Complete Sayings of Hazrat Inayat Khan*, 165.

Spheres and Bodies

Sufi	Jewish	Tibetan	Hindu
Hahut (paramount)	Hayoth	Truth body	
Lahut (archetypal)	Archangels		
Jabarut (splendor)	Cherubim	Body of bliss	Anandamaya kosha
Malakut (celestial)	Seraphim	Emanation body	Vijnanamaya kosha
Mithal (metaphor)	Ophanim		Manomaya kosha
Ajsam (subtle)	Galganim	Illusory body	Pranamaya kosha
Khayal (mental)			
Nasut (physical)			Annamaya kosha

Chapter Two
Embodying the States of Awakening

Those who think that the heavenly knowledge is sufficient are mystical, but the joy of the heavenly knowledge and the full understanding of it come from being able to express it in this world's medium of expression.[1]

Hazrat Inayat Khan

But when meanings are embodied and become manifest in shapes and measures, they assume forms.[2] *The Real discloses Himself within forms and undergoes transmutation within them.*[3]

Muhyi ad-Din Ibn 'Arabi

Advanced Practices

The attainment gained at each step in meditation, as your realization breaks new horizons, has immediate consequences in your subtle and celestial bodies, and even your physical body.

Having earmarked and explored the counterparts of your being at different levels, and their modes of functioning in the corresponding spheres, you now undertake the next step: to translate your realizations and attunements into the corresponding structure of those subtle sheaths.

The Sufis and Buddhists outline clues to applying our creative imagination in the shaping of our subtle and celestial bodies, which eventually restructure our personality, and even our countenance, transpiring through our bodily expression.[4] You need to involve your whole person in the creative process, releasing latent potentials, unfurling them, and interconnecting your different subtle and celestial bodies, starting at the highest level of your being and working down; we have seen this operating in all artistic creativity.

---

1 Inayat Khan, *The Sufi Message* series, *In an Eastern Rose Garden*, 86.
2 Chittick, *The Sufi Path of Knowledge*, 354.
3 Ibid., 230.
4 See Gyatso, *The Clear Light of Bliss*.

We are studying the skills needed to embody states of consciousness by fashioning our higher bodies, rather as a sculptor models a statue; except that here we are the sculptor, the clay and the statue. Moreover, the form of the statue keeps on changing, and the fabric becomes more intangible as one moves up the scale of the celestial spheres. The slightest shift in our attunement or realization reshapes our subtle effigies instantaneously and unwittingly. In reinforcing this action by our will, we can attain a greater degree of perfection and also ensure that the changes become more durable.

While these formative processes are, in the main, programmed beyond our personal volitional participation, we can customize their programming by our incentive, or attunement, or degree of awareness.

In man the Creator has, so to speak, completed nature; yet the creative faculty is still working through man, and thus art is the ultimate step in Creation.[5]

As the whole of nature is made by God, so the nature of each individual is made by himself.[6]

Hazrat Inayat Khan

The work performed first in meditation and followed by real life, consists essentially in envisioning, very concretely by your creative imagination, the features of your subtle bodies that would, for example, express the qualities, attunements, or realizations attained in your meditations, for example, on the waza'if; and then identify with the subtle body corresponding to that level. And so on, all the way down to your physical body.

Let us keep in mind our objective: to fashion our subtle bodies and celestial sheaths in such manner as to extrapolate between their transcendental models hailing from the celestial spheres, and the formative processes resulting from the maturity gained by our earthly experience. Consequently, we need to work from the top, moving downwards, recollecting our perinatal and transcendent origins. Then, in a further step outlined in the next chapter, we will be transmuting our subtle bodes with a view to anticipating resurrection. To this end, we need to shift our identity upwards, distilling the gist of the wisdom gained by experience as it matures the subtle bodies on the way up.

'Alam al-Hahut

To prepare yourself for the creative work in fashioning your subtle bodies, you need to first proceed as in the preceding chapter, shifting your consciousness and attunement upwards, from one level to the next.

Tracing back your steps, recall that you first remember the physical scene or scenario, while having freed yourself from your representation of it because

---

5 Inayat Khan, *The Sufi Message* series, *Sufi Mysticism*, 159.
6 Inayat Khan, *The Complete Sayings of Hazrat Inayat Khan*, 35.

it now seems deceptive. Then the memories of the physical world evaporate. Presently, even the images that flash upon your subliminal consciousness disintegrate, leaving a residue reminiscent of kaleidoscopic sparks. You find yourself in an airy emptiness. It appears as if peripheral impressions are drawn into a vacuum, a black hole in the center of the vortex that coincides with the solar plexus. You are aware of being awake—highly perspicacious.

Carry your recollection further and further back, by retrieving your memories of transnatal celestial, or perinatal states,[7] until you reach the paramount root of your being, which has its seat in the heavenly spheres called *hahut*. You will find it easier to direct your thoughts back into a distant past rather than earmarking your subtle bodies as they are now; however, you are still what you were then, while much has accrued to you since. To understand this, think that there is a second dimension of time moving from transiency to transcendence and vice versa, in addition to the arrow of time moving from the past to the future. Imagine time fanning out at the base and converging at an apex at the summit.

As we have seen, to achieve this, you will need to bear in mind that you do harbor a recollection of the state you were in prior to your birth—and actually, prior to your conception—in deep memory. This requires you to sink into a state of tranquil serenity together with beatitude, a state which corresponds to awakening in deep sleep.

If you manage once more to capture some fleeting impressions of your pristine state, it will appear as pure intelligence, endowed with an inherent grasp of the programming behind the universe prior to the stage where this intelligence generated the act of consciousness, which may be considered as a derivative of it. This generation made you aware of the existential state. You will be able to tell the difference between consciousness and intelligence; your consciousness seems to be the projection and personal focalization of the divine consciousness, whereas intelligence is to be found in you as your supermind, which is of the same nature as the mind of the universe in its initial planning, and therefore, is impersonal. The Sufis define this state as the one in which God apprehends or cognizes the principle of Divine Being, unmediated by attributes, qualities, names, forms, and potentialities, which only convey some clue as to God's essence by qualifying it. At the lahut level, God's inscrutable essence is disclosed, but in a somewhat derived manner.

We recognize intelligence in its manifestation, but we do not know it in its essence.[8]

Hazrat Inayat Khan

---

7 See Grof, *Ancient Wisdom and Modern Science.*
8 Inayat Khan, *The Sufi Message* series, *Philosophy, Psychology and Mysticism*, 64.

As we have seen, when our cognizance does not rest on the feedback of experience, an inherent knowledge is revealed to us.

Intelligence confined to this knowledge becomes limited, but when it is free from all knowledge, then it experiences its own essence.[9]

Hazrat Inayat Khan

In the previous chapter, at the hahut level, we encountered a dimension of our mind that we called the supermind, so encompassing that we had to recognize that our conscious mind is only a sub whole. Our conscious mind cannot grasp it; rather it is the supermind that gauges the inadequacies of our conscious mind, as viewed from the very subtle level of jabarut. When we have let go of our sense of individuality, the supermind can take over, because, at that level, our thinking is impersonal—that is, it does not refer to the concept of the personal *I*. And that is why Sufis call it the *divine mind*.

You will know that you have reached the pinnacle of your being if you have not only lost your sense of what we commonly understand by matter and space and time, and of your thoughts or emotions regarding events, or your personal idiosyncrasies, including your subtle double or even celestial countenance, but even of your individuality as a discrete entity. Therefore we cannot, at this stage, speak of fashioning our subtle bodies. Yet since we are meditating downwards instead of upwards, somehow we wish to take advantage of this invaluable attunement and realization, to observe how all the strata of our bodiness, at each level, appear from this vantage point.

We can also hope that, thanks to our awakening beyond the perspectives of those levels, we will be inspired to recreate ourselves more effectively than ever.

What would be the clue to maintaining this crest of attunement and realization while being aware of all the levels, all the way down, including the physical? The clue is realizing that it was our identification with those materializations of our being, which we have called our subtle or celestial bodies at the different levels, that precluded our acting upon them creatively. This was the crucial delusion.

Mankind is clothed in the garb of an angel, of a jinn, and of a human being; but when he only sees himself in the garb of a human being without seeing the other garbs, he believes he is nothing but a human being.[10]

Hazrat Inayat Khan

Identify with the essence of your being instead of trying to get to know it, because we are so programmed that by trying to know it, we ordinarily

---

9 Inayat Khan, *The Sufi Message* series, *The Way of Illumination*, 162.
10 Inayat Khan, *The Sufi Message* series, *The Sufi Message of Spiritual Liberty*, 91–92.

project it as the object of our cognizance. It would prove incongruous to try to grasp the essence of your being at the hahut level, because you are that essence.

The spirit distinguishes everything except itself.[11]

Hazrat Inayat Khan

Therefore, keep being wary of this natural tendency to slip in your awareness, into identifying with the substructure of your being. Try being aware, for example, of your physical body without identifying with it, and so with your etheric body, and even so with your celestial demeanor, while considering these as a support system. However, since they do unfurl your latent potentialities, you must not consider them as totally foreign to yourself. This is true to a lesser extent regarding our creative works, which are an extension of ourselves. They are not ourself, nevertheless not altogether foreign to ourself, as, for example, our clothes or the furniture in our room; and even here, our choice does reflect something of the nature of our being.

You now know if you question that things are the way they appear, you will awaken beyond life; however, you will be oblivious of the existential levels of reality,[12] which is what we needed to do in the practices of the previous chapter. But in our present step, we need to see what things are, while being aware of our involvement in them.

Apply the same to your identification with your personality. You will be able to ascertain that by taking your opinion for granted, you descend into identification with your thinking; and thus you slip down from the pinnacle of your being, where you are endowed with an innate knowledge, which the Sufis call *revealed knowledge.*

If the soul could see independently of the mind and body it could see infinitely more.[13]

Hazrat Inayat Khan

It is your sense of the fundamental unity of being, which you reach by losing a sense of your individuality; and this opens access to divine revelation.

Once more, the clue to maintaining yourself at this pinnacle is to keep trying to see things from the divine point of view, which requires you to first discount your point of view. This is until such a time as you are able to extrapolate it with the divine point of view; but that belongs to the next stage: lahut.

---

11 Inayat Khan, *The Sufi Message* series, *Philosophy, Psychology, Mysticism*, 66.
12 This is the state which the Sufis call *al Adam*, the void. See Al-Jili, *De l'Homme Universel*.
10. One likes to parallel this with the Buddhist *sunayata*.
13 Inayat Khan, *Esoteric Papers*.

'Alam al-Lahut

The Sufis describe lahut as the level at which the divine essence permeates all things, by imprinting each sphere in the descending order with the seal of the attributes on which this divine essence is predicated. The practice of the wazifa consists in highlighting these attributes (*sifat*) by invoking their names (*asma ilahi*).

Every form you see has its archetype in the placeless world.[14]

Jalal ad-Din Rumi

The key to gaining access to this plane is thinking archetypal thoughts instead of topical thoughts.

You are touching here upon a much more fundamental aspect of yourself than your personality. Imagine the stump of a tree felled to its roots. A new tree grows from it, and the form it assumes may be very different from the previous one. These outgrowths are secondary, derivative: the root is the primal reality. It is the same with this archetypal ground of your being, which the Sufis ascribe to the level of lahut, and which Hazrat Inayat Khan calls our *divine inheritance*.

You will be struck by the impersonal effect of this dimension of your being at this level; yet to maintain yourself at this level, you need to reconcile it in your mind with your sense of individuality. You find yourself at a transitional threshold between unity and multiplicity; the Sufis speak about the multiplicity latent in unity, or the unity dwelling in multiplicity.

The Unicity is a revelation of the Essence, which appears as a synthesis because of the distinction of my qualities. All in it is unique and differentiated at the same time. So admire the multiplicity essentially one.[15]

'Abd al-Karim al-Jili

Inheritance is a very good illustration of this. Our DNA may potentially carry the code of the entire universe, but customized in each of us in our uniqueness. At the initial stage of the embryo, the blasthema, the cells are not yet differentiated. If you touch upon this level of your being, you will realize that, just as in the blasthema, the all-possibility lies in wait in our being, while we have reduced those possibilities by confining our identity to our personality.

From the vantage point of this level (lahut), you can actually witness the way that the bounty in the seedbed of your personality is continually trying to manifest and actuate itself in your personality; and by the same token,

14 Nicholson, *Selected Poems from the Divani Shamsi Tabriz*, 47.
15 Al-Jili, *De l'Homme Universel*, 46.

you will reinforce that flow. It will seem to you as though it were flowing down from a timeless level to a transient one. Doing this—that is, grasping a vertical chain of causation—will open a whole new outlook, because we are so used to thinking of causality as a horizontal sequence of inference, based upon the inexorable advance of becoming.

At this level, you may capture hunches of the divine intention at its inception. The Sufis call this *being invited to the court of the king*, which signifies being apprised of the divine intention, revealed under conditions of silence, solitude, fasting, and watchfulness. The dervishes try to capture the mark of God in all things.

You will notice that these archetypal attributes, which are latent within the depth of your own being as in all of nature, already carry at this stage the promise of prospective beauty and majesty.

There is a difference between the one who is burned in the fire of love and the one who is illuminated by His beauty in the light of contemplation. If intimacy (uns) is possible, it is possible only with the praise of Him, for uns involves love. Haybat (awe), on the other hand, arises from contemplating greatness, immensity ('azima), which is an attribute of God. Therefore God annihilates the souls of those who love Him by revealing His majesty and endows their hearts with everlasting life by revealing His beauty.[16]

Abu'l-Hasan al-Hujwiri

If you can maintain yourself at this lofty level, as you contemplate the way the divine attributes unfurl as your personality, you will discover the divine consciousness discovering aspects latent within God's nature, heretofore unknown to God, that emerge when actuated in you and thus manifested by you.

He manifested Himself to the possible things according to the preparednesses and realities of possible things.[17]

Muhyi ad-Din Ibn 'Arabi

You will be thrilled by discovering your participation in God's Self-discovery. But in so doing, if you remember your state at the hahut level, you will realize that from the pinnacle of the divine vantage point these qualities are only devices or clues predicating the divine essence, eschewing all manifestation thereof.

With us the name of everything is its outward form; with the Creator its inward essence.[18]

Jalal ad-Din Rumi

---

16 Al-Hujwiri, *Kashf al-Mahjúb.*
17 Chittick, *The Sufi Path of Knowledge*, 101.
18 Nicholson, *Rumi Poet and Mystic*, 97.

You will remember that at the hahut level, your *I* was coextensive with the divine *I*. At the present level, lahut, you are aware of being invested with the divine inheritance, so that you only know God through the mediation of the divine attributes. These are archetypes present in the seedbed of your personality, but only knowable through their exemplars in the idiosyncrasies of your personality.

To achieve this, you need to acquiesce to the fact that these qualities are present in the seedbed of your personality. This is because, among the bounty of qualities in our divine legacy, we carry within us the gift of the divine creativity.

Concentrate on a particular quality that you feel is particularly relevant for you, i.e. mastery, wisdom, truthfulness, energy, or spirit. Now consider that these are the models upon which the corresponding idiosyncrasies in your personality are modeled, and the magnificence of what comes through the forms of the world. Granted that these models are perfect, and your idiosyncrasies are only relatively conformable to the original, and in fact, remotely approximate these archetypes; yet identify with these models, envisioning them as representing the seedbed of the idiosyncrasies of your personality, which you now observe instead of identifying with them. You will rejoice in discovering that they carry the promise of beauty lying in wait to manifest in the world.

If you match your being at the lahut level, your divine inheritance, with the idiosyncrasies of your personality, you will notice that:

In the depth of that soul there is the quality which it has brought with it; on the surface is that quality which the ancestors have given. If that innate quality is greater, then it may also manifest on the surface, covering that quality which the parents and ancestors have given.[19]

Hazrat Inayat Khan

You will also notice that the exemplars (your idiosyncrasies) tend to lose touch with their archetype, your divine inheritance. Sometimes, though not always, the legacy of your ancestors is stronger, or the influence of the social environment. Hence, if you are committed to your spiritual ideal, you will nurture the need to dissolve your personality, so that it may be replaced by a new dispensation from the source of your being.

'Alam al-Jabarut

Jabarut is the level of the very subtle psyche of our celestial bodies (malakut). At this stage, while your mind gets individuated by emerging out of your supermind, it has not yet structured itself to the degree of envisioning forms,

19 Inayat Khan, *The Sufi Message* series, *Healing, Mental Purification, The Mind World*, 276.

as our mind does at the level of mithal in fashioning our subtle body; but it does exercise an ubiquitous impact upon our imponderable effigy in the malakut sphere. Let us call it the sublime mind, because it evokes and embodies the emotional drive behind the cosmos, as a nostalgia for pure splendor, which, at the subsequent levels, gets configured as beauty.

You activate this level of your being when you feel moved by that nostalgia into an act of glorification, as in prayer. Here lies your access to this plane. In that high attunement, you feel that somehow, anticipating the outburst of life in the cosmos, you are resonating with the divine intention at its inception; here the divine attributes you encountered at lahut arouse those emotions at a cosmic scale and beget forms at the existential level. Yet at the level at which you are now attuned, beauty eschews all forms. Here you will sense a degree of perfection such as could never be constrained within a perceptual image.

You will know that you are functioning at this level (jabarut) on your way down through the planes leading to the existential level, by the fact that, since thinking as an individual has not yet gelled, you are exulting in what may be called a symphony of emotions; the enormous variety of overwhelming emotions encountered confer upon you an astonishing sense of realization. The Sufis call it the *understanding of the heart*. Although not personal emotions, it is the wellspring of emotions that will manifest as personal emotions lower down the scale of spheres. Exult in this cosmic celebration, but also let yourself be moved by the power of love to self-generate beauty in yourself and create beauty in the world.

In so doing, you are fulfilling the programming of your being, which is that of the entire universe; because according to the Sufis, God reveals the many-splendored potentialities of the virtuality of beauty inherent in God's essence, by manifesting these to and in beings. And responding to this divine action upon us, we glorify the divine artist whose features are latent within us, by actuating them in our personality and body.

We respond to the initial act of God imagining the world, by imagining God, and thus creating God by our imagination, in our very nature, as the *God created in the faiths (al-Haqq al-makhluq fi'l-i'tiqadat)*.[20] Thus, by glorifying God, we create God as our being, and reciprocally, we facilitate God's creating God's own Self as us.

As we have seen, the Sufis distinguish between the light that can be seen and the light that sees. If indeed, our celestial bodies are constructed in the fabric of a super-physical light,[21] we understand why the Sufis describe the light of the sphere of jabarut as the light of intelligence (*nur-i 'aql).*

20 Corbin, *Creative Imagination in the Sufism of Ibn 'Arabi*, 188.
21 The uncreated light of Gregory of Nyssa.

To spark the structuring of our celestial, subtle, and eventually, physical body, we need to connect up these two dimensions of light: the light of jabarut with the light of malakut.

A light upon a light.[22]

Qur'an

You need to translate the emotion that moves the universe and stirs our souls into thought patterns at the ajsam level, which molds our subtle and physical bodies. You are in sync with the attunement of the archangels, whose inheritance you carry within you.

If our soul is indeed an angel, it would reflect the archetypal images of the archangels; consequently, these images in one's imagination must carry within themselves the hallmark of the angels who projected them.

'Alam al-Malakut

Since at this level, the splendor of the sphere of jabarut configures itself into forms, our true being manifests to our superior vision in a high state of meditation in a tangible way; yet it does not sport a profile, and therefore, you will notice that it bears a resemblance to Walter Chapell's photographs of flowers under ultraviolet light. It is somewhat of the nature of a countenance rather than a face; and it is effulgent, translucent, and diaphanous, like gossamer. Such is our celestial counterpart which reveals a transcendent meaningfulness hailing from the jabarut level and shrouded in pervasive beauty.

The form of an angel projects itself into a human form, in the same sense as a form projects itself upon a mirror. At this level, you do not seem to have assumed a definite form with a profile; yet you may reminisce some sense of your celestial nature, which, if you happen upon it, would strike you as being authentic. This may be arrived at while still being in what one understands as the awakened state. However, the Ariadnean thread of memory registered in the deep unconscious can only be retrieved if you are extremely calm and relaxed—almost as in autohypnosis. The sense of identity that you thus uncover is so sublime that you will find it difficult to accept that it is your own immaculate counterpart.

Thus the Imago Terrae *is indeed here the very image of the soul, the image through which the soul contemplates itself, its energies and its powers, its hopes and its fears.*[23]

Henry Corbin

---

22 XXIV:35.
23 Corbin, *Spiritual Body and Celestial Earth*, 83.

Beauty reveals to us the transcendent meaningfulness buried in our celestial counterpart at the sphere of malakut.

The key to envisioning how things look at this level is to think of yourself as being thought of, rather than thinking. For example, someone is thinking of you; now you can imagine how you look or appear to that person. But think of it as God (or the transcendental pole of your own being) who is thinking of you. Imagine that from this vantage point, you appear as a work of art, as the product of the imagination of that Being whose body is the cosmos.

You will, of course, have to give up your commonplace notion of the features of your face and body, based upon the use of the mirror, and accept the possibility that you would look quite different if you shifted your perspective, for instance, to your dream state.

If you muse upon your state prior to your conception, realizing that you would look different as seen from the vantage point of your higher self, the semblance of a face will suddenly dawn upon you. It appears as an ineffable impression that transpires nebulously, and sometimes with compelling evidence. It may surprise you that, by some paradoxical contrivance of the programming of the universe, it might, in fact, resemble your aura. How the extraterrestrial and the existential concur in us never ceases to astonish one. Chen Fu's metaphor could be rephrased as follows: *I thought I was a grub, but suddenly realized that I had wings.*

If you hit upon it, there can be no doubt; you will be convinced that this is really *me*, whereas your face is simply a mask over the reality of your being. You will also be intrigued by a paradoxical aspect of what you discover when you encounter your celestial double: it is multi-tiered, or rather features an ubiquitous admixture where several forms are intermeshed, like a wave interference pattern in which the eddies permeate and suffuse each other. You will indeed be able to earmark the immaculate condition of your celestial being, hailing from your paramount being within its defilement; moreover, its innocence is conjoined with its sophistication.

Visualization of your aura at the ajsam sphere, immersed in realms of light, will trigger off the memory of having always been a being of light on the sphere of malakut.[24] Imagine that you are a hybrid: you are a denizen of the heavens, the face of your celestial body being fashioned in the fabric of the light of the heavens, but having inherited from your human ancestry.

Contrive to superimpose these three images: your immaculate core, your physical face, and the countenance of your celestial face matured by the earth experience. You will notice that your pristine, celestial countenance appears

---

24 The concept of the light field utilized in physics, rather than thinking of light rays, may prove helpful in freeing ourselves of our commonplace representations of light that stand in the way of this experience, since our concepts do forestall experience.

ingenue, embryonic, in contrast to your matured celestial countenance. You will remember that our objective is not to return to our pristine state, but to maintain the innocence of the child while developing the wisdom of the master. While at first it seemed that the higher sheaths of your being act as templates for the lower ones, it will occur to you that the opposite is also true. You will notice that your subtle bodies unfurl within the physical body, like the butterfly in the cocoon. For that which has been gained in the existential state in our bodies to survive, it needs to be recycled into the cosmic programming, passed upwards from one sheath to the higher one. Consciously incorporate into your psyche the bountiful inheritance of our cultures, the inspiration of countless beings who left us the legacy of their creative thoughts; see how they have imprinted not just your physical face, but left their hallmark all the way up into your celestial body at the level of malakut, while being transmuted so as to become quintessential.

If you have practiced the stages in ascent through the spheres in the previous chapter, you know that the physical world looks very different when looked upon from the vantage point of malakut. You will spot in the environment, and also in the prevailing circumstances, signs and traces (ayat) of a splendor and meaningfulness, which you had already encountered beyond the existential level at the sphere of jabarut. What you took to be events will seem simply to be illustrations of the way that a deeper reality manifests at the surface. If you are able to maintain your attunement, you will realize the extent of the world view, which you had been entertaining by allowing yourself to be subjected to the usual conditioning of our societies; and how it has limited your understanding, and hence your grasp, of the meaningfulness of your problems, by what science calls reductionist thinking. For example, instead of thinking of matter as dead, you will envision the atoms, molecules, cells, stars, and galaxies as endowed with intelligence, emotion, and will. Instead of reducing your representation of light to what your senses can perceive, you will experience yourself as constructed in the fabric of a nonphysical light.

Things which seem real to an average person, are unreal in the eyes of the mystic; and the things that seem unreal in the eyes of the average person, are real in the eyes of the mystic.[25]

Hazrat Inayat Khan

As you go about your chores, imagine that you are a denizen from the heavens walking upon Planet Earth with light in your eyes. Wherever you go, consciously project your light upon all situations and upon the minds of the people you meet.

---

25 Inayat Khan, *The Sufi Message* series, *Sufi Mysticism*, 14.

Represent to yourself those masters, saints, and prophets, or angels who epitomize what you imagine to be an illuminated being, as we did in the previous chapter; but now, attuning yourself to their attunement, try to imagine what it would be like to be illuminated yourself.

Meditate on different divine attributes, archetypes of inborn qualities, which we exemplify in our being, in others and in the world in general; and see how concentrating upon these affects the way you envision your countenance at the malakut level. Then think of the effect of the qualities you develop in your interface with your life situations—for example, perspicacity, self-motivation, initiative, responsibility, solidarity, courage, and forbearance—and how they affect your countenance at that level.

'Alam al-Mithal

This is the plane where our creative imagination functions as an extension of the self-creativity of the cosmos, the divine creativity. If you wish to function at this level, and hence enhance your own self-creativity, you need to reverse your usual mode of thinking, which is normally concerned with the feedback of experience, and highlight the feed forward of your inventiveness and incentive— to act upon the world rather than reacting to it. To trigger off this breakthrough, you will need to keep imagining how things could be, instead of simply observing the way things are.

If you capture the flimsiest clues as to the thinking of your mind at this level, it will occur to you that it relishes imaginations, fantasies, and sometimes, random phantasmagorias of pure fantasy that could easily elude control, but which are sometimes beautifully integrated and meaningful. It seems to be dabbling in processing the thinking of the collective unconscious in a tangible way.

Watch the thinking of your ordinary mind (khayal) while entertaining creative ideas; you will realize that it is contriving to concretize the metaphors erupting from your mind at the level of ajsam. It is a subsidiary of your mind at the level of mithal, and your mind at the level of ajsam is a subsidiary of your mind at the level of malakut.

The soul produces the mind out of its own self, and yet the mind is constructed fully after the formation of the body.[26]

Hazrat Inayat Khan

Avail yourself of the service of the faculty of your ordinary mind; but being appraised of the way it tends to limit the spontaneous outburst of creative thought, do not let it take over. Maintain your attunement.

26 Inayat Khan, *The Sufi Message* series, *Spiritual Liberty*, 253.

Concomitantly, imagine that your intelligence is superimposed upon your consciousness and throws light upon your understanding of what is being enacted in the prevailing circumstances. Consequently, instead of simply assessing your problems, you will endeavor to see them in the perspective of the overall intention motivating them. This is what the Sufis call *prioritizing the act of intelligence over the act of consciousness.*

You will, therefore, be anticipating the future. This will open a breach, giving you clues to the divine intention; it triggers off in you a similar perspective to the divine one: planning ahead. You will notice that, to some degree, this programming is delegated to you in your free will, within the overall orderliness of the universe; contrariwise, it has an impact on the overall programming. Furthermore, you will realize how, by bad judgment, greed, poor taste, and profligacy, we can obstruct and even sabotage that programming, as we may now observe in our pollution and abuse of the environment.

To train yourself to be creative of yourself and in your activities, you may model yourself on the amazing creative process in the universe, breaking through into configurations and structures. If you follow the sequence of attunements and modes of thinking in the course of the descent through the spheres, you will capture the originating divine intention erupting as an emotion as you resonate at the level of splendor (jabarut), then as a quintessential template (malakut), then breaking through to your creative mind (mithal) as a kind of archetypal meaningfulness. If you follow this further, you will observe this meaningfulness gelling into actual forms at the level of ajsam.

When meanings are embodied and become manifest in shapes and measures, they assume forms.[27]

I know God in proportion to the Names and attributes which are epiphanized in me and through me in the forms of beings, for God epiphanizes Himself to each of us in the form of what we love.[28]

Muhyi ad-Din Ibn 'Arabi

It will appear to you as though the miracle of life were a maze of cosmic thinking, powered by cosmic energy and coded into living atoms, molecules, cells, galaxies, nebulae, force-fields, celestial beings, biological beings, and endowed with a psyche, prodigies of art and craft, and creative imaginings.

Why do we think that a flower or a crystal or a piece of music is beautiful? The petals follow some kind of meaningful distribution of space, in which the multiaxial symmetry of the petals is bent by a certain measure of fluctuation

27 Chittick, *The Sufi Path of Knowledge*, 354.
28 Corbin, *Creative Imagination in the Sufism of Ibn 'Arabi*, 124.

from perfect order. In the crystal, unless using spectography, we perceive only subliminally the geometrical coherence of the light waves registered through our retina, and the departure from that coherence due to the fluctuations of the electrons from one orbital to the other. Even more complex is the patterning of our body cells; and even our thinking matches the selfsame cosmic harmony, and also the fluctuations from that harmony. To grasp that harmony in matter, match it with the orderliness of your thinking processes. You will recognize your thinking in the orderliness of matter.

At this level, do not allow your understanding of events to be limited by your interpretation of impressions inputted by your consciousness, but cast the light of your inborn intelligence upon events; and behold how the software behind the universe manifests and actuates itself in its hardware. As you attuned to the higher spheres, you relished the discovery of the software; now see that the purpose of the software is the hardware. The existential scenario should not be dismissed as illusion (maya), but seen as the fulfillment of the purpose behind it all.

The purpose of the soul is that for which the whole of Creation has been striving, and it is the fulfilment of that purpose which is called God consciousness.[29]

Hazrat Inayat Khan

This will have an immediate consequence on the way you envision your problems. Envision events and circumstances in your life as the projections of virtual realities that can never be the object of the act of consciousness. However, we can now match our grasp of the divine intention, culled in the higher spheres, with the issues enacted in our problems. You will realize that handling your problems in a creative way will have an effect upon the programming motivating them; and you will develop an insight into the deep springheads behind your thoughts, concerns, activities, and relations with others.

'Alam al-Ajsam

The experience [the mind] has gained through the body as its vehicle becomes its knowledge; and it is knowledge that makes mind.[30]

Hazrat Inayat Khan

---

29 Inayat Khan, *The Complete Sayings of Hazrat Inayat Khan*, 217.
30 Inayat Khan, *The Sufi Message* series, *Healing, Mental Purification, The Mind World*, 134.

At this stage, take advantage of the insight you have gained in the descent through the spheres to fashion your subtle body.

You will find yourself in the state of reverie experienced in the course of your ascent, with the difference that you have not lost sight of the physical world.

With open eyes, train yourself to continually keep stalking that which transpires behind what appears; try to espy in the material world, also in the circumstances that you are involved in, the traces or signs of a splendor often obscured by the appearance of matter and situations. The only way to achieve this with open eyes is to offset your glance as we have learned to do. This is to maintain, ever present in your awareness, your inherent intuitive notion of the celebration in the heavens, which we solemnize in our worship together with its correlate: the celebration of the earth, of which the scenario of the physical cosmos is a dramatic, and often disappointing, projection.

Vision requires implicitly a creative act on the part of the one seeking it. To do this, you must straddle several, in fact, all spheres; because our appreciation of beauty calls upon a resonance at the higher levels of our being.

If you proceed thus, you will be enraptured by the discovery of beauty in its ineffable condition, eluding all form and yet transpiring through its mediation. Indeed, if the forms reveal meaning, it is because they serve as expressions of a language that articulates that meaning. However, you will notice how the forms of the physical world, while translating the motivating emotion and the originating meaningfulness behind the formative processes in the existential world, fall short of achieving this. One could offer several reasons for this: the very conditions in which the software of the universe is actuated at the existential level are limiting, i.e. the space-time framework; the difficulty for we creatures, including atoms and molecules, to grasp the magnitude of that emotion and meaningfulness; the personal bias. A defilement sets in, particularly in the measure in which the creature develops free will.

Knowing this, you will endeavor to translate more effectively the emotion you experienced at the jabarut level, and the sense of the divine intention you experienced at the lahut level, into the actual form of your subtle body.

To exercise some impact on your subtle body, you will have to exercise some measure of detachment regarding your identification with it, which you developed in the ascent at the ajsam level. Consequently, even though aware of the physical plane with open eyes, your imagination will be idling somewhat, irrespective of your perception of the physical environment.

All the while, you will notice that your etheric body is interspersed with the cells of your physical body, like high frequency light waves filtering through the spaces between the molecules of a crystal. Now imprint this force field, which one tends to think of as subtle matter, with the sense that you have acquired of the countenance of your effigy at the level of malakut; and see how it changes with your thoughts and emotions.

The fabric of this etheric double responds to the fashioning of our creative imagination much more readily than that of our physical body, of which it is both the template and distillate.

In, or rather as it, our being gels in a tangible, though malleable, form. Granted that it is a hybrid, and therefore, does not just reflect the genetic form of your ancestors, but also replicates its malakut template. Notwithstanding, we can reshape it just as a sculptor could improve a statue. To ascertain how easily it changes with your thoughts or emotions, you could watch in a mirror the way the muscles of your face change according to your thoughts and moods.

Providing you maintain your glance so as to grasp that which transpires behind what appears, the reflection of your physical face in the mirror can serve as a useful feedback system to give you some clues as to the countenance of your subtle body. Experiment on yourself by thinking of the way you have suffered from the abuse of a person of your acquaintance. See how it affects the expression that transpires through your face. Then think of a person whom you love or admire, and observe the difference. Now think of a quality like compassion, and see how the countenance of your face expresses that archetypal quality. Now think of your nostalgia for beauty. See the effect. Now truth. Now mastery. Now perspicacity, alacrity, and so on.

As we have seen in our personality, the divine attributes (sifat), invoked by their names (asma'-ilahi) as contemplative musings (waza'if), are not endowed with a form, but are manifest in our etheric double as a form.[31]

'Alam an-Nasut

The body is a wonderful instrument in which to foster illumination, providing one transforms it.

Tibetan adage

You will say: can one change one's physical body? Can one change one's face? One can.[32]

Hazrat Inayat Khan

The physical body is the key to working with the subtle and celestial bodies, since these influence each other reciprocally. The clue is to tap into the process

---

31 Since, according to the Sufis, the etheric body survives the disintegration of the cells of the body at death, we have, thanks to the incentive of our creative imagination, the chance of fashioning it the way we wish to be after this episode of life on Planet Earth. Therefore the Sufis, and also the Tibetans, have developed skills for working with this body of resurrection.
32 Inayat Khan, *Esoteric Papers*.

that interconnects your mind and your body, seen as two poles of the same reality. We have seen that the mind of the physical body is the gross mind, as compared with the mind of the etheric body (ajsam), which is the subtle mind of the plane of metaphor (mithal)

To work with the mind-body connection, rather than dismissing your interpretation of your experience, extrapolate it with the feed forward of your creative mind, the subtle mind. Since the purpose of the software of the universe is in its hardware, rather than dismissing the existential scene as illusory, think of it as the fulfillment of the divine purpose; and by the same token, consider your circumstances as the chance of fulfilling your purpose.

Our imaginings are extensions of the divine imagination behind the fashioning of the universe. Let us bear in mind that these evanescent formations have their existence regardless of whether or not they are actuated in physical matter. Our appreciation of beauty, as perceived through the mediation of the world, brings us in contact with the celestial spheres of pure forms.

Nature protects us from overstress by taking care of numerous functions through automating them. But as you evolve, you can use your free incentive to take over more and more of these functions consciously and willfully, so as to ensure the impact of the higher levels of your thinking over your body, which concretizes them and communicates the clarity thus gained, all the way up through the spheres. To achieve this, we need to earmark the links between mind functions and their underpinnings in the plexus of the autonomic nervous system, and also the connections between these and the central nervous system. Paramount among these is the impact of your higher modes of thinking upon your pituitary gland, and the connection between the posterior pituitary and the hypothalamus.

To demonstrate that you can impact the cells of your body with your thought, it suffices to represent to yourself your arm being lifted to spark the mechanism that fires the relevant motor nerves. Think of the cells of your body as endowed with consciousness, and infuse the consciousness of these cells with your overall consciousness.

The first step consists in concentrating on a particular plexus (chakra); for example, the cardiac plexus (anahata chakra; latifa sirriya), or the pineal gland (ajna chakra; latifa khafiya), etc. Concentration is reinforced when exhaling.

Now try to represent to yourself the cells of that plexus. Each plexus is related to an endocrine gland, or a whole organic interrelationship between endocrine functions.

Concentrate on your solar plexus. Envision it as the threshold leading into a vacuum. Let your psychological or physiological tensions be resorbed in this vacuum. By so doing, you will be affecting the pancreas, which processes proteins. There is some cryptic relationship between our digestion of food and our ability to process psychological impressions. Under stress, both can get blocked. The sheer mental representation of the vacuum, which is your capacity for absorption, will unblock the bottleneck.

Concentrate on your cardiac plexus. Think of it as an outgoing outlet. Broadcast warm thoughts of goodwill. Reach out into the environment, the world, and the cosmos, broadcasting emotions of love, compassion, joy, and peace. You will be affecting the thymus gland. Being the key to the immune system, it serves as an underpinning for your sense of identity, which now reaches beyond its commonplace boundaries.

Concentrate on your pituitary gland—actually the posterior pituitary. This will instantly give you a sense of being in control—in control of your thoughts, your emotions, your consciousness, and your life situations. The pituitary enjoys some kind of prevalence over all endocrine functions, co-ordinating them. Its interface with the limbic brain, partly through the mediation of the hypothalamus, is situated at the pinnacle of the interface of the autonomic and central nervous system along the spine. It is, therefore, a key to assuring sovereignty.

Thus you will be able to ascertain that by impacting key functions of the body by dint of pure mental representations, you will make the body more efficacious in serving the awakening of your consciousness and your mastery. Even if there is wear and tear in the body, its template does not deteriorate; in fact, it can improve while the body cells deteriorate. Therefore, the Sufi dervish Shams-i Tabriz called it *a palace in a ruin*.

When a soul arrives at its full bloom, it begins to show the color and spread the fragrance of the divine spirit of God...Once man has arrived at that pitch, he begins to express the manner of God in everything he does. And what is the manner of God? It is the kingly manner, but a manner which is not known even to kings.[33]

Hazrat Inayat Khan

---

33 Inayat Khan, *The Sufi Message* series, *The Unity of Religious Ideals*, 96, 111.

Chapter Three
Preparing for Life After Life

Every form has its archetype in the placeless [spaceless] world; if the form perished, no matter, since its original is everlasting.[1]

Jalal ad-Din Rumi

People are beginning to ask more questions about death and its process. This is because people today are more bent on confronting feelings honestly, rather than dismissing them out of fear.

Our notion of death is perhaps the most nonsensical of all our notions! Exploring the software of the universe, physicists never cease to be amazed by the smartness of the planning. How could we possibly believe that all that has been gained not only by our know-how, but the uniqueness of each of our personalities, should get lost to the universe?

If we are unaware of our immortality, we will think that we die. It is all in our way of looking at things. Our fear of death is linked with our failure to grasp more advanced paradigms of thinking.

The first step in learning how to resurrect consists in widening our sense of identity, which eventually proves to be coextensive with the universe. We commonly think of ourselves as a distinct individual; but if we are updated with the holistic view of our day and age, we realize that every fraction of the totality carries, virtually, the code of the totality.

Envision yourself as the keyboard of a piano, most of whose keys are taped so that you can only play a simple melody. Realize that if you can tear away more and more of the tape, and awaken previously latent, many-splendored features invested in you by the universe, then you will exult in self-validation.

In addition to the holistic paradigm, we need to consider the transcendental one. Our commonplace thinking thinks in terms of categories: mind, body, and perhaps the soul, that mysterious unknown.

---

1 Nicholson, *Selected Poems from the Divani Shamsi Tabriz*, 47.

The consequence is that our thinking breaks up in a dualistic or pluralistic view: the bodies dies, but we hope the soul continues to live—two categories.

The advanced way of thinking is in terms of polarity: I am also my body. In our spiritual beliefs, we are so old-fashioned. We still think in terms of one time-dimension.

If we invoke the new paradigms and are able to extrapolate between two or more dimensions of time, then we may envision ourselves as a pendulum, of which one pole is moving in space-time, and the other remains unchanged. In between these two poles there are numberless transitional stages. Information, imputed from our perceptual interface with the physical environment, is processed upwards, so that ultimately, the quintessence is recycled into that level of our being where meaningfulness prevails over perception and is eventually recycled into the software of the universe.

As we shift our sense of identity upwards, our feeling of the process of becoming merges into a sense of being a continuity in change. Indeed, the very cellular structure of our bodies, particularly our faces, which configures our emotional attunements and insight, will imprint the fabric of the subtler levels of our being; for example, our electromagnetic field, the sparkling of our aura, the morphogenetic field that acts as a template of our body, and further upwards, in degrees of subtlety in infinite regress. Thus our bodies will outlive the dispersal of the building blocks of our body: the electrons and protons that survive and carry some bytes of memory. This could be illustrated by the fact that not one cell of our body is today the same cell as a few years ago, yet we think it is the same body, because its basic structure survives the disruption of the cells.[2]

Consequently, like a sculptor, we can consciously and willfully fashion in a creative way, our bodies of resurrection—that is, our celestial bodies that maintain the gist of the countenance, which sometimes transpires through our face when we are aware of the bounty and thinking of the universe coming through us.

---

2 The same water never flows under the same bridge, yet the river remains. If a magnetic field structuring metal filings into a pattern were to undergo a momentary depolarization, and then get repolarized, perhaps under a different voltage or amperage, the metal filings would disperse, then reform again. It will never be the same metal filings that will return to their initial position, but the overall configuration of the magnet will remain constant. Behind the dizzy flickerings of the building blocks of our bodies, the morphogenetic field of the body remains constant. The electrons within the atom rearrange themselves more meaningfully and efficiently as a support system for the advance of intelligence in the evolutionary leap from the inorganic to the organic, than in the inorganic mode. At first sight, the falling apart of the given structures could be misconstrued as an irretrievable catastrophe, yet the components self-organize themselves in a new structure.

By identifying with our self-image, which is a fallible notion of ourselves, we are obstructing the shift in our thinking that enables us to bypass our transiency, which, in turn, is the condition of learning how to resurrect. The resulting misassessments of our involvement in our problems stands in the way of our realization, because we are ultimately our realization; and it is this transcendent dimension of our being that survives its support system.

This would then require that we would need to stretch our minds beyond their middle range, and see what the implications of our problems are from the point of view of those involved in them; and while surveying ourselves with a bird's eye view in the context of the cosmic drama in all its extent, grasp the dovetailing of our lives and beings with theirs.

Do you ever feel that your body cannot contain you, or constrain you, or live up to the thrust of your mind, or withstand the exhilaration of your soul? Such are the vistas attained in the further reaches of the mind, maybe during meditation—a foretaste of life after life.

In this perspective, our way of looking at ourselves and our participation in the human drama will aver itself to be just the kind of thinking that will prepare us for the experience of resurrection. We would cease to limit our assessment of our problems to causation in a linear fashion in the arrow of time, or succumb to the conditioning of our personality; but we would grasp, as Speiser says, a *pre-causal stage*, out of which the programming of the universe arises behind the apparent universe or our own self-image.

Viewing things from this perspective, we would see ourselves in the universe, not just on Planet Earth or in our personal dramas, our storms in our teacups; and we would interrogate ourselves: *What are you doing on Planet Earth? What is your place in the universe?*

The body then, rather than being our spacesuit on Planet Earth, which we will discard at death, is seen as a support system. To borrow a metaphor: Pegasus could not reach Olympus, but he imprinted upon his rider, Bellerophon, the thrust that hoisted him aloft. The bodiness of Pegasus was transmuted into energy.

Admittedly, while many of the recollections in Dr. Moody's *Life after Life* and its sequels could be accounted for by the residual exercise of brain functions, the out-of-body overview of the physical shroud gives us some clues as to the aftermath of this episode.

Kabir typically refers to this in his verse: *I have learned from Him how to walk without feet, to see without eyes, to hear without ears, to drink without mouth, to fly without wings.*[3] May I add: *and think without the brain.*

---

3 Kabir, *Songs of Kabir*, Tagore, trans. 75–76.

However, we cannot be creative of a work of art, or of ourselves, just by willing it; we have to be moved and shattered and bewondered and bemused. In fact, we need to find our role in the cosmic celebration, not in the mavens imagined to be up there, but enacted right here and now, behind the apparent scenario of the drama of our own lives.

Reciprocally, the know-how and experience gained at the existential level is transmitted upwards, but is distilled at each upward level. For example, experience is distilled as know-how, and further upwards, as wisdom. There needs to be a way in which transient experience may be eternalized, so that it may update and enrich the programming behind the existential universe. To this end, it needs to be assimilated, made quintessential. The substrate of the know-how gained by experience, now distilled, becomes the very substance of the subtler planes that accrues to that which your subtle bodies inherit from the spheres hierarchically above them; thus they move up into the process that is called resurrection. Hence the importance of working with these higher bodies. This is commonly called *working with the body of resurrection*. Since according to the Sufis, God, descending from his transcendent form, becomes immanent in us, and then He is resurrected in us through our resurrection.

This work needs to be done during one's lifetime. This is the reason for the Sufi injunction: *Die before death and resurrect now.*

Should we parallel the views elaborated by the Sufis regarding the descent actuated by individuation, and the ascent, featuring resurrection of what we might call the essential core of one's being, through the spheres, with those of the Buddhists, we are heartened and, in fact, thrilled by the crossovers that corroborate each other.

Through and in our beings, spirit and matter interact, interfuse, cross-pollinate; and that which is thus gained is then recycled into the totality through the process of resurrection, releasing our counterparts trapped in the fabric of the universe with which we are intermeshed.

Chronicles of the past evidence flashes of genius in outstanding beings, in whom the intelligence of the universe broke through dramatically, sometimes jolting civilization into a sudden leap forward. Although they live, in a sense, in our memories, and their thoughts have percolated into our thinking today, in our commonplace perspective they have vanished from our reach. The same is true of great civilizations, which flashed in history and left a mark on the evolutionary march. Yet they too vanished, leaving traces now highlighted by anthropologists.

The discovery of the very least thing is the discovery of the whole of humanity.[4]

Hazrat Inayat Khan

---

4 Inayat Khan, *The Sufi Message* series, *In an Eastern Rose Garden*, 224.

Just like humans who carry a disintegrating hormone in their pituitaries in order to ensure an optimal turnover to foster evolution, even so do civilizations, however mighty, carry within them the seed of their own destruction. And so, over a large stretch of time, does the human species on Planet Earth. One can already spot the viruses of self-destruction and decadence in the corruption in our modern societies: the slovenliness and vulgarity where everything goes, crime on an unprecedented scale, menacing overpopulation, vying with the nobility of a minority, together with the lethal spoliation of our planet. On the other hand, never has there been such a genuine spiritual awakening and upgrade of human values. Since it is these values that have been gained by the very act of existentiation, how could one accuse the planning of the universe of letting it get lost? We are now speaking not just about the resurrection of individuals, but of values.

We usually grasp the causal, horizontal impact of creative genius, whether in art or technology, upon the progress, both cultural and technical, of life on the planet; yet we find it difficult to figure out the other dimension: the vertical. Even though civilizations sometimes avail themselves of the resourcefulness of their predecessors to make further steps, sometimes their past achievements are buried in oblivion. Much of the archives of the past are subject to conjecture. In the overall perspective, it does not make sense that anything achieved at any time in the universe should get lost. Yes, that energy should be expended to upgrade information, that makes sense. Yes, that the gist of experience should be extracted from its contingency and retrieved is the only view that makes sense. And this is what is meant by resurrection.

We limit our understanding of life by representing the universe as simply a physical reality; it is a many-tiered reality.

The next world is the same world as this, and this world is the same as the next; only, what is veiled from our eyes we say is a next step, and we call it the unseen world.[5]

Hazrat Inayat Khan

In addition to having left a mark upon us, the quintessential aspect of the beings whom we ascribe to the past have their being on higher planes; and there we can encounter a pool of resourcefulness for our creativity on earth, while ourselves contributing to this pool by our realization.

---

5 Inayat Khan, *The Sufi message* series, *Philosophy, Psychology and Mysticism,* 55.

Part Six

Working With the Psyche: Personal Transformation

Chapter One
Introduction to the Alchemical Process

transformation
      mutation
           transmutation
                regeneration
                     transfiguration
                          resurrection

Achievement, however great, does not seem to grant most people a complete sense of satisfaction. Perhaps the greatest human need is transformation, no doubt because, unconsciously, we are tugged by the inexorable forward march of the evolutionary process, of which we are participants.

Since time immemorial, the best brains of our species have vied to unearth means of promoting and accelerating the process of human transformation, at both the physical and psychic level. Alchemists searched their deep unconscious for clues, while believing that the coveted secret must be culled from a study of the processes that regulate the transmutations of metals, crystals, elixirs, or chemicals in general; because they posited that there must be a unified principle governing all transformation, whether at the level of the body or the psyche. This unwritten law governing life was emblazoned in the Hermetic tablet in the formula: *as above, so below.*

Arguments in favour of attributing the etymology of the word *alchemy* to *chem*, the black earth of the Nile, rather than to the Greek *chyma* (smelting), are reinforced by the fact that the oldest extant alchemical drawings are on Egyptian papyri. Furthermore, the attribution of the authorship of perhaps the most hallowed text, called the *Emerald Tablet,*[1] which defines the very

---

1 According to a legend, the *Emerald Tablet* (*Tabula Smaragdina*) was found in the first century by the Greek Apollonius of Tyana, in a grotto, in the hands of the corpse of Thoth, written in Phoenician characters. See Ruska, *Tabula Smaragdina*, 138–139.

basic principle upon which alchemy is founded, to Thoth-Hermes, points to it having originated in the Egyptian initiatic tradition, which was later transmitted to Greece and the Christian and Islamic worlds.[2]

Foremost in the text are the words:

As above, so below; as below, so above; to make possible the fulfillment of the One reality.

We have here a basic axiom affirming the unity of principle governing all transformation. In consequence, alchemists held that the processes they discovered in the manipulations of matter in their laboratories in order to transform raw material called *materia prima* into gold, would yield clues as to the processes that foster human growth.

While exploring means of transmuting metals in their laboratories, they were really discovering their own psyche, and an infinite number of valuable clues as to how to promote the transformation of the psyche. These are embodied in the royal art: *ars regia*.

The Muslim alchemist, Jabir ibn Hayyan,[3] postulated that the differences between lead and gold could be accounted for by the fact that the latter underwent a longer process of incubation in the womb of the earth under the effect of the planets, by the union of sulphur (hot and dry) and mercury (cold and moist); and he inferred thereby, that there must be a progression in the states of matter ranging from lead to gold.[4] The early alchemists, who were blacksmiths, the ancestors of the industrial revolution, posited that we humans could intervene in the operation of nature and accelerate the process in the *athanor* (the oven) or the *alembic* (the distiller). The secret was providing heat, which we know in physics is a form of energy. As the alchemists substitute the athanor, and sometimes, the alembic, for the womb of the earth in the incubation of metals or crystals or elixirs, in like manner, the meditator uses the body, magnetic field, aura, and other aspects of our total being, as constituting the vessels in which transmutation may be effected. In the esoteric view, fashioning these subtle personal substitutes of the athanor is regarded as building a temple to safeguard the sanctity of the divinity of our being. This is the psychic substitute for the athanor, and our subtle bodies form the altar of the temple.

Moreover, the alchemists posited that if we could only grasp these principles, we could not only accelerate the processes of transformation in the

2 See Burckhardt, *Alchemy*, 16–19.
3 Jabir ibn Hayyan, (Geber in Latin) (d. 815), of Tus and Kufa, was the first to intuit quantitative relationships between chemical elements rather than qualitative, thus prefiguring the Mendeleev serial law. See Holmyard, *L'Alchimie* 65 seq.
4 They thus forestalled the Periodic Table of Mendeleev.

laboratory, but by the same token, enhance the process of transformation in the psyche of humans. Therefore, the methods that they applied by learning how to trigger off the creative process in nature, using energy called *quickening*, throws some useful light on the skills we develop in meditation when enhancing our life field.

Since the heyday of the alchemists, scientists and physicists, chemists and biologists, physiologists, psychologists and meditators have carried that early research a great deal further. While the tenets of the mechanistic and positivistic theories neglected much of what the alchemists were conveying, albeit cryptically, the mind-body axis is now appearing increasingly on the scene. In general what one might define as a psycho-physics is emerging in our day and age.[5]

Yogis have been working with methods, both mental and physical, designed to promote the influence of the mind upon the body and the impact of the body upon the mind. For Buddhists, the body provides us with a most resourceful vehicle in which to foster illumination, providing its potentialities be exploited and its fabric transmuted.

We would like to know more about precisely how our thoughts configure the very cells of their support system, which is our body; and what we can do to promote this transformation. For example, we could achieve it by dint of the influence of our thinking and emoting upon that sophisticated network of nervous circuits that mediates between our thinking and body functions.[6]

These changes, which are mediated further by the endocrine glands, induce in turn, an effect upon the enzymes that supervise the replication of the DNA by the RNA. Moreover, the impact of our joy or sadness upon the light that we emit as an aura, or our electromagnetic field, can now be measured in laboratory conditions

Present-day advances in science and technology have opened up new vistas as to the way thoughts, imagination, and emotions affect brain, and particularly, endocrine functions. In fact, it may be said that the choreography of the molecules, atoms, even the electrons and photons of our bodies, ensure the miracle by which the splendor of the cosmic software endeavors to emerge through the structures and functions of matter.[7] But what we mean by subtle bodies, or acupuncture meridians, or the *chi* force still eludes the grasp of our middle-range thinking.

We are only beginning to investigate the transducers whereby our resentment, guilt, violence, and our self-image affect the immune system. Instead

---

5 See Bohm, *Unfolding Meaning*, 73.
6 Ibid., 95.
7 See Murchie, *Music of the Spheres*.

of thinking in terms of the psychosomatic, Dr. David Bohm considers the psyche and the body as the two constellated poles of the same reality, which he calls the *soma-significance*.

Such far-reaching research triggers off in us prospects of numerous procedures, devised to improve ourselves, and consequently, fulfill our purpose in the universe. This way of looking at ourselves challenges us to explore new ways of fostering transformation.

The Six Stages
Methods Applied in the Opus of Transformation

To promote transformation, alchemists of the ars regia, the royal art, point out the need to first dissolve (*solve*), and then rebuild (*coagule*), consciously and intentionally.

Applying the model arrived at in the transmutation of metals to personal transformation, Basil Valentinus divides each of these two phases in six stages.

1) purge any extraneous elements from your being;

2) distill the desired elements;

3) identify with the quintessence of your being;

4) integrate the constituents of your being (the alchemical marriage);

5) consolidate the transformation that has occurred;

6) eternalize what has been achieved by incarnating, by constructing your body of resurrection.

First Stage in the Alchemical Work:
Separatio
♄ Epitomized by Saturn, the Cross over the Crescent

In the initial purification, to purify the raw material (materia prima) used at the outset, alchemists start by subjecting it to a process of putrefaction, fermentation and trituration. Then they sift the dross or filter it, pouring it through a sieve. Alternatively, they subject it to a more stringent process in the athanor, called *calcinatio*, calcination.[8] By fusing base metals, the extraneous elements are scalded and drained as the sludge found in the ashes.

In their early attempts to make sense of the physical ingredients encountered in the manipulations of the prima materia, the alchemists distinguished three principles in matter, epitomized by mercury, sulphur and salt. It would be a simplistic interpretation of the ars regia of alchemy to advance that the alchemists elected mercury as the symbol of intelligence (our sense

---

8 Pulverization by fire.

of meaning or realization); and sulphur, which is easily fused, ephemeral, and transient, as exhibiting the features of the psyche; and salt,[9] which fixes the volatile elements, as the body. However mercury, the catalyst of life, according to alchemy often linked psychologically with consciousness, acts ostensibly upon sulphur, which is often held as the metaphor of the psyche; and the resultant product, salt, is ascribed to the body.

What consequences can we derive therefrom, regarding personal transformation? In our ordinary state, our notion of our trans-existential being gets immersed within that which has accrued to us from our ancestry, inherited on Planet Earth. Consequently, we carry within our nature the assets, and also blemishes, which have developed in the evolutionary march through the mineral, vegetable and animal realms, including the early fumblings of *homo sapiens*. Therefore, we need to first spot and earmark those elements in our nature that are unwholesome and detrimental to our progress, and then avail ourselves of the impact of our higher self to eject or drain them away.

The psychological practice advocated by the Sufis at this stage is called *muhasaba*, self-examination. This auto-cross-examination is enhanced by a strong attitude of confrontation as opposed to complacency.

1) Earmark those idiosyncrasies in your personality which you do not feel too happy about, but have difficulty in changing.

2) Surveying your life's curve by recalling reminiscences, try to spot those patterns in the events in which these idiosyncrasies have proven unfavorable to your activities.

With courage and honesty get in touch with your suffering. Acknowledge it; own it.

For the purpose of this practice it is better to let it hurt than bury it under a stiff upper lip. Later, perhaps, you can hold a better grip on the reins of your emotional steed.

Having let go of that trammel, you may discover areas of despair, agony, exasperation, destitution, hopelessness, to which you had never acquiesced. In fact, the words of Christ on the cross will gain a particularly vivid, painful, pertinent significance as they have been brought home to you in your own life.

Think of those instances where you have been let down and suffered abandonment, particularly by someone you trusted, or someone you loved, or someone you felt you completely depended upon. *Why hast Thou abandoned me?*[10]

---

9 Salt was added by Razi (in Latin, Rhazes) to the classical twin alchemical elements, quicksilver (mercury) and sulphur. Rhazes (825–925) was a famed doctor and pharmacologist in Bagdad. See Holmard, *L'Alchimie,* 92.
10 Matthew 27:46.

Are there cases where you have done precisely the same to another person? Imagine that person's suffering. You may find it more difficult to forgive yourself than to forgive those who harmed you. If only you could reverse what happened, turn time around! Could retribution offer some atonement? Not even a chance. There is nothing you can do but fret and denigrate yourself further.

Remember failing a test, an exam, a challenge. Remember evading a challenge out of fear, feeling like a coward. Remember being insulted, humiliated, derided. Remember being ashamed of yourself; and if there is no such case, simply not having lived up to one's highest ideal.

Remember being offended, maligned, unjustly treated, betrayed and deprived of any means of redress or retribution.

Take stock of those aspects of yourself that you do not like. Remember those times that you felt you were good for nothing, or at least below par, and consequently, frightened of facing the challenges of supporting yourself in competition in a competitive world.

Have you had childhood trauma? Were you victim of abuse, or worse? Did you try to put it out of your mind until it erupted, shattering your whole being? Believing that you were psychologically damaged will reinforce the trauma. If you are in therapy, you know that recovery is a painstaking process. What we are now supposed to call disability is not really so; it is simply a handicap. It is a higher hurdle than the usual ones, but simply a greater challenge. Stress is written into our programming; by challenging our resources, it awakens them and reinforces them, and spurs our resilience. *Be of good cheer ye who are fainthearted!*[11] It is the challenge that makes heroes. Throw down the gauntlet to high stakes. You can turn the tables on adversity to your advantage, overcompensate, and beat your records and those of the timid.

Wherever you look, you will see suffering, but you might have to plug into the consciousness of those who are more desolate, more severely tested than yourself. This can prove even more devastating than wallowing in one's own desolation.

O ye brave men, let go, allow yourself to cry at least just this one time. And if your valiance holds back your tears, let the tears of your heart flood your body with compassion for the victims of aggression!

And think of those cases where you feel that it was bad luck or ill fate that let you down, with the ensuing chain of misfortunes that escalated your suffering further; see how this affects your faith in God, or simply that there

---

11 Paraphrase of John 16:33: *In the world ye shall have tribulation: but be of good cheer; I have overcome the world.*

is some well-meaning intention behind life. In fact, the fear that we are delivered into a whimsical, heartless universe, void of sense, lurks in the dark depths of one's psyche. Yes, it can escalate beyond fear, and in fact, lead to terror when imagining being trapped in a concentration camp.

If you run into the darkest part of the night and hit rock bottom, your overstressed mind will be in turmoil; your thoughts will flash and pummel your psyche as in a raging storm. Out of control, your emotions have run amok. This is where the process of dissolution has reached its extreme disruption. It is well nigh impossible, at this stage, to presage that it carries the promise of a rebirthing, a new integration. Does not the grain have to dissolve that a new plant may arise?[12] It may appear as though one's mind were rent asunder. In pathological cases, it may even perhaps spill over in the body cells, which may seem to disperse in outer space, like a forestalling of what will happen to the electrons of our body after death. Paradoxically, the opposite may strike one: thoughts may crowd in, jumbled, random and deceptively meaningless, although fancifully interpreted, like being sucked into the void in the vacuum of one's psyche.

Why hast Thou abandoned me....

These words of Christ embody the whole drama of life, the deep quandary in our soul-searchings, when even the flimsiest flicker of light in the form of faith is being tested in the extreme.

Applying the know-how gained in the opus, the actual operation in conducting the process of transformation of the psyche, Jabir ibn Hayyan inferred that since putrefaction or fermentation takes place in the dark, one needed to let the dark forces of the unconscious take over in the dark night of the soul[13] until a point was reached where the sifting could be carried out usefully. Alchemists call it *mortificatio*, mortification, It is the experience of many that unpredictably, and sometimes unaccountably, their psyche, falters into a gruelling breakdown. All transformation requires a falling apart of sclerosed structures to allow their components to reconfigure themselves in an improved way. Does not Jesus say that the seed needs to die so that the plant may live?[14]

The way in which nature pummels our psyche to effect its transformation process, may take over in us, following its inevitable course; but it can be precipitated by the mystic through subjecting the psyche to drastic austerity, as illustrated by the alchemical process of calcination. The adept has a fore-taste of death or annihilation, whether in the dismembering of the body

---

12 See John 12:24.
13 See St. John of the Cross, *The Dark Night of the Soul*.
14 John 12:24.

(symbolized by the story of Osiris), or the collapse of the construct of one's personality, or the bankruptcy of the mind—a dark night, *nigredo*.[15] In the case of some mystics, castigation to the point of masochism was advocated as a means of atonement. Some justified whipping up their suffering, by projecting upon the model of Christ's suffering as an act of propitiation, just as the sacrificial slaying of an idol that we find in various pagan traditions.

The first night or purgation is bitter and terrible to sense...
St. John of the Cross[16]

However, it is a good thought to look upon a crisis as an opportunity to bring about a change, rather than to consider oneself as the victim of blind fate.

Breathing Practices

To reinforce the sense of forcibly evacuating unwanted ingredients in one's body, life field, or psyche, it is helpful to eject them as one exhales,

1) Let us adopt a Yoga practice called *bhastrika,* sometimes referred to as the *practice of the bellows of the blacksmith.* It is most appropriately described as follows:

Force all the air out by a sudden contraction of the abdominal muscles. Automatically they will return to their natural position; so there is no need of any conscious effort for the inhalation...It is best to prepare the body for bhastrika by first practicing uddiyana. *After emptying the lungs, with breath out, forcibly contract the abdominal muscles, raising the viscera until a large depression is made under the diaphragm. On should be able to place both fists in the pocket that is made, then suddenly relax. Repeat this alternating contraction and relaxation ten times before taking another breath.*[17]
Theos Bernard

2) As you exhale, imagine: a) the polluted energy in the energy field of the body (the etheric body) being drained, i.e., toxins eliminated by the lymph glands, as in a human drainage system; b) the emotions of resentment, disgruntledness, spite, hatred, envy, jealousy, the thought of being wronged, or self-pity are also being drained.

3) Apply the breathing practices already defined in Part One, Chapter 3, to enhancing the dispersal of your life field.

---

15 The notion of the value of darkness is to found in Gregory of Nyssa.
16 St. John of the Cross, *The Dark Night of the Soul,* Book 1, Chap. VIII.
17 Bernard, *Hatha Yoga,* 42, 45–46. Theos Bernard was an American relative of the author who practised Hatha Yoga in India, subjecting himself to severe discipline.

We have already encountered the effect of the dispersal of the magnetic field, or the diffraction of the aura, as you exhale. But you can enhance the process of dislocation even further by placing the accent on the absorption or assimilation of the psychic toxins, such as resentment and guile, and other fields, into the void at the center of that vortex constituted by our life field, at the end of your inhaling, culminating in the retention of your breath.

If, indeed, the central nucleus of one's being is immaculate, all dross must be absorbed into it. Therefore, assimilate the deleterious elements in your psyche, and resorb them in the void inside, thinking of your solar plexus as the threshold into the vacuum in the center of that vortex that you are. You can now contrast the dispersal at the jagged ends of your being with the assimilation at the center.

Second Stage in the Alchemical Work
Distillation
♃ *Epitomized by Jupiter—the Crescent over the Cross*

In the second stage, the fluid or fused products obtained after completion of the first operation is now distilled, sometimes repeatedly, in the alembic or retort. Alternately, the ashes remaining after the elimination of the base metals by fusion, are now put through a mysterious process in the hope of capturing the volatile spirit, mercury—the phoenix rising through the ashes. The volatile gas thus produced, before it is condensed as a liquid, is epitomized as mercury—the winged dragon. Great precautions are taken to avoid that the winged dragon should not be allowed to escape from the retort.

As applied to the psyche, having rid ourselves of the heavier, burdensome idiosyncrasies of our personality, we now proceed to transmute those that lend themselves to the sublimating processes and may, as such, be harnessed usefully, instead of being discarded.

Consequently, we transfer the center of our notion of ourselves to a higher level of our being in our scale of values. Meditation may, at this stage, lead to feeling etheric, like vapor. We are now called upon to abandon our crutches, unmask the hoax of the games wreaked upon us by our minds, and more so, by our emotional fancies and addictions. This accounts for the increasing need for detachment as adepts advance in their spiritual journey.

Instead of rescuing one from despair, one's commonsense logic throttles one under water, thwarting one's efforts to surface. It is only by doubting the validity of our commonplace thinking in adversity that we can escape the grip holding us down. But doubting the mind's ability to grasp meaningfulness beyond the middle range, still bespeaks of the dark night of understanding, not yet the dawning of the flicker of the saving light of realization: St. John of the Cross' *living flame of love*.[18]

Even if it flickers but hazily, remotely, and intermittently like a safety buoy in the mist, cleave to it in your floundering, even if by being eclipsed by the terrifying waves of obsessive and uncontrollable emotion, it seems to keep on letting you down.

When confronted and awakened, your personal emotion will mow you down mercilessly; rise again, and keep at it. Unchallenged, it will whittle your zest surreptitiously from inside, leaving you desensitized, apathetic, sceptical, fossilized, low-key. Therefore take courage; do not demur. Just keep remembering that you might be missing out on your ultimate rescue if you discounted that light as a hallucination, a mirage, wishful thinking.

It was because one lost touch with the intuition of the cosmic celebration; because one became bogged down by one's personal emotions that had overwhelmed one, alienating one from one's saving grace: the celebration in the heavens.

You are crossing the dark night. If you were blindfolded you might have a better chance of calling upon your innate resourcefulness, instead of looking for crutches outside. Maybe that light is inside, in a kind of hunch that *there is meaningfulness in all of this; but for the time being, I cannot see it.* Your friends cannot help you much, since they cannot be presumed to be where you are; and even if they were, you can only find help inside, and only if you trust a kind of idiosyncratic self-organizing faculty. However, in your terrifying destitution, the feel of a safe hand in the fiasco offers some solace even if that friend cannot pull you out of the mire. Besides, the realization that there is goodness to be found in the world, will prove ultimately heartening.

Only faith in yourself, when there is no foothold for a ledge that you can rely upon outside, will save you. The *God within*, rather than *God other*, up there: the God manifesting as you. Maybe you can only reach the *God beyond* from inside, by identifying with God. Defy your logic: you are both excellent and flawed, like an eighteenth century cracked cello, a palace in a ruin, yet sublime, divine and human. If you could just espy the beauty within you, buried under so much that you dislike! Avoid dismissing your pride in the aristocracy of your soul, by priding your ego in your humility.

A slender rope of hope offers itself to hoist you from despair, if you give it a chance by reminding yourself that you value beauty and kindness, and that you could not have any idea what this means unless it were a reality somewhere. Looking upward seems to turn you in the opposite direction to gravity; and gravity makes you aware of your body, of matter, with all that this involves in terms of constraint and limitation. If you think that matter is

---

18 See St. John of the Cross, *The Living Flame of Love*.

only meaningful for the body; if you become less aware of your body or feel the magnetism surrounding your body; or think of yourself as etheric and gossamer; and if you think that your psyche, your thinking, your personality is not really your real being but like the unfurling of that seed unknown to you that is your real being; then you have a ladder to rescue you from the phantasmagoria of your daunting, deceptive representations of yourself.

This is the second stage in the alchemical process: ridding the quintessence of the materia prima from its dross, by distillation. Highlight the essence of your being from all that has mixed with and tarnished it.

You may feel a sense of levity, as though you were lifting yourself above the heavy, constraining burdens of your earthly underpinnings. Consequently, you begin to become aware of your subtle body, and at a further stage, your celestial body.

Alchemists picture the body as the athanor, the oven, while hermeticists look upon it as a temple. The psyche is pictured as the alembic, the retort, the altar in the temple in which the work of transformation is carried out.

Alchemists recognize the role of heat in powering the transmutation, and heat is energy. For the Sufis, this energy can be felt as the streamers of energy in our breath, *pas-i anfas*.

1) Think of yourself as a plant. Having eliminated, as you exhale, the waste products (in psychology, those aspects of yourself that were ejected in the previous stage), now siphon the telluric forces of the earth, transferring your attention up your spine. You will sense the difference between the grosser vibrations and the more subtle ones, and that indeed, the grosser ones can be refined. This is obviously the Yogic practice of kundalini. But in this second phase in the alchemical process, do not simply lose yourself in an uncanny void, but let the forces released thereby hoist you up through the spheres.

2) You may now appropriately apply the practices in this book on the celestial spheres, specifically in shifting one's consciousness from one plane to the next.[19]

(i) Start by becoming vividly aware of, for example, your heart, your liver, your kidneys, your lymph glands, your arteries, your brain. Then more specifically, the cells of, for example, your fingers.

(ii) Now become aware of the zone of energy surrounding your arms and shoulders, and projected by your cardiac plexus and above your head. Imagine that your body extends to this zone. It appears to be of the nature of a force field. It feels volatile, nebulous, unstable, floating, amorphous, like gossamer. Identify with it while considering your body as a crystallization thereof. Yet you will realize that it permeates the cells of your body, interspersing with

---

19 See Part Five, Chapter One, "Exploring the Spheres."

the very electrons of the atoms of your body. You will have the impression that you can think and be aware and experience without a body.

(iii) You will notice that your mind now thinks differently, archetypally. You will, moreover, enjoy intense euphoria, a sense of freedom.

(iv) After identifying with the physical radiance surrounding your body, shift your attention to a subtler effulgence, both adumbrating and permeating your physical aura. It appears to be non-physical in nature; and it can only sustain itself if you maintain your attunement in a non-worldly state, and offset your consciousness from the perception of the senses.

6) While doing this, represent to yourself those idiosyncrasies that you can transmute, and envision them thus sublimated. If you find difficulty in transmuting them, you might find it easier to rise above them by affirming your freedom. This can be achieved by disidentifying with them, considering them to be extraneous to your pristine being.

7) At a further step, you find that, having selected those features of our human cultures with which you feel an affinity, you can even sublimate these further so as to literally ingest them in your psyche.

The alchemist's concern that extreme care should be taken lest the winged dragon escape from the retort, could well be substantiated by the concern of modern psychotherapists that, should one shift one's sense of identity into its boundless dimensions, as one does in meditation, to the point where one has a feeling of merging with the totality, one cannot harness consciousness to foster a rebirthing of the psyche.

Third Stage in the Alchemical Work
The Immaculate State
☽ *Epitomized by the Moon— the Lunar Crescent*

The process of dissolution, the lesser work,[20] culminates in the acquisition of a product of rare beauty, sometimes described as the philosopher's stone that has the power to transform dramatically all that it comes in touch with. It is this vade mecum that is supposed to transform base metals into gold. Although it would seem foolhardy to validate claims to this effect, one may well treasure the view that the principle that it represents in the hermetic traditions, the Holy Spirit—the immaculate state—carries the clue to transformation.

This quicksilver, when it was sublimated, was clothed in so pure a white that it looked like the snow on a very high mountain. It had a fine crystalline lustre,

---

20 Corresponding to the minor mysteries.

from which, when the vessel was opened, there emanated a perfume so sweet that nothing resembling it could be found on earth... I wept with joy and astonishment at so great a wonder...What kind of a nature can that be which, coming from a corruptible thing, nevertheless contains in itself a wholly celestial thing?... Perhaps, however, there will come a time when I can tell you a number of things about this nature which the Lord has not allowed me to communicate in writing.

Bernard Trevisan[21]

Trevisan's soul-searchings spark troublesome interrogation in our own minds: we had endeavoured to rid ourselves of our material nature to discover our spirit, only to find that it was embedded in matter all the time.

It takes, however, this step into the unknown beyond our usual body consciousness, to discover our spirit in its purity. Here lies the clue to this third stage in the alchemical process of transformation. You have, or will have, the impression of having lost from your view the perspectives, not only of the existential state, but even of the celestial spheres, as though you had kicked the ladder which had hoisted you into the unknown. Typically, you have lost the sense of location in space and the passage of time.

You will remember that at the level of malakut, you had the impression of having at last grasped your real being while remembering your earthly self-image, which seemed like a mask. Now, since you have a hunch that you were immersed in a hoax, and have at last awakened to reality, you dismiss your memory, which is thus totally obliterated; and you have a sense of at last discovering your true being. Paradoxically, it is so totally impersonal, so cosmic, that you have lost your sense of personal identity; and while incorporating virtually the bounty of the many-splendored qualities, you are, at this level, immaculate

One can understand that Christian alchemists elected the Virgin Mary as epitomizing this state. Obviously, the reason why we lost our memory of existential states is that it would have been so difficult to reconcile this virginal condition of our being with its defilement in our personality. However, it is precisely this extrapolation that we will have to achieve in the course of the next phase, coagule, starting with the alchemical betrothal.

Now, as you rise like the phoenix out of your cinders, and shake off the dust, you will rediscover the child in you, which is innocent, defenseless, untarnished within its own defilement in your adulthood; it is hidden under your mask, buried under the elaborate defense system you built up, which not only proved ineffective, but turned the tables on you.

---

21 Trevisan, "The Forgotten Word" (*La parole delaissee)*, in *Le Voile d'Isis*, 461.

You will discover that you have wings, like the butterfly that thought it was a cocoon. But to discover this, you had to shift your identity and believe that you need not be the person you thought you were. You are liberated; you can dance with abandon, round and round. and up and up. spiraling into the fresh breeze of freedom! Hurtle into outer space, beyond the earth sphere like a rocket freed of its launching station, in infinite regress beyond the beyond.

You are pure spirit. You have awakened! You are pure intelligence, untrammeled by earth consciousness. You have also loosened the grip of transiency; the essence of you is gifted with the nature of eternity.

1) Cease to identify yourself with your psyche, which now appears as a support system. Imagine that the countenance of your celestial counterpart has already conveyed to you a sense of innocence, without blemishes—like distilled water.

2) It will now seem as though you awakened backstage of the universe. Our practices scanning the stars and the galaxies having freed us from our parochial purview, we make the next leap, reaching out for the celestial spheres. A clue to doing this would be to imagine that, standing on the earth, you reach aloft; and having done this, standing on the plane thus acceded to, you reach further, then still further.

3) The practices under Part Four, Chapter Four, outlining the stages according to Patanjali's *Yoga Sutras* regarding the modes of our thinking as we venture beyond our commonplace thinking, constitute landmarks leading the way to the level corresponding to the immaculate state, which is precisely the samadhi state in Hinduism.

4) Tune into the mode of thinking associated with your memory of the celestial spheres.

5) Realize that, ultimately, you are your realization, irrespective of body or even personality or a brain. Discover that your human realization is only the projection of the realization of your celestial being; and that beyond the celestial perspective, you could touch upon a still higher one. At the pinnacle of thought, you have the feeling of rising further and further in the realms of significance behind the thinking of the universe.

6) Instead of thinking of your consciousness as the spectator, or the lens of that Spectator that is God's consciousness, think of your consciousness as simply a reflection of the divine *I* (eye). Now cogitate on the implications of Mahmud Shabistari's statement:

Not being is the mirror, the world is reflection, and man is as the reflected eye of the Unseen Person. In that eye, His eye sees His own eye.[22]

Fourth Stage of the Alchemical Work
The Alchemical Betrothal
♀ *Epitomized by Venus — the Sun over the Cross*

Now we transit from the stage aiming at dismantling the elements of our being, *solve*, to the rebuilding or rebirthing, *coagule*, epitomized by Venus.

*At first, the volatile power of feminine Quicksilver prevails over the solid bodies....
Later, however, the fixative power of Sulphur prevails over volatile Quicksilver
and effects a new, and this time active, crystallization of the soul-body form.*

Titus Burckhardt[23]

Here we touch upon the crux of the whole operation: how do we inter-weave this imponderable quintessence of our being, which we have at last captured by probing the depths of matter, with the material underpinning of our being, such as it has become in the course of our making?

This is, of course, idyllic; but was there not something wonderful about life at the existential level, something challenging, something gained—an evolutionary thrust into further dimensions of reality than the splendid isolation in the bliss of the heavens? Were we not building something that was not there before, out of our incentive, our endeavour, hewn out of the pristine promise of all potentiality by dint of blood and tears, of imagination, incentive, labour, suffering and hope in a better world? Doubtless it is af-flicted with constraint and frustrations, but is freedom from all of this the only freedom? Is there not freedom in our creativity—freedom from the past, from conditioning, from conformism, from our own self-made illusions and self-deception, from what we are? Is there not freedom in becoming what we want to be, rather than going along with what we have been?

We can rebirth ourselves, and make a new picture out of the material at hand. We can earmark traces of the heavens in us, without escaping our material underpinnings. We can see value in our humanness. We can combine the two, willfully, consciously and intelligently, with the skill of a sculptor, of an artist.

The entire objective of the ars regia, the royal art of the alchemists, is to grab a handle on the creative process in order to recreate ourselves the way we wish to be, rather than being the victims of what we might suspect are the unpredictable whims of the destiny that constituted our making.

22 Shabistari, *Gulshan-i Raz.*
23 Burkhardt, *Alchemy*, 190.

Indian alchemy, rasayana,[24] fosters the art of going through each step that led to our conception and birth, consciously and willfully. Indian alchemy is a form of Tantra. The practitioner transmutes body functions, and even cellular configurations, by the impact of *purusha,* spirit, also identified with mercury. This requires a regression into the primeval state[25] followed by a rebirthing, followed by an immortalization. After separating purusha from prakriti, as we have seen in the practices leading to samadhi advocated by Patanjali, the tantrist works to transmute the body by awakening miraculous powers called the *siddhis.*[26]

Let us now examine the skills that are devised to foster rebirthing.

We are a hybrid. The alchemical betrothal highlights the union of our heavenly and earthly inheritances.

At the moment of birth two currents meet: all that the soul has inherited from the spheres in the course of its descent, and all that has been inherited through one's ancestors.

Hazrat Inayat Khan

If we look deeper into these two groups of factors constituting the building blocks of our being at all levels, we find a plethora of ingredients so infinitely rich that we could never list them exhaustively. Obviously, we inherit from the whole universe; the universe converges into each focal point of itself, as in a hologram.

We may invoke the model of a hologram to illustrate heredity. As we have seen, if you fraction a hologram, each fraction behaves like the whole hologram rather than as a portion thereof; although the smaller the fragment, the less well it performs the functions of the whole hologram. The simile of the human being with the hologram of matter differs, however, in that it is the scope of our awareness that determines the degree to which we can actuate the functioning of the whole universe.

According to the ars regia, our primary nature, prior to its transformation, is still present within the materia prima, which the alchemists are trying to transfigure. If indeed, *as above, so below* is true, then, just as in the blastema (the original cell in the embryo) all genes are present without yet a determination as to which will be turned on and which turned off to diversify the cells of the unfolding embryo, so only a few of the infinite potentialities invested in what the Sufis, quoting Christ, call our *divine inheritance,* are actuated in our personalities; most of the divine qualities are recessive. The same applies

---

24 See Eliade, *Yoga, Immortality and Freedom,* 283.
25 *Regressus ad uterum.*
26 See Eliade, *Yoga, Immortality and Freedom,* 274.

to our subtler bodies that embody infinite possibilities—the angel hidden within us.

Just as the initial cell in the embryo is a hybrid in which the universe, having converged in umpteen scores of beings, cross-pollinates with that of numberless other beings, so the substrate of our subtle bodies carry the many-splendored bounty of untold denizens of the heavenly spheres. However, this primeval material of which we avail ourselves, whether bodily or psychically, has both evolved and deteriorated in the course of its involvement in the existential condition. Yet, just as the voice of Caruso is still buried in its pristine glory in the bad recording of the time, so the celestial counterpart of our being is unscathed under its peripheral defilement.

According to the Sufis, our personality is composed of the exemplars of those divine archetypes (sifat) that predicate the divine nature. It may then be posited that we inherit the plethora of the divine qualities, which are infinite and perfect. We need to add to these those idiosyncrasies that we inherit from the outcome that ensued from the way these primeval qualities were unfolded by our celestial counterparts. We need, therefore, to account for the qualities that accrued to us at each step in our descent through the spheres. Let us ponder upon the inborn knowledge with which we are invested at birth. This is one more remarkable feature of our cosmic inheritance—to wit, Mozart's or Handel's or Chopin's genius. These are the talents referred to by Christ.[27]

In addition to all of this, we need to account for the fact that our bodies are made of the fabric of the Planet Earth, which is made of the fabric of the stars, even of the whole universe. Our bodies, therefore, carry the nature and features of the atomic structures of matter. Furthermore, we need to account for all the racial, social, cultural, and psychological features that we have inherited through our ancestors, including animal, vegetable and mineral. We are normally only aware of an infinitely small slice of all the richness that lives in us.

Our problem is this: how do we integrate all this material in a congruent way? The ingredients composing our being are extremely diverse, and some-times contradictory, conflicting, antagonistic, and even mutually exclusive, unless we find a way of reconciling the irreconcilable. This was the quandary of the early church fathers who were epitomizing this very issue in the being of Christ, meshing both the divine and the human. Since there was no way in which ordinary minds could see how opposites could be combined,[28] the Vatican Council declared a dogma that one needs to believe even if one can-

---

27 Matthew 25: 14–30.

28 *Coniunctio oppositorum.*

not understand it. Nowadays we experience a need to stretch our minds to grasp challenging thoughts. Congruence in space could best be illustrated by the locksmith who needs to match the key with the tumblers so that they may snap into position. Another example could be found in a constellation of stars, or more generally heavenly bodies, where they coincide from the perspective of Planet Earth, in a syzygy. Hindus ascribe great power to the junction between two rivers, or a confluent and a river, *pralaya*, or the polar points where the lateral trunks of the spinal cord connect. Congruence in time could be illustrated by the many examples given by C. G. Jung of apparent coincidences in time, which he called *synchronicity*. Congruence becomes even more impelling to our understanding in Euclid's algorithm: it is the largest number that divides into two given numbers.[29]

A pertinent example of congruence in physics is a wave interference pattern based upon the rule according to which, if the crests of two waves concur, they reinforce one another; and if the crest of one wave coincides with the trough of another, they cancel out. Dr. David Bohm's theory of the implicate order is the very epitome of congruence at a cosmic scale. In genetics, the linkage and crossover between the DNA of the father and mother requires either a compromise in which there is a lot of dovetailing, or the dominance of the phenotype of one parent and recessiveness of the other. An aesthetically agreeable example of congruence is consonance, illustrated by a musical chord in which the intervals between the components have a common denominator. A particular euphoria is sparked when human minds cohere, or when the emotions of two or more people are on the same wavelength. In logic, congruence is challenging to our commonplace thinking. Our minds are programmed in such a way that we ordinarily pigeonhole our thoughts in categories. To reconcile thoughts that seem irreconcilable, we need to stretch our minds into what might be called an all-encompassing, integrating mode.

Since the cases in the above example, where there was concurrence, are exceptional, we need not be surprised if there is a lot of maladjustment and incongruity, and hence, conflict within our own minds and personalities. This is illustrated by the cases in which we inherit from an irate father and gentle mother (or the opposite); or we are pulled in two directions by our passion, as opposed to Dantean love; or by our need to involve ourselves in life and our need for seclusion. Hence the importance attached by C. G. Jung to the integration of the personality. May the above serve as models of ways and means that we may adopt to integrate the perinatal[30] and existential components of our being, so that the qualities of our celestial counterpart

29 The original term *algoritmi* derived from the name of the Arab mathematician Muhammad ibn Musa al-Khwarizmi. See Penrose, *The Emperor's New Mind*.

30 Before or at the time of birth. A term coined by Dr. Stanislav Grof in 1984.

may cross-pollinate with those of our planetary inheritance. To achieve this, it may prove helpful to call upon some of the skills developed in the art of meditation.

Practices

1) To start with, having had a whiff of that imponderable breath we conceptualize as the Holy Spirit,[31] we have now reached the point where we need to feel in our meditations whether we can grasp the quickening witnessed by many mystics.

If no carnal attachment subsists in him, then that spirit of which Jesus, son of Mary, was born, descends upon him.[32]

Mansur al-Hallaj

After the dismal gloom of the darkest of the night, comes the breakthrough of light.

Oh! flame of the Holy Spirit, that so intimately and tenderly dost pierce the substance of my soul.[33]

St. John of the Cross

This same light that appeared as darkness, because it dazzled and blind-folded him, now avers itself to be comforting:

Thou dost not afflict me and cause me the suffering and the anguish which Thou didst before, anymore.[34]

St. John of the Cross

Could St. John of the Cross' esteem for a gracious lady, Dona Ana de Penalosa who was a benefactor of the Carmelites and for whom he composed *The Living Flame of Love*, have opened the way to his soul, out of the seclusion of monastic otherworldliness and into the discovery of the Divine Beloved transpiring though the human channel?

The soul always undergoes transformation through love.[35]

St. John of the Cross

2) We have already tried in previous lessons to connect up the idiosyncracies of our personality with their archetypes; for example, we considered the degree to which we are generous, and then tried to represent God as

---

31 In Islam, *Ruh al-quds.*
32 Massignon, *La passion d'al-Hosayn-ibn-Mansour al-Hallaj,* Vol. III, 48.
33 St. John of the Cross, *La vive flamme d'amour,* Stanza I. Cf. my translation.39.
34 Ibid., 53.
35 Ibid., 36.

being generous to the extreme limits; this is, indeed, what we mean by the archetype. Let us do this again, earmarking one idiosyncrasy after another.

3) To observe clearly the contrast, and indeed, the incongruities between your perinatal inheritances and earthly one, interface the features of the countenance of your subtle bodies with those aspects of your being that you have gained, not only by dint of your ancestral heritage, but by your experience of life on the planet. You will become vividly aware of the incompatibility between these two aspects of your being, which you are now trying to inter-mesh.

4) To do this, as already seen, we need to try to retrieve our memory of our celestial condition, at the level called *malakut* by the Sufis. If you remember, the very thought of the eyes of a baby or child could trigger off this memory; or alternatively, highlighting an attitude of innocence or guilelessness in your handling of situations; or again, in the attunement you achieved in the exercises relative to the second stage we have just practised. You will be moved by the very thought of splendor, enamoured with the grasp of beauty, bewondered by the extraordinary intelligence programming events, and emboldened by the power of our life field. Realize that these states are all present within you. They highlight your celestial inheritance.

5) Working with another person, apply the practice that we have already learned, of the violet and blue effigy.[36] You could imagine that person's physical face in blue and superimpose, as in a hologram, that person's celestial countenance in violet.

6) Now you can do the same with your own image.

7) You will need to take two steps. (i) Correct the distortions, which have incurred in the course of your descent through the spheres by the impact of your perinatal self upon your existential self; (ii) appraise the pool of resourcefulness gained by incarnation, which, in turn, feeds back into your trans-existential, or perinatal, being.

8) See how these reciprocal adjustments facilitate the intermeshing of the feed forward with the feedback, in what is called the *alchemical betrothal*.

9) Working with those idiosyncrasies that you estimate having inherited from your celestial inheritance, and those from your parents and ancestors, you have two options. You will find that the simplest method is simply to find a compromise; for example, not be too otherworldly and yet not be too worldly. It is much more difficult to manage to reconcile the irreconcilable,

---

36 Part Two, Chapter Two, "Working With the Glance."

to be in the world and yet, as in the words of Christ, not of the world.[37] You could value material things, yet not be attached to them. To apply some of the methods we have practiced, you could be aware of the personality features of a person, while at the same time, grasping their celestial being. In your own case, you could be aware of both.

10) Working to integrate the inheritances of the idiosyncracies of both parents in order to integrate your personality: if there is or was incompatibility or conflict between them, since the idiosyncrasies of both are in you, then you again have an option. You could compromise; for example, if your father was overly generous and your mother stingy (or the other way round), you could find a nice middle way. However, how could you find a way of reconciling the irreconcilable here? You could be wholeheartedly generous to the deserving and parsimonious with those who might take advantage of your generosity. You could be magnanimous yet unyielding, or compassionate without being accommodating. From the above, we see the advantage of inheriting very diverse qualities, even if they appear incompatible at first. This is precisely what is meant by reconciling the apparently irreconcilable.

Fifth Stage in the Alchemical Work
Making the Gold Adamant
♂ *Epitomized by Mars—The Sun under the Cross*

We may enjoy high moments in our meditations, moments of euphoria, have a peak experience and then fall right back where we were. It is a steep climb to get back to the crest again. Therefore, to maintain some measure of equanimity, we must keep remembering how we felt, what was our outlook when high. Once more, our logic is defied. Can we believe that the child within is still there, untarnished, even if our assessment of ourselves has reasserted itself? Can we believe in the aristocracy of our soul while people's treatment of us will remind us to honor the democracy that our ego holds us to in our personal self-evaluation? Can we believe, beyond the proof of the contrary, the realization grasped in our high moments?

We may be a new person, but people will still hold us to the image they have always entertained of us. If we are fainthearted, that hackneyed image will destroy our more recent one, which is more precarious, like a fledgling. In our modesty, we may demure to what now appears as commonsense, forgetting that it is the commonplace mentality, unless we believe in our new self, identify with it, and declare *urbi et orbi* that we are different now, we are a new person. Maybe they will see it and support us in our newness.

---

37 John 18:36.

At this stage you need to do two things:

(i) You need to extrapolate between, on one hand, all that we have encountered so far, with, on the other hand, the considerable input from the natural and social environment, education, upbringing, and prevailing circumstances.

(ii) Instead of limiting yourself to incorporating your inheritances, you need to freewheel in order to brainstorm what you want to be.

Let us remember that to be creative, you need on one hand, to assimilate the bounty of the wealth of the input from the environment; while on the other hand, you need to be self-motivated, spontaneous, and inventive. However, to galvanize this emerging aspect of your being, you do need to downplay the input, treating it rather like a catalyst, so as to concentrate mainly on what is coming through: your own uniqueness and incentive.

This is the way of fulfilling the purpose of your life: making your dreams come true by actuating realizations or visions into reality at the existential level.

Practices

1) Consider the bounty that you have inherited at all levels, including all that you have acquired through your environment, education, culture, acquired skills, and wisdom, as a pool of resourcefulness that you could avail yourself of at your own discretion. This might require a paradigm change in your way of thinking. Instead of thinking of yourself as having been conditioned, highlight your free will.

2) The considerable diversity of factors in your vast inheritance provides you with not only (i) infinite options, but also (ii) a palette of infinite combinations.

3) Therefore, (i) being fully aware of the presence in the seedbed of your personality of a virtual quality, called by the Sufis the *divine inheritance*, inherited from the very programming of the whole universe, decide which of these resources you wish to prioritize.

(ii) Being aware of your idiosyncrasies inherited from your parents or ancestors, decide which of these resources you wish to prioritize.

(iii) Being aware of the idiosyncrasies which you have acquired from the environment on Planet Earth, decide which of these resources you wish to prioritize, which you wish to downplay, and which you wish to discount or reject.

2) Sort out in your mind whether the qualities that you are concerned about developing evidence: (i) your concern about adapting yourself to the environment; or (ii) the way that your particular programming unfurls the potentialities lying in wait in the seedbed of your personality; (iii) the way you want to be. The first option evidences our concern about adapting ourselves to the environment; the second, the way that as we unfold we adapt the environment to our own internal conditioning; and third, our freedom from the environment and from our own programming.

3) Now to enhance your creativity. Scan the vast spectrum of qualities, values, and attunements that you have ingested from the environment, and more-over, those impacting you at present. Decide (i) which strike you forcibly; (ii) which are those that typically display the present trend; (iii) and which are those that bear an affinity to your own nature.

4) To be creative, you have the choice between (i) reacting to whatever impinges upon your consciousness from outside, and describing it in your work of art or manifesting it in your being; (ii) brainstorming ideas that emerge impromptu from within;[38] or (iii) availing yourself of the input from outside as a catalyst to trigger off fresh impulses from within. The latter option implies that you do not simply react—that is, boomerang back the impressions wreaked upon you from the environment; but by dint of a paradoxical association process, different impressions awaken subliminal thoughts that acquire thereby a new dispensation of energy. You thus call upon that inherent faculty in all nature to self-organize, in the measure in which it is not constrained from outside pressure.

5) Your emphasis on your own incentive is now going to give you a clear vision of your new self-image that definitely reflects tangible changes in your personality. But you realize that people around you, not realizing this, still think you are the way you were. Therefore, you have to affirm your new personality, actually spell out to your mate or friends that you are not the same person as before, and request of them to take this change into account. Otherwise you incur the danger that you will loose faith in whatever has been achieved in the alchemical process, and slip back to the way you were before by conforming to the hackneyed image that people have built of you.

Such is the characteristic of the fifth stage in the alchemical process: making the gold adamant.

---

38 Traditionally called *ex nihilo*, out of nothing. In the view of Dr. David Bohm re the holomovement, one would refer to emerging from the implicate to the explicate state. See Bohm, *Unfolding Meaning*, 12.

Sixth State in the Alchemical Work
The Spiritualization of Matter, and the Materialization of Spirit
☉ *Epitomized by the Sun—the Solar Disk*

Death is swallowed up in victory. O death, where is thy victory? O death, where is thy sting?[39]

St. Paul

Here the whole process attains its completion. This stage is often described as *the spiritualization of matter, and the materialization of spirit.*

If we look at the process we have undergone so far, it becomes clear that in the first three stages, we mentally dismembered the components of our being in order to recombine them anew, in keeping with the realization we have gained. In the next two stages, our objective was the transformation of our being and the incorporation of all its potentialities, including the celestial ones, in the psyche, and even in the body. There is an underlying assumption that whatever is gained at the existential level is what life is about. But what value is there in something that is ephemeral, transient? Therefore, the only way that life could make sense is if the gist[40] of what is achieved can be perpetuated. This is already illustrated in the fact that the seed ensures that the features of the plant will survive its death. But if the cycles of existence were limited by this rule, there would never be any progress. Evolution is only possible if whatever is gained by the plant, owing to its interfacing with its environment or its adaptation to the environment, is fed back into the seed. This can be accounted for by the process exhibited in nature called *mutation*, which ensures new genetic variability. As we have seen earlier,[41] the Sufis point out the programming whereby the plus gained at the existential level is fed back into the celestial levels of our being, which survive the demise of the body.[42] This presupposes, in the language of the esoteric Sufis, that the gist of experience at the existential level is fed back into the divine programming. But if the know-how of an individual survives death, it does not follow that the individual survives as an individual. That the altered chromosome would lead to a new form of the species, does not indicate that the individual is reincarnated. From the fact that the seed does undergo a mutation in its structure, can one infer that the individual flower survives

---

39 I Corinthians 15:54–55.
40 In alchemy, the term is *quintessencia*, quintessence.
41 Part Five, Chapter Two, "Embodying the States of Awakening."
42 Mutations can sometimes be detected cytologically in the chromosomes, but one could legitimately theorize that they have their springheads at a deeper level; for example, the scaler level or the morphogenetic field. Maybe if we probe deeper into this nebulous subterranean underpinning of our being, we will arrive at something of the nature of what the traditions mean by *other planes* or *spheres* or *subtle bodies*.

in a different seed to the one it unfurled in the first place? Does this really give us a clue to what the Sufis mean by resurrection? I think not, because according to them, the change need not be imprinted into morphological structures, but rather in the code.

In Sufism, as in Tibetan Buddhism, skills are taught to extract the gist of the know-how gained through experience, and to ensure its transference into the subtle bodies.

When you have now ensured the input of your extra-existential counterpart and the overall programming of the universe infiltrating your personality, thoughts and emotions, and which is manifesting creatively in your activities, as in the previous stage, you are better able to feedback the gist of everyday experience, transfiguring it into your higher being. An analogy would be how spelling out one's thoughts in speech or writing will help gestate the ideas, but conversely, the impact of language on thought is equally valuable. This is why, at this stage, you need to be aware of the actuation of your perinatal being in your psyche and body; keep reminding yourself of the fact that you are incarnating, and at the same time, observe and enhance the transfiguration of your psyche, and even the cells of your body, into the fabric of your subtle bodies. That is to experience resurrection.

Chapter Two
The Creativity of the Personality

What an opportunity life offers us to be creative! Besides, the only way to find fulfillment in our life is to be creative, to give a tangible expression to our uniqueness. The universe is enriched by the diversity of the infinite manifestations of the One and only Being, in and as each of us.

Wherever you turn, there is the face of God.[1]

Qur'an

We are those faces, each different, unique, and each, potentially, a further contribution to the richness of that marvelous totality, of which we are all an expression. But what do we do with this precious gift?

We may claim that our life is so busy simply surviving in a highly competitive world that we cannot afford to be creative. But why do we assume that to be creative we need to have the training and develop the skills of artists or musicians or writers? The most wonderful work of art is the human being, or at least, it lies in wait in the human being. The compositions of great composers, the paintings of great painters, and the poems of great poets are simply the reflections of their own being in a language that can be communicated to others. Their creativity is the means whereby their uniqueness is shared with those who resonate with them. We are enriched by the cross-pollination that takes place when the meaningfulness and excellence in the universe flows from one being to another. Creativity is the way through which the thinking and feeling of that Being who is the universe, passing though us, is customized by us in our idiosyncratic way. We all carry that potentiality. Unfortunately, in most cases, people do not harness its full capacity. What a waste of cosmic potential! What a waste of the wonderful gift of life!

To be creative, whether of a work of art or of ourselves, we need to let ourselves be moved by ecstasy. Music is ecstasy. Poetry is ecstasy. Dance is

---

1 II:115.

ecstasy. Arts and crafts are inspired by ecstasy. Even scientists are enraptured by the discovery of the elegance of the software of the cosmos.[2] But there is a wide range between bliss and euphoria, between noble emotion and vulgar feelings. And there is no accounting for taste; one may pay pearls for pebbles.

We are born with the gift of ecstasy. We lose it by our frustrations, our disappointments, our defeats, by the derision or humiliation to which we may have been subjected. We lose it by our greed, our guile, our lack of charity, our cynicism. Truly enough, we are living in a cruel, decadent, and violent world; but intertwined with all of those things that sicken us and offend our sense of propriety, nobility and kindness, flashes of beauty, heroism, and idealism strike the eye of those who are on the lookout for it. We see that which we are attuned to; it just depends upon what our values are. Everything is to be found right here and in each one of us, in the form of our potentials.

Remember, it is your ecstasy at the discovery of the beauty behind the expression at the existential level that will spark the beauty in yourself, and eventually, may spark the latent beauty in others. Conversely, it is because the virtuality of beauty is within you, that you are able to discover its semblance in the universe.

If you seek beauty, you may become a consumer of beauty and dependent upon it, addicted to it; you will want to possess it, and it will either confine you or escape you, or it may even evaporate in your grip. If you create beauty, people will be looking for the beauty they are seeking through your gift of what you actually convey of the divine beauty, which underlies all manifest beauty. What you have to give will live in those who have valued it and been enriched by it, and it will spread further afield—perhaps anonymously—and you will even continue to live in this way after you die.

To spark your creative impulse, let yourself be carried by a state of be-wonderment, stalking a reality hidden behind the apparent scenario of life. You attune yourself to a state of reverie, the twilight state of the mind. Here the mind thinks in a holistic instead of linear mode; thought is enfolded in its implicate mode. The priority is given to affinity rather than contrast, and thereby, thinking becomes multidimensional instead of reductionistic.[3]

Furthermore, as you turn within, emotions become imponderable; the mind is able to extrapolate thoughts by recognizing similarity. A multitude of thoughts, with their emotional load and corresponding images vying for our attention, emerge simultaneously rather than in sequence, including

---

2 See Chandrasekhar, *Truth and Beauty.*

3 An example of reductionist thinking is syllogistic logic based in the *categories of reason* of Immanuel Kant.

suppressed or frustrated emotions. When the mind is plunged more deeply into the state of reverie, it is able to superimpose all these images. As our consciousness surfaces toward the threshold state, it finds it difficult to reconcile these discrepant images, but toggles between them back and forth, rather idly.[4]

In the state of reverie out of which creativity arises, thoughts and images do not just fan out horizontally, but also vertically—that is, not just in the cosmic dimension, but also the transcendental.

Know that there is no form in the lower world without a likeness (mithl) in the higher world. The forms in the higher world preserve the existence of their likeness in the lower worlds....Between the two worlds there are tenuities which extend from each form to its likeness.

These are like ladders for the angels, while the meanings that descend in these tenuities are like angels.[5]

Muhyi ad-Din Ibn ʿArabi

In the twilight of consciousness, our unconscious straddles several tiers of our being and the corresponding spheres, which include suppressed or frustrated emotions. In deep sleep these impressions are also interspersed. In the state of reverie, the impressions from different spheres are often super-imposed, and it requires the cohering impact of the beam of consciousness to highlight one or the other of our celestial bodies, thus enabling us to pan from one landscape to another. However, should we attempt this unprepared, we could easily find ourselves precipitated back into the ordinary diurnal state, and lose our focus on our subtle bodies and our perspectives on the celestial spheres in the same way that, when the sun rises, we cannot see the stars any more. Even though impressions from different levels of our being are intermeshed, still it is the dominant emotions lurking in our unconscious that stir impressions from one level rather than another, to the surface.

---

4 To illustrate this mode, Bohm suggests a paper so crumpled that more and more fragments are juxtaposed with one another. In theory there would be no limit to this, even though there would be in practice. This model simply serves as an analogy. But for our minds to follow this, we would have to grasp that space can be envisioned as having a fourth dimension in which everything intersperses with everything else, as in a wave interference pattern. And then, conceivably, there could be a fifth dimension of space and so forth, in infinite regress. This mode gives an incomparably greater—in fact, infinite—scope to our thinking and feeling, and consequently, frees the mind from the constraint of clichés in our commonplace thinking and our sometimes stilted emotions, which have become fossilized by the force of conditioning. Hence it fosters new ideas, unthought so far—precisely what creativity is about.

5 Chittick, *The Sufi Path of Knowledge*, 406.

Since we are not only interfacing landscapes or scenarios of little-known spheres, but also touching upon different levels of our identity, there can be no doubt that our self-image—and hence our self-esteem—is precariously suspended on these elusive impressions. While in our diurnal focus, we are able to talk ourselves out of our negativity, or someone else may boost our self-esteem; while in these nebulous, sometimes murky regions, we normally do not enjoy any control. In some cases, thoughts can be obsessive, particularly in the case of people suffering from psychological stress. The only way of exercising any influence upon these imponderable conditions is by auto-suggestion prior to sleep.

How Do We Proceed?

Through the kind of training learned in Yoga Nidra, we can indeed illuminate these areas, and even single out the spheres we wish to highlight. The clue consists of knowing how to activate intelligence instead of consciousness, as we have already learned to do.

Practice discounting the ordinary scene of the world, considering it to be maya in day consciousness, because this is where the personal will can operate. Capture that which transpires behind that which appears, and then shift your own sense of identity from the existential level to the subtle, then to the celestial. Your unconscious will pick up the programming of the conscious and carry it into the dream state.

This cannot be achieved simply by disciplining your will and training your mind. It is your emotional attunement that powers your will and modulates your thinking. It is by your love for beauty that you attune yourself to the higher levels of your being, which, in turn, affects your thinking. It is also your innocence that resonates with the condition of the heavenly counterparts of your being, making you aware of them. Therefore, there is a great deal of work that we need to do with ourselves before we can have any impact upon what our ordinary conditioning is doing to our unconscious in the dream state or the state of reverie: overcoming greed, hatred, vanity, guile; pledging ourselves to service; being caring, loving, and forgiving. This, as we know, is going to affect our creativity.

This is why the music of some composers or the pictures of some artists simply reflect their inner conflicts, which are sometimes the garbage of repressed emotions, random, fanciful thoughts, and sordid and distorted images thrust upon the public. These will find resonance in those who are wallowing in the same kind of netherworlds. In contrast, there is a sense of integrity in great works of art.

In the degree to which we reflect the intention behind the cosmos and exult in its splendor, in the values that we uphold, in the intensity of our nostalgia for sacredness, we mold our personality into a beautiful work of art.

Creativity is born in that twilight state—reverie—where emotions, ideas, and their corresponding forms abound in profusion, germinating, proliferating and procreating unrestrained. In that subliminal state where our minds free themselves from linear thinking, we discover that the horn of plenty that unfolds in the universe is replicated in the infinite dimensions of our minds.

We witness here the role of freedom from constraint that drives the mutations in the evolutionary advance of the cosmos, and which can burst forth through our creativity, even in a violent way. Sometimes upheavals ensure progress, freeing the programming of our lives from conformity to its own self-originated patterns, lest they become fossilized and arrest further growth. Similarly, to be creative, you need to keep beating your records by freeing yourself from their patterns. For the Sufis, the granting of freedom is the ultimate act of divine generosity. It is inbred right into the electrons of the atoms of our bodies, which avail themselves of the energy of light to slip away from the constraint maintaining them in their orbitals. But free will needs to be balanced by orderliness to avoid running amok, which would prove counterproductive.

You will notice a quality of innocence or, shall we say, the ingenue, in the very spontaneity of creativity at its inception; an unsophisticated trust in the bona fide of the intention and the meaningfulness behind the universe, which Sufis call the *divine intention*; a regard for authenticity, taken for granted. It is only as the creative patterns move down into the existential realm and adapt themselves to it, that they become contaminated by earthly conditions in which abuse of the gift of freedom has opened the door to guile and defilement—a challenge to the sacredness of our original immaculate state. And then an inherent, cosmic wrath may emerge as a defense in the form of outrage, which comes through in our creativity, including our personality, in confrontation, aggressiveness, violence, and even cruelty.

To manifest at the existential level, emotions have to be translated into forms; for example, they configure our countenance, modifying the complex tensions in the muscles of our face, or in the inflections of our voice. It is during this transit between the initial emotional impulse and the way it gels into a form, that our intellectual faculties are called upon. But it is a fine art to learn to shift our sense of meaningfulness from the enfolded state into concrete, discrete thought-patterns. Some of the mental templates behind great works of art are masterpieces of intellectual ingenuity.

To be creative then, we need to follow the selfsame process that governed the sequence of states in our descent through the spheres. In so doing, we will be nurturing our creative imagination, which is the selfsame power that projects the software of the universe as its hardware.

Practices

1) First, get in touch with your intuition of an immaculate, nascent sacredness, in its pristine state prior to its having become tarnished by interfacing with the world.

2) Then attune yourself to your highest nostalgia for splendor, recognizing the values that you cherish most.

3) Earmark qualities that are latent in the seed of your personality, while realizing that we can only know these archetypes by exemplifying them in our personality.

4) Then marshal a strong determination to actuate these qualities more than ever before, not only in your personality, but also in your way of handling your problems.

5) Listen silently to what is coming through; having given yourself over totally to rapture, you need to translate that emotion into a language, a form, a structure. In the case of the artist, it is obvious: musical themes or rhythms are also forms, and so are words and thoughts; the idiosyncrasies of your personalities are subtle forms.

6) Now give vent to your self-organizing faculty. Our minds and wills are also part of an inherent, self-organizing thrust. Sometimes we believe that to be creative, we need to bypass the mind and the will. Actually, they are sorting things out, working under cover of the unconscious in a way that we could not achieve consciously. However, by the fact that this self-organizing faculty is customized in us, the creativity of the mind of the universe gains further excellence. The choice between playing it by ear and intervening with our incentive is at the very crux of the creative process.

Represent to yourself that we are paradoxically involved with, coextensive with, and isomorphic (of identical nature) with a web of interspersed and superimposed strands. These converge from the infinite variety of aspects of the ultimate reality. And in fact, you are those strands yourself, and will discover yourself in them through your creativity.

A formidable power lies wasted at your doorstep. The qualities latent within the transcendental pole of your being excel, beyond imagination, those actuated in your personality. And as you capture something of the immensity of the cosmic dimensions of your being, you realize that you inherit from the genes of the entire universe, including the stars, the galaxies, cosmic rays, the Big Bang, the orderliness of the molecules in a crystal, or the disruption in the harmony of the spheres in a solar or galactic storm, or the majesty of an elephant, the diligence of a bee, the playfulness of an otter, the sensitivity of a butterfly. But you also inherit the thinking of the universe, the cosmic planning, the creativity, the ecstasy, the psyche of the universe, the will—in fact, what we mean by the soul of the universe, where the mystic in us discovers the traces of the divine inheritance.

Sufis consider these archetypal principles, which govern our human nature, as our divine inheritance. These crowning features, lying in wait in the very roots of our being, strike us as infinite and perfect.

Divinity is like the seed which grows in the heart of the flower: it is the same seed which was the origin of that plant and it comes again in the heart of the flower.[6]

Hazrat Inayat Khan

To possess that which you have inherited from your ancestors, you have to conquer it.[7]

Johann Wolfgang von Goethe

It is not enough to have inherited the bounty of the totality; you still have to do something to translate latencies into actuality, to unfold the implicate into the explicate. That is precisely what creativity is about.

To be creative, you need to weave these strands into a tapestry—that is, to cohere elements that seem at face value heterogeneous, and make sense of them. This is where your sense of meaningfulness proves its relevance.

For there to be some congruence in your creativity, rather than randomness—pure fantasy, which is not attractive or enriching—you need to find a way of joining similarity with diversity, or even discrepancy. Even if two patterns do not interlock like a key and tumbler, there is often some point at which they do match, although *in extremis*, even in infinite regress; for example, at some point we are all expressions of the totality we call God.

Examples in mathematics abound: for one, the common denominator between two numbers, or between two sums, as in an algorithm; or there may some similarity in the dynamic patterns of arithmetic, geometric, or harmonic progressions. Further fascinating illustrations of this principle are found in music when, after having spirited dissonant chords which evoke discordant impressions in the listener, the composer shifts the musical chords into harmonic consonance; a resolution has been clinched, tensions are relieved; and suddenly, we grasp a sense of harmony or orderliness behind the programming of the universe. This is what is called congruence.

---

6 Inayat Khan, *The Sufi Message* series, *The Unity of Religious Ideals*, 118.

7 *Was du ererbt von deinen Vätern hast, erwirb es, um es zu besitzen.*

Creativity is the fruit of insight into collating divergent elements in what they have in common: coordinating while contrasting similarities and dissimilarities in meaningful permutations. Musical analysis can give us invaluable clues as to how to work creatively with ourselves.

When we look at all that we have inherited, the enormous variety of factors seems unwieldy in the extreme. Say we had an irate father and a gentle, loving mother (or the opposite): we inherit in our very personality the problem they experienced in their relationship. Your task is now to integrate two seemingly opposite and contradictory idiosyncrasies within your own personality. It is not surprising that we encounter internal conflicts, as C.G. Jung points out. But this is just the start. Consider not just your parents, but all your ancestors, including the animals, vegetables, and minerals. Moreover, recognize the need to reconcile your ancestral inheritance with your celestial inheritance. If indeed, you do inherit from the celestial spheres, have you ever considered that you may well have had parents in those spheres? You may find yourself confronted with the problem of reconciling the innocence and purity that lies at the celestial and immaculate core of your being, with the guile inherited from your earlier ancestors, which they developed in their struggle to survive primitive conditions.

If you scan your cosmic horizon further, you may discover more and ever more heirlooms in the unknown dimensions of your being. In fact, you inherit from the whole universe. Since our commonplace self-image is typically idiosyncratic, we have difficulty in recognizing these as inheritances that have accrued to our being in the course of its descent through the spheres. They strike us as being ultimate, archetypal. Al-Hallaj refers to lahut, the plane from which we derive this legacy and which is beyond the celestial plane, malakut, and even beyond the plane of splendor, jabarut:

O take away this nasutiyat *(human nature) so that only Thy* Lahutiyat *may prevail in me.*[8]

While the divine nature latent in our inheritance is limited and defiled in our personality, it is still present, although recessive. Here again, we have the problem of reconciling those two natures co-present within us. An admittedly not totally satisfactory example of creativity would be comparing a high resolution picture of a landscape with a bad reproduction, and then bringing more and more detail into the bad reproduction.

For the wave interference pattern of the holograph to be meaningful to our mind/brain, a new laser beam having the same frequency as the original beam, needs to be thrust across it. In our state of reverie, the plethora of

---

8 Massignon, *La passion d'al-Hosayn-ibn-Mansour al-Hallaj.*

intermeshed, variegated strands that we wish to weave into a tapestry needs to be cohered congruently until they can emerge as a nicely integrated personality. Failing this, our personality would be incoherent, incongruent, fanciful, or freakish. That beam is, in terms of the mind, our innate sense of meaningfulness; and in terms of the emotions, our innate sense of aesthetics. Therefore, it is our realization and our love for beauty that will make our self-creativity of our personality into a precious work of art, and make us grow to great stature. Creativity is born, not just out of the intermeshing between numerous latent, inherited ingredients in the seedbed of our personality, but out of the coincidence between these on the one hand, and on the other, the congruence between the light of our intelligence and our striving for excellence. This is precisely what David Bohm means by the super-implicate order.[9]

We now see the importance of working in meditation with both the cosmic dimension of our being and the transcendent, and of coordinating them. We also see the need of enhancing our grasp of meaningfulness by consciously casting the light of our intelligence upon the idiosyncrasies of our personality, rather than simply observing these with our consciousness.

Clearly, at least at first, you cannot cope with all the overabundance latent within you. That is why you are programmed so that only a few qualities dominate in you, the others being recessive. This is precisely what makes for the uniqueness of each person and the great variety of personalities. If you intervene in your self-creativity, then you need to pick those qualities you wish to prioritize. The consequence is that those we downplay will consist of your deficiencies or foibles. If you wish to progress, you will eventually have to deal with these.

The Sufis consider that we are on a journey, and pass through different phases (*maqamat*) in our itinerary. The more you use your incentive, the less you are subjected to a programming beyond your control. But should you take things in hand, then there is a likelihood that you will give priority to the concern about adapting yourself to the challenge of situations around you, rather than cooperate consciously and willfully with the way you are programmed to unfold.

Therefore, ask yourself:

1) *Which is the quality that has emerged in me lately and is uppermost in my thoughts at present?*

---

9 Renee Weber, *Dialogues with Scientists and Sages,* 33. A model that you may find useful to foster your creativity could be found in collating Dr. David Bohm's theory of the holomovement, calling for a to and fro alternation between the implicate and the explicate state, with an alternation between what he calls *soma* and significance.

2) Then ask yourself: *Should I reinforce this quality? Would it make me better able to deal with the tests I am subjected to in my life at present than if I apply the quality that I thought I needed to develop?* If we just go along with our programming, we are not being creative.

3) Therefore, ask yourself the third question: *What is the quality that I would like to develop, regardless of whether it makes me better able to adapt myself to the environment, or whether it is the quality that corresponds to the stage I am passing through in the natural course of my development?*

Nature itself breaks the continuity of its progression, sometimes in a kind of quantum leap as, for example, from the inorganic to the organic. We find the same in music: J.S. Bach often takes us in the flow of a harmonic progression, then breaks the pattern, transporting us into a whole different attunement. Incidentally, as we have seen, we encounter here the difference between the moment of time where a continuity is felt within the change, and the instant of time where any sense of continuity has been interrupted abruptly and decisively. Personal incentive frees us from the kind of continuity programmed into evolution by conditioning, transposing us into a more intensive evolutionary rate. What is more, our decision affects the whole programming of the universe to a degree varying with its relevance to the whole.

If you model yourself on composers, you will find that after developing a musical theme (that is, after making the most of its potentialities), the composer will bring in another theme. Very often this second theme is in some way related to the first, while contrasting with it in a complementary way. Indeed, you will find in your work with your personality that you need to balance one quality with another. Simply highlighting one quality may create an imbalance; for example, should you enhance your generosity, it would be taken advantage of unless you, at the same time, build up your strength to ward off abuse. Or telling people what you think of them by highlighting your truthfulness, would need to be tempered with compassion and love. Or should you simply reinforce your mastery, you would become stubborn and fail to listen to guidance. There is a difference between striking a balance where a quality would need to be tempered and thereby impoverished in order to accommodate another one, or reconciling the irreconcilables, where the qualities complement each other like the poles of a magnet.

To be creative, the composer needs to make use of the psychological trend as a catalyst, to spur innovative ideas emerging from within. It is not enough simply to adapt to the challenge of the environment, or just to do one's own thing.

Process the impressions from outside deeply (like the way our liver breaks down and builds new amino acid chains), rather than responding to them in a perfunctory way, in which case you would not avail yourself of the pool of the resourcefulness of your being.

Apply the same to the creativity of your personality. Circumstances are always challenging us. Should you simply adapt yourself to the environment, your personality would become stereotyped, and you would not be enhancing your uniqueness, which is your greatest gift. On the other hand, if you are oblivious of what is happening in the world, you are not likely to contribute to your environment. In fact, it is just this concern about the relevance of the idiosyncrasies of our personality to the psychological environment, that marks the difference between random, whimsical fancifulness that purports to qualify as art or capriciousness in our personality, and a meaningful masterpiece. The criterion is integrity. It is our concern for usefulness—actually service—that makes all the difference.

That is why the development of your personality has to take into account your problems. In addition to all those inherited factors that we have been scrutinizing, our personality incorporates the social and psychological environment: our upbringing, our education, our culture, our hobbies, our friends, those who have exercised an intense influence upon our way of thinking, emotional attunement, and being. People we love or admire have somehow spilled over in us; they sometimes continue to live, in a sense, in us and through us. This is why Ibn 'Arabi warns that should we segregate ourselves in seclusion, we may fail to pick up a divine revelation that takes place in our interfacing with real life circumstances.

How do you train yourself to incorporate more of the wealth that comes from outside? Naturally, you need to love and care, and become involved in venture and risk, success or defeat, adulation or contempt, encouragement or frustration, life or death. But we sometimes reduce the contribution of the environment by our assessment of it. This is one of the benefits of meditation, which teaches us to get in touch with our thinking, scrutinize it, unmask the hoax of our mind games, update our assessments, and confront our motivations; these interpose themselves between the input from outside and our realization, disfiguring the data ingested from the environment. By learning how to cast the light of your intelligence upon problems rather than observing them with your consciousness, you will find that you are gradually uncovering the springheads behind the programming of occurrences, disclosing the issues being enacted in the relationship between your problems and your personality. The insight gained by this can trigger off sudden changes in your personality.

Practices

1) Try to earmark in your personality, the psychological features and emotional attunements of your father. Now your mother. Now your grandfather

and grandmother, if you knew them personally, or from impressions picked up through your parents.

Observing that your parents exhibit similar, even identical qualities as their parents, you will not need much convincing that the chances are that you carry these same qualities in your genes. By the same token, you may well infer that some of our idiosyncrasies, which you cannot pin down to your parent's features, may have hailed from much farther back in your ancestry.

2) Try to distinguish, among the features of your personality, those which obviously reflect your upbringing, your education, those persons whose thoughts have played a significant role in your psychological unfoldment, your way of thinking and feeling, your culture, the psychological environment in which you move, the courage and sometimes heroism, know-how, wisdom, or verve of people you admire, and the circumstances that you are adapting yourself to. See how they may tally or differ from your parental or ancestral inheritance, and also from your own innate nature.

Now consider your the impact that your teachers have had upon you. Did it ever occur to you that you exercised an impact upon your teachers?

Consider now the impact of your exposure to the great achievements of our civilizations: art, music, poetry, theater, architecture, and the new technology. You might observe how those qualities from the environment that are most penetrating are the ones which resonate with those that typify your core being, and consequently, reinforce them. Ask yourself whether those which predominate are those which evidence your concern about adapting yourself to the environment, rather than adapting the environment to your own sense of purpose. Are you seeking outside reinforcement for what you intuit is already within? This tendency seems to be based upon a principle of cosmic mirroring.

He brought the cosmos into existence upon His own form. Hence it is a mirror within which He sees His own form....God has told you that man is his brother's mirror. Hence man sees in his brother something of himself that he would not see without him.[10]

Muhyi ad-Din Ibn 'Arabi

However, we need to be warned of the deceptive nature of the mirror.

Know that mirrors are diverse in shape and that they modify the object seen by the observer.[11]

Muhyi ad-Din Ibn 'Arabi

---

10 Chittick, *The Sufi Path of Knowledge*, 297, 351.
11 Ibid., 351.

3) Now follow your recollections back in retrospect, as you prod your unconscious depths; regress into childhood, then babyhood. You may discover that the infant is still present at the core of your being, untarnished, sacred, and innocent, while the outer shell has been marked by the stains of worldly life.

4) If you now relax to an extreme degree, as in autohypnosis, you may be able to push your memory right back, prior to your birth in perinatal states. You may recall uncanny, insubstantial landscapes whose fabric appears to be phosphorescent, incandescent, volatile and diaphanous like gossamer, and illuminated by diffuse light. They resemble the pictures in which Gustav Doré strove to describe the heavenly spheres. You will entertain a strong sense of déjá vu. Even if those recollections seem elusive and evanescent as they flash in your remote memory, their afterglow will strike a significant note in your heart, because they confirm your intuition about an idyllic reality behind the physical world. This can help you validate the features of your personality that emerge when your thoughts and feelings are uplifted; for example, through an act of glorification.

5) Now imagine that this was indeed your condition prior to your descent through the spheres down to the Planet Earth. If you downplay or discount those idiosyncrasies that have accrued to you through your parents or through interfacing with the planet, you will be able to identify yourself with the angelic counterpart of your being, and thereby highlight those qualities in your being that feature your celestial inheritance. When they are interspersed with your earthly counterpart, you have difficulty in earmarking them.

6) Now if you discount even those qualities that may be ascribed to your celestial inheritance, you may feel that you have at last singled out your core being. You will find that these qualities contrast with those which you have inherited from your earthly or celestial ancestry, or whatever has spilled over from your interface with the environment, in that they strike you as permanent, fundamental, germane, essentially you after having shed 22,000 veils, as the Sufis say.

The real discloses Himself within forms and undergoes transmutation within them.[12]

Muhyi ad-Din Ibn 'Arabi

We carry our eternal inheritance within our earthly incarnations. The power of these essential qualities that typify our being is incomparably greater than any of the qualities that have accrued to us.

12 Chittick, *The Sufi Path of Knowledge*, 230.

7) If you hoist your consciousness, as we have learned to do in what we called the transcendental dimension, in infinite regress, it will occur to you that these qualities that constitute the seedbed of your personality (even though only a finite measure of their bounty ever comes though your personality) are endowed with an infinite range; and it is our choice that limits which ones we highlight in our personality.

8) If you sit for a very long time in one posture without flickering your eyes, and blank out any thoughts impinging upon your mind, you will shift into a trance-like state. This is the clue to sounding your unconscious to its utmost depths. You will be overwhelmed with the over-abundance of jumbled impressions converging from the whole physical universe. The secret of this is that the motionlessness of the body contrasts with the unceasing turbulence of the outside world; besides, by settling your mind into a state of quietude by dint of detachment and indifference, you will free yourself from the conditioning of your mind that constrains your experience, both perceptual and conceptual, within a very narrow range. Further skills consist in widening the field of your consciousness by representing to yourself a vast panorama, while refraining from panning. Another method would consist in highlighting your sense of always having existed, rather than thinking in terms of the short-lived span of your sojourn on the planet. A further skill would be countering disturbance by frustrating, annoying, or even outrageous circumstances, by remaining unruffled and unperturbed, while at the same time being involved with people and situations.

In this attunement, you envision yourself as a continuity in change. We could illustrate continuity in change by a tree. Having felled a tree, you may find that the stump grows another trunk and branches that appear quite different from the previous one. Capturing that continuity of the unique core of your true being, which you have always been, still are, and always will be, prior to, during, and subsequent to your sojourn on the planet, puts you into a magical state. You will be brought to the point of having to acknowledge that this crowning feature of your own being is perfect, while at the same time you are aware that changes owing to incarnation have affected the surface of your personality.

9) It is baffling and troubling to discover that the perfection, which we ascribed to God, constitutes the very foundation of our own being; in fact, it is the ultimate dimension of our being. If you have grasped the implications of the holistic paradigm, then you can acquiesce to the fact that the totality of the archetypal qualities exemplified in the universe—the divine nature—is virtually present in each of its parts in the form of our nature, which remains

unchanged in its seedbed; but it is transient and perishable at its surface as it unfolds as our personality. This leads the mystic to honor the divine status of one's own being. This is crucial to our self-validation. Even if faced with our personal misgivings about our worth, faith in our potentials will flash hope through the prospect of improving.

In addition to this, if you have grasped the significance of the super-implicate order, then it is clear that our intelligence, embodied in our sense of meaningfulness, is not a fraction of the divine intelligence; but while it is funneled down and focalized, it is still, essentially, the divine intelligence itself.

10) At this point we attempt quite a tour de force, reconciling the perfection and splendor of our divine inheritance with the inadequacies of our personal idiosyncrasies, which are actually what we have so far made of ourselves.

Divinity is human perfection and humanity is divine limitation.[13]

Hazrat Inayat Khan

11) Pay attention to the fact that by drawing you into your personal vantage point and self-image, your involvement in life does tend to downplay your awareness of your divine inheritance. To unfold the qualities lying in wait in the seedbed of your personality, keep matching a quality in your personality with the corresponding archetype of which it is the exemplar. To achieve this, toggle to and fro from the transcendental setting of your consciousness to its personal setting.

12) Since to discover the divine qualities invested in our being we need to actuate them, to discover the divine power latent in the seedbed of your personality, envision how your personality would be if you were to:

a) enhance the quality which you have been working with; for example, your compassion or your authenticity or your mastery, etc.

b) confront the challenges that you are called upon to overcome, rather than trusting that destiny will solve them;

c) to discover the compassion latent in you, tend a wounded patient, physically or psychologically;

d) to discover the perspicacity latent within you, try and envision how things would look from the divine vantage point.

There is a kind of knowledge that comes from doing, which then feeds forward into improving our performance.

13) Observe how the idiosyncrasies that you inherited from your ancestors may prevail over and conflict with those which feature your real being, your divine inheritance being recessive, but which you may yet espy. Perhaps their

13 Inayat Khan, *The Complete Sayings of Hazrat Inayat Khan*, 19.

idiosyncrasies are the very qualities of their divine inheritance, which they customized and which, therefore, became limited, perhaps distorted or defiled, in them. Now you may retrieve those qualities that you ascribe to your divine inheritance simply by being intensely aware of them, concentrating upon them and identifying with them, while downplaying those inherited from your ancestors. This is the reason why St. Francis or Ramana Maharshi, and in general monks and nuns, renounce their family dynasties. The way that inherited features can be metamorphosed is illustrated in the induced mutations in plant and animal breeding. The seed carries within itself the potentiality of infinite variations. Your personality is one of those variations that affect the whole programming.

14) The next step is to envision how your personality would be if you were to try blending two complementary qualities; for example: generosity and strength, mastery and intuition, truthfulness and compassion, joyfulness and peace, sovereignty and indifference. Work with more and more qualities of your own choice. Then work with more tandems of qualities, as previously done. Here lies the hallmark of your freedom. Freedom is something that we discover by availing ourselves of it in self-creation. Creativity is projecting ahead possibilities that we may hitherto have failed to entertain. By observing that the qualities you work with by concentrating upon them, actually are enhanced, you discover that you can be the way you want to be!

15) You will notice that sometimes people's qualities concur with and reinforce qualities already latent in your inheritance. Notice how the emotional attunement of people affects your attunement, which in turn affects the quality you wish to highlight; how their thinking influences your thinking, and consequently, the pursuit of your objective.

16) Envision those circumstances in your daily life that call for a particular quality. There can be no doubt that it is under stress that our latent resourcefulness is discovered and actuated; and that it is being prepared to take responsibility that will release these potentialities.

17) Now recall some of the situations in your life that you perceive as challenging. Envision in what way a quality would alter the situations and relationships you are involved with in real life situations. How you would handle situations and relate to people with this quality?

18) Ask yourself: i) what are the values you cherish that prompted you to foster one quality rather than another; (ii) what are the values that are being enacted in the problems that you are facing, while realizing that every situation in life involves those connected with it, in infinite regress.

19) Consider what is the influence exercised by the role you want to play in life, in your choice of the quality you wish to work with. When you see this clearly, then the challenge that you take upon yourself will release the appropriate latent quality in you.

20) Ask yourself: *What are my true motivations?* Here the real person is revealed, unadorned and authentic. Unmasking your intention serves as an invaluable feedback system, and proves to be the ultimate criterion evidencing your readiness to confront yourself and call your own bluff. At this point, you may discover some conflict between your idealized values and your wishes. Behind the thrust of our motivations lie deeper roots: our innate qualities and our foibles. If we fail to confront ourselves, life itself unmasks them. Besides, they emerge to the view of those endowed with deeper insight into human nature.

21) Now you may have reached a point where you may espy a cosmic intention behind your intention. Grasping the cosmic dimension of your intention is a step towards enlightenment.

22) Having acquainted yourself with all the influences, various sources of inheritance, the conditioning, the motivations that have played a role in the formation of your personality, decide how you would like to be irrespective of any concern about adapting yourself to the circumstances or unfurling the potentialities you are programmed with. You may choose the kind of personality you want among the infinite variety of potentials at hand. Creativity of the personality is comparable to composing variations on a theme, which you may fluctuate inventively, at will. Thus you will be affirming your ultimate freedom.

Chapter Three
Preventive Healing: Immunity

However peacefully inclined one is, there can be no doubt that if we do have a role to play in life, it is in upholding our treasured values. In so doing, according to the Sufis, we are taking responsibility, acting as guardians of the orderliness governing the cosmos, safeguarding it from chaos. Thus we participate in the sovereignty of the paramount government of the world. In fact, this is the only thing that makes sense of our life. In Islam, this way of thinking is based upon a statement in the Qur'an affirming our allegiance to that aspect of God wielding paramount sovereignty in the cosmos.

The first is the form of the knowledge of declaring God's incomparability,... while the second is the form of the knowledge of declaring His similarity, that is, it is the servant's assumption of the traits of the divine names and his becoming manifest in His kingdom through the lordly attributes. In this station, the created thing is a creator and manifests the properties of all the divine names. This is the level of the viceregency and the deputyship of the Real in the kingdom. Through it the servant can exercise governing control among the existent things by acting through his Resolve.[1]

Muhyi ad-Din Ibn 'Arabi

If we honor that assignment, then wherever we possibly can—that is, within our jurisdiction—we need to intervene to uphold those standards upon which the order of the universe is founded, against the efforts to disintegrate it or sabotage it by people abusing their divine gift of freedom. Here lies the commitment that makes for that ancient, though perennial, tradition of knighthood (futuwwat), upon which Sufism is based .

Should we stand up valiantly for what we believe to be right and true, and protect the victims of abuse, we may well ourselves fall victim to those with

---

1 Chittick, *The Sufi Path of Knowledge*, 313.

whom we take issue. Thus we will need to protect ourselves. It is remarkable that the defense system with which our bodies are programmed, namely our immune system, is based upon the difference between self and non-self, *me* and *not-me*, differentiating between isomorphic and heteromorphic elements.[2] In a further step, the body's sense of its singularity is extended to accommodate more and more of the universe.[3] Applying the same principles would give us a clue as to how to avail ourselves of our psychological defense system. Scrutinizing these principles should give us insight into healing in general, and in particular, self-healing.

We find precisely this concern in the psychotherapists' effort to ensure that their patients have a clear sense of identity, defined by boundaries distinguishing it from other-than-self; whereas, meditating in the cosmic dimension, our sense of identity overflows into the universe, merging with the totality, and the boundaries evaporate.

The human immune system accounts for both, because should we simply reject everything that is other than ourselves, we could not eat—that is, ingest the universe—and the crossover of genetic information in reproduction could not occur. At the psychological level, we would remain bigoted, and we would fail to avail ourselves of the resourcefulness gained by our interface and osmosis with other minds and opinions and cultures. On the other hand, we need to distinguish between ingredients, thoughts, and emotions accruing from the environment that are harmful and disturbing, or enriching and enhancing.

Our immune system takes care of these needs and safeguards our integrity. At the psychological level, our heritage provides us with a sampling faculty by which we may decide which of the elements ingested from the environment are in sync with our sterling idiosyncrasies and interests, and favorable to our growth, and which are discrepant and even harmful. The sensitivity of the enzymes governing the replication of the DNA in RNA is based upon the model of a lock and key. The key has to match the pins and drivers of the tumbler. The measuring rod upon which this sampling is built is constituted by our scale of values. This is why meditation aims at making us more aware of the qualities and idiosyncrasies of our being at different levels.

Spotting the harmful elements heightens our perspicacity, consequently stimulating the growth of leukocytes in our immune system. In our psyche, it incites us to devise a protective strategy. Just as the receptors at the periphery of our body cells alert the immune system of the presence of a detrimental agent, so in meditation, Buddha enjoins us to place a sentinel at the doors

---

2 See Weir, *Immunology*, 3.

3 Ibid., 36.

of perception. Consequently, one is able to arrest the advance of harmful elements into the deeper regions of our psyche, where they are more difficult to eradicate.

Like our physiological immune system, our psychological immune system provides us with a means of differentiating among those elements from the environment which are alien, not idiosyncratic:

a) those which we can adapt to and ingest (if transmuted); and

b) those which would prove detrimental to us even if we tried to adapt to them; and finally,

c) those which, unless defeated, would take over and disrupt our related nature altogether.

Let us first mention that the presence of the immune system acts as a deterrent without even having to be activated. Likewise, it is our detachment which will protect us from the impact or sway of unwanted impressions; but this is only effective if our defenses are solidly in place.

One's defense is rejection. Just as our bodies reject implants of heterogeneous cells, in the same way we have a natural hunch as to those impressions from our interfacing with the environment that are deleterious. We react to them congenitally by rejecting them.

Our built-in physical immune system is endowed with genes that will repel harmful foreign agents. Likewise, our built-in psychological immune system is programmed with defenses. For example, anger is a deterrent against untoward actions by others that would prove harmful to our psyche, though we must distinguish between rage and outrage. Our scale of values provides us here with the measuring rod to determine whether our action is appropriate or not. But there is more to it than judgment or judgmentalism; it has to do with our inherent aesthetic sense, illustrated by the clothes that suit us, or the interior decoration of our choice, or our favorite music.

Moreover, we instinctively protect ourselves against people or impressions that make us feel uncomfortable. This is a feature of our basic defense system. At the psychological level, we are exhibiting a primeval instinct by ostracizing people who are incompatible with our way of being, or by turning away or shielding ourselves from impressions; for example, certain music or art which disturbs our inner harmony. Through meditation, we develop a perspicacity with regard to the human psyche, warning us in our relationship with a person about how their attunement, thinking or values would deter us from pursuing our objective. Nature warns us against involving ourselves with people or circumstances which might prove harmful to us, or even precipitate disaster.

Yet there is sometimes a fine line between those factors that are unquestionably harmful, and those that could be made good use of, if transmuted. Our psyche has the faculty of digesting impressions—that is, breaking them down and rebuilding them in a way that is meaningful to us or in harmony with the nature of our being, just as amino-acid chains are broken down by the liver and rebuilt in accordance with the code of our DNA. This is the way of turning the tables on adverse factors and putting them to good use. The principle upon which this is founded is transmutation. Both matter and thought have the faculty of transmuting themselves. This is illustrated by the story of the *Ramayana*. To retrieve Sita, his silver queen (higher self) who had been abducted by Ravana (the devil), Rama built a bridge of monkeys over troubled waters. When the monkeys had fulfilled their task, they developed wings; and thus primitive nature was transmuted.

Our immune system is even endowed with the capacity of mutating its genes to provide defense against yet unknown antigens, unless overstressed, as in the case of the illnesses of the autoimmune system. At the psychological level, this corresponds to our ability to foresee possible obstacles that have not yet materialized.

Both our immune system and our psychological immune system are programmed to be able to bypass the first line of defense, the innate system, by habituation, and to build a further line of defense called the acquired immune system. The innate immune system does not depend upon the feedback of experience, but is genetically determined, just as our tastes are, in the first instance, determined by our culture and our ancestral inheritance, and at a higher level, by our divine inheritance. However, our psychological defenses get eroded and warped by constant exposure to the grossness that develops in our civilizations.

As we evolve, we learn to get along with increasingly diverse people and put up with the most invidious circumstances. By habituation, we adapt ourselves to the environment. Our immune system is endowed with the capacity to adapt itself to the unfamiliar by accommodating more and more of those factors that were originally incompatible. However, if we become overly accommodating and undiscriminating, as in the case of codependence, we may find that our overtolerance hinders another person in trusting their own resourcefulness and becoming self-reliant; and it may act self-destructively upon our own psyche. Paradoxically, some people rejoice while agonizing over having made themselves dependent upon us, thus making us dependent upon them. From the moment that we can see this, we will find it difficult to continue to adjust ourselves to situations previously taken for granted or even coveted.

Obviously, as we grow, we need to adjust our relationships accordingly. We are not the same person we were when we involved ourselves with the other, nor are they. Relationships must never be taken for granted. We need to apprise those close to us of the way our values have been updated as we evolve. This might help them in reassessing their own values. Those we love need to be re-wooed. Redressing current situations and relationships after reassessing them, requires even more insight and courage than dealing with new situations; we need to safeguard people's pride, lest we damage their vulnerable psyche. Loving those with whom we are incompatible, or whom even dislike, will alleviate some of the self-imposed stress we wreak upon ourselves by our self-righteousness.

Here we see the need to balance adaptability to the environment with adapting the environment to our own purpose.

To accommodate more and more of the environment and thus enriching ourselves, the immune system mutates; and our notion of identity extends. Since this extended sense of identity results from developing more and more features in ourselves that have affinity with what we have encountered in the universe, we begin to discover a holistic relationship with the totality, which we had not hitherto grasped. The more we evolve, the more universal our sense of identity. This accounts for the fact that, as the thinking of our civilizations progresses in the course of evolution, our notion of God shifts more and more from a sense of God as *other,* to honoring the divine status of our being and that of others. Indeed, if we identify with the personal dimension of ourselves, we are less accommodating than should we identify with our divine inheritance. By identifying ourselves with our divine inheritance, we find the ultimate common denominator that maximizes adaptation and renders our defenses obsolete through the power of love. This was the message of Christ.

What is more, as species evolve they not only adapt to the environment but innovate, finding new ways of being and thus updating the very programming of the universe. In our creativity, we need to strike a balance between reflecting the trend of things and being totally innovative. Moreover, we must reconcile our individual originality with our cosmic and transcendental dimension. As our minds become increasingly sophisticated, countenancing a richer web of ideas and realizations, our psychological defense system becomes more and more precarious and needs further development. Consequently, our immune system needs to develop new genes to cope with the havoc wreaked upon us by opening the door to more and more complex diversifications. This accounts for the increasing need of both psychotherapy and meditation techniques, both being complementary and mutually enriching.

The immune system can be reinforced clinically by administering drugs that convey additional protection when the immune system is overstressed, and therefore, insufficiently effective. The qualities that the Sufis are working with in repeating certain waza'if, function as antigens to overcome the psychological equivalent of viruses. Having spotted our foibles, we reinforce the quality that overcomes them; for example, developing mastery over addiction, or truthfulness against guile, or magnanimity against hatred. In the same way, we can reinforce our psychological immunity by propping it up, drawing on the qualities that we admire in beings we hold in esteem, and which spill over in us.

Perhaps the most hopeful prospects for the future of medicine are embodied in the vaccine, an actively acquired immunity and a form of preventive medicine. The immune system can be reinforced by injecting into the body the very fiend that it is being armed to fight, but it is neutralized as it lives in the body. By this means, the immune system recognizes the features of its antagonist and prepares its defenses accordingly. In the realm of psychology, familiarity with that which is detrimental to us sometimes puts us on guard, providing that we have earmarked it as harmful. Having engulfed the antigen, the macrophages incorporate the know-how of the strategy in the body's memory. This could serve as a clue to preventive therapy. Otherwise, we might simply adapt to it, not realizing the damage that it is doing to us by attacking and neutralizing our very defenses and taking control of us. In fact, if our ability to identify the enemy breaks down the immune system, it works against itself, as in autoimmune deficiency diseases.

The secret lies in unmasking the hoax of our attacker, and having mastered its strategy, turning the tables on it by harnessing our disability as an asset. Some of the world's best piano tuners are deaf, orators stutter, thinkers have impediments in their nervous system, tycoons have lived in penury, commanders experience defeat, geniuses were "retarded" children, and clowns have defeating self-images.

Furthermore, we may test ourselves by confronting challenges within our capacity, and then at the edge of our capacity, thereby increasing the capacity and always hovering at the leading edge. In terms of psychology, the enemy is already lurking in the unconscious in the form of self-destructiveness that results from self-defeatism, which, in turn, results from self-denigration. Clearly this is where we need to build up or rebuild our discriminatory faculty. This is why, in meditation, by discovering our potentials at all levels and extending our identity holistically, we gain self-validation, honoring our divine status.

Practices

1) Ascertain cases in your life where people are victimizing you because you are standing up for what you believe is right.

2) To protect yourself to some extent, feel clear about the idiosyncrasies of your being, as opposed to evident disparity with the ones of those who oppose you. However, you will need to adopt the same attitude with the adversary to your ideal within your own psyche. Do not try to demur in either case, because this will weaken your sense of who you are.

3) Do not lay yourself open to the influence of adversaries, including the shadow in your own self. They may use arguments which are ambiguous and could easily confuse the issues. Unmask the strategy whereby your opponent may maneuver you into becoming dependent. This is also true about one's own helplessness facing those aspects in oneself which one dislikes.

4) Try to differentiate that which is positive in your opponent's motivations from that which is simply discrepant, or even friendly, by matching them with identical idiosyncrasies in yourself.

5) Keep confronting your motivations with a certain mistrust for the justifying faculty of the mind. You will thus become increasingly discerning, reinforcing your conviction in the rightness of your stand.

6) Since all qualities are inflicted with their shadows, earmark clearly any elements in your opponent's point of view that you could incorporate in your psyche by eliminating its shadow.

7) Watch that you do not adopt your opponent's defects to counter him or her—you may indeed find these in your own psyche.

8) Counter valiantly anything that is clearly evil, cruel, dishonest, sacrilegious.

9) If you take up a wager, your anger will inevitably be increasingly aroused; and if allowed to boil over as personal rage, it may get out of control and turn against you. Therefore distinguish between rage (the personal dimension) and outrage (the impersonal dimension); you feel the conscience of humanity being outraged by cases of violation and contempt of the sacredness of fellow human beings.

10) Your sensitivity to the attunements of people will become increasingly refined, which will steer your relationships more wisely.

11) In your self-examination, clearly distinguish between the idiosyncrasies that are reprehensible, and those which hail from your inheritance of your precursors in the perennial evolutionary procession and which now serve as

a primeval underpinning of the superior qualities you have acquired—between Ravana, the monster and Hanuman, the monkey.

12) As we progress, we become more cautious and forestall the kind of obstacles we might encounter in our strife to uphold righteousness, thus reinforcing our defenses.

13) Since our psyche is continually ingesting the psychological environment, be careful to screen the impressions that invade the unconscious before they have had a chance of settling in your unconscious; for example, watching TV, or simply walking in the street. Habituation allows impressions to take root in our psyche unawares. This is where keeping oneself watchful, alert, and discerning, processing impressions by matching them with our scale of values, will ensure the integrity of our psyche. Consequently, we will need to balance our accommodating tendency with a degree of severity, honoring boundaries.

14) Eventually you reach the stage where, instead of isolating yourself to protect yourself from disturbing factors, you will strengthen yourself by familiarizing yourself with whatever you consider harmful and foreign to your nature. Espy the assets of your opponent, where your opponent is strong and where you are vulnerable; any sense of inadequacy or self-denigration could spell defeatism.

15) Watch whether you are allowing a person to weaken your resolve by making themselves dependent upon you. If not on the lookout, one tends to allow oneself to pride oneself of a person's dependence upon one.

16) Keep articulating very clearly, particularly to those more closely related to you, how you feel, what your values are, what your motivations are, and keep them apprised as these get updated.

17) By being clear about all the above, you will find it easier to love people you disagree with, without giving in to them, while safeguarding their pride even though they may be so different to ourselves. They still are integrally intermeshed in our psyche.

18) If you work with yourself, earmarking latent qualities and thus awakening them, you will become increasingly universal and all-encompassing, while reconciling this with your uniqueness.

Chapter Four
Cosmic Emotion

There is yet a further stage in personal transformation: working with cosmic emotion.

Practices

1) Rather than being pummeled by your personal emotions, precariously poised upon the whimsical flux between likes and dislikes, success and disappointment, hope and despair, love and hate, attachment and rejection, if you allow your consciousness to shift into its transcendental setting, you will be resonating with emotion at a cosmic scale. You will resonate with the emotion of the trees, of wildlife, of the sea, of the atoms, including those of your own body (even the cells of your body), the emotion of the planet, of the peoples inhabiting the planet, and of collective emotion at an enormous scale: the emotion of the stars, the galaxies, the immensity of outer space. You will be overwhelmed with the power of that emotion.

2) Now imagine that these beings, whether mineral, plant, animal, or human, whose emotions you are now resonating with as your consciousness becomes increasingly all-encompassing, are the expressions of the emotion and intention that has programmed them. That is, you experience the emotion that manifests in the structuring of a crystal, for example, or a snowflake, or a flower, or a symphony, or a person, or a planet, or a galaxy.

In the transcendent meditations, we tried to grasp clues to this programming. But at the stage that we have now reached, no sooner do we glean a hunch as to the intention behind it all, than we get a sense of the amazing emotion that expresses itself and actuates itself in these existential formations. This could be exemplified by imagining what it would be like to experience the emotion of Bach that found its expression in the Mass in B Minor, or Beethoven in his Ninth Symphony, or Brahms in his Sonata for Cello and Piano in F Major.

This is the pinnacle in meditation, which will transfix and transfigure your being.

3) Not only let a sense of meaningfulness dawn upon your understanding of the paradox of life, but realize that there is not only astonishing intelligence behind all of this, but also splendor, and ultimately, sacredness motivating the intention.

For the Sufis, the universe is the fulfillment of the divine nostalgia for excellence; splendor manifests existentially as excellence. That splendor is, unfortunately, curtailed by our shortsighted activities, limited by the reach of our realization of this very intention, and warped by our personal desires that have alienated themselves from the divine nostalgia. However, that splendor does burst forth in our creativity, whenever the human being is uplifted by a sense of bewonderment in the pursuit of excellence.

4) Envision the whole universe as just the projection of what one might call a symphony of emotions. The software of the universe works it all out beautifully, and clearly would not have any purpose if it were not to serve something much more ultimate than itself, which is the ecstasy of splendor. For the Sufis, this is the divine nostalgia, the springhead of creation and of creativity.

5) Can you see that all the different levels of the universe, not only the physical plane, are devices whereby that splendor is made known and concretized?

Why did you laugh or cry when viewing the film E.T.? At the physical level, there were shadows on the screen; they represented a hoax. E.T. was outfitted with the head of a turtle and the voice of an old woman; or did you see E. T. through the eyes of that lovely child? Actually, through these devices, you were gaining access to the thinking, imagination, and emotion of Steven Spielberg.

If you extend this view to the universe as a whole, you will realize that the universe is a marvelous system of beautifully planned devices to translate into concrete terms, the intention and emotion behind it.

Traditionally, this intention and these emotions are ascribed to God. In our present perspective, we see how easily one slips into confusing God with our conception of God.

Theoretical knowledge of a subject can never take the place of experience, which is necessary for realization.[1]

Hazrat Inayat Khan

---

1 Inayat Khan, *The Sufi Message* series, *The Sufi Message of Spiritual Liberty*, 14–15..

If we were to envision the universe as a being, then this being would be endowed with a global intelligence and motivations and emotion. However, if we adopt Shabistari's model updated, it is clear that we must not confuse that image in Gabor's hologram, however real it is as a discrete entity made of the fabric of light, with the object that it projects.

The reflection of Absolute Being can be viewed in this mirror of Not-Being.[2]
Mahmud Shabistari

If the universe may be illustrated by this projection, then let us not reduce our concept of God to this projection. So can we leave room in the symphony of emotions for transcendent emotion beyond cosmic emotion. This is corroborated by the insistence on transcendence in most religious traditions.

6) Realize that your lower mind is simply grappling with those devices, trying to make sense of those devices whereby a superlative intelligence, intention, and emotion are trying to come through to our understanding. Meanwhile, we still keep trying to figure out our concepts of our problems, rather than our problems. The emotional springheads spurring those problems would give you a better clue than your assessment of them.

7) By questioning the assessments of your lower mind, you will gain access to the higher levels of your thinking: the understanding of the soul. You may notice that your thinking extrapolates not only between the nature of the holistic paradigm (contrasted with the syllogistic logic, based upon categories bolstered by our usual sense of causality in the process of becoming), but also the nature of a transcendental mode of cognizance, and beyond this, a subtle sense of emotional values.

8) Keeping the cosmic motivations you intuit ever-present in your awareness, maintain your attunement in resonance with the emotion driving the universe, and uphold the vision of the splendor trying to break through in the form of excellence.[3]

9) You can see that it was the awareness of the body that entrapped your notion of yourself in a skin-bound identity. If you realize that your body is just the extension of the intention behind it, just as the hardware of a computer is simply the concretization of the software behind it, if you realize that your

---

2 Shabistari, *The Secret Rose Garden of Sa'd ud Din Mahmud Shabistari*, Part VI.

3 Quantum physicists never cease to be flummoxed by the intricacies, (actually, by the intelligence) of the programming evidenced by the paradoxical behavior of matter, and in general, physical phenomena, which keep defying our commonplace thinking. Consequently, they are continually revising their thinking, stretching the mind beyond its middle range by carrying it past the limits we impose upon it by our self-image. If you are prepared to do this, life makes sense, with all its contradictions, paradoxes, soul-searchings.

faculty of imagining belongs to the level at which the software is planned, it represents a deeper reality of your being than your body and psyche. Yet we must bear in mind that the hardware—your house, for example—is what the blueprint is all about.

10) Observe that your creative imagination is doing precisely the same-thing as the imagination behind the universe. In fact, it is the nostalgia of the universe, customized through you into your aspirations, which will, in fact, mutate the very software of the universe of which it is the expression.

11) Envision the software of the universe as dynamic instead of static, continually mutating. And think that we are the ones in whom and through whom the overall cosmic software is carried forward in the evolutionary process. We are the laboratory of the divine experiment.

Now hoist yourself a degree higher. It will become evident that even creative imagination, with which you had previously identified yourself, is just a projection monitoring an effort to translate your realization and attunement into images, so as to make them more tangible.

As we have seen, the Tibetans distinguish three levels of mental activities: a) the gross mind, b) the subtle mind, and c) the very subtle mind. We have seen into the relative inadequacy of the gross mind in trying to figure out events. We then identified with the subtle mind, which is that activity in us that is creative and inventive, and of which our psyche is a projection. And we have had elusive hunches about the very subtle mind that represents the level of our being at which we can touch upon the programming directly, without trying to infer it from its actuation in existential events.

Thus you have shifted your sense of identity from being the creative mind to being your realization. One could say that every being is in life according to that being's degree of realization. Furthermore, one needs to account for a realization of one's own or another's emotional attunements, and a still deeper realization of the soul. Realization is the basic reality; that is what you are, gauged by the degree to which you are awake.

12) With this in view, try to see yourself in the universe, instead of thinking of yourself within the confines of your planetary inheritance.

13) Here comes the crucial breakthrough, when you realize that bodiness and creative imagination are just concretizations of the cosmos. When you can see your participation in the cosmos, then you can evaluate the impact of your realization upon both your creativity and your body functions. Upon reflection, the realization dawns upon you, that if you observe a high attunement as you fashion your personality, you have the ability to become what you want to be.

14) As you try to recollect always having existed beyond time and space, you will find that one of the assumptions obstructing us from availing ourselves of the higher levels of our thinking, is our notion of space. We have difficulty in assuming that two objects could occupy the same space, interpenetrate, or dovetail. A little present-day physics will point out that waves intersperse, forming wave interference patterns, whereas particles collide. We think of the matter of the universe, including our bodies, as particle-like. Envision your body as wave-like rather than solid and bounded by a boundary.

15) Now embolden yourself to challenge your notion of time. So far, we seem to have referred to our temporal being as opposed to our eternal being, as though they were two entities. But if you take the model of a pendulum, one moving pole alternates as time goes on, whereas the other stationary pole remains unchanged. Both are poles of the same reality, not separated but representing a continuity. Once more, the difficulty that we experience in accepting the co-presence of eternity and transiency, is similar to that which obstructed our sense of being interspersed in space.

An event that took place at a moment in time is eternalized in our memory. Memory is, therefore, a faculty that transits from transiency to eternity. By the same token, incarnation is the process whereby our eternal being interjects into transient modes, while remaining unscathed. A good example is that the whole ocean emerges each time as each wave; it is untrue to say that one wave causes another.

16) Try to reconcile being eternal and transient at the same time. You will realize that you can reconcile the perfection of your eternal being with the inadequacies of your temporal being.

17) Remember that the code, not only of the body but of the universe, is written right into the DNA of each of our cells; but to ensure the diversity of cell functions, only some genes thereof are active, and the others are turned off. Since a similar principle applies to the code of your psyche, you will find that the key to turning on or off the genes of your cosmic heritage is in the representation that you make of yourself. This is what is holding the potentialities of your being back from unfurling. Turn them on.

18) Can you earmark the eternal core of your being, embedded within its distortions in your transient being owing to the influence from other beings, and in general, the social pull towards the lowest common denominator?

If conditions are unfavorable, a seed can unfurl as a weedy plant; yet at the culmination of the life cycle of the plant, the seed will reemerge unscathed. Such is the breakthrough of realization accompanied by the promise of rebirth, as one awakens from the dream of maya.

19) Now for the next step. Of course, unfurling the seed of your being, blossoming as a bountiful and beautiful personality, seems indeed to be the objective; but there is yet a further, as a matter of fact, radical step, which is to foster the mutation of the seed of your being, rather than work with your personality. Interestingly, this procedure will manifest immediately in your personality. It marshals a whole other dimension of your being into action; and since the mutations start having effect at the inception in the shoots as they emerge from the seed, this is where you will need to work. Capture creativity as it emerges, at its inception in the deep layers of your being.

20) Intuit the intention, the orderliness, the emotional attunement at a cosmic scale that initiated your being, and then customize it. Be careful to avoid indulging in fantasy. Follow the whole creative process right down into the very structuring of your personality. Be sure that, rather than satisfying yourself with observing how it works, you intervene in the process with your incentive and inventiveness.

There can be no doubt that even our inadequate concept of God will have a contribution to our creation of ourselves, because we are really projecting aspects of ourselves that we do not know how to express or actuate in ourselves, upon this archetypal level of ourselves, on the model of what we project upon God. This occurs at those moments when we are carried beyond ourselves, moved by cosmic emotion.

21) The emotion aroused by the sense of the sacredness of the divine status of your being will enhance your personal creativity.

22) What would be the applications of this in everyday life? Curiously enough, you will realize that you did not have to set off in Challenger to arrive at the outer space perspective: Planet Earth is in outer space!

You also don't have to be special, or belong to a spiritual group: everybody is special, or holy. Perhaps the changes in you are not visible. According to the Tibetans, a change in the subtle body of a person cannot be perceived except by a few, although it will eventually pervade your body. What is important is that you should hang on to your new identity. It would be difficult for most of us to pronounce Abu Yazid Bastami Bastami's words: *How great is my glory!*[4] But we can still say: *O God, all thanks to Thee for investing me with such glory and bounty!*

It might be helpful to point out to your friends that you have changed, that you are not the same person as before; otherwise they will hold you to the way you were in the past.

4 Massignon, *Essai Sur Les Origines De Lexique Technique De La Mystique Musulmane*, 249.

This only holds true if you will have more light sparkling from your eyes, and will be enshrouded with peace, casting the light of luminous intelligence upon all things, seeing beauty behind appearance to the contrary, handling ugly situations beautifully, conveying a kind of life-sustaining energy around you, and communicating your high to all those you encounter.

Chapter Five
The Mass as Therapy and Transfiguration

Some of the more traditional religious ceremonies are preceded by a procession, exhibiting festive pageantry. Participating in a procession features our need to discover whatever is holding us back from our quest and release ourselves from it.

But it is in the custom of performing ablutions that our sense of guilt is sparked. It brings home to us the importance of confronting our conscience as we recollect having offended or abused or harmed a fellow being. By the same token, it draws our attention to the immaculate nature of that deep core in our being, in which we discover the sacred.

Man may retain angelic qualities even in his life on the earth as a human being; and it is the angelic quality which can be traced in some souls who show innocence.[1]

Hazrat Inayat Khan

Just as in the Mass, we first need to go though the *Kyrie Eleison* before participating in the *Gloria*; we cannot approach the immaculate center of our being without coming to terms with our guilt. To be honest with ourselves (otherwise it would be a masquerade), we resort to ponderous soul-searchings. Memories of forgotten incidents besiege our minds and pummel our emotions. Our reason will come to our rescue, furnishing us with the most unconvincing arguments intended to justify ourselves. We may fall for these unawares, yet our conscience may not feel totally assuaged.

Our assessment of our guilt proves to be not very reliable. It easily overlaps with our resentment. We may feel guilty for having allowed ourselves to be abused or codependent. Anger serves as our defense system, but we need to clearly distinguish between rage and outrage. Consider rage as the personal

1 Inayat Khan, *The Sufi Message* series, *The Way of Illumination*, 116.

dimension of outrage, and outrage as the impersonal dimension of rage. Rage can degenerate as hatred; outrage can erupt into heroism.

Toying with the impelling emotions generated in the drama of our lives, religion avers itself to be our saving grace, since grasping the splendor in the heavens behind the iniquity in the earthly drama, lures us out of our self-pity, helping us to heal. Is it worth missing out on the *Gloria* by being waylaid by our hurts in our tempests in our teacups, when life in all its glory beckons us to participate in the cosmic celebration?

The act of glorification, rising aloft as incense from the fervor of the congregation, into the high vaults amidst the rafters adorning the colossal masonry of the nave, echoes the celebration in the heavens—or is it our incantations that enchant those celestial beings, by an eerie divination into an upsurge of jubilation? It is a though a skylight had been suddenly opened between earth and heaven.

The *Gloria* of the Mass serves as a reminder that it is only out of an act of glorification that we can raise ourselves above our commonplace self-image, in which we are encapsulated by our trite emotions, our greed, our lack of mercy and compassion. It brings home to us that it is our ability to honor our intuition about a splendor, which is continually trying to breakthrough the painful circumstances constraining us in the existential condition, and which is fostering our transformation.

Of course, those realms that we ascribe to the heavens are not located elsewhere; they are not confined to us either. But we accede to these by constructing that very temple built in the fabric of our own person, our body, magnetic field, aura, psyche, thus securing a psychological area offering us protection against the sacrilege rampant in the world and also within ourselves.

It is indeed our faith in our intuition—a kind of inborn sense of meaningfulness not based upon the judgments of our limited minds—that gives us access to the higher dimensions of our being, and by the same token, of the universe. Incidentally, let us not confuse faith with belief, which is based on authority.

This is where the *Credo* comes in, bolstered by the power of our personal convictions. It is a mode of cognizance, not based upon our assessment of situations, but upon the fact that our thinking is of an identical nature to the thinking of the universe when not limited by our personal focal center. This perspective emerges only when we are able to grasp the cosmic and transcendental outreach of our being.

It is prayer, the act of glorification, that shifts our thinking from the commonplace mode to this cosmic and transcendent mode. The effect of prayer is challenging to our minds, by revealing to us hidden causes behind events that do not make sense in our lives or those of others. In our ignorance of that which is enacted behind situations, sometimes dramatically, we tend to make serious mistakes in our handling of our affairs, with dire consequences for ourselves and others. It is difficult for our minds, functioning in their limited fashion, to grasp the interaction between destiny and free will. It is difficult to gauge the cosmic laws whereby the interplay between our covetousness and our dedication to service affects our destiny—or how this effects our personality, our attunement, and our fulfillment of our life's purpose. That the act of giving, sacrifice, relinquishing, even to the point of surrender, should be the ultimate issue in our lives, defies rational commonsense. Why should we not simply pursue our personal interest? Why this moral injunction about sacrifice, epitomized in the rituals of all religions and illustrated in the oblation of the *Agnus Dei*, the Lamb of God, or the immolation of Isaac, culminating in the *Crucifixus* of the Mass?

Those who are crucified on earth will be free in the heavens, and those who are free on the earth will be crucified in the heavens.

Hazrat Inayat Khan

It is not much use trying to argue with whatever we ascribe to destiny—that is, the enigmatic intentions of the programming of the universe; but it is clear that we cannot appraise this intention from our limited perspective. However, I think that we can agree that charity makes people's personalities appealing and welcoming.

The only sense renunciation could possibly make is in resurrection—*Resurrexit*. That the quintessence of whatever has been achieved in the process of becoming is fed back into the pool of resourcefulness of the cosmos, makes metaphysical sense. That which has been achieved by existentiation is that the virtual totality should be diversified in each of us; this points to the original contribution of our personal dimension—that the quintessence of our personality and know-how must be resurrected.

It becomes obvious to one's soul-searchings that one cannot expect one's being to be resurrected unless it is purified of its blemishes. To extract the quintessence, alchemists need to drain away the dross. This is where one finds that asking for forgiveness is not good enough; one needs to repent, which means renewing one's pledge never to repeat the offense: the *Confiteor*.

The pledge to service illustrated by Isaiah's *send me* is a commitment to accept whatever the office asks of one in terms of sacrifice, to the point of persecution, torture, and martyrdom. There is a feeling that those called to cosmic service are being eulogized by heavenly beings: the *Sanctus*. Moreover, something in the human spirit surges forth to honor, venerate, and sanctify our heroes who have lived up to their higher calling: the *Hosanna*. They figure in our sacred treasure house as living examples of the value we treasure most.

Only after this in the *Introit*, may the celebrant approach the altar, the Holy of Holies, to partake of the Eucharist.

Hic es enim Corpus Meum; Hic est enim Calix Sanguinis Mei.
This is my body, this is the chalice of my blood.

According to Pierre Teilhard de Chardin:

The body of Christ represents the matter of the universe that is continually being transmuted into spirit (energy), and the blood is the suffering implied by the incarnate condition, being transfigured into joy.

The ritual serves as a reminder that we do carry within us the inheritance of the whole universe, which may be looked upon as the body of God. But if we are not aware of our divine inheritance, it remains recessive in us; and we cannot actuate it in our personal idiosyncrasies.[2]

Be ye perfect as your Father in heaven is perfect.[3]

Jesus Christ

The celebrants now return to their seats replenished by the many-splendored bounty lying in wait in their own being. Conversely, by following the psychological stages celebrated in the Mass, the contemplative may, in personal orison, experience this Holy Communion with the whole universe at all its levels.

The altar is amongst the stars.

Pierre Teilhard de Chardin

The kind of peace that passeth all understanding in the *Dona Nobis Pacem*, could not possibly be reached unless one has gone through the cosmic drama, enjoying the privilege of the gift of life, and suffering defeat, humiliation, and despair. There is no peace equal to that at the aftermath of a storm, when

---

2 Reference could be made here to the Greek myth of Zagreus, the son of Zeus. When Zeus vacated his throne, his son Zagreus sat upon it. While stupefied at the discovery of his resemblance to his father as he looked into the mirror presented to him by the Titans, they precipitated him into the abyss and devoured him. Zeus shattered the Titans with his thunderbolt, and men were born out of the ashes of the Titans who had ingested the body of the son of God.

3 Matthew 5:48.

one has confronted the challenge and come to terms with it. Hence the last words of Christ: *It has been fulfilled.*[4]

> *Ite, Missa est.*
> *The Mass is completed.*

---

4 John 19:30.

Part Seven

Forestalling the Future

Chapter One
Updating Spirituality

What would be the features of an updated spirituality? Always give precedence to your own and other's need for sacredness. Here lies the commitment to the spiritual quest.

1) Foster genuine experience, as in meditation, rather than dogma. However, we need to take into account that experience is influenced by our interpretation of it; moreover, we preclude experience by our assumptions. Our inborn intuitive faculties get blunted by our mind games.

A way of avoiding this is to clearly distinguish between faith and belief. Belief rests on authority, and faith rests on a proto-critical knowledge, emancipated from the constraints of our commonplace logic.

2) To update spirituality, one needs to:

a) question the efficacy of past procedures by marking their defects;

b) however, to avoid throwing the baby out with the bath water, earmark the elements among those used in the past that are not time-bound, bearing in mind that our current structures are the sequence to their predecessors;

c) see how time-honored procedures fit into the present trend;

d) reconsider things taken for granted, and restructure, renovate, and brainstorm new procedures that would constitute an improvement over the current ones.

We need to strike the right balance between innovation and conservation, regulation and freewheeling. We miss out on a lot of resourcefulness by forcing things into a rigid pattern, which is exactly the danger of institutionalization. The cycles of plant life perpetuate themselves repeatedly. Successful mutations are rare, but plants can grow a spin-off that enjoys a relative autonomy, and thanks to this relative freedom, can update itself more easily. We may find that those human institutions that are obviously spin-offs from their predecessors, which had lost their inventive motivation, are often more successful because they are not constrained by outdated customary procedures.

3) The members of the institution need to be empowered with responsibility, rather than conforming blindly to prescriptions. We cannot take responsibility if our decisions are determined by conformism. This applies even to consensus or public pressure. Nonconformism is often ostracized, and this is the way the common denominator obstructs originality and suppresses people's honoring their personal conviction. When freed from this moral imposition, people are able to discover their conscience and consult their conscience as their ultimate criterion.

4) Train in skills with those who have mastered the know-how leading to the excellence we are seeking, providing that they encourage your initiative and creativity. Open yourself to their attunement only if they walk their talk and honor the freedom of your conscience. Applying this principle, counseling guides will act more as facilitators to help you probe your own hearts and minds, help you untangle the incongruities in your assessments, unmask your real motivations, and inspire you. In every field there are people more schooled or more skilled than others, but by telling their pupils what to do, they rob their pupils of their own judgment and incentive.

5) Moreover, be wary of evaluating a person's degree of spirituality or spiritual rank by their appearance, position, claim, title or prepossessive manner. However, offer recognition to degrees of proficiency in know-how and skills, and leadership qualities.

Claiming a high spiritual rank or being divinely special is out of order in our times; it may have had its place in more credulous societies to ensure one's credibility and is, unfortunately, still prevalent amongst the more innocent and gullible dear beings. The world is graced with beautiful people without any pretense to spirituality, often more inspiring than those purporting to hold a spiritual rank. Spiritual guides will have to prove themselves by germane realization and the soul qualities that help you tune to your spiritual ideals and bring it into practice in your life.

Nurturing one's ideal for the sublime and the sacred is most important for so many people in helping them to overcome their disenchantment in the sordidness of much of our society, and to overcome their own inadequate self-image. But the one who triggers off this catharsis and transformation in you needs to be not just charismatic, but selfless. If the one whom you trust to help you fails to make the connection between the sublime level of reality and the existential conditions, by escaping from real situations into wishful thinking that person believes himself to be special and induces you into believing it too. Everyone is special in their own way. And you run the risk that, when the concupiscence and vanity of the one upon whom you made yourself dependent for your inspiration surfaces, you will doubt your very ideal.

It is of no use to try and prove to be what in reality you are not.[1]

Hazrat Inayat Khan

Living up to an exemplary image to nurture the need of the guru image in people forces those in a leadership position into a role in which one runs the danger of neglecting to confront one's own defects, weakness or inadequacies. Because of a pupil's awe in the face of the aura of eminence of the guru, it is sometimes difficult to espy the justifying faculty of the mind resorted to by a person who is looked upon as an example. The arguments offered often scramble the issue by flaunting contradictions, instead of striking a balance between clearly defined choices. This is a typical guru syndrome that we are witnessing in our time: masking contradictions instead of recognizing their incongruity and correcting them.

The consequence of masking contradictions is the conflict and confusion that these ambiguities arouse in oneself and in others. Since in the drama of real life one senses how important one's image is for people, those in a leadership position fear that, should they admit criticism, they would spoil that image. However, by justifying oneself, one deprives oneself of the opportunity of ever progressing; and this self-deception spills over to the pupils who tend to deceive themselves instead of confronting themselves, thus hindering their progress too. The image cannot hold for long unless matched by the reality of one's personality. Consequently, in the end, one's effort to uphold one's image to help people defeats its own end.

Those who try to make virtues out of their faults grope further and further into darkness.

The way to overcome error is first, to admit one's fault; and next, to refrain from repeating it.[2]

Hazrat Inayat Khan

Anybody volunteering to embody the archetype representing people's higher self, will have to choose between artfully concealing one's shadow, and when discovered, stand on one's high horse, justifying it hypocritically; or alternatively, by putting oneself on the line, open to be exposed to scrutiny and criticism by all.

1 Inayat Khan, *The Complete Sayings of Hazrat Inayat Khan*, 12.
2 Ibid., 14–13.

Should one have the honesty and courage to confront one's shortcomings, one will better understand people's problems through seeing oneself in others and others in oneself, thus affording real help to those who also need to transmute their shadow. Clearly, how could one expect to help another if one has not experienced their problems oneself and dealt with them constructively?

By justifying oneself, one blunts the ability to earmark one's defects. If one is not extremely scrupulous about being honest to oneself, one tends to fail to recognize this distortion and firmly believes that one is acting under the higher impulse.

It is only if one is able to recognize one's inadequacies as a distortion of that very ideal to which one pays lip service, that this ideal can operate in transmuting the shadow of one's pupils by transmuting one's own shadow. One's divine legacy is hidden behind that shadow, which stands in the way of it becoming a reality in our personality.

To know what one's defects are, all one needs is to recognize one's qualities and earmark the distortions of those qualities in one's personality. It is this very distortion of a quality that stands as an obstacle to developing that very quality.

There is a pair of opposites in all things; in each there exists the spirit of the opposite.[3]

Hazrat Inayat Khan

Should one fail to admit and confront the defect, that very defect will, by the synchronistic interplay in our relationships with people, call forth a situation in which we are placed before the choice either of applying the defective idiosyncrasy in handling the situation, or the divine quality of which the former was a distortion.

Moreover, as pupils often confuse the guru with the image they have projected upon the guru, they run the risk of going wrong if they assume that guru's advice is absolute.

Do not take the example of another as an excuse for your wrongdoing.
One should take oneself to task instead of putting one's fault upon another.
Overlook the greatest fault of another, but do not partake of it in the smallest degree.[4]

Hazrat Inayat Khan

Paradoxically, one may err in the opposite direction. When pupils tend to model themselves upon the life pattern that prioritizes service above anything

3 Inayat Khan, *Esoteric Papers.*
4 Inayat Khan, *The Complete Sayings of Hazrat Inayat Khan*, 17, 13, 22.

else, this sets a challenge that people tend to emulate. Here once more, the guru transference image acts adversely: people get burnt out and develop a sense of frustration and self-pity. One becomes increasingly aware of the stress incurred by accumulating the responsibility of service with the needs of their job and the care of their families, and people need to give some satisfaction to their personal emotions.

Every soul has its own way of life; if you wish to follow another's way, you must borrow his eyes to see it.[5]

Hazrat Inayat Khan

---

5 Ibid., 28.

Chapter Two
Future Spirituality

Planet Earth and we, as the decision-making members of the planetary population, are right in the midst of a revolution. For the evolutionary thrust of which we are the beneficiaries to advance, the status quo inevitably has to break down; but this breakdown triggers off a breakthrough.

Scanning our evolutionary advance in retrospect gives us some clues as to how we could improve. Clearly we progress through an increase in the scope of our consciousness. Whereas the tree is locked into its immediate environment, the awareness and the thinking of pioneers among human beings encompasses the galaxies. Thinking big will get us out of the rut if we can see in terms of global consciousness and realize that we are all in this together; the well-being of the whole also promotes our personal interest.

If the planet on which we live had no intelligence, it could not have intelligent beings on it.... The collective working of many minds as one single idea, and the activity of the whole world in a certain direction, are governed by the intelligence of the planet.[1]

Hazrat Inayat Khan

Our experiments with political institutions have proven how crucial freedom is to promote progress—in fact, freedom from conformity generates creativity. On the other hand, there is nothing in the world more abused than freedom. We see its consequences in the decadence, vulgarity, slovenliness and permissiveness of our modern societies; while on the other hand, we witness a raising of the consciousness of people to the dignity of life that begets nobility. There is no accounting for taste.

Religious parochialism has caused the death of thousands of innocent people and wreaked havoc on the environment. In many areas, advocating tolerance in the interest of a global religious vision would be interpreted

1 Inayat Khan, *The Sufi Message* series, *Philosophy, Psychology and Mysticism*, 41–42.

as treason to one's religious loyalty. How can we reach a global sense of the unity of the human family, if we cling to our divisions?

To advance, we must not, like the wife of Lot, look back, with the risk of being sclerosed by thinking as we did in the past. It is a positive vision of the way the future could be, the way we could make the future, that will propel us forward.

It takes courage to let go of many ways of thinking that one has built up over the years. To network with those who are not in the race, we need to integrate even old ideas into the wider web of new ideas, rather than rejecting the old, like throwing the baby out with the bath water.

Paradoxically, the very technology we have in our grip, which is destroying the environment, could be harnessed to save it. But only a very small portion of the population of the planet is prepared to prioritize the interest of the whole over individual greed, failing to see that the wellbeing of the whole does reflect upon the living standard of the individual. It is our way of thinking that is the determining factor, and more so, our values. We have not grown on a par with the potentialities that, as the apprentice sorcerer, we have unleashed. It is really a matter of both consciousness and conscience. Vested interests have regularly sabotaged technological breakthroughs; we have often succumbed to complacency, habit-forming, and sectarianism. Yet indeed, we never cease to be amazed by the dramatic upheavals in our day and age that have overthrown abusive practices. This being so, there is hope!

New Vistas

Our way of considering the cosmos, and Planet Earth in particular, has taken a quantum leap. Instead of looking at the stars as viewed from Planet Earth, we are now able to imagine how Planet Earth looks as viewed from the stars. This has surreptitiously revolutionized our way of considering our planet, which, in turn, revolutionizes our way of seeing ourselves.

We imagine outer space to be out there, but has it ever occurred to you that actually Planet Earth is in outer space? It all depends on how you look at it.

Since we can now see our live cells in powerful microscopes, our whole perception of the fabric of our body has undergone a dramatic change. While the ancients who had not yet acquired our knowledge of matter, witnessed the decay of the body after death and considered it to be like dust returning to the earth, we now know that matter is convertible into energy.

Instead of dismissing our bodies as other than ourselves, we are beginning to honor the involvement of our innate sense of meaningfulness with the very fabric of our bodiness. We are intrigued by the manner in which these two sides of the same coin interact and modify each other reciprocally. It is not just mind over body, but body over mind as well.

Psychology

In the realm of psychology, by the same token, we realize that our sense of personal inadequacy, or our pessimistic judgment in our assessment of a situation, were due to our mind having become entrapped in a way of thinking from which we failed to see a way out. Yes, one can get trapped in one's thinking and ascribe the prison to one's fate. The bind is in the mind.

To escape from this prison takes two things: a flash of insight and resolve.

How do we trigger off the flash of insight? We need to first ask ourselves: *What if my assessment of my life situations, or of people around me, upon which I have relied all this time and which I have always taken for granted, was wrong?* If we therefore forego not only previous assessments, but any attempt at a reassessment, then faced with the collapse of our opinion, we find ourselves hopelessly groping our way in the dark night of understanding. Bereft of any crutches, a different mode of understanding dawns upon us; and when we cease to interfere with our commonplace mind, we discover a self-organizing faculty, written right into our programming.

The New Spirituality

In a large number of human activities, the know-how must be continually updated. Meditation also needs to be updated. Armed with the plethora of information in the enormous pool of published material available in our day, we are now able to make a comprehensive study of the methods of meditation taught in the classical schools. By taking this opportunity to compare all these methods, we can gain a whole new grasp of the core issues facing our pioneering meditating predecessors. This, in turn, will help us to look ahead, and to brainstorm perspectives on the future of meditation at the scale of present-day thinking.

Since the challenges of our times are, in some ways, more demanding than those faced by our predecessors, we will need to take into consideration futuristic views in physics, some of which have not yet gained acceptance in the party-line of physics, or the latest developments in psychology. Meditation needs to give us means of stress reduction, help in decision-making and ways of overcoming resentment and a poor self-image. In meditation, we need to honor our concerns about the environment, population explosion, crime, and political oppression. We need to gain insight into the disenchantment about institutionalization, particularly in the field of spirituality, and join the nascent trend to explore new expressions of our need for the sacred, emancipated from hackneyed forms, power trips, and superstitions. We need to replace belief by faith, dogma by experience, encourage people to take responsibility rather than follow authoritarian prescriptions, and adopt honesty rather than sanctimoniousness.

Consequently, we need to brainstorm a new method of meditation that incorporates the earlier methods and carries them into the future.

To achieve this, instead of modulating consciousness from one vantage point to another, we will need to learn to extrapolate between several vantage points. The consciousness of future humanity may well be called *stereoscopic consciousness*. This applies equally to the mind, which will learn to extrapolate between thinking in terms of categories and grasping the wholeness of a situation.

Furthermore, we need to hoist our vantage point from the commonplace narrow range of the immediate environment, and look at things in a wider context. This is where some of the meditation skills can prove helpful. It is somewhat like witnessing how different a familiar landscape looks when flying over it. Doing this, we realize that our assessments of our life situations change with the altitude of our purview and with our scale of values.

Instead of aiming at escaping the here and now to scan transcendental levels of reality, as in samadhi, we will endeavor to look at the way the everywhere and always manifests—not just in the here and now, but manifests in the forward march of becoming.

Science

The revolution in science, apart from updating our technology to the leading edge, must of necessity affect our day-to-day thinking. In our commonplace thinking, most people still think as ever before, in categories. If you think holistically, you are not a fraction of the totality, but a relatively permanent expression of that totality in its wholeness, which is potentially present in you. Should we apply this way of thinking to our relationship with the environment, we would not think of it as something one can exploit without spoiling one's very underpinning, right under one's feet.

Time

Applying the new dimensions of scientific thinking to our day-to-day thinking, we will even need to account for further dimensions of time in our understanding of causal inference; for example, include a transcendental vector of time to the simplistic process of becoming, as illustrated in Jung's synchronicity.

Space

Everything in the cosmos is connected with everything else, as in the holistic paradigm. It is simply easier for our minds to see the connection between the motion of a billiard ball and that of the one it has hit, than to see how the surge of a wave we think is in the Pacific, could have any relevance to a wave in the English channel. These are the nonlocal laws of modern physics.

Causality

The revolution in the thinking at the prow of the evolutionary advance has changed our way of looking at causality. Instead of the simplistic view, it is now understood that each wave in the ocean is not simply the result of the previous one, but the whole ocean rises as each wave; and each wave is interjected back into the ocean; and the whole ocean arises as each new wave. Causality is now seen as a concatenation of causes.

Quantum Leap

Sometimes we find ourselves confronted with the choice between situations that progress gradually, like a bud unfurls; or where things remain at a standstill; or run the chance of reversing into decay; or where nature proceeds by leaps and bounds. There are situations which one cannot change in their outer circumstances, but which will change by one's changing oneself, or by a new way of handling them. In exceptional cases, there is no slow transition from one perspective to the other; the transit is sudden. Here lies the difference between the moment of time, in which there is an overlap between past and future, and the instant, in which there is a sudden and irreversible break of continuity.

These threshold or rare conditions occur in our lives and in our thinking. They may be illustrated by a sunrise or sunset, or the equinoxes or solstices, or a singularity in astrophysics. They are best illustrated by a solar or lunar eclipse, where there is an alignment in space between two luminaries at a given time, called a *syzygy*. Let us bear in mind that the coincidence is only meaningful from our vantage point, and therefore, relates the objective world to our subjective dimension.

The French physicist Olivier Costa de Beauregard is looking into the subjective factor in scientific research:

The symmetries past-future and knowledge-organization imply that the observer is also an actor.[2]

Rebirthing ourselves requires us to extrapolate between our celestial and human inheritance, the psychosomatic axis.

C.G. Jung spent much ponderous inquiry upon this paradoxical conjunction between our psyche and the physical world. In paradoxical cases, rather than a perception or an event that impacts our psyche and gets processed by our psyche, it is our psyche that participates in the event. He was intrigued by series of events, undoubtedly similar, occurring in a short span of time, which could not possibly determine each other, and which are too remarkable

---

2 Costa de Beauregard, *Retrocausality and Conditional Probability*, 68.

to dismiss as accidental—*the simultaneous occurrence of two meaningful but not causally connected events.*

If they do not fit into our understanding of causality, he thought, there must be other parameters to Laplacian determinism: our psyche must have a role here. This requires another principle of explanation.

By the same token, he sees a synchronistic connection between our personality and what we ascribe to our fate.

If you do not confront your shadow, it will appear to you in the form of your fate.

Carl Jung

But how does our mind affect the outer physical world? This is what it meant by psychokinesis.

After years of painstaking research in psychokinesis, Dr. J. B. Rhine arrived at conclusions that throw some light on the problem. For Rhine, space and time are dependent upon psychic conditions, and therefore, can be reduced to almost a vanishing point.

We are touching upon a most important point: for the psyche, space is only meaningful when one is experiencing or reminiscing physical occurrences, or when the mind functions creatively without images in the act of imagination.

Dr. Bohm sees the same in our sense of time,[3] and for Speiser, at a certain level of our thinking, our psyche touches upon a level prior to causality. It is an initial state, which is not governed by mechanistic law, but is the preconditioning of law, the chance substrate upon which law is built.[4]

Dr. Bohm sees how, in turn, changes at the existential level affect the software of the universe, thus corroborating Dr. Rupert Sheldrake's controverted morphogenetic resonance gedanken experiment:[5] Remarkably, this astonishing view echoes the verse of the Sufi poet Jalal ad-Din Rumi:

For tonight, the teeming world gives birth to the world everlasting.[6]

We therefore realize the implications of our interventions, not only in the hardware, but also in the software of the universe. And we see how intervening in one area of the psycho-ecosystem affects every other.

One could define creativity as the act of exploring uncharted regions of the mind, while grasping a correspondence between the mental constructs thus gleaned and a form or configurations or scenarios in the fabric of matter.

---

3 See Bohm, *Unfolding Meaning*, 17.
4 See ibid., 17; and Speiser, *Über die Freiheit*, 28.
5 See Sheldrake, *A New Science of Life*, Appendix.
6 Rumi, *Selected Poems from the Divani Shams-i Tabriz*, trans. Nicholson, 143.

Creativity is a congruent conjunction between the timeless and the transient, the heavenly and the earthly. It is a sudden sense of meaningfulness that sparks our innovative faculty. What we mean by our sense of meaningfulness is our mind's ability to click when it grasps a correspondence between two thoughts that had hitherto appeared unrelated. To be creative rather than just fanciful, one's vision needs to click with the possibility of its actual realization at the existential level. The grasp of congruence sparks our being with delight, because it gives us a sense of thinking in sync with the thinking of the universe, and feeling in resonance with the emotion of the cosmos, and hence, makes us aware of our holistic connectedness with the totality which we call God, not just at the physical level but at all levels.

When the unreality of life pushes against my heart, its door opens to the reality.[7]

Hazrat Inayat Khan

---

7 Inayat Khan, *The Complete Sayings of Hazrat Inayat Khan*, 163.

May the path be open and
smooth before you.

Glossary of Names and Terms

'Abd al-Karim al-Jili (1366–1424): Sufi mystic of Baghdad in the school of Ibn 'Arabi.

Abu'l-Hasan al-Hujwiri (c. 990–1077): Central Asian Sufi scholar buried in Lahore.

Abu Sa'id al-Kharraz (d. c.890): Sufi scholar of Baghdad.

Abu Yazid Bastami (804–c.878): Persian Sufi known for his ecstatic utterances.

afferent neurons: sensory neurons carry signals from sensory organs to brain and spinal cord

Ahmad al-Ahsa'i (1753–1826): Arab mystic who founded the Shi'ite Shaykhia school.

akasha (Sanskrit): sky: in Sufism, an accommodation.

ajsam: bodies. In Sufism the plane constituted by subtle templates.

Anfortas: the wounded Fisher King who guard the Grail at Munsalvaesche.

alembic: alchemical vessel of distillation.

athanor: alchemical oven.

baqa (Arabic): subsistence; the stage following *fana*.

Bohm, David (1917–1992): Innovative American theoretical physicist.

chakra (Sanskrit): center of subtle energy.

chi force: universal energy in Chinese tradition.

dervish: Sufi practitioner.

dhikr: (zikr, Persian): remembrance; in Sufism, the ritual of divine remembrance.

dhakir: the adept repeating the dhikr.

efferent nuerons: motor neurons sending signals to muscles of body.

explicate state: diurnal, overt state of consciousness

fana (Arabic): annihilation.

hahut: the transcendent plane.

haqq (Arabic): Truth.

hal (Arabic): meditative state.

Hassidim: members of a mystical Jewish path established in 19th century in Eastern Europe

hologram: three-dimensional image.

implicate state: covert, inverted state of the unconscious.

Inayat Khan, Hazrat (1882–1927): Sufi teacher who brought Sufism from India to Europe and North America; father of Pir Vilayat Inayat Khan.

'ishq (Arabic): divine nostalgia, love.

jabarut: the plane of splendor.

Jalal ad-Din Muhammad Balkhi Rumi (d.1273), famed Persian Sufi poet of Konya and founder of Mevlevi Order of the whirling dervishes.

John of the Cross, Saint (1542-1591): Spanish Carmelite friar and mystic.

khanaqa: Sufi headquarters.

khayal: plane of the reflexive mind.

kundalini (Sanskrit): force of subtle energy in Yogic tradition.

lahut: the plane of archetypes.

latifa (Arabic. pl. *lata'if*): subtle energy center.

Mahmud Shabistari (1288–1340): Persian Sufi poet.

malakut: the celestial plane

Mansur al-Hallaj (c.858–922): Persian Sufi poet, executed for heresy.

mantram (Sanskrit): repetitive spiritual practice.

maya (Sanskrit): illusion.

mithal: plane of metaphor.

Muhammad Ibn 'Abd al-Jabbar an-Niffari (d. 965): 'Iraqi Sufi mystic who wrote on spiritual states and waystations.

Muhyi ad-Din Ibn 'Arabi (1165–1240): Andalusian Sufi mystic, writer, and philosopher.

nasut: the physical plane.

Nur-ud-Din 'Abd-ur-Rahman Jami (1414–1492): Sufi poet buried in Herat.

noetic: relating to the mind or intellect.

Parsifal: the hero of the Grail romance of Wolfram von Eschenbach.

pir (Persian): spiritual director.

prakrit (Sanskrit): matter.

pranayama (Sanskrit): Yogic breathing practices.

purusha (Sanskrit): commonly translated as the Self.

rishi: Sage in the Yogic tradition.

Sahl Tustari (c. 818–c. 896): early Persian Sufi scholar.

samadhi: transcendental state.

sannyasin: Hindu renunciate.

shahadat: Islamic profession of faith.

Shibli (d.946): a prominent Sufi of the Baghdad school.

Shihab ad-Din Yahya Suhrawardi (1155–1191): Persian Sufi, founder of the Illuminationist school. Executed for heresy.

siddhis (Sanskrit): mystical powers.

somatic: relating to the body.

Speiser, Andreas (1885–1970): Swiss mathematician.

Sufi Order: Founded in 1910 by Hazrat Inayat Khan, the Sufi Order grew out of the Chishti Order in Ajmer, India, which was established in the 13th century.

tawhid: plane of unity.

Teilhard de Chardin, Pierre (1881–1955): French philosopher and Jesuit priest.

Trevisan, Bernard (1406–1490): Italian alchemist.

Vedanta: the Hindu texts known as the Upanishads; also, the philosophy originating from them. Advaita Vedanta is non-dualistic school.

syzgy: an alignment in space between two luminaries at a given time.

wazifa (Arabic. pl. waza'if): Sufi mantram.

Sources and Selected Bibliography

'Abd Allāh ibn Muhammad Ansari al-Harawi. *Kitāb at-Tamkīn fī sharh Manāzil as-sa'irin (Book of Waystations for the Wayfarers)*. Cairo: Dar Nahdat Misr li'-t-Tab'-wa-n-Nashr, 1969.

———and de Beaurecueil, Serge, ed. *Khwādja 'Abdullāh Ansārī (396-481 H./1006-1089); mystique hanbalite*. Beirut: Impr. Catholique, [1965].

'Abd al-Karim al-Jili. *De l'Homme Universel: Extraits du livre Al-Insan Al-Kamil*. Titus Burckhardt, commentary and trans. Lyon: Derain, 1953.

Abdel-Kader, Dr. Ali Hassan. *The Life, Personality and Writings of al-Junayd: A Study of a Third/Ninth Century Mystic*. London: Luzac, 1976.

Abu Bakr Muhammad al-Kalabadhi. *Kalabadhi: Traité du Soufisme*. R. Deladriere, trans. Paris: Sinbad, 1981.

Abu Hamid al-Ghazzālī. Manuel Alonso Alonso, trans. *Maqasid al-Falasifa: o, Intenciones de los filósofos*. Barcelona: J. Flors, 1963.

Afnan, Soheil, M. *Avicenna: His Life and Works*. London: George Allen and Unwin, 1958.

Ali ibn Uthman al-Hujwiri. *Kashf al-Mahjúb; the Oldest Persian Treatise on Súfism, by Ali B. Uthmán al-Jullábí al-Hujwíri*. Reynold A. Nicholson trans. London: Brill and Luzac, 1911.

Allison, Edgar Peers. *The Mystics of Spain*. London: George Allen and Unwin, 1951.

L'Annuaire de l'École Pratique des Hautes Études, Section des Sciences Religieuses, 1938-1939.

Attar, Farid ad-Din. *The Conference of the Birds: Mantiq ut-tair*. Berkeley: Shambhala Publications, 1971.

Avicenna, *Kitab al-'Isharat wa'l-Tanbihat*. A.M. Goinchon, trans. Paris: UNESCO Collection of Arab Texts, Vrin, 1951.

Basu, Shrabani. *Spy Princess: The Life of Noor Inayat Khan*. London: Sutton, 2006; and New Lebanon: Omega Publications, 2007.

Bayrak al-Jerrahi, Sheikh Tosun, com. *The Most Beautiful Names*. Putney: Threshold Books, 1985.

Beauregard, Olivier Costa de. *Retrocausality and Conditional Probability: Reply to C.I.J.M.Stuart*. Paris: Institut Henri Poincare, 1991.

———*Cosmos et Conscience* in *Science et Conscience*. Paris: Stock, 1980.

Beck, Hermann. *Boeddha en Zihn Leer*. Groete Phoenix Pocket Nr 59. W. De Haan Zeist, 1961.

Becker, Robert O. and Gary Selden, Gary. *The Body Electric: Electromagnetism and the Foundation of Life*. New York: William Morrow, 1985.

———and Andrew A. Marino. *Electromagnetism and Life*. Albany: State University of New York Press, Albany, 1982.

Bernard, Theo, *Hatha Yoga*. London: Rider, 1950.

Bhikshu, Vijnana. *Yogasara, Sangraha of Vijnana Bhikshu.* Bombay: Tatva-Vivechaka Press, 1894.

Bingen, Hildergard von. *Hildegardis Bingensis Liber divinorum operum.* Derolez, Albert and Peter Dronke, eds. Turnholti: Brepols, 1996.

Bohm, David. *Wholeness and the Implicate Order.* London/Boston: Routledge and Kegan Paul, 1981

——Factor, Donald, ed. *Unfolding Meaning: A Weekend of Dialogue with David Bohm.* Gloucestershire: Foundation House Publications, 1985.

Buber, Martin. *I and Thou.* New York: Scribner, 1958.

Burckhardt, Titus, *Alchemy: Science of the Cosmos, Science of the Soul.* Shaftesbury: Element Books, 1967.

Carus, Paul. *The Gospel of the Buddha; Compiled From Ancient Records.* Chicago, London: Open Court, 1915

Casaril, Guy. *Rabbi Simeon Bar Yochai et la Cabale, Maitres Spirituels.* Paris: Seuil, 1961.

Chandrasekhar, Subrahmanyan. *Truth and Beauty: Aesthetics and Motivations in Science.* Chicago: University of Chicago Press, 1987.

Chappel, Walter. In *Caduceus Journal Ltd.* West Sussex.

Chittick, William C. *The Sufi Path of Knowledge: Ibn al-Arabi's Metaphysics of Imagination.* Albany: State University of New York Press, 1989.

Chodkiewecz, Michel ed, *The Meccan Revelations*, William Chittick and James Morris, trans., New York: Pir Press, 2002.

Corbin, Henry. *Creative Imagination in the Sufism of Ibn 'Arabi.* Ralph Manheim, trans. Princeton: Princeton University Press, 1969.

——*Spiritual Body and Celestial Earth: From Mazdean Iran to Shi'ite Iran.* Nancy Pearson, trans. Princeton: Princeton University Press, 1977.

——*The Man of Light in Iranian Sufism.* Nancy Pearson, trans. Boulder: Shambhala Publications, 1978 and New Lebanon: Omega Publications 1994.

——*Cyclic Time and Ismaeli Gnosis.* London/Boston: Kegan Paul in association with Islamic Publications, London, 1983.

——*Suhrawardi d'Alep: fondateur de la doctrine illuminative (ishraqi).* Paris: G.P. Maisonneuve, 1939.

——*Histoire de la philosopphie islamique.* Paris: Gallimard, 1964.

Cousins, Norman. In *Nobel Prize Conversations With Nobel Prize conversations with Sir John Eccles, Roger Sperry, Ilya Prigogine, Brian Josephson.* Saybrook/Dallas/New York: Norton, 1985.

Dara Shikuh, Prince Muhammad. *Majma'-ul-Bahrain.* Calcutta: Asiatic Society of Bengal, 1929.

Davies, Paul. *Superforce: The Search for a Grand Unified Theory of Nature.* New York: Simon & Schuster, 1984.

Deikman Arthur, J. and Charles Tart, ed. *Altered States of Consciousness.* Garden City: Doubleday, 1972.

——*The Observing Self: Mysticism and Psychotherapy.* Boston: Beacon Press, 1982.

Digby, Simon. "Encounters with Yogis in Indian Sufi Hagiography." London: London School of Oriental Studies, Jan. 1970.

Eliade, Mircea. Willard Trask, trans. *Yoga, Immortality and Freedom*. Princeton: Princeton University 1958.

Evans-Wentz, Walter Yeeling. *The Tibetan Book of the Great Liberation*. London/New York: Oxford University Press 1968.

Fahkr ad-Din Muhammad ibn 'Umar Razi. *Traité sur les Noms Divins: le livre des preuves éclatantes sur les noms et les qualités*. trans. Maurice Gloton. Paris: Dervy-Livres, 1986.

Fulcanelli. *Le Mystère des cathédrales et l'interprétation ésotérique des symboles hermétiques du grand œuvre*. Paris: J.J. Pauvert, 1964.

Ferguson, Marilyn. *The Aquarian Conspiracy: Personal and Social Transformation in the 1980s*. New York: J.P. Tarcher, 1980.

Gambidharananda, Swami, tr. *Mandukya Upanishad*. Calcutta: Advaita Ashrama, 1979.

Gardet, Louis. *Expériences mystiques en terre non-chrétiennes*. Paris: Alsatia, 1954.
———*Études de philosophie et de mystique comparées*. Paris: J. Vrin, 1972.

Gardiner, Martin, *The Ambidextrous Universe: Mirror Asymmetry and Time-reversed Worlds*. New York: Scribner, 1979.

Gatlin, Lila L. *Information Theory and the Living System*. New York: Columbia University Press, 1972.

Gilchrist, Cherry. *The Elements of Alchemy*. Rockport: Element Books, 1991.

Gleick, James. *Chaos: Making a New Science*. New York: Viking, 1987.

Gödel, Kurt. *Paper On the Incompleteness Theorems*, 1931.

Cf. Gribbin, John. *In Search of Shrödinger's Cat: Quantum Physics and Reality*. New York: Bantam, 1984.

Grof, Stanislav, ed. *Ancient Wisdom and Modern Science*. Albany: State University of New York Press, 1984.
———*Beyond the Brain: Birth, Death, and Transcendence in Psychotherapy*. Albany: State University of New York Press, 1985.

Gyatso, Geshe Kelsang. Tenzin Norbu trans. *The Clear Light of Bliss: Mahamudra in Vajrayana Buddhism*. London: Wisdom Publications, 1982.

Hadot, Pierre. *Plotin ou la Simplicité du regard*. Paris: Études augustiniennes, 1973.

Hermes. Le Vide, expériences spirituelles en Occident et en Orient, in *Hermes*, Vol. 6. Paris: Minard, 1968.

Hirtenstein, Stephen and Michael Tiernan, eds. *Muhyiddin Ibn 'Arabi: a Commemorative Volume*. Rockport: Element Books, 1993.

Holmyard, Eric. *L'Alchimie*. Paris: Arthaud, 1979.

Idel, Moshe and Jonathan Chipman, trans. *The Mystical Experience in Abraham Abulafia*. Albany: State University of New York Press, 1988.

Inayat Khan, Hazrat. *The Complete Sayings of Hazrat Inayat Khan*. New Lebanon: Sufi Order Publications, 1978; Omega Publications, 2005.
———*Esoteric Papers* (unpublished).

———*The Music of Life: The Inner Nature and Effects of Sound*. New Lebanon: Omega Publications, 1983.

———*Song of the Prophets: The Unity of Religious Ideals*. New Lebanon: Omega Publications, 2009.

———*The Sufi Message of Hazrat Inayat Khan* series. London, Barrie and Jenkins, 1973.

———*The Sufi Message of Hazrat Inayat Khan* series. Netherlands: Servire, 1979.

———*The Sufi Message of Hazrat Inayat Khan* series. Alameda: Hunter House Inc. 1982.

Jalal ad-Din Muhammad Rumi. *Selected Poems from the Divani Shamsi Tabriz*. R.A. Nicholson, ed and trans. Cambridge: Cambridge University Press, 1898.

———*The Teachings of Rumi : the Masnavi of Mauláná Jalalu'd-Dín Muhammad i Rúmí*. E. H. Whinfield, ed. and trans. New York: Duttton, 1975.

Jalbani, G.N. trans. and D. B. Fry, ed. *Sufism and the Islamic Tradition: the Lamahat and Sata'at of Shah Waliullah*. London: Octagon Press, London, 1980.

John of the Cross, St. *The Ascent of Mount Carmel*. Benedict Zimmermann and David Lewis, trans. London: Thomas Baker, 1906.

———*The Dark Night of the Soul*, in *The Mystics of Spain*. Peers, E.Allison, ed. London: Allen & Unwin, 1951.

———*La vive flamme d'amour*. Paris: Cerf, 1994.

———*The Living Flame of Love*. Peers, E. Allison Peers, ed. and trans. Garden City: Image Books, 1962.

Jung, Carl. *Psychology and Alchemy*. G. R. F. C. Hull, trans. Princeton: Princeton University Press, 1968.

———*Synchronicity; An Acausal Connecting Principle*. Princeton: Princeton University Press, 1973.

Kabir. *Songs of Kabir*, Rabindranath Tagore, trans. New York: Weiser, 1977.

Kaku, Michio and Jennifer Trainer. *Beyond Einstein: The Cosmic Quest for the Theory of the Universe*. New York: Bantam, 1987.

Koestler, Arthur. *Janus: A Summing Up*. New York: Vintage Books, 1979.

———*The Act of Creation*. London: Hutchinson, 1970.

Korzybski, Alfred. *Science and Sanity: An Introduction to Non-Aristotelian Systems and General Semantics*. Lakeville: International Non-Aristolian Library, 1948.

Krippner, Stanley and Daniel Rubin, eds. *The Kirlian Aura: Photographing the Galaxies of Life*. New York: Doubleday, 1974.

Lacape, R.S.. *A la recherche du temps vécu*. Paris: Hermann, 1935.

Le Saux, Henri. *La rencontre de l'hindouisme et du christianisme*. Paris: Seuil, 1965.

LeShan, Lawrence and Henri Margenau. *Einstein's Space and Van Gogh's Sky: Physical Reality and Beyond*. New York: Macmillan, 1982.

Lewisohn, Leonard, ed.: *The Legacy of Mediaeval Persian Sufism*. London; New York: Khaniqahi-Nimatullahi Publications, 1992.

Lindquist, Sigurd. *Die Methoden des Yoga*. Lund: Hakkian Ohlssons Buchdrukerei, 1932.

Lory, Pierre. *Alchimie et mystique en terre d'Islam*. Paris: Verdier, 1989.

Mahmud Shabistari.*Gulshan-i Raz, The Mystic Garden of Roses of Sa'd ud Din Mahmud Shabistari.* E. H. Whinfield, trans. London: Trubner & Co. 1880.

——*La roseraie du Mystere.* Djamshid Mortazavi and Eva de Vitray-Meyerovitch, trans. Paris: Sinbad, 1991.

——*The Secret Rosegarden of Sa'd ud Din Mahmud Shabistari.* Florence Lederer, trans. London: J. Murray, 1920.

Maimonides, 'Obadyāh b. Abraham b. Moses. *The Treatise of the Pool.* Paul Fenton, trans. London: Octagon Press, 1981.

Mansur al-Hallaj. *Diwan.* Louis Massignon, trans. Paris: Éditions du Seuil, 1981.

Massignon, Louis and P. Kraus. *Akhbār al-Hallāj, texte ancien relatíf à la prédiction et au supplice du mystique musulman al-Hosayn b. Mansour al Hallāj.* Paris: Éditions Larose, 1936.

——*Essai Sur Les Origines De Lexique Technique De La Mystique Musulmane.* Paris: Librairie Philosophique J. Vrin, 1954.

——*La passion d'al-Hosayn-ibn-Mansour al-Hallaj, martyr mystique de l'Islam, exécuté à Bagdad le 26 Mars 922; étude d'histoire religieuse.* Paris: Gallimard, 1975.

——*The Passion of al-Hallāj : Mystic and Martyr of Islam.* Herbert Mason, trans. Princeton: Princeton University Press, 1982.

Meyerovitch, Eva de Vitray. *Mystique et poésie en Islam.* Paris: Desclée de Brouwer, 1972.

Michael, Salim. *Les obstacles à l'illumination et à la libération.* Paris: Éditions Guy Trédaniel, 1992.

Mishra, Rammurti. *The Textbook of Yoga Psychology: The Definitive Translation and Interpretation of Patanjali's Yoga Sutras for Meaningful Application in All Modern Psychologic Disciplines.* New York: Julian Press, 1987.

——*Fundamentals of Yoga: A Handbook of Theory, Practice, and Application.* New York: Julian Press, 1959.

——*Yoga Sutras: The Textbook of Yoga Psychology.* Garden City: Anchor Press, 1973.

Monroe, Robert. *Journeys out of the Body.* Garden City: Anchor Press, 1977.

Morris, Richard. *Time's Arrows.* New York: Simon & Schuster, 1985.

Muhammad Ibn 'Abd'l-Jabbar an-Niffari. *The Mawakif and Mukhatabat of Muhammad ibn 'Adi'l-Jabbar al-Niffari, with other fragments.* Arberry, Arthur J. trans. London: Luzac. 1935.

Muhyi ud-Din ibn 'Arabi. *Études Traditionelles.* Michel Valsan trans. (Periodical publishing series from works of Ibn 'Arabi over several years.) Paris: Chacornac.

——*Les illuminations de La Mecque (Futuhat al-Makkīyah): textes choisis, présentés et traduits de l'arabe.* Chodkiewicz, Michel, trans. Paris: Éditions Sinbad, 1988.

——*The Seals of Wisdom.* Norwich: Diwan Press, 1980.

——*Whoso Knoweth Himself... from The Treatise on Being (Risalat-t-ul-wujudiyyah):* Translation of T. H. Weir (1901). Translation of an Arabic Manuscript in the Hunterian Collection, Glascow University 1901.

——*The Wisdom of the Prophets (Fusus al-hikam) / Muhyi-d-din, Ibn 'Arabi*. Titus Burckhardt and Angela Culme-Seymour, trans. Alsworth: Beshara, 1975.

Murchie, Guy. *Music of the Spheres: The Material Universe from Atom to Quasar, Simply Explained*. New York: Dover Publications, 1961.

Nasr, Seyyed Hossein. "The Spread of the Illluminationist School of Suhrawardi," in *Studies in Comparative Religion*, Vol. 6, No. 3. London:1972.

Nicholson, Reynold A. *Rumi, Poet and Mystic*. London: George Allen and Unwin, 1964.

——*Studies in Islamic Mysticism*. Cambridge: The University Press, 1921.

Nikhilananda, Swami, trans. *The Mandukyopanisad*. Mysore: Sri Ramakrishna Ashrama, 1955.

Nur-ud-Din 'Abd-ur-Rahman Jami. *Lawa'ih*. London: Royal Asiatic Society, 1906.

Nysenholc, Adolphe and Jean-Pierre Boon, eds. *Redécouvrir le temps*, in *Revue de l'Université de Bruxelles*. Brussels: Universite de Bruxelles, 1988.

Nwiya, Paul, com. and trans. *Trois oeuvres inédites de mystiques Musulmans*. Beirut: Dar El-Machreq Ed. 1973.

——*Ibn 'Abbād de Ronda, 1332-1390; un mystique prédicateur à la Qarawīyīn de Fès*. Beirut: Impr. catholique, 1961.

Ornstein, Robert E. *The Psychology of Consciousness*. San Francisco: W.H. Freeman, 1972.

Otto, Rudolph, and Bertha L. Bracey, Richenda C. Payne. *Mysticism East and West*. New York: Meridian Books, 1957.

Ouspensky, P.D. *Tertium Organum: The Third Canon of Thought, a Key to the Enigmas of the World*. New York: Vintage Books, 1950.

Pagels, Heinz R. *The Cosmic Code: Quantum Physics as the Language of Nature*. Simon & Schuster, 1982.

Palacios, Miguel Asin. *L'Islam Christianise*. Paris: Guy Trédaniel, 1982.

Paquda, Bahya ben Joseph ibn. *The Book of Direction to the Duties of the Heart*. Menahem Mansoor, trans. London: Routledge & Kegan Paul. 1973.

Patanjali. *Yoga Philosophy of Patañjali: Containing His Yoga Aphorisms With Vyāsa's Commentary in Sanskrit and a Translation With Annotations Including Many Suggestions for the Practice of Yoga*. Swami Hariharananda Aranya and Paresh Nath Mukerji; Vyāsa. Albany: State University of New York Press, Albany 1983.

Penrose, Roger. *The Emperor's New Mind: Concerning Computers, Minds, and the Laws of Physics*. London: Vintage, 1990.

Pribam, Karl H. *Brain and Behavior*, New York: Penguin Books, 1969.

——"Some dimensions of remembering: Steps toward a neuro-psychological model of memory," in J. Gaito, ed. *Macromolecules and Behavior*. J. Gaito, ed. New York: Appleton-Century-Crofts, 1966.

Prigogine, Ilya. *From Being to Becoming*. San Francisco: W.H. Freeman, 1980.

Qur'an, The Holy. Maulvi Muhammad Ali, trans. Lahore: Ahmadiyya anjuman-i-ishaat-i-Islam, 1920, 1948.

Rabten, Geshe. *Echoes of Voidness*. London: Wisdom Publications, 1983.

Reeves, Hubert. *Poussières d'étoiles*. Paris: Seuil, 1984.

Restak, Richard M. *The Brain, the Last Frontier*. Garden City: Doubleday, 1979.

Rhys Davids, C.A.F. , trans. *Tipitaka. Abhidhammapitaka. Dhammasangani: A Buddhist manual of psychological ethics of the fourth century B.C. being a translation, now made for the first time, from the original Pali, of the first book in the Abhidhamma pitaka, entitled Dhamma-sangani (compendi um of states or phenomena)*. London: 1900.

Rhys Davids, T. W. Rhys and C.A.F. Rhys, trans. *Dialogues of Buddha*, Part I and Part III. London: Pali Text Society, 1898–1921.

Rizvi, Athar Abbas. *Religious and Intellectual History of the Muslims in Akbar's Reign*. Delhi, 1975.

Ruska, Julius. *Tabula Smaragdina*. Heidelberg: Carl Winter's Universitätbuchhandlung, 1926.

Sangharakshita, Bikshu Sthavira. *A Survey of Buddhism: Its Doctrines and Methods Through the Ages*. London: Tharpa Publications, 1987.

Schaya, Leo. *L'homme et l'absolu selon la Kabbale*, in *La Barque du Soleil*. Paris: Buchet/Chastel Corrêa, 1958.

Schimmel, Annemarie. *Mystical Dimensions of Islam*. Chapel Hill: University of North Carolina Press, 1975.

Scholem, Gershom. *Zur Kabbala und Ihrer Symbolik*. Zürich: Rhein-Verlag, 1960.

Schuon, Frithjof. *Sufism Veil and Quintessence*. Bloomington: World Wisdom Books, 1979.

Sheldrake, Rupert. *A New Science of Life: The Hypothesis of Morphic Resonance*. Rochester: Park Street Press, 1985.

Schrödinger, Edwin. *What is Life? The Physical Aspect of the Living Cell; Mind and Matter*. Cambridge: University Press, 1967.

Shihab ad-Din Yahya Suhrawardi. *Oeuvres philosophiques et mystiques de Shihabaddin Yahya Sohrawardi*. Henri Corbin ed. and trans. Paris: A. Maisonneuve, 1952.

———and Qutb ad-Din Shirazi, and Mulla Sadra Shirazi. *Sohravardi: Le Livre de la Sagesse Orientale*. Henri Corbin ed. Lagrasse: Verdier, 1986.

Sivadjian, Joseph. "*Le problème métaphysique*," in *Actualités scientifiques et industrielles*, 616. Paris: Hermann, 1938.

Speiser, Andreas. *Über die Freiheit*. Basel: Basler Unversitaetsreden, 1950.

Sulami, Muhammad ibn al-Husayn; Tosun Bayrak: *The Book of Sufi Chivalry: Lessons to a Son of the Moment*. The Hague: East-West Publications, 1983.

Teilhard de Chardin, Pierre. *The Phenomenon of Man*. New York: Harper & Row, 1959.

Trevissan, Bernard. "*La parole delaissee*," in *Le Voile d'Isis*. Paris: 1931.

Vajda, Georges. *Isaac Albalag*. Paris: J. Vrin, 1960.

Valiuddin, Mir. *Contemplative Disciplines in Sufism*. Gulshan Khakee ed. London and The Hague: East-West Publications, 1980.

Weber, Renée. *Dialogues with Scientists and Sages: The Search for Unity*. London; New York: Routledge and Kegan Paul, 1986.

Weir, D.M. *Immunology*. Edinburgh: Churchill Livingstone, 1973.

White, John, and Stanley Krippner, eds. *Future Science: Life Energies and the Physics of Paranormal Phenomena*. Garden City: Anchor Books, 1977.

Wilbur, Ken, ed. *The Holographic Paradigm and Other Paradoxes: Exploring the Leading Edge of Science*. Boulder: Shambala, 1982.

———*The Spectrum of Consciousness*. Wheaton: Theosophical Pub. House, 1993.

Wilkinson, J.L. *Neuroanatomy For Medical Students*. Bristol: John Wright, 1986. San Francisco: Harper & Row, 1981.

Zaehner, R.C. *Mysticism, Sacred and Profane*. New York: Oxford University Press, 1961.

———*Hindu and Muslim Mysticism*. London: Athlone Press and New York: Schocken Books, 1969.

———and Nicol Macnicol. *Hindu Scriptures*. London: Dent & Sons, 1966.

———*Hinduism*. Oxford: Oxford University Press, 1966.

Zajonc, Arthur. *Catching the Light: The Entwined History of Light and Mind*. New York: Bantam, 1993.

Index

A

C

F

Pir Vilayat Inayat Khan

Biographical Note

Pir Vilayat Inayat Khan (1916- 2004) was the eldest son and spiritual successor of Hazrat Pir-O-Murshid Inayat Khan, the first Sufi master to teach in the West. Born in England, Vilayat Inayat Khan was educated at the Sorbonne, Oxford, and École Normale de Musique de Paris. During World War II he served in the British Royal Navy and was assigned the duties of mine sweeping during the invasion at Normandy. His sister, Noor-un-Nisa Inayat Khan served in the French section of SOE as a radio operator. She was captured and later executed at Dachau concentration camp.

After the war, Pir Vilayat pursued his spiritual training by studying with masters of many different religious traditions throughout India and the Middle East. While honoring the initiatic tradition of his predecessors, in his teachings Pir Vilayat continually adapted traditional Eastern spiritual practices in keeping with the evolution of Western consciousness. Throughout his life, he was an avid student of many religious and spiritual traditions, incorporating the rich mystical heritage of East and West into his teachings, and adding to it the scholarship of the West in music, science, and psychology. He taught in the tradition of Universal Sufism, which views all religions as rays of light from the same sun.

Pir Vilayat initiated and participated in many international and interfaith conferences promoting understanding and world peace as well as convening spiritual and scientific leaders for public dialogues. In 1975 he founded the Abode of the Message in New Lebanon, New York, which continues to serve as the central residential community of the Sufi Order International, a conference and retreat center, and a center of esoteric study. He also founded the Omega Institute for Holistic Studies, a flourishing learning center, and published many books on aspects of meditation and realization.

For more information on Sufism
and the Sufi Order International please visit:

www.sufiorder.org